AMERICAN DIOGENES

AMERICAN DIOGENES

A Life of Brigadier General Mott Hooton, 1838-1920

KEVIN BROWN

Amy King

Brown & King

For

ROB & DIANE

with thanks and humility

Your memories live on through the impacts you've made on the lives of others.

Contents

Preface

Situated less than a mile north of the small borough of West Chester, Pennsylvania, Oaklands Cemetery stands like a memorial to the town's nineteenth-century social scene. Though still an active burial ground, its aesthetics feel distinctly Victorian. The entrance is flanked by two large granite stanchions but is otherwise hidden from the road blocked by trees and a tall embankment. The front section of Oaklands is relatively small consisting of a low hill covered in memorials and surrounded by a perimeter of trees. As the cemetery road wends circuitously around the hill, it descends into a small valley and crosses a creek. On the other side, this deceptively small place suddenly opens up to reveal hundreds of monuments of varying sizes and designs dotting a series of rolling hills under the leafy protection of seemingly ancient trees. The cemetery lane diverges in multiple directions, each moving organically among the hills.

Unlike many cemeteries which are little more than open fields arranged in strict rows of headstones, Oaklands was conceived as a garden cemetery. Following the Victorian ethos surrounding death, garden cemeteries challenged the idea that cemeteries be grim, macabre places. Garden cemeteries like Oaklands were intended to be beautiful places of repose where one might go for a pleasant stroll or even have a picnic beside the resting place of a loved one. Indeed, the whole of Oaklands cemetery is enclosed on all sides by woodland such that visitors might feel as if they've stumbled into a secret world. In its heyday, a small gothic chapel stood at the apex of the tallest hill and two large ponds, long since filled in, once added to the peace and beauty of the location.

Amy and I first discovered Oaklands in the spring of 2006. We were both on opposite ends of our final year of undergraduate school at West Chester University. We had met the summer before as archaeology students participating in a field school run by the university and became quick friends. The next year, we volunteered to join the field school again. When we learned that part of the work would involve mapping the graves of Civil War veterans at Oaklands, we drove out one weekend to get a sneak peek. As we walked the paths, admiring the setting, we couldn't help but recognize prominent local families whose names grace street signs throughout town to this day.

We eventually wandered towards a back corner of the cemetery where we spotted a tall, rounded marble headstone near the path. The name on the stone immediately caught our attention: Mott Hooton. It was an unusual name and, to be honest, our first reaction was to chuckle at its strangeness. But we also noted the headstone identified the man as a Brigadier General in the United States Army and it bore a lengthy inscription highlighting an illustrious military career. This man instantly piqued our curiosity. That night, we each went home and typed his name into Google believing that surely someone who had attained the rank of general would be well-documented. We were wrong. Our searches turned up nothing.[1] But it did not dissuade us. On the contrary, it had become a mystery we felt compelled to solve. Shortly thereafter, we decided to stop by the Chester County History Center in downtown West Chester to see if they had any records or information that could tell us more about this enigmatic general.

The Chester County History Center (CCHC) is a highly professional local cultural institution with impressive collections of locally-crafted early American decorative arts and other material culture representing the county's history. The research library contains an impressive manuscript collection with materials dating back to the seventeenth century, an unprecedented newspaper clipping collection and a large photograph archive. It is not the image one might expect to conjure in their minds when they think of a small town historical society. With the help of Diane Rofini, the librarian, we quickly located a bit of information on the wayward Mott Hooton. It wasn't much. A copy of his frustratingly brief military memoir and a few newspaper articles gave us only a general sense of the arc of his professional life. Then we discovered one particular article that made us think he was no ordinary soldier. Mott had traveled the world, met fascinating people and even experienced a chance encounter with a Siamese King. We were hooked.

During that same trip, Diane located a photograph of Mott in the photograph collection. We waited impatiently while she left the reading room to retrieve the photograph that would make this mysterious gentleman "real" to us. When it arrived, we donned our required white cotton gloves and the photograph was placed in a mylar sleeve for us to handle. It was a carte de visite portrait taken during his Civil War service and was not at all what we had expected.

In the sepia-toned photograph, Mott is seated wearing a dark—most likely navy blue—unmarked, military-style coat with light-colored trousers. With government-issued uniforms in short supply, his garb was likely a homemade imitation and featured an unusual slash pocket on the left breast filled with unknown contents. His gaze is aimed directly at the camera as his left-hand rests on the hilt of a sheathed sword which is propped up against his knee. The most striking part of the portrait, however, is his big, bushy beard. Far from the dapper military officer we had envisioned, the man staring back at us from the photograph seemed to project the gruff severity of a reclusive mountain man. Of course, facial hair of that nature was not uncommon in the mid-nineteenth century, but even by contemporary standards, the coif of hair hanging from his jaw was impressive to say the least. In fact, the closely cropped hair on the top of his head created such an odd juxtaposition against the untamed beard below that even his comrades did not fail to notice as we soon learned. In a letter home to his family, William Henry Darlington, a private in Mott's Civil War company wrote, "Mott cut his hair, but not his beard or mustache, which now exceeds his hair in length."[2] That Darlington would make the observation and take the time to mention it when writing home is telling of the impression Mott's appearance made.

Though his appearance was unexpected, we felt as if the photograph was in keeping with all of the rest of the scant sources available. Photographs have a way of making the past tangible and bringing to life those who are long gone, yet the intensity of that beard seemed to only further obscure the man beneath it. As we got to know Mott over the next few years and as we uncovered other photographs of him, we came to appreciate another striking feature—his eyes. Slightly hooded beneath long, hooked eyebrows, his eyes appear at once soft, yet convey a sense of determination and strength of purpose. In nearly all the photographs taken throughout his life, his eyes always project the same placid expression that epitomizes the phrase "still waters run deep." In photographs taken towards the end of his career and even in retirement, though his hair had grayed and the beard had long been removed, leaving only a large handlebar mustache, his eyes remained remarkably the same—wizened by life, yet still youthful and filled with the same depth and serenity of his twenty-four-year-old self. In many ways, it was this initial photograph that inspired the work to come. We had looked into his eyes. This unusual name etched in stone in the local cemetery had become real for us and despite the paucity of source material at the time, we were determined to learn more. Who was he? What else had he done and experienced in his life? What was he like as a person? Why was there so little information about him? We got into a conversation with Diane about where to go next and she told us she thought his name sounded familiar, but she couldn't quite place it.

A First Glimpse: Mott Hooton, 1861 (Detail)
Courtesy of the Chester County History Center, West Chester, PA

Among its manuscript collections, CCHC holds many significant Civil War-related manuscripts and correspondence. The men he commanded in the Civil War were all local volunteers from Chester County and so we thought perhaps if there are any contemporary writings of theirs, they may have written about their commanding officer from time to time. We cross-referenced a muster roll of Mott's company with the CCHC collections and discovered a treasure trove of letters from several of his men. We began the arduous, yet exciting task of wading through their letters from the war.

On one Wednesday evening, when the library was open late, I stopped by to continue our perusal through the company letters. Diane approached me with a grin on her face. She had remembered why Mott's name had sounded so familiar to her. Years earlier, an elderly gentleman had come to CCHC from out of town and donated a large cache of letters and other materials belonging to his great uncle, Mott Hooton. Knowing West Chester was his uncle's hometown, it seemed only natural his papers live there. The collection had not been completely processed at the time, which explained why we didn't find it in the manuscript catalog. It was like Christmas morning as Diane wheeled out a cart of several boxes of letters from throughout his life. I immediately called Amy to tell her and dropped what she was doing and raced to CCHC to see the collection. It was incredible. His personality, his family and friends, his experiences, were all encapsulated in those records. Yet as revealing as the collection was, it was still not entirely comprehensive.

Diane was able to broker contact with Mott's great-nephew on our behalf. We sent a letter to the gentleman hoping to learn more, only to receive a reply from his widow. Hazen Park Chase, Mott's great nephew, had died just a few years prior and the bulk of the family knowledge on Mott went with him. Still, his wife, Dorothy, was willing to help us where she could. Through her, we were able to contact her children and nephew who had additional photographs of Mott and his Civil War diary from 1863-1864. She also kindly shared with us what she had been told about Mott by her husband.

Despite the new materials now before us, we continued digging through the correspondence of his soldiers from the Civil War. It had started as a means to an end to learn more about Mott, but as we read, we became endeared to these young men, seeing their personalities shine through and learning of their hopes and fears. The utter humanity of the letters drew us in. We had resolved to write a biography of Mott eventually but felt the collective story of these men who fought for the Union deserved to be told as well. The source material was all local and more readily available than what we would have to uncover for Mott. With the sesquicentennial of the Civil War just a few years away, it was the perfect time to do it. This led to our first book, *A Small Company of Faithful Ones: The Brandywine Guards of Chester County"* self-published through Amazon in June 2011, one hundred and fifty years—almost to the day—of their muster in for service in 1861.

Conceived as a collective biography of a group of young men from the county who shared a major life-defining moment, the book provides a history of their three years of service in the war as seen through their eyes. Our interest in them as people inspired us to dedicate nearly half of the book to brief biographical sketches of each of the one hundred thirteen men who comprised the company. We wanted to reveal what became of them after the war, who their families were, and where their final resting places lay. It was an accomplishment we were both proud of, but we never lost sight of our original goal: telling Mott's story.

It's been over fifteen years since Amy and I first looked into Mott's eyes in that carte de visite at CCHC. Life interruptions for both of us—graduate school, careers, families, even an overseas move for one of us—turned the project into an on-again-off-again venture. But Mott's story remained an insistent voice in our minds. Somehow, we would find a way to get his story out. Over the years some additional sources have come to light online, we located collectors of military memorabilia with materials related to Mott, we corresponded with family, and even helped a small historical society in Maine solve a long-held mystery about Mott's identity after they discovered a small grave in their county memorializing one of his dogs.

There were times we thought we would never finish this work, but it's gratifying to have finally completed the book so we finally have something to show for all of the help and support we have received along the way. It was that encouragement that kept us going all these years. First and foremost, we want to thank the Chester County History Center not only for the important work they do in preserving and promoting the county's local history but for the unending assistance they provided. In particular, the now-retired former photo archivist Pam Powell and assistant librarian Margie Baillie took great interest in our discoveries and continued to offer help and research insights along the way. More recently, Judy Ng, current librarian was instrumental in supplying several of the photographs included. We also want to thank August Marchetti, President and Founding Director of the Pennsylvania Reserve Volunteer Corps Historical Society as well as Ed and Faye Max, local collectors and all historians in their own right, whose enthusiasm and openness in sharing items, including letters and photographs, from their collections have allowed us to flesh out Mott's life. Their friendship and cheerleading have kept us going all these years.

We also must thank Mr. Hazen P. Chase for believing his great uncle's papers were worth preserving and sharing with the people of Chester County. Although we never met Mr. Chase, we hope he would be gratified to know someone has made good use of his donation. We cannot forget to thank his wife, Dorothy Chase, who corresponded with us enthusiastically and shared what knowledge she had. She, unfortunately, passed several years ago, but we remain indebted to her for humoring these two local historians all those years ago and showing us such openness and kindness. Finally, no acknowledgment of the family would be complete if we did not include Richard Palamar, Clayton Chase, and Richard Chase, all great grandnephews of Mott who shared with us copies of Mott's Civil War diary, photographs of Mott and family, and images of relics passed down to them including swords and medals. We hope they will be pleased with how we've written about their predecessors.

Another collector of militaria deserves our gratitude as well. In 2017, we finally connected with Decker Landry, whose possession of a trunk of Mott-related materials we had heard about for years, but could not track down. We greatly appreciate the time he spent copying and mailing documents and photographs to us which helped us to fill in several gaps in Mott's life.

We would be remiss in not mentioning our families here as well. George and Maureen Brown and Wayne and Linda King. Not only have they encouraged us in this work, but they also willingly listened as we excitedly told them about new facts or interesting events we had uncovered. We could never have done this without their love and support. Thanks must also go to my wife, Christine, daughters Clara and Lucy, and Amy's son Noah for putting up with all the time spent away from them finishing this work. We are grateful for their patience.

Finally, we have to thank two individuals who are no longer with us and to whom this book is dedicated. Dr. Robert Lukens, former president of CCHC, was one of the most energetic and passionate champions of public history we have ever met. We will never forget how Rob elevated our work after the release of our first book, interviewing us on his local history radio show and inviting us to be guest speakers at an installment of his "History on Tap," an engaging monthly lecture series that hosted speakers discussing various topics in local history and supported local businesses by using area restaurants and bars as the venue. Rob was always willing to vouch for us and write letters of introduction in his official capacity as CCHC president if we ever needed to access a private collection or establish communication with institutions that might not have responded to unsolicited requests for information from unaffiliated historians.

Our second dedication remembers Diane Rofini, the former librarian at CCHC. There are no words to express our gratitude to her for all of her help over the years. If it were not for her, we would never have uncovered all the information we did and Mott's collection might never have seen the light of day. She also showed great patience as we spent day after day, sometimes all day at the library researching. The first summer we worked on this project, we spent nearly all day, every day for weeks at a time in the library researching. She probably pulled more manuscripts for us that summer than she had pulled for patrons all year. But she put up with it patiently and with grace. In truth, we think we amused her as we later found out she would talk about us to her sister, Laurie, the archivist across town at the County Archives.

Both Rob and Diane were taken from the world well before their time. We regret that they will not be able to see the finished product, but we hope they would be proud of it. The fruits of their labor and the personal impact they both had on us are evident throughout this book.

A Word about Terminology

Language is a powerful, dynamic tool for communication and it is constantly evolving. The words we use matter, particularly when it comes to describing or identifying groups of people, and so care must be taken to not perpetuate terminology that is either no longer acceptable or represents a particular lens of understanding that is not accurate. Mott lived at a moment in time in which racial inequity allowed for the use of language that is not appropriate for the twenty-first century. Mott and his contemporaries were products of their time. It was not uncommon for them to use pejorative language when referring to African Americans or Native Americans. Such language was largely acceptable in white society at the time and where such terminology is used in a direct quotation, the original wording has been retained for authenticity.

In regards to our language, however, we have endeavored to hold our writing to twenty-first-century standards of propriety. For example, when referring to people of African descent, you will see the use of the terms "African-American" or the capitalized "Black." Wherever possible we have tried to speak of "the enslaved" rather than simply "slaves," to reflect bondage as a condition imposed on a person rather than a marker of their identity.

Writing about Native Americans is particularly sensitive given the vast diversity of peoples, traditions, and opinions about what they prefer to be called. Guided by Gregory Younging's *Elements of Indigenous Style,* we have favored the use of "Native Americans" and "Indigenous Peoples" over "Natives," "Indians," or "American Indian." A caveat is where such terms exist in a proper name, such as the Bureau of Indian Affairs, Indian Agent, or "the Indian Territory," the latter term referring specifically to the geographical area covered by modern-day Oklahoma.

We have also tried to use language that reinforces the dignity of Native American civilization, preferring the word "Nation" over "tribe" or "band," though we recognize that these latter words are not universally eschewed by every Native American community. More importantly, whenever appropriate to do so, we have tried to be specific about the particular Nation or group of Native Americans in question and have opted to use the names they use for themselves, rather than the more familiar names applied to them by European settlers, unless it has become commonplace for them to do so. The terms in bold below reflect the terminology we have chosen to use.

Of all the Indigenous nations Mott would encounter, the **Lakota** were the most prominent. Historically, the Lakota were a sub-group within the broader Oceti Sakowin, also known historically as the "Great Sioux Nation." However, the term Sioux is problematic as it was adopted by the French from the Ojibwe word for "little snakes." The Ojibwe and the Oceti Sakowin were enemies of one another. Additionally, the Lakota broke down into seven main "Oyate" or sub-groups:

- **Hunkpapa:** To which the famous Chief Sitting Bull belonged
- **Oglala:** This included notable figures such as Red Cloud and Crazy Horse
- **Mnikowoju:** More commonly known as the Miniconjou, included leaders such as Lame Deer and Spotted Elk
- **Sicangu:** Known also as the Brulé. One particular Sicangu figure, Plenty Horses, appears in Mott's story.
- **Itazipcho:** Also known as Sans Arc
- **Sihasapa:** Also known as Blackfoot/Blackfeet
- **Oohenunpa:** Also known as Two Kettles.

Throughout the book, unless appearing in a direct quotation or a proper name, you will see "Lakota" used instead of "Sioux" and where possible, the name of the specific Oyate is used.

Other nations that figure prominently in this story, but who go by names likely less familiar to the reader include:

- **The Three Affiliated Tribes:** A historic alliance of three Native American groups on the northern Plains who came together to form a united nation after a devastating Smallpox outbreak in the 1830s decimated their populations. They are also known as the Mandan, Hidatsa, and Arikara (MHA) Nation.
  - **Mandan**
  - **Hidatsa** (also known as the Gros Ventre of the Missouri)
  - **Arikara** (also known as the Ree)

Mott encountered several other Native American nations throughout his military career, whose more familiar names still seem to be the most appropriate, including the Cheyenne, Navajo and Paiute. In these cases, the more familiar names remain the same. Mott spent a good deal of time in Colorado and Utah, a region heavily populated by the Ute people. Although they call themselves "Nuche," they do employ the name Ute when identifying themselves.

We are not experts in Native American nomenclature and so this terminology represents our best attempt to portray the various nations Mott encountered in as accurate and respectful a light possible. Any missteps are unintended.

Introduction

In every age, there are a select few who define the times in which they live. They are the movers and shakers, the drivers of national and world events. They influence their cultures in ways that reverberate throughout society. These are the people who find their way into textbooks, museums, and the popular consciousness.

But what of the rest of us—the vast multitudes who are left to navigate the times that are shaped by others? You won't find these names in history books. Their possessions do not become prized relics for which people journey far and wide to gaze upon behind a museum vitrine. Historical societies and other small institutions throughout the nation are dedicated to remembering the lives of people within their local communities, though they would appear to mean little beyond the borders of their localities. What is the value in retaining their stories? Are they not merely actors in someone else's play?

This is a key question that many historians debate. For some, there are only a precious few whose lives rise to the level worthy of study. The broad historical forces in the continuum of time toss the average person about as they live their lives in little actual control of their fate and so the study of an individual is seen as almost folly compared to the bigger concepts that create significant change over time. For these scholars, it is these broad forces that should be explored as they hold the only real implications for the development of humanity. This kind of inquiry is important and incredibly valuable, but for the general public, who are by and large the successors to the anonymous, unstudied individuals of history, the value of a regular person's story is in its relatability. It is a link to history in a more tangible way by experiencing events through something—someone—more accessible. This link can be quite literal, for example in the case of genealogical study, or it can be tangentially anchored by familiar locations across time within a common local community. But even on a wider stage beyond blood relations and local audiences, the study of the historically anonymous offers a different, more personal perspective of the events of history in a way that feels real to non-historians.

The life of Brigadier General Mott Hooton offers such a perspective. To follow his story is like having a personal tour guide to nineteenth-century American history. He was a witness to many significant events in his time and felt the effects of still more. His direct impact on national and global affairs was relatively small, but to say he was merely pulled along the current of time with no personal agency would be an unfair assessment. There is nothing passive about negotiating the unchangeable reality of one's world to create meaning out of one's life. In an 1899 letter to the war committees in both chambers of Congress, Mott wrote "my service is my life." But forty years earlier, such conviction was not a given. Deciding what path he would take in life at first vexed him. Mott was keenly aware of the world into which he was born. He knew the expectations others placed on him based on his gender, education, and socio-economic status, but he would always forge his own path and think for himself. As he experienced new cultures and met people different from him, whether they be Lakota warriors on the field of battle, African-American Troops under his command, or the howling dervishes of Turkey, Mott challenged prevailing notions that he easily could have taken at face value and thought no more deeply about. While not immune to the conventional social and cultural mores of his day, Mott harbored a natural skepticism that made him an independent thinker. The author of an 1895 article in a writer for Anaconda Montana's *Anaconda Standard* once described Mott as "a very genial and approachable gentleman, a 'Simon Pure' American of the old school who thinks the United States is good enough for anybody."[1] While not untrue, it was an overly-simplistic assessment. The author had clearly never heard about the time Mott threatened to expatriate himself over frustrations with his government or roundly criticize his superiors for the sufferings of the country's indigenous peoples.

Throughout the course of his military career, Mott experienced life like few others could. Though a native of Philadelphia, Mott grew up in West Chester, Pennsylvania where he was educated under a militaristic French headmaster. In his early twenties, the South seceded from the Union and he commanded a company of volunteer soldiers in the subsequent Civil War, fighting in some of that conflict's most horrific battles—from famous engagements like Gettysburg to smaller skirmishes like Bethesda Church, unsurpassed in its savagery yet obscured by the relatively small number of soldiers involved.

After the War, Mott joined the ranks of the regular army on the recommendations of prestigious generals.[2] Mott's long career in the army brought him face to face with the likes of George Custer and Sitting Bull, storied figures in the history of the American West. He encountered numerous dangers of life on the frontier, at times fighting for his life in engagements with various Native American nations or keeping settlers in their place.

In the 1870s, as part of several forces called to quell labor unrest, Mott was witness to the birth of unionization which would shape labor relations in the country. A brief stint in New Orleans during the city's White League Insurrection reminded Mott that emancipation and the Confederate surrender at Appomattox was just the beginning of a tumultuous reconstruction of the South and the struggle for civil rights. His travels abroad exposed him to new cultures and new people bringing him to the dazzling sites of the ancient world, the holiest places at the heart of Christianity, the lavish halls of Asian royalty, and the barren immensity of the Siberian plateaus.[3]

Yet for all of this, Mott's military memoir, written towards the end of his career in 1899, comprises a grand total of sixteen pages, the last several being occupied by appendices. By that time he had only three years left in his career, but those three years would find him commanding troops in Cuba and the Philippines during the Spanish-American

War. Given Mott's penchant for brevity and humility, it is not likely these events would have enlarged his book much had he chosen to amend it later. The memoir was likely written as a resume of sorts in furtherance of attaining a promotion, but although it covers the important milestones of his career, it is wanting when trying to really understand Mott as a person. It doesn't help that even in his own time, his life was tantalizingly shrouded in mystery. In the mid-1880s, an anonymous contributor to West Chester's *Daily Local News* wrote, "Captain Mott Hooton is a man of retired disposition, but he has led a most eventful life if one could get at his career...he is a genuine hero, but a modest one."[4]

The modesty and near anonymity he created around an otherwise exciting life present a vexing challenge for the historian. Indeed it is often a significant challenge when looking to focus less on the famous and more on the everyday. Fame often comes with at least one advantage for the historical biographer- a proliferation of source material. We are fortunate that a fair number of letters and other primary source materials exist by which to reconstruct Mott's life, but at times we are also painfully aware of how non-comprehensive that material is. It takes more careful analysis of the sources that do exist and creative research to fill in the gaps. For example, if the subject was tightlipped about who they were, perhaps a close friend or family member might have been more forthcoming.

Perhaps the most honest and perceptive estimation of Mott's character is revealed in a brief 1871 letter from a young woman named Justine Ingersoll who referred to Mott playfully as a "miserable old Diogenes," an allusion to the ancient Greek philosopher and father of Cynicism.[5] It was a telling observation, perhaps more than she knew. Born about 412 BCE in the time of Plato and Alexander the Great, Diogenes of Sinope eschewed the trappings and social mores of civilized society. Skeptical of authority and the merits of arbitrarily prescribed social convention, he believed that "civilization" denied the fundamental animalistic nature of humankind. As such, Diogenes chose to live an ascetic life of self-reliance, adaptability, and poverty, wandering the streets virtually naked, sleeping, as popularly purported, in a tub or large ceramic jar. He rejected notions of fame, personal exceptionalism, and what he saw as artificial political boundaries, preferring instead to think of himself as a citizen of the world. In an era in which a person's identity remained intrinsically linked to their city-state (Athenian, Spartan, Corinthian, etc.), it was a bold and unusual statement.

Taken literally, such a comparison would seem a bit hyperbolic. After all, Mott did not eschew society, deny himself the acquisition of wealth, or wander the streets naked sleeping in a tub. As a member of the Army, an organization decidedly strict in its formal hierarchy, Mott could hardly be accused of rejecting authority and social stratification. However, viewed within the context of Mott's life, the allusion bears some merit. At its heart, the ancient philosophy of cynicism posited that true happiness could only be achieved through "self-sufficiency, freedom, detachment, [and] training aimed at instilling physical and moral toughness or endurance."[6] Mott knew how to take care of himself in some of the harshest and remotest environments. Though bound by the dictates of his army, the frequent movement to new locations offered, in a sense, a freedom that many of his cohort back east, their roots firmly planted, would never know. It also isolated him from society in a way that could be considered detached. That he never married further exemplified his reticence at being pinned down. Moreover, the lifestyle attributed to the ancient Cynics, including "relying on nature...traveling the country with little protection against the elements," in many ways parallels the "roughing-it," Spartan nature of Mott's life in the army.[7]

Mott could be a man of convention, but he never shied away from iconoclasm when it suited him. He remained steadfastly loyal to the Army and its command structure, but he was not afraid to denounce any superior officer he disliked. In an age where most members of his socio-economic status were God-fearing Christians, Mott's attitudes toward religion were, at best, ambivalent, sometimes inciting the admonishment of relatives. Exhibiting a skepticism that the ancient Cynics would respect, he refused to assume that the worldview with which he was raised was necessarily the correct one simply by virtue of being born to it. Similarly, though loyal to his government, he didn't shy away from being critical of its policies if he believed them to be wrong.

In terms of marriage, Diogenes was purported to have said that a young man should wait to marry and an old man should never marry—a paradoxical statement ultimately intended to suggest that one should not marry.[8] Mott was quite popular with the ladies, but he would stay a confirmed bachelor his entire life. Diogenes' self-identification as a citizen of the world likewise jives with the restless wanderlust that Mott consistently exhibited, living a transient, pseudo-Bohemian lifestyle, traveling the world and moving between forts, almost never staying in one place for more than a year or two. Although the nature of army life hardly makes the latter movements Mott's personal choice, it may have been part of what attracted him to the Army in the first place.

Diogenes was said to be in constant search for "an honest man." Among the bizarre behavior he was purported to exhibit, Diogenes supposedly traveled around carrying a lantern, lit even during the day. When passersby would ask him about it, he would simply tell them he was in search of an honest man, though in true cynical fashion, he claimed never to have found one.[9] For his part, Mott also held honesty and personal honor in the highest regard. He suffered no fools and had little patience for cowardice, dishonesty, or treason. In this, Mott could be almost zealous.

What follows is not an academic history. It is an account of an ordinary man who lived an extraordinary life. He was a career soldier with an impressive record, a world traveler with a keen and open mind, a confirmed bachelor, yet ever the family man, and a modest figure with a habit of crossing paths with some of the most important people of his day.

This is the story of Brigadier General Mott Hooton.

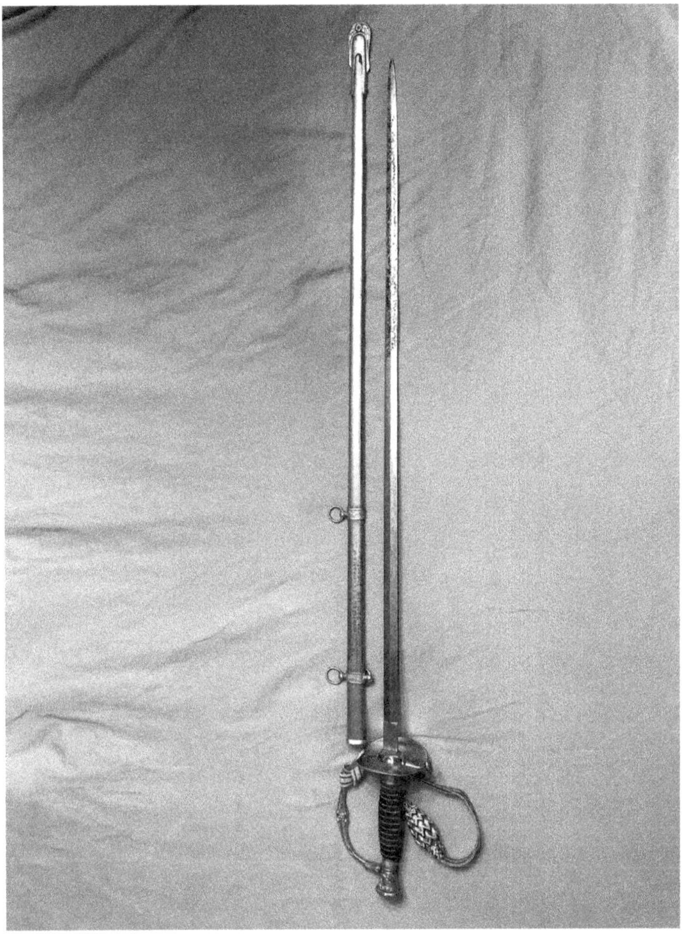

Symbol of service: Mott's Presentation sword from the 22nd Infantry
Courtesy of Decker Landry

Mott's wayward trunk: Dating from the Civil War, he later used it to
store letters, photographs and other paraphernalia

Courtesy of Decker Landry

I

A Childhood of Opportunity

The Philadelphia hardware merchant was only twenty-five when "with Christian firmness and resignation," he succumbed to Consumption on October 20, 1838.[1] It should have been the prime of his life. Just three years earlier, he stood before Reverend Samuel A. McCrosky in St. Andrew's Episcopal Church where he exchanged vows with Ann Eliza Carpenter, the daughter of a respected Philadelphia lawyer and businessman.[2] In the intervening years two sons were born, the hope of a bright future for the young family. But Mott Hooton would barely get to know them. The youngest was only six months old when Ann laid her husband to rest in St. Andrew's Episcopal Cemetery at Fifth and Spruce Streets in Philadelphia.[3]

The funeral cortege set out from the stately row home of Ann's father, John Carpenter, located on Union Street just above Third Street.[4] There are no accounts of the funeral, but assembled around the grave one would have expected to see those family members closest to him in life. Mott's father, Andrew Hooton, was an alderman in Moyamensing, a neighborhood in South Philadelphia. Born in Nova Scotia in 1786, Andrew moved to Moorestown, New Jersey as a young man before relocating to Philadelphia to work as a real estate agent and conveyancer. Andrew had lost his wife, Mary, several years before, but he would not have stood alone at his son's grave. Four daughters—Rebecca, Elizabeth, Catherine, and Rachel—as well as another son, Isaac, were likely all there to pay their last respects to their brother.[5]

The young widow Ann relied on her own family for support. Her father, John was a lawyer and businessman in the city, though his roots lay in the small village of Marshallton in West Bradford, Chester County, Pennsylvania about forty miles southeast of Philadelphia.[6] Like Andrew Hooton, John was also a widower having lost his wife Sally several years earlier. Ann's siblings stayed close and took to heart the adage that it takes a village to raise a child. Emily, William, John Jr., and Frank would each play a role in the lives of their two fatherless nephews, but none would have the same impact as Ann's eldest sister, Susan. Born in 1802, Susan Carpenter was thirteen years Ann's senior. Possessing a keen mind, fierce independence, and more than a little love of town gossip, Susan never married. Though childless herself, she would become no less a second mother to the two boys. Her warmth, her strength, and her wisdom would prove vital in the development of Ann's two boys.

As the final funeral rites were said, the eyes of those in attendance drifted toward those two young boys. Just a week shy of his second birthday, Francis Carpenter Hooton, called Frank by family and friends and later F. C. in professional life, was born on October 31, 1836. The youngest had been born just that spring on April 16, 1838. At only six months old, the baby was entirely unaware of what was happening. Bearing his father's name, Mott Hooton Jr. would honor his namesake's legacy by living the long and full life that had been denied his father.

As Mott grew, the two halves of his family—the Hootons and the Carpenters—presented an interesting dichotomy. Both families were originally of English Quaker stock. The Hootons traced their genealogy to Oliver and Elizabeth Hooton, the latter purported to be the first female preacher in the Society of Friends. Elizabeth visited the American colonies several times in the seventeenth century and her daughter would settle in New Jersey, establishing the American branch of the family.[7] The Carpenters hailed from Gloucestershire and settled in Chester County Pennsylvania in the early eighteenth century where the family would remain until the late nineteenth century.[8]

During the Revolution, the two families landed on opposite sides of the War for Independence. The Hootons cast their lot with England. Mott's great-grandfather, Jacob Hooton, served as a Captain in the King's American Dragoons. After the war, Jacob and his wife, Rachel Mott, left the newly-created United States of America and headed for Canada, where they established their family. Meanwhile, Mott's Carpenter great-grandfather, Thomas Carpenter, supported the cause of independence. He joined the 6th Pennsylvania Militia as Captain of Company A, serving in Long Island, New York and participating in the Battle of Monmouth before settling down in Marshallton to raise his family.[9]

The two families had not been connected during the Revolution, but the ideological divide between them would recur during the Civil War. The Carpenters, who remained in Pennsylvania, settling in Chester and Delaware Counties with close ties to Philadelphia, were staunchly pro-Union. Meanwhile, most of the Hootons moved south into Maryland where the state's formal connection to the Union during the conflict belied the Confederate sympathies of its citizens. Rachel Hooton, the elder Mott's sister, married David Crane Blackiston, a prominent farmer from Kent County, Maryland who would later serve as a Maryland State Senator for most of the 1860s. Their home, Bright Helmstone, would become the family seat of sorts for the Hooton clan.

Not long after the funeral, as many of the Hootons ventured south, Andrew Hooton left the eastern seaboard entirely to take up farming in Iowa where he would serve as a delegate to the state's first constitutional convention in 1844.[10] Ann remained in Philadelphia to begin raising her two boys with the help of her family. Living in the city, Ann could provide her boys first-rate education. Both Mott and Frank attended the Friends Select School, a Quaker institution then located on Orange Street between Seventh and Eighth Streets near Washington Square for their early schooling.[11] After a few years, Ann found herself in a predicament when she fell in love with the brother of her sister's husband. In 1842, Ann's sister Emily married a gentleman from Delaware County named Thomas Rhoads. Aunt Em and Uncle Tommy, as Frank and Mott knew them, maintained a constant presence in Ann's life and the upbringing of the two boys. Through their union, Ann met Maris Rhoads, Uncle Tommy's brother. The two fell in love and within a few years, on April 1, 1845, Ann and Maris were married in Philadelphia in a ceremony officiated by the mayor, Peter McCall.[12]

The marriage was a happy affair. The next year, Ann gave birth to a girl, Sallie Rhoads, named after Ann's mother. Five years later, a second girl, Ann Eliza "Annie" Rhoads was born. But it was not long after her marriage that Ann realized she could not remain in Philadelphia. Her new husband was a farmer and there was little Maris could do in the city. His land was in rural Springfield, Delaware County about ten miles to the southwest. Ann could not bring herself to move her boys out there. Although Pennsylvania had established public education throughout the state with the Free School Act of 1834, the educational opportunities in a place like Springfield paled in comparison to the private education available in Philadelphia. For families that could afford it, private schools remained the preference over the new public education system. Ann valued education too highly to sacrifice her boys' futures on account of her marriage and so she made the difficult decision to leave Frank and Mott in the care of her sister Susan and father, John.

Despite the separation from their mother, the boys continued to flourish in Philadelphia for the next three years until 1848 when their grandfather John decided to retire and move back to his native Chester County. His bachelor son, John Jr, owned a farm just outside of the borough of West Chester and as the town was quickly gaining a reputation as the "Athens of Pennsylvania" due to the quality of private education in the borough, it was an acceptable place to relocate Frank and Mott.[13] So the elder Carpenter brought his daughter Susan and the two boys to live with John Jr. The farm consisted of approximately forty-three acres with a stone farmhouse, a large barn and other small outbuildings. The land was arable and included a small apple orchard.[14] Not more than a mile or two down the road, John Sr. enrolled the boys in Bolmar's academy.[15] Its headmaster, a former officer in the French cavalry, ran the school with military precision and attracted students from prominent families throughout the United States and abroad to study under "the Napoleon of Teachers."[16]

Jean Claude Antoine Brunin de Bolmar was born in 1797 in Bourbon-Lancy, a town in Burgundy, France. He served in the 6th Hussars during the 1823 French invasion of Spain to restore the Bourbon King, Ferdinand VII, to power after a revolt by the Spanish military. After a six-year stint in the army, Bolmar traveled throughout Europe before sailing to America and settling in Philadelphia in the late 1820s. Truncating and anglicizing his name to Anthony, Bolmar established himself as a French teacher and wrote several well-regarded textbooks. In 1832, Bolmar fled a Cholera epidemic in the city and found himself in the small village of West Chester. At that point, the town was little more than a sleepy crossroad, but he enjoyed it so much he decided to stay.[17]

Bolmar expanded his teaching role in West Chester, taking over the West Chester Academy in 1834, the predecessor to the West Chester Normal School.[18] Six years later, he learned of the closure of an all-girls boarding school at the north end of town. Bolmar decided to purchase the property and establish his own boarding school for boys. Occupying twenty-three acres along Marshall Street near Franklin Street, the school consisted of a large, four-story building, a working farm, and several outbuildings for staff residences.[19]

"Old Bollie," as the students affectionately referred to their headmaster, ran his new school with militaristic discipline. He demanded students adhere to a strict moral code and expected honesty and peer pressure to control troublemaking over more traditional methods of corporal punishment. Drinking and fighting were not permitted and all spending money allocated to the students by their families were impounded and doled out by Bolmar on the weekends for spending in town—usually for ice cream and candy at Lydia Pyle's shop on Gay Street.[20] Any student who could not abide by his rules or was found lacking either academically or morally was summarily expelled.[21] Mott would later adopt a similar no-nonsense policy throughout his career when it came to the conduct of those under his command. His instruction under Old Bollie likely influenced his own approach to discipline.

Frank and Mott received a well-rounded education at the academy. The standard curriculum included English, history, mathematics, Latin, and geography. For an extra fee, one could take an additional language class in French, Spanish, or German.[22] Only a minority of students at the academy were local. Students from as far away as Cuba and South America came to West Chester to study under Bolmar. Many prominent military families in the American South sent their sons for instruction as well, including Robert E. Lee, the future Confederate general whose son William Henry Fitzhugh "Rooney" Lee attended the institution.[23] Born in 1837, William H. F. Lee would have been a contemporary of the Hooton boys. It is entirely possible they overlapped.

In 1859, well after Frank and Mott had left the institution, Bolmar temporarily closed the school to attend to some business back in France. He returned the following year and attempted to reopen, but fomenting tensions between North and South meant that he had lost many of the Southern aristocrats who had formed a particularly solid base for new recruitment. In 1861, the year the Civil War broke out, Bolmar stabbed himself in the heart with a dagger, taking his own life. The militaristic reputation he built the school on continued as it subsequently became the home of the Pennsylvania Military Academy in 1862 and then later a military academy run by William Wyers in 1866.[24]

That both Mott and Frank could attend such a high-profile school reflects the level of affluence to which they were both born. The average tuition was about $250 per year, which accounting for inflation, equates to a little over $8,200 in purchasing power in today's money.[25] Assuming the boys' time at the school overlapped, the tuition would have been quite costly. However, it seems the family could afford it. John Carpenter's household included Irish domestic servants and between two and three African-American laborers, as did the household of Mott's stepfather, Maris.[26] In 1850, their Aunt Susan alone possessed real estate valued at around $20,000, or just over $667,000 today. Her brother had real estate valued at about half of that.[27] Mott himself would claim a personal wealth of nearly $100,000 in today's money as a young, thirty-two-year-old Lieutenant in 1870.[28]

The family supplemented their income with property ownership. Mott, personally, would make oblique references throughout his life to properties he owned at one time or another in Chester County and elsewhere. He came to own at least two farms in Chester County and one property in St. Paul Minnesota, though he did not hold on to the latter for very long as the distance complicated the management of it.[29] Frank would likewise own several investment properties, mostly farms, in western Chester County, though through financial mismanagement he would later have to sell off at various times.[30] Their Aunt Susan shared ownership in a building on 3rd Street north of Chestnut in Philadelphia with Ann and Maris. The rent from the ground-level store and the several stories of apartments above provided a decent income. The value of that property alone totaled $28,000 by 1872, or nearly $600,000 today. Mott and Frank would later inherit her share.[31] Finally, Maris and Ann owned additional property in Camden, New Jersey.[32] They would not have been counted among the highest echelons of the social elite, but they were respectably comfortable in their finances.

Although they benefitted from hired labor to help maintain the farm, both Frank and Mott spent time working on the land. In 1854, Mott kept a farm diary. Though unremarkable in content—consisting primarily of brief statements about animal sales, purchases, breeding and births—the diary reveals a sixteen-year-old young man perhaps beginning to think of his place in the world. Mott scrawled variations of his signature along several of the pages, trying to perfect his personal mark. On other pages, he doodled images of military officers shouldering their muskets as if betraying a fascination that foreshadowed the direction his life would eventually take.[33] Bolmar's influence likely played a role in Mott's eventual interest in the military, but there was another role model nearby who might have inspired his drawings.

In 1853, the year before Mott's diary doodling, George Archibald

McCall purchased the farm next door. McCall had come to West Chester to enjoy a quiet retirement with his wife after a long career in the military. Born in 1802 into a prominent Philadelphia family, McCall graduated from the United States Military Academy at West Point in 1822. For thirty years, he served with the army, participating in the Seminole Wars in Florida in the 1830s and the Mexican War in the 1840s. He rose steadily through the ranks, earning a brevet Major and then Lieutenant Colonel for his actions at the Battles of Palo Alto and Resaca de Palma, respectively during the Mexican War. By 1850, he was granted a Colonelcy and appointed Inspector General of the Army. After his service in Texas, McCall's health began to suffer. Just three years into his post as inspector general, McCall retired to convalesce and live a quiet life in the country.

McCall's health gradually stabilized and improved during his time in West Chester. From his estate, which he named 'Belair,' he pursued an active interest in natural science and authored his *Letters from the Frontiers*, an account of his service out West. McCall frequently entertained visitors to talk about the old days in the military. He had a particular fondness for meeting fellow veterans and those who served under him, famously sending them away with a bit of extra pocket money at the same time. As the reputation of his generosity became widely known, some asked him how he knew his visitors weren't lying about their service just to squeeze some money out of him, to which McCall calmly replied, "if a man has the cheek to claim to have fought under me, I cannot refuse him. I never yet sent one of them away as poor as he came, and I never will."[34] Mott certainly knew McCall, the latter referring to Mott as "my young friend," but their exact relationship is not known.[35] Given McCall's penchant for reminiscences with social callers, it would not be surprising if at times the colonel regaled the young teenager with tales of his travels and military exploits.

***

An inspiration next door: George A. McCall

National Portrait Gallery, Smithsonian Institution, Frederick Hill Meserve
Collection

In 1851, Mott's Uncle John passed away at only thirty years of age. The farm was initially offered for sale, but the family seems to have held on to at least some of the property for the rest of the 1850s in Susan's name.[36] But as the decade of the 1850s progressed, Mott and Frank approached the age of maturity at which point they would each have to decide how and when to leave the farm. For all intents and purposes, they grew up wanting for nothing, but ultimately reached very different conclusions about what to do with the opportunities and privileges they had been afforded. For Frank, the level of respectability he had as a member of the burgeoning professional middle class would never be enough. As a young man starting out on his own, he directed all his energies to change that, determined to make a name for himself. He read law and was admitted to the bar in late 1857, the day before his twenty-first birthday. By early 1859 at the age of twenty-two, barely having begun his professional life, he stood as a candidate for county District Attorney.[37] Though unsuccessful in that first bid, throughout his life he would continue to seek public office and hobnob with the upper echelons of West Chester and Philadelphia society in furtherance of his own social and political advancement.

Mott, on the other hand, lacked the clear ambition of his brother. When the Civil War broke out in 1861, Mott was twenty-three and still working the farm.[38] There is no evidence of any other professional vocation. While he may have been content to farm and own property, it is more likely he either did not know what he wanted to do with his life or, if he already felt drawn to the military, did not want to admit his ambitions to his family for fear of their disapproval.[39] Mott lost his grandfather the previous year, which may also have contributed to Mott's reticence to leave his Aunt Susan alone.

As political tensions grew after Abraham Lincoln's election in the fall of 1860, it became increasingly clear the country was hurtling toward war. This changed Mott's vocational. When a young lawyer in town started soliciting volunteers to join his company of soldiers in defense of Pennsylvania against the looming conflict, Mott answered his call.

Old Bollie's School: Bolmar's Academy, West Chester, PA
Library of Congress

2

The Brandywine Guards

"I have never had a Confederate flag, but when I go to Baltimore I intend to buy one and wear it!" Kate seethed to Mott. "Then, if your cousin is sent to Penitentiary to wear her life away, I shall send for you and get you to do my work while I sing 'secession' songs!"[1] The correspondence from Kate Blackiston, the daughter of Mott's paternal Aunt Rachel, reflected the beliefs of much of his Hooton relations in Maryland who believed the federal government in Washington to have devolved into tyranny and the Union soldiers to be nothing more than a "lawful band of murderers."[2] Kate's brother, Hooton Blackiston, had quickly traveled south at the opening of hostilities to enlist in the Confederate army from a state that had seceded. Kate only wished she could join him. "If I were a man, I would have long since gone south armed like David of old with the five smooth stones from the brook, trusting in the name of the Lord of Hosts, would have willingly have met their Goliath!" she declared. Mott's Aunt Rachel shared her daughter's convictions blaming the Union for the destitution of so many innocent civilians caught in the middle of the conflict. "Can you, darling, see an American woman hungry and not feed her?" Rachel questioned Mott's brother Frank. "Why Frank, when Yankee soldiers pass here and ask for food, I always give it to them and I know I detest them more than you can those poor, helpless women. And what made them poor and ragged and hungry? The invasion of their once fruitful country by an enemy."[3] The ideological divide in Mott's family lent credence to the allusion of the American Civil War as a Cain and Abel story and it mirrored the country's implacably deep divisions.

The election of 1860 was one of the most tumultuous elections in the nation's brief history. In the years leading up to the campaign, the westward expansion of the United States had raised questions regarding any corresponding expansion of the South's "peculiar institution" into the new territories. Should slavery be legal in a newly-created territory or state or not and whose decision was it? They were not academic questions. For the North, the moral soul of the nation depended upon the answers. For the South, their way of life and power in government hung in the balance. Various compromises in the decades before the election tried to balance slave-owning and non-slave-owning interests through legislation such as the Missouri Compromise which divided the country in half at about the 36th parallel. Under the compromise, all territories or states above the line, with the exception of Missouri, out-lawed slavery, while those below allowed it. In the intervening years, as a result of the annexation of Texas and other territory in the Mexican-American War, the issue of slave status for new territories continued to be a hot-button issue. Further compromises had kept disunion at bay through a variety of concessions including strengthening fugitive slave laws and allowing new territories to determine their slave status for themselves. However, these were temporary fixes that never addressed the heart of the matter. The enslavement of human beings was a moral issue for which there could never truly be a compromise.

The Republican party emerged in response to this very issue in 1854 and it coalesced around a platform of opposing the expansion of slavery. The emergence of this new party, whose raison d'etre in part fundamentally threatened a key component of the Southern economy and way of life, did nothing to lower the temperature over the issue. When the party nominated the Illinois lawyer and former United States Representative Abraham Lincoln for President in 1860, the tense relationship between the pro and anti-slavery factions in Congress quickly deteriorated. Lincoln had no plans to abolish slavery outright, but nor was he interested in placating the Southern desire for perpetual balance between slave-holding states and non-slave-holding states. The Republican platform challenged expansion, not abolition. Their strategy was one of containment. They had resolved to allow slavery to exist where it currently did but sought to forbid its expansion elsewhere. The South perceived this strategy as a war of attrition. As more and more free territories and states were admitted, the representation of slave-holding interests in Congress would become diluted. Once weakened in influence, the only logical conclusion for the Southern legislatures was the eventual extinction of slavery.

In November 1860, Lincoln won the presidency handily. Carrying eighteen states and one hundred eight more electoral votes than the second-place candidate, Southern Democrat John Breckinridge, Lincoln demonstrated the power of the relatively new Republican platform. Many Southern states responded by seceding from the Union. South Carolina was the first to leave on December 20, over three months before Lincoln took office. By inauguration day—then in March—six more states had followed. Some in Congress made attempts in late 1860 during the lame duck session to pass constitutional amendments permanently enshrining slavery in the states and territories where it existed in a last-ditch effort to stave off disunion and prevent the Federal Government from ever abolishing the institution, but their efforts ultimately failed.

The separated states formed their own union, the Confederate States of America, with their capital in Richmond, Virginia. Jefferson Davis, United States Senator from Mississippi turned Confederate President, quickly sought the peaceful transfer of all federal property in their territory, including military installations, to Confederate ownership. Lincoln refused to negotiate with a government he did not recognize as legitimate and ordered the garrisons in the southern forts to remain at their posts. On April 12, 1861, the Confederates decided to take them by force opening fire on one particular fort in South Carolina—Fort Sumter. With that act, the Civil War had officially begun.

***

Confederate soldiers were acutely aware that the motive for secession was to preserve slavery. Though not blind to the issue of slavery at the forefront of the conflict, many northern soldiers fought, initially, simply to suppress a traitorous rebellion. Abolition would not be an expressed goal for the Union until President Lincoln passed the Emancipation Act in 1863.

For Southerners, secession was always about slavery. Flowery speeches espousing lofty goals such as the right to self-determination, states' rights, freedom from the tyranny of Northern policies, and the preservation of their way of life sounded noble, but they belied the issue of slavery at its core. The right they were afraid to lose was the right to keep slaves. The right to self-determination was the right to determine themselves as keepers of the enslaved. The only way of life under threat by an overwhelming Republican majority in Congress was the reliance on slave labor.

Jefferson Davis understood that the containment policy that the Republicans sought would eventually choke out the influence of slaveholding states until the institution could be easily extinguished. It was for this reason, the threat to slavery, that he justified the South breaking away. Containment would render "property in slaves so insecure as to be comparatively worthless, and thereby annihilating in effect property worth thousands of millions of dollars," Davis would write to the Provisional Congress of the Confederate States of America in April 1861.[4] Alexander Stephens, Vice President of the Confederate States of America, in his famous "cornerstone" speech from March 1861 shortly before the attack on Fort Sumpter, stated the case more bluntly. Stephens emphatically declared that slavery and the threat to the institution posed by Lincoln and his political ilk was "the immediate cause of the late rupture and the present revolution."[5] The Confederacy was not formed simply to maintain slavery, Stephens noted, it was entirely built upon the notion that slavery and racial inequality were irrevocable moral truths to be enshrined. "Its foundations are laid, its cornerstone rests, upon the great truth that the negro is not equal to the white man; that slavery, subordination to the superior race, is his natural and normal condition. This, our new government, is the first, in the history of the world, based on this great physical, philosophical, and moral truth."[6]

Of course, northerners hadn't forgotten about slavery in those early days. Despite the official stance of the Government not to abolish slavery outright, many still hoped to see abolition as the end game. William Henry Darlington, a volunteer sergeant who would fight with Mott and a member of one of Chester County's oldest, most prolific, and most respected families, wrote home from Camp Carroll outside Baltimore in 1861:

I am content to work and wait, and the longer the contest the more certain the issue. We need defeat to bring about the proper issue of this war, anything less... would be a disappointment to me, however easily gained. I hope the contest may go on through defeat, and through victory, through blood and misery and death, till not a single shackle shall remain in all America, and every human being shall be free.[7]

Darlington's identification of the "proper issue" of the war and the idea that they would not have completely done their job if the rebellion were simply stymied and reunification was achieved without emancipation for the enslaved suggested at least some northerners saw the conflict from the beginning as the final reckoning over the institution of slavery.

Mott's family, like many others who found themselves on opposite sides of the national conflict, struggled to maintain the familial love they still felt for each other in the face of such disparate political ideologies. "Oh Frank, when will these horrid times be over?" Rachel Blackiston wrote to her nephew in West Chester. "When will friends meet as once they did?"[8] Rachel felt the tensions particularly acutely as her sister, Rebecca who lived in Philadelphia was one of the few in her immediate family who had not sided with the Confederacy. "I have worried about Rebecca lately," She wrote. "I believe she has a hard time. I have half a mind to go see her when I go to the city, how will it do? David and the children are opposed to my doing so. They say I will lay myself open to insult."[9] Rachel's conciliatory attitude towards her sister led to her children jokingly calling her a Yankee, though even Mott's cousin Kate, for all her vitriol, tried to make allowances for family. "Mott, what a pity that you and I should each be devoted to different sections with such fervor!" she lamented. "I candidly believe you think you are right (all I think fault of education). And you show it by your willingness to give up your life."[10] However, no one felt the pain of the rift like that family patriarch, Andrew Hooton.

Mott's seventy-six-year-old grandfather, still in Iowa in early 1862, deeply regretted the conflict in the family. "How bad it looks for relatives to quarrel about politics or religion. That's the one thing I will not do. I leave all free to act, think, and do as they see fit. All I ask is the same privilege."[11] Mott held a special place in Andrew's heart for he remained one of the only tangible links to his deceased son. "I love you dearly, not only for your warmth but for the name you bear," he would later write to Mott. "You cannot but know you have long since found the bottom of my heart."[12] Andrew did not offer his own opinion on the political climate, but at his age, his priority was simply keeping the family together. "We shall be so happy when you shall be able to return to visit your relatives and friends. May God speed that happy time," he wrote two years later as the war raged.

Let us again extend the hand of love across the troubled land between us and strengthen that silver cord of love which I trust naught but Death can sever. I, my dear, was 78 on New Year's Day. I think I hear my darling son say, 'Grandpa, your race is very near run.' Time's hourglass, which he never reverses, and suspended over my head must be near exhausted and as the last sand falls, I must then pass to another and I hope better world unless this Christianity be a fable, and that cannot be. Then let us so live that we may be

amongst the blessed and loved ones who have proceeded us and you are aware
we have many in the spirit land.[13]

Relations between Mott and his southern family though strained
were never actually severed. Mott would never be as close to his Hooton
relatives as his Union-loyal Carpenter connections, but he would continue to keep in touch with them for the rest of his life.

***

On April 15, 1861, three days after the assault on Fort Sumter, President Lincoln called on volunteers from across the Union states to take
up arms. The regular army of the United States at the time stood at just
over 16,000 men. It was a paltry amount, especially considering that
no small number of officers native to the South defected to the Confederacy in defense of their home states. Volunteer enlistments were set
at three months, a naïve reflection on the length of time the government believed it would take to put down the rebellion. Pennsylvania
answered Lincoln's call more than any other Union state, not just out
of loyalty to the Union, but also for its own protection.

Pennsylvania occupied a particularly delicate geographic position
in the conflict and its people knew it. Although their southern neighbors, Maryland and Delaware, remained Union states in practice, most
Marylanders would have preferred to have seceded with their southern brethren and the sympathies of Delaware's citizenry were divided.
With the exception of Washington D.C., Pennsylvania realistically
represented the gateway to the north. Being on the state's southern
border, the people of Chester County felt particularly anxious about
their geographic reality. In Kennett Square, a small town in southern
Chester County, citizens flew into action doing whatever they could to
prepare for the worst. Women sewed uniforms while men, armed with
whatever they could find, conducted nightly patrols. Bayard Taylor, a
renowned diplomat, author, world traveler and Kennett native turned
Cedarcroft, his stately home just north of town, into a fortification

of sorts, keeping watch on the immediate area from its tower. Armed with his "African swords," he too patrolled with his fellow townspeople. "Everything here is upside down," Taylor wrote about a week after the Fort Sumter attack. "We live almost in a state of siege, with the rumors of war flying about us. At present, we don't know what is going on. We have reckless secessionists within twelve miles of us...The excitement and anxiety is really terrible. We are so near the frontier that if the damnable Maryland traitors are not checked within three days we may have to meet them here."[14]

Less than ten miles north of Kennett, Mott witnessed a similar level of activity in West Chester, though not everyone in the borough was content to wait for the fight to come to them. A Benjamin Sweeney, a local grocer, met with James Given, a tobacconist in town, and decided to raise such a company of so-called "three-month men" in answer to Lincoln's call. They dubbed their small unit of volunteers the West Chester Rifles and sent word to Governor Andrew Curtin in Harrisburg that the "baker and his rowdy mechanics," as one historian referred to them, stood ready to fight.[15] Additionally, Henry Guss who commanded the county's two-hundred-fifty-member militia likewise reported their readiness to the governor. Communities across the state formed similar volunteer units and Curtin quickly filled the quota Washington had set him. In fact, he greatly exceeded it. He had more men at his disposal than he knew what to do with.

Curtin did not let the outpouring of support go to waste. Although he had met his obligations to Lincoln, he believed the extra men could be of vital importance in defense of the state against potential invasion, which inspired the governor to form a home guard comprised of the excess volunteers. On May 15, 1861, in response to Curtin's proposal, the Pennsylvania State Legislature approved the creation of the Pennsylvania Reserves, an all-volunteer unit of thirteen regiments of infantry, one regiment of cavalry, and one of artillery.

Once again, Chester County responded robustly. Young men from communities all around the county began organizing their own volunteer companies, giving themselves descriptive nicknames like the Exton

Guards or the Phoenixville Artillerists. In West Chester, Henry McIntire, a twenty-six-year-old lawyer and native of Cecil County, Maryland took it upon himself to form his own company drawing on men from the town and throughout the Brandywine Valley to the south and west. It did not take McIntire long to fill up the roster for his Brandywine Guards, as the company was christened. Among the first to sign up was Mott Hooton.

In some ways, the Brandywines represented the professional class of West Chester. Being a lawyer, it's not surprising that McIntire would attract his peers in the town. No less than six other lawyers and a law student joined him. Other white-collar professions filled out the ranks —clerks, merchants, teachers. He even counted a dentist on the rolls. By far the most frequently listed occupation among the men was "farmer," but many could be more accurately described as gentleman farmers as opposed to toilers in the fields.[16] At the time of his enlistment, Mott fit within this last category. News of the company's formation spread far and wide amongst their social circle even as far as Nebraska where William Bowen, a friend of Mott's who had recently moved there, had heard of the Brandywine Guards and the social class they represented. He was pleased to see Mott enlisted and particularly so as a non-commissioned Sergeant. "This...relieved a fear I had that only the lower classes were enlisting, those of better fortune only going as commissioned officers," Bowen remarked to Mott. "While I do not deny that the officers should be filled by the most capable and intelligent, I don't see why a gentleman shouldn't serve his country as a Private."[17] Still, the demographic trends were not absolute. Amidst the Darlingtons, Hoopeses, Matlacks, Brintons, and Copes in the muster, representing some of the county's most prominent families, there was no shortage of laborers and tradesmen including blacksmiths, pump makers, molders, cabinet makers, printers, painters, and one young man listed only as a "tinkerer."[18]

Founder of the Brandywine Guards: Henry McIntire (Detail)
Courtesy of the Chester County History Center, West Chester, PA

The Brandywines quickly coalesced into a tight-knit group. Indeed, many of the men were already friends or relatives. Philip Price, one of the company's sergeants, referred to the band of men as "a small company of faithful ones" and in writing to the anxious mother of a young recruit, Price extolled the virtues of the men.[19] "Being in our company, the Brandywine Guards," Price wrote, "he is among men, who as a body, in morals I have never met their superiors. I say this honestly without boasting or a desire to mislead thee."[20] Joseph Way, a private in the company, offered this description of the men:

This company is composed principally of stout, hearty young fellows and of about the right stripe too at that...Their motto is onward to victory of their glorious country's cause or death and you may rest assured that the Brandywine Guards will never return to their homes as long as their glorious republic is in danger, nor ever turn our backs to the enemy but will return without a blot on our character.[21]

Less than a month after the attack on Fort Sumter, McIntire counted close to eighty men on his rolls, mostly in their late teens and mid-twenties with a few outliers in their thirties and forties.

On May 2, Mott reported to McIntire in West Chester for inspection along with the other Brandywines. Many of them proudly stood at attention in their homemade or previously-purchased uniforms consisting of a "dark blue cloth coat and pantaloons, trimmed with braid, and blue cloth cap, with oil cloth cover."[22] As was common practice for the next couple of years in volunteer units, the Brandywines likely held their own elections to determine the company's chain of command. Not surprisingly, Henry McIntire assumed command as the company's first Captain followed by John Nields as First Lieutenant and Charles Lamborn of Kennett Square as Second Lieutenant. Mott became the first of the company's four sergeants, followed by eight corporals and the rank-and-file privates.

The majority of the Brandywines had no prior military service, but they found a worthy advisor in local war hero George McCall, who took a keen interest in the Brandywines, not least of which because the company's first sergeant had been a close neighbor of his. When McIntire brought the Brandywines together, McCall came to their aid to help them drill, eager to train them to give them a fighting chance in the conflict.

A couple of weeks later, McIntire traveled to Harrisburg to meet with Governor Curtin and officially offer the Brandywines in service to the state. Without hesitation, Curtin graciously accepted the Brandywines into the Pennsylvania Reserves. The timing of being presented with a volunteer force from West Chester was fortuitous. The Chester County Horticultural Society had recently donated a large swath of land south of West Chester to the state for use as a military camp of instruction. Today the site is primarily occupied by the dormitories of West Chester University, but in 1861, the large open field would play host to hundreds of new recruits. Camp Wayne, as it was christened, became one of a handful of such camps throughout the state.

The first military occupants of Camp Wayne were three-month men. Two regiments, the 9th Pennsylvania and 11th Pennsylvania, were briefly organized at the camp before being shipped out at the end of May. With the Pennsylvania Reserves being organized in earnest, the camp would play host to an even greater number of citizen-soldiers beginning with the Brandywine Guards.

On June 3, 1861, Mott and the Brandywine Guards officially mustered into military service. Captain McIntire marched his home-grown West Chester company through the town to Camp Wayne where unsurprisingly they were the first of the Reserves to occupy it. As the ranking officer, Captain McIntire took command of the camp until the designated staff officers arrived from Harrisburg. As units from the surrounding towns and counties arrived in the succeeding days, the bustling activity around the camp became a spectacle for the local population and the soldiers, in their eagerness to show off, encouraged it. Shouldering their muskets and drilling in their crisp, new uniforms, their drilling was meant to impress their friends and family who regularly came down to spectate as much as it was to prepare for war. Music drifted through the air, the men socialized with each other, and on more than one occasion some young ladies found themselves arrested for certain indiscreet behaviors having gone down to give the young men a good time.[23]

What the camp lacked in military precision it made up for in enthusiasm. "O Lord, Alf, this is great, isn't it?" Luther Mendenhall, a young law student and member of the Brandywine Guards, exclaimed to his tent mate, Alfred Rupert.[24] If they didn't already know one another from their local communities, most of the men quickly bonded with their tent mates. All along the "streets" of white tents scattered across the campground, the men added personalized touches to their accommodations. In particular, many of them bestowed nicknames for their tents posting signs such as "Buckingham Palace," "The American Heroes," and "The Insane Devils."[25] The novelty of Camp Wayne soon grew wearisome for the citizens of West Chester as the rowdiness of the soldiers at times became disruptive and dangerous. Recruits were wounded with some frequency by men getting used to their muskets and the weathervane atop the county courthouse suffered considerably from its attraction as an object for target practice.[26]

Within a couple of weeks, as staff officers arrived to take command and the regiments began to formally organize, discipline improved. The individual companies present at Camp Wayne were divided and organized into two of the fifteen regiments that would make up the Pennsylvania Reserves, the 1st Regiment and the 7th Regiment. The Brandywine Guards were designated Company K in the 1st Reserves. The captains of the companies that made up the newly organized 1st Reserves convened to elect the staff officers that would command the entire regiment. In a bittersweet moment for the Brandywines, the collected captains chose Henry McIntire as Lieutenant Colonel, the regiment's second in command. They were sorry to see him leave the company but were also proud to have one of their own in such a position of honor. McIntire's elevation left a command vacancy in the company. First Lieutenant John Nields, a thirty-one-year-old printer, succeeded McIntire as Captain with Charles Lamborn as First Lieutenant and allowed Mott to assume the rank of Second Lieutenant.

The final staff officer named to the regiment was its commander, but that appointment fell to Governor Curtin who installed Richard Biddle Roberts, a lawyer from Pittsburgh, as colonel of the regiment. A rotund individual with a tired, drooping face that belied his relatively young age, Roberts was thirty-six years old when he joined the staff of Governor Curtin to assist in the raising of the original three-month men from around the state. He proved deeply unpopular with the Brandywines. "This man Roberts is this day the most perfidious black-hearted and malignant-natured man I ever knew," Mott once fumed to his brother.[27] Mott did not disclose what exactly Roberts had done to earn such vitriol, but he was not alone in his feelings. In their personal letters home, several of the Brandywines would privately question both Roberts' courage and competence at various times.

Curtin redeemed himself of Roberts' appointment in Mott's eyes when he convinced George McCall to come out of retirement to serve as a brigadier general in command of the entire Pennsylvania Reserve Corps. There could not have been an appointment more appropriate for the Brandywines. That McCall was local automatically put more than a few checks in his favor, but they remembered the aid he provided them during their early drilling. His devotion to honor and integrity earned him the unmitigated loyalty of the Brandywine Guards. "We don't belong to nobody but General McCall," one of the men would later exclaim in a letter home.[28] Unlike some other commanders under whom they would serve, the soldiers of the Pennsylvania Reserves respected McCall's willingness to ride at the head of the column and encourage the men, rather than bark orders from behind. Alfred Rupert, a member of the Brandywines would later offer this description of McCall and his inspirational soldierly bearing:

An unpopular commander: Richard Biddle Roberts
Courtesy of the Pennsylvania Reserve Volunteer Corps Historical Society
(PRVCHS)

His beard is gray and his mustache gives him a different and more soldierly look. He is a very graceful soldier. As he galloped down the line last evening, his great cloak flying and waving his cap, he seemed to inspire the men with the greatest ardor and a wild shout went down the line such as I have never heard.[29]

McCall reciprocated the affection his men felt for him. He conversed as easily and willingly with the lowliest private as he did with a high-ranking officer and with the same deference. Early in the war, there would be rumors that the army wanted to split up the Pennsylvania Reserves, but McCall would successfully lobby to keep the "family" together. Not surprisingly, McCall harbored a particular soft spot for the Brandywines. Once, during a troop inspection by Simon Cameron, President Lincoln's Secretary of War, McCall announced proudly "there goes a Chester County company!" as the Brandywines passed by the secretary.[30]

Mott and the Brandywines remained at Camp Wayne drilling and training for nearly two months, but to say they were settling into army life would be a bit disingenuous. They may have been living in tents, but the center of a bustling West Chester mere blocks away provided them with a level of comfort they would not see in the field. On the contrary, the town did all it could to shower the men with warmth and praise. On the fourth of July, the town pulled out all the stops. Citizens planned a large party in honor of and featuring the troops at Camp Wayne. During the day, the men paraded through town, chests puffed out and pride gleaming in their eyes. Later, throngs of people flooded Everhart Grove, a park on the western edge of town. Betwixt the various patriotic songs performed by the local bands, an orator read the Declaration of Independence and numerous local personages delivered speeches espousing the righteousness of the Union's cause and thanking the assembled troops for their sacrifice. Governor Curtin himself attended to review the troops and offer words of thanks and encouragement.[31] Perhaps more than a little naïve about the realities of the war they would soon face head-on, these Fourth of July festivities were the crown of one of the most exciting times in the lives of most of the soldiers.

At the end of July, shocking news reached Camp Wayne. The Union Army had been defeated at Bull Run. The Battle made it clear to President Lincoln and his administration that the war would not be as short and swift as everyone had hoped. The three-month term of service for the volunteers the Union had previously raised now seemed totally inadequate. Fortunately for Lincoln, when the Pennsylvania legislature approved the creation of the Pennsylvania Reserves, it included a provision in its charter that Lincoln could federalize the reserves to become part of the United States Army if they were needed. Bull Run convinced Lincoln that they were.

On July 21st, Mott paraded through the streets of West Chester alongside his company mates to great fanfare. Citizens lined the streets to cheer them on as they made their way down Market Street to the train depot while a band played "The Girl I Left Behind."[32] Packed like a sardine into one of a series of train cars, Mott watched the country unfold in front of him as he waved to cheering well-wishers through all the towns they passed along the way to Harrisburg. Once in the capital, Governor Curtin officially mustered the Reserves into federal service for a three-year tour of duty. Within a few days, Mott and the Brandywines marched into Maryland, headed for war.

Mott's family naturally feared for his safety, but they were proud of him for standing up to defend the Union. "O how much the country is indebted to you all for all these risks to save our beloved country," Aunt Susan wrote Mott. "You may well say you look with disgust upon those able-bodied "men" I cannot call them, who are lounging satisfied with their false position."[33] Susan went on to name some young men she saw about town whom she believed were bringing shame to their families when they ought to have been out on the front. Mott appreciated the support, but it would be some time before he truly felt he earned Susan's pride.

3

A Feather Bed Company

The sun shone warmly on the hills overlooking Baltimore as a light breeze gently caressed Mott's face and lulled him into a sense of calm. Surrounded by gardens in the shade of old trees, he watched as his comrades laughed and joked with each other. Some were writing home to loved ones and others simply lay in the grass enjoying the weather. Mont Clare mansion, the stately former home of Charles Carroll, a signer of the Declaration of Independence, provided an elegant backdrop to the scene. Mott may as well have been attending a garden party instead of occupying a military camp in the middle of a war. Mott could not deny the comfort and ease their first camp in the field afforded him, but it came with a measure of guilt. He was not on the front doing his part to suppress the rebellion. War was not meant to feel luxurious.[1]

Over the next week, Mott's subsequent camps would not be nearly so pleasant, but nor was he any closer to the front lines where he felt duty-bound to be. When Colonel Roberts assigned the Brandywines to guard a railroad at sleepy Annapolis Junction, several of the men suspected Roberts of cowardice for managing to find such a quiet assignment. "I always knew the Colonel was a scoundrel, now I am fully convinced of it," wrote Charles Speakman, a private in the Brandywine Guards, after their move to guard duty.[2] "Our colonel R. B. Roberts was frightened very much indeed. He is so much of a coward that he has succeeded in getting us ordered to guard a railroad," Charles Sheaff echoed in writing home to his wife.[3]

The Brandywines remained at the junction for about a month before moving for Tennallytown, Maryland via a brief stop in the nation's capital. There was a certain excited energy in the air as Mott marched into the capital. Most of the men had never been to Washington before and the city strengthened their resolve to protect the Union. Given some time to explore, Mott and the other Brandywines visited many of the iconic places of note, including the White House, the Capitol, and the Smithsonian. Upon leaving the capitol that afternoon, Mott beamed with pride as he paraded with the troops through the crowded streets of the most important city in the Union before departing for Camp Tenally. Colonel Roberts humbled that pride when he instructed the men to march as "heavy infantry," something they had never done before having only drilled as "light infantry." The sudden change made for an awkward and less-than-impressive showing for the regiment. If Mott or the other Brandywines had any second thoughts about their negative feelings towards Roberts, making an embarrassment of them on the streets of the capital quickly dispelled any notion of that.[4]

When the Brandywines arrived in camp, General McCall ordered Colonel Roberts to announce a reorganization of the companies in the 1st regiment. As part of this reorganization, McCall had not consulted the colonel before making changes to the regiment, a fact Roberts inappropriately made clear to all his men. After reading the orders out loud with a measure of resentment in his voice, Roberts concluded by telling the men in no uncertain terms that they were not his orders. The public clarification angered McCall who was already disappointed with Roberts for the bungled march he had led through DC. It pleased Mott to hear later that McCall gave Roberts a dressing down, exclaiming in his tent that he was "not accustomed to his Colonels taking such liberties."[5]

As part of the reorganization, McCall changed the designation of the Brandywine Guards from Company K to Company A, the designation they would hold for the duration of their service in the war. The move was a great honor for Mott and the Brandywines as they now held the first position on the right of the regiment. But for others in the regiment—particularly the Union Guards of Lancaster County who had previously occupied that position but were now designated Company B—it was a blatant display of favoritism. Everyone knew the Brandywines were McCall's hometown boys. The charge became more difficult to deny when Mott personally received a letter from McCall shortly thereafter asking the Brandywines to act as the General's personal bodyguard. Mott gladly accepted on behalf of the company, but the accusations of favoritism tempered the pride and honor he and his fellow Brandywines felt.

As the men settled into their new position, Mott began to take on more and more responsibilities. His immediate superior, First Lieutenant Charles Lamborn, had been appointed the adjutant for the regiment and therefore spent all his time with the regimental staff. Captain Nields, meanwhile, spent little time among the men and neglected their drilling. Nields' lack of engagement with the men concerned Mott. Mott and several of the men approached their captain to address the lack of drilling, but Nields responded by flying into a rage. If they wanted to be drilled so badly then he would drill them for four hours a day every day, he threatened. It was an empty threat as army regulations stipulated that a company could not be drilled more than one hour twice a day, but it was clear they could not rely on Nields to ready the company for battle.[6] Neither Mott nor the rest of the Brandywines disliked Nields per se, but there were suspicions he struggled with alcohol.[7] In any case the men refrained from troubling the Captain further and Mott realized if the company were to be prepared, it was up to him as third in command to do it. Mott did not have the drilling experience that Nields had, but he did his best to fill in the void left by the absence of his two superiors. The Brandywines would not forget Mott's devotion to them.

In October, Captain Nields left the Brandywines to accept the position of Lieutenant colonel of the 104th Pennsylvania Infantry. As was the practice with volunteer units at this point in the war, the company organized an election to decide Nields' successor. While rank was certainly considered, it was not a foregone conclusion that the next in line would become their next captain. Several officers among the Brandywines were in contention for the captaincy. First Lieutenant Lamborn was an obvious possibility given his seniority in the company's chain of command, however, he was generally not well-liked among the men and as adjutant, he had not spent much time with them.[8] Mott, as second Lieutenant had in many ways already been acting as de facto captain. The Brandywines liked him personally and they respected his initiative in stepping up in responsibility in light of Nields' shortcomings. However, not everyone believed he possessed the executive ability or clear-headedness required, particularly in drilling, which he still had not mastered.[9] First Sergeant Cheyney Nields, the younger brother of the outgoing captain, made another attractive choice. Like Henry McIntire, the company's founder, Cheyney was a lawyer, intelligent and likable. Though his elevation to captain would require disregarding the chain of command, he remained a serious contender.[10] In the weeks since Nields' departure, the election became a topic of great interest and anticipation amongst the Brandywines.

In early fall, the Brandywines settled into what would be their winter quarters at Camp Pierpont near Langley, Virginia. As the election neared, Lieutenant Lamborn withdrew his name from consideration. General John F. Reynolds had offered Lamborn a more prestigious position as his aide de camp, but he also may have known he would never have received enough votes and simply wanted to save face. Lamborn sent a statement home to the local Chester County papers "for the gratification of [his] friends at home" claiming he had been offered the captaincy, but graciously turned it down because of his appointment with Reynolds.[11] No other existing accounts of this election corroborate Lamborn being previously offered the captaincy.

When the Brandywines cast their ballots on October 16, the choice ultimately came down to two men: Mott Hooton and Cheyney Nields. Though both were strong choices, deference to rank won out and Mott was elected Captain with sixty votes to Nields' seventeen. Nields had not campaigned strongly for the position and was well-pleased with the result believing Mott deserved the command. Nields did not go without recognition, however. With Mott's promotion, the company needed a new second Lieutenant to replace him. Nields moved into the position unopposed. Nominally, Lamborn retained his position as first Lieutenant of the Brandywines, but as he would remain detached from the company serving with General Reynolds, Nields effectively became Mott's second in command.

The company spent the next five months at Pierpont quartered in a grand hotel, a luxury afforded them as McCall's bodyguard. Despite the unusual creature comforts they were enjoying because of their honored position with the General, their inaction frustrated Mott and his men. They were acutely aware of the battles occurring elsewhere and felt a certain amount of guilt over their lack of contribution in combat. Additionally, as McCall's bodyguard, they not only had the best accommodations but were also exempt from many of the other fatigue duties like cutting logs or digging entrenchments. They were not even required to drill as frequently as their comrades in the other companies. There was nothing to do but "eat, sleep, and be merry and cheer for victories gained by other men," wrote Joseph Way, one of Mott's privates. "We might as well be home. We do not seem to be anything more than home guards."[12] This feeling of uselessness played into sensitivities Mott and others in the company felt regarding the way other people perceived them. They were largely of a professional class and people recognized the privilege with which many of them had lived. "Before we left West Chester, the cry was 'the feather bed company,'" Way wrote to his father, "but if they show us a chance, we will let them see that the 'feather beds' are not afraid of noise!"[13] They were eager to prove themselves, but as the men simply stayed in camp all day writing letters, reading books, and playing card games, there was little opportunity to do so. The nearest to combat they had come was a snowball fight with a neighboring unit.

Duly elected: Captain Mott Hooton of the Brandywine Guards
Courtesy of the Massachusetts Commandery, MOLLUS

***

On a crisp winter day at Pierpont, a lone Black man entered the Brandywines' camp. He explained that had been enslaved in the service of a Confederate Captain and fled while on an errand to take wheat to Mechanicsville. His family was to attempt an escape as well, but as he had escaped while on a lone mission, he did not know their fate. Rather than move on without them, the man, Known only as "Old Nat," approached Mott as the company commander and asked to stay with them, offering his services as a cook to the Brandywines' captain. Nat had resolved to contribute what he could to help the Union bring an end to slavery, even if it meant playing servant to a Union officer.[14] Mott accepted Nat into the camp and he became a popular fixture among the Brandywines. He likewise came to know the men, quickly learning who the troublemakers were, like Sergeant William Hammond. The sergeant was a friend of Mott's but liked to play the occasional practical joke on his captain. Among his frequent pranks, he would sneak up behind Mott's tent and stuff up the chimney to his stove to smoke him out. After a few such occurrences, Nat began to keep a small pile of stones by the entrance to Mott's tent and any time he caught Hammond sneaking around the tent looking to do mischief, he'd grab the stones and hurl them at the sergeant until he retreated.[15] Later that month, a regiment of cavalry bound for Washington passed through camp accompanying a group of so-called contraband—southern African-Americans who had escaped enslavement. Craning his neck to see if he recognized anyone, Nat quickly spotted several relatives including his children. He sprinted through the mud as fast as his legs would take him, relieved and over-joyed at their escape. "He soon came back smiling for the first time since he has been here saying that 5 of 'dem dere' were his children," wrote Private Charles Speakman to his sister.[16] After a brief respite in camp, the group moved on with its escort to Washington D.C. Nat's fate is lost to history. He did not remain with the Brandywines long, but when he left Mott's service was never recorded. It is entirely possible he followed his family to Washington.

In March, when the regiments finally broke camp and moved onwards, they passed through Manassas Junction, where the Battle of Bull Run had been fought. Their brief stay at the junction was humbling as they surveyed the area where the battle took place and where bones of the dead could still be found littering the ground in front of them. It was another stark reminder of the sacrifices of other people. As the Brandywines settled in Falmouth, Virginia, they once again idled away their time with little to do. Their uselessness seemed to be a fait accompli.

In June, as summer approached, Mott led his men into camp at Dispatch Station, eleven miles from Richmond. They had been moving steadily west towards the southern capital for the last couple of months. Though unaware of it within the ranks, it was all part of an ambitious offensive plan drawn up by George McClellan, commander of the Union Army. The plan was risky, particularly for McClellan who had been laboring under immense public criticism of inaction. McClellan convened a war council to whom he presented a grand plan to capture Richmond quickly and decisively by pulling all the troops around Washington D.C. and sending them down the Rappahannock River to take the Confederate capital by surprise via the Virginia Peninsula. Many of his generals questioned the plan. The success of McClellan's Peninsula Campaign was predicated on the assumption that the Confederate troops stationed in the vicinity of Washington would pull back to pursue the Union army to stop them from taking Richmond. If they did not withdraw, however, Washington would be left defenseless. President Lincoln could not risk the Confederates not taking the bait. He provided his approval on condition that one corps remain behind and any enemy batteries along the Potomac be neutralized before the rest of the troops left their positions.[17] With Lincoln's conditions met, the Brandywines began the move that had brought them to Dispatch Station near Richmond.

The trip down the Rappahannock towards battle had proven quite pleasant for Mott and his men. The thought of finally playing their part in suppressing rebellion kept morale high. One of Mott's Privates likened the sail down the river as more of "a pleasure party" than a troop movement.[18] When Mott received orders to take his men off bodyguard duty and rejoin the regiment, the Brandywines believed their time to fight had finally come. They stacked their knapsacks to lighten their load and moved toward the front.

The Brandywines experienced their first taste of battle at Mechanicsville, Virginia. The rest of the third division under General McCall had been posted to the fifth corps under General Fitz John Porter on McClellan's right wing. Reaching the outskirts of the battlefield at dusk, the Brandywines could see the flashes of cannon fire lighting the sky and could hear the projectiles crashing into the Union lines some distance away.[19] Mott quickly located the rest of the 1st Reserves on the extreme right of the field and moved the Brandywines along with the 3rd Reserves to join them. That evening, the Brandywines lay on their guns with bayonets affixed ready to support the nearby battery of artillery. As Mott lay on the ground, immobilized by the threat of artillery fire passing above his head, all he could do was watch the enemy shells soaring through the air, tearing nearby trees to shreds and some of them landing perilously close to his position.[20] The Union artillery managed to scatter the rebel forces attempting to overtake them, but neither Mott nor his men moved for the rest of the evening.

Sleep evaded Mott that night amidst the din of wounded men screaming and crying for aid in the distance.[21] Around midnight, the first and third regiments were relieved to fall back. During the retreat, when the Brandywines fell behind to retrieve the knapsacks they had stacked earlier. Hearing gunfire, they looked around to see the 8th and 10th Reserves heading their way in a hasty retreat pursued by Confederate forces. Amidst the shot and shell, Mott ordered his men to join the retreat.

The next day, as the Union continued to withdraw, Mott and his men provided cover for the retreating troops until they too were compelled to fall back and regroup with the regiment at Gaines' Mill. They moved on to a series of low hills near Gainesville to cover the retreat of supply wagons crossing the Chickahominy. Later that day, McCall rode by with his staff and acknowledged his bodyguard. The Brandywines responded by giving McCall three cheers as he rode on.

Throughout the rest of what became known as the Seven Days Battle, Mott led his men in a fatiguing retreat while guarding McCall's wagon train, once again separated from their regiment who were at the front fighting a losing battle. By the morning of June 30, only a third of Federal forces had reached their retreat destination on the James River. The rest of the army remained in the vicinity of Glendale, a small town at a crossroads, where they held the line to allow the rest of the supply train to reach the river. Five days of mounting losses with no ground gained to show for it had proven to McClellan that his plan on the peninsula had failed. The demoralized general left the battlefield on the pretense of securing the supposedly precarious position in the rear at Malvern Hill.

McClellan's hasty departure created confusion about the chain of command. The line across Glendale and the surrounding crossroads was uneven, spread apart, leaving each corps and division commander to fend for themselves. General McCall took the worst of this situation being positioned in the middle of this haphazard line. The Pennsylvania Reserves had borne the brunt of the combat at Mechanicsville and Gaines' Mill and were once again thrust into the middle of the battle.[22] McCall could not repel the attack and his three brigades became scattered and disorganized as the Confederate forces punched through the center.

Mott was frustrated that he and his men could not be at the front with the rest of the regiment, but he continued to follow McCall's orders protecting the baggage and supply wagons as they retreated. Without knapsacks, a change of clothes, or even sleep, the Brandywines eventually made it to Harrison's Landing on the James River where the Union had set up its base. Mott did not lose any men. In fact, the company suffered almost no casualties. Only minor flesh wounds were reported. In many ways, their position as McCall's bodyguard had insulated them from much of the horrors of the Peninsula Campaign. Had they remained with their regiment after Mechanicsville and

Gaines' Mill, they would likely have suffered the same severe losses as the rest of their regiment at Glendale. As Mott received reports of the aftermath, he learned their days as McCall's bodyguard were done. His men would finally get their wish to rejoin the regiment, participate in fatigue duties, and fight in its battles. The cost for the privilege, however, had been high.

During the battle, the Brandywine's founder Henry McIntire, suffered a gunshot to the foot, shattering his ankle. McIntire was pulled from the field, but there was no going back. The surgeons had no choice but to take his foot. General John F. Reynolds, the commander of the brigade in which the Brandywines were part and whose aide de camp was the company's first Lieutenant Charles Lamborn, was captured during the retreat and sent to Libby Prison. The biggest blow for the Brandywines was revealed when Mott learned that General McCall had been taken prisoner. McCall had ridden out on the evening of the 30th with several aids to try to round up his scattered men. He ran into a contingent of men from the 47th Virginia Infantry who surrounded him and brought him back to General James Longstreet. It was an icy reception between the two generals who had served together in the 4th infantry in the 1840s. Longstreet extended a hand to his old friend, but McCall scorned him. Longstreet ordered McCall taken away and sent to Libby Prison in Richmond where both he and Reynolds would remain for the next month and a half.[23]

With low morale and their hero gone, the Brandywines remained at Harrison's Landing until August 15. Both McCall and Reynolds were freed in a prisoner exchange, but McCall would not be returning to his men. His confinement in Libby had exacerbated the health problems that led to McCall's first retirement in the 1850s. Although he returned briefly to address the men and thank them for their devoted service, he took his leave and returned home to West Chester for good. All the men of the Pennsylvania Reserves respected McCall and they gave him a deafening cheer for a sendoff, filling the sky with their caps.[24] Such was the loyalty McCall inspired that even after command of the Reserves was transferred to General Truman Seymour, a career soldier from New York and McCall's artillery chief, some in the Brandywines insisted their families still address mail to them as "McCall's Division."

After leaving Harrison's Landing, the Brandywines traveled by steamship to Acquia Landing where they joined the command of Irvin McDowell's third corps in Pope's Army of Virginia. They continued to Falmouth and afterward towards Fredericksburg. Meanwhile, with his service to McCall concluded, Mott decided to seek further advancement. Being a Captain was not without some prestige, but it did not match that of an officer of a regimental staff like a major or Lieutenant colonel. It would have paid better and eased him of more physical duties. However, despite multiple appearances before different Boards of Examiners, his bids for a higher position were unsuccessful and he began to feel jaded. Shortly before arriving in camp near Fredericksburg, Mott learned that his brother, Frank, was considering joining the army. "If you do intend on going," Mott wrote to his brother making no attempt to hide his disillusionment, "I would advise you to try and [get] a commission in the line for it is no fun in being a Private in this army. It is, like all armies, a despotism."[25] Mott wrote as if from the voice of experience, though Mott was no Private and never had been. Nevertheless, the fact that his hopes for advancement had yet again been dashed when he wrote to Frank likely explained his cynicsm. "I have been before another Board of Examiners some time since and have not heard of the result, but guess it will not amount to anything," Mott wrote pessimistically.[26] For a man who appears to have held little particular ambition prior to the military, the palpable frustration Mott felt having been passed up for promotion suggests that he had finally found a calling that suited him. Yet it seemed to be going nowhere. Just ten days later, however, Mott would face a more serious setback that would take him out of the army for the next six months.

The Brandywines arrived on the field with the rest of their division near the Warrenton Turnpike on August 24. Over the next few days, they pressed forward along the turnpike, occasionally skirmishing with Confederate soldiers, before turning towards Manassas Junction where the second battle along Bull Run was about to take place. On the morning of the 29th, General Reynolds took his division of Pennsylvania Reserves up towards Groveton to support General King's division near the town. The Brandywines had not been at Groveton long before General Reynolds realized that the Confederates were beginning to turn the army's left flank. Reynolds ordered a retreat to hold the line along Chinn Ridge but General Pope, refusing to believe Reynolds' word that the Confederates were advancing on the left, was slow to send reinforcements to the ridge leaving four brigades numbering about eight thousand men against a force of nearly twenty-five thousand rebel troops.[27]

During the fighting the next day, Mott experienced the first significant casualties of his command. Nine of his men sustained serious, though not life-threatening wounds, while Corporal Thomas Nields, a younger cousin of Lieutenant Cheyney Nields, was killed while skirmishing. Lt. Nields had little time to mourn his cousin as command of the Brandywines would soon fall to him. As Mott skirmished alongside his men, he suddenly felt a searing pain in his left thigh. Falling to the ground, unable to walk, Mott dragged himself to a nearby ditch for cover. One of his men found him shortly thereafter and pulled him back behind the lines. When the army surgeons examined his leg, they were pleased to discover the ball had passed straight through. They were able to control his bleeding and bandage the wound to spare his leg, however, he would not be fit for duty for quite some time. The surgeons recommended furlough and sent Mott home to recuperate. Mott trusted Nields to take good care of his company in the meantime, but he vowed to return as soon as humanly possible. Mott's unrealistic assessment of what was possible would lead to a six-month absence before the Brandywines would see him again.

4

On the Front Lines

Mott hobbled into Dr. W. D. Hartman's office in West Chester on October 17 reverberating with frustration. Just a few weeks before, the Brandywines had participated in the Battle of Antietam, a confrontation that would go down as the bloodiest single day of battle on American soil. The Brandywines were spared the decimation that other units experienced, but several of them were seriously wounded and one had died. The guilt of his absence plagued Mott, but as Hartman examined his leg, the doctor could offer no reassurance. The wound remained unhealed. Hartman ordered him confined to his room for the next thirty days to allow his body the time to properly heal.[1] It was a naïve order. Dr. Hartman attended Mott's bedside the following month only to find that despite Mott's general respect for authority, he had all but ignored Hartman's prescription of rest. "...in consequence of unduly exercising the left leg, in which he was wounded," Hartman reported to the army, "inflammation set in and sloughing of the wound followed which rendered confinement to the bed necessary."[2]

Continued news from the front only further fueled Mott's impatience to heal. In early December, the Brandywines entered the fray at Fredericksburg where they once again faced additional casualties. Yet Mott's wound was stubbornly slow in healing. On Christmas Eve, Dr.

Hartman once more went before a Justice of the Peace to attest to Mott still being unfit for duty noting that Mott could still not walk without crutches.[3] Hartman couldn't even hazard a guess as to when he expected Mott to be able to return to duty. By the end of January, even Mott was forced to admit the truth and accept that he needed to allow himself time to heal. He wrote to request an additional 30 days' leave having been examined by a military surgeon.

The pain and debility of his injury notwithstanding, Mott's return to West Chester was not without its welcome pleasures. For the first time in over a year, he was once more amongst family. Home-cooked meals and a comfortable bed felt luxurious compared to his living situation in the army. When he eventually became more mobile, able to get about on crutches, he enjoyed the company of his many social acquaintances in town. He changed up his style, shaving off his bushy beard in favor of a large, yet neat mustache and found time to do a little flirting in Everhart Grove with Flory Ebbs, a local girl who had caught his eye.[4] The community welcomed him as a war hero, though Mott likely felt the distinction undeserved. The Brandywines were just beginning their active role in combat and he was an absentee commander. For all the creature comforts of home, his reception was a reminder that it was not currently where he belonged.

On February 26, Mott traveled from his home in West Chester to Philadelphia to meet with Dr. Gibbons, an army physician who oversaw invalid officers. Though much improved, Gibbons still could not tell Mott what he wanted to hear, declaring him unfit for duty and sending him home again for yet another month. A couple of weeks later, Mott opened his copy of the local *Village Record* to a headline reprinted from the *Washington Star* that shocked him.

Regiment Disarmed

We hear, and have no doubt of the truth of the statement, that last night the 1ˢᵗ Pennsylvania Reserve Regiment went out on picket duty in the vicinity of Union Mills, and instead of performing it, the whole regiment went to sleep![5]

The article went on to condemn the soldiers of the 1st Regiment for mutiny and called for "Every officer of the regiment who cannot signally clear himself from suspicion of sympathy [to be] summarily reduced to the ranks and forced to serve with musket on shoulder..."[6] Additionally, the paper demanded that the rank and file be split and reassigned to units where insubordination would be met with a firing squad.

Though originally published in the *Washington Star*, publications throughout Pennsylvania and beyond picked up the story. It would have enraged Mott to read what he most likely assumed to be a libelous lie and so he was pleased to see the following week the name of his second in command, Cheyney Nields, affixed to a stern rebuttal by company officers throughout the regiment:

THE FIRST PENN'A RESERVES
Every friend of the gallant and tried soldiers of the First Regiment of the Pennsylvania Reserves, will be glad to know that the charge of "insubordination" and "disgraceful conduct" reported against them in the Washington Star, is not only untrue, but that it is really without a shadow of foundation in truth.

Camp 1st Regt. Inft, P.R.V.C.
Union Mills, VA, Feb. 28, 1863
Editor Evening Star: Great injustice has been done this Regiment by the gross mistreatment published in your issue of Friday, the 27 inst, in reference to an occurrence that took place here on the morning of that day, and we trust that you will give this a place, that the injury to the officers and men may be corrected. This regiment has been on duty here under Brig. Gen. Alex Hays commanding 3d Brigade, Casey's Division, 22nd Army Corps, now fourteen days, during which time not a single case of insubordination has occurred. The duty assigned to it thus far, has been to guard at Brigade Headquarters, occupy two picket posts, and fatigue duty requiring a daily detail of two officers and about sixty men. Every duty was promptly and faithfully performed by officers and men, and frequently received the commendations of

the General and his staff. On the night referred to in the article, the regiment was not on picket duty, but was in their encampment- one post only, as picket, by order was occupied by a corporal and three men, who did not sleep while on duty and their arms were not taken from them. There were but eight officers in the regiment at the time, two of those being unfit for duty, leaving the number so small that they came on duty in some cases every other day, and in one instance the officer performed duty seventy-two hours out of ninety-six, and the men forty-eight consecutive hours. The officers and men of the 1ˢᵗ Regt. Penna. Reserves have not been guilty of sleeping on their post, neither have they been guilty of "disgraceful conduct," or of "insubordination." The officers, we are glad to say, can "signally" clear themselves from suspicion of sympathy with insubordination, and if twenty-two months' service has not made better officers and men than the article in your paper indicates, we agree with you, that we "should be summarily reduced to the ranks," or "drafted into regiments." We ask an insertion in your paper, that our friends may see, that we are not yet fallen into "an unorganized mob," but that we stick to our glorious old flag, which leads to duty.[7]

In truth, the Brandywines and the other companies of the 1ˢᵗ Regiment had technically mutiny over a misunderstanding of orders. A hard winter of frequent movements frustrated the men who felt they were being treated as little more than cannon fodder. They had even been asked to relieve units of fresh recruits so the latter could go into winter quarters instead of the exhausted Reserves. There was merit to their anger. General Abner Doubleday had even traveled to Washington on behalf of the Reserves to entreat Secretary of War Stanton to relieve them but to no avail. Finally, in late February, when the 1ˢᵗ Regiment received what they thought were orders for yet another deployment to picket duty, many stacked arms and refused to go. However, they had misunderstood the orders, which were relieving them to go into winter quarters. Once the confusion was cleared up, the men complied. But this insubordination was not the alleged mutiny reported in the *Star*.

Mott's right hand: Lieutenant Cheyney Nields (Detail)
Courtesy of the Chester County History Center, West Chester, PA

The Commandant of their new camp, General Alexander Hays, quickly gave the regiment new reasons to feel abused. Hays frequently drank himself into a drunken stupor and woke the men up at all hours to disarm them or send them out against a threat he had invented, simply to harass the men. They had not been disarmed in camp for any insubordination and it was Hays who provided the *Star* with the false report.

Back in Harrisburg, Governor Curtin had received an account of the incident from Hays himself, which of course mirrored the skewed facts presented in the *Washington Star*. Ironically, the Brandywine Guards found a savior of their reputation in a man they had roundly despised when in the field. Colonel R. Biddle Roberts, who had resigned from the field in November 1862 before the Battle of Fredericksburg, was serving on Curtin's staff when the incident occurred. When Roberts learned of the article, he immediately challenged Hays' account on behalf of his former soldiers to set the record straight for the Governor.[8]

Mott felt relieved to hear the truth come out and the honor of his men restored, but it expended his last bit of patience for his recuperation. He desperately wished to get back. At his monthly evaluation in March, Mott finally heard the news he had been waiting months for. His wound was sufficiently healed, and he was cleared once more for duty.

On March 26th, Mott left home and headed for Washington to catch a transport to the front. Allowing himself one more indulgence of home, he stopped at his cousin Sallie Rogers' home where he stayed all night in the company of his cousin and her husband. The next morning, Sallie sent him away with some sugar bags and a bottle of whiskey courtesy of her husband, Evans.[9] He made his way to Washington D. C. where he remained until Friday morning. Though anxious to return to his men and continue the fight, he confessed to his Aunt Susan that as soon as he left West Chester, his heart grew heavy. "I never had the blues so badly in all my life as I had [in Washington]," he wrote to Susan.[10] His journey to the front was lonely and more than a bit frustrating because no one could seem to give him a straight answer as to where his company was positioned. On Friday morning, Mott left Washington, crossing the Potomac by boat to Alexandria. From there, he boarded a train for Fairfax Court House only to be told his company had moved on to Union Mills. Mott pressed on, arriving in the early afternoon, but did not see his men. He enquired about his regiment and was directed to an old camp some small distance away where members of the Keystone Battery were on guard who might know the whereabouts of the 1st PA Reserves. "I plunged over through the mud and when I got near it I saw two fat and dirty artillerymen conversing," Mott wrote his aunt.[11] As Mott approached the two men, one of them gestured in a familiar way and Mott suddenly recognized Harry Carpenter, his cousin. Harry warmly welcomed Mott and invited him to join them for their afternoon meal of ham, roasted on a bayonet, with tea, bread, and butter from home. Harry had informed Mott that he believed the Brandywines had left for Centerville with their regiment and that he might find them there. After a few hours spent catching up, Mott got back on the road.[12]

Mott boarded a train again headed for Centerville but made a fortuitous stop back at Fairfax Court House. Upon his arrival, he discovered that the Brandywines had just returned to Fairfax from Centerville and they were in camp just four miles away. At eight o'clock that evening, Mott finally walked into camp and approached his men, none of whom recognized him at first without his beard. "The men seemed very glad to see me," he wrote to Susan, "but none of them recognized me until I spoke."[13] Mott enjoyed catching up with his old company and he took supper with friends. The reunion buoyed Mott's spirits and lifted him from the funk that had plagued him since Washington. "I feel well and in better spirits than I have since I left home," he informed his Aunt.[14]

As pleased as he was to be with his old friends again, Hooton returned to a very different company than the one he commanded the previous summer. Going into Second Bull Run in August 1862, Hooton commanded a force of ninety-nine men, but upon his return, only seventy-eight remained, none of whom would be replaced.[15]

Throughout the spring, Mott engaged in a seemingly endless string of aimless movements. In mid-June 1863, Mott and all the Reserves were told the unthinkable. Pennsylvania faced an invasion by the Confederates. This was what Governor Curtin had feared; this was the very reason for the existence of the Pennsylvania Reserves: to protect the Commonwealth as a first line of defense against an incursion into the North.

The army that Lee brought with him into Pennsylvania was an invasion force, not an occupying one. Lee could not have mustered enough men to carry out such a task even if he had wanted to. His victories at Fredericksburg and Chancellorsville had in many ways proved more costly than not. They had brought him no closer to winning the war. Lee convinced Confederate President Jefferson Davis and Secretary of War James Seddon, that the South needed a decisive victory behind enemy lines to change the course of the war in their favor.[16] With enlistment terms for Union soldiers expiring creating mounting losses in his enemy's army, Lee felt the time was ripe to move north and feed off the enemy's terrain as the Union had done so often in the South. At the very least, by entering Pennsylvania and taking Harrisburg, Lee hoped to shatter the North's morale and inspire the voices of northern peacemakers to grow louder.[17] If, however, the fear and panic this Southern incursion fostered did not bring Lincoln to the negotiation table, Lee could redirect his army eastward and then descend upon Washington D.C. from the north.[18] For the Brandywines, such a movement by Lee could mean Confederate troops marching through their homelands in Chester County. It was a horror they could not allow. Mott readied his men for the most determined march of their service thus far.

Mott and the Brandywines marched for five days through rain and mud. Such conditions would typically have engendered grumblings of abuse among the ranks, but not this time knowing what was at stake for them. "This is a spirit-stirring march," Mott recorded in his diary that evening. "With fifes screaming and drums rattling and roaring some patriotic air which makes us forget our sore feet and tired limbs and march shoulder to shoulder and keep to the step, the people fairly line the roadside to greet us as we pass and give us Godspeed and refreshments."[19]

On July 1st, at three o'clock in the afternoon, the Reserves crossed the state line into Pennsylvania. Fighting had already commenced near the small town of Gettysburg in Adams County. Company K in the Brandywine's regiment was dubbed the "Adams Infantry" after the home county of the soldiers who comprised it. Mott dreaded the mere thought of enemy troops traipsing through his homeland, but he need only look down the line to his regimental comrades to catch a glimpse of what it would be like for those fears to become reality. Many in Company K were not just from Adams County but from Gettysburg itself. Their families, friends, and homes were on the line and they were determined to fight to protect it, but the regiment would not arrive at the battle until the next day. That night, Mott made special note of the events and activities in his own camp,

I never saw [the men] display such pluck and determination as our men displayed today notwithstanding we marched nearly all night halting long after midnight. They were joking and ridiculing each other for looking so absurd... We laughed although suffering agony from bruised and feverish feet... I can compare our men on this march to nothing but the Crusaders. They seemed to be filled with a patriotic fervor which stimulated them to make physical efforts almost beyond the powers of endurance of Man. They were singing this night 'hoist up the flag' and other songs. Cheyney and I would join in the chorus.[20]

The revelry and merriment in the camp that night did much to raise the morale of the men and to inspire enthusiasm for the next days' trials.

The Brandywines arrived in Gettysburg at noon on July 2, the second day of battle, a day Mott referred to in his diary as simply, "a memorable day."[21] As part of the Third Division under General Samuel Crawford in General George Sykes' Fifth Corps, the Brandywine Guards along with the rest of their regiment joined the First Brigade under Col. William McCandless. Around five o'clock, Crawford brought the men

A small company of faithful ones: the Brandywine Guards shortly before the Battle of Gettysburg, 1863
Courtesy of Ed & Faye Max

to Little Round Top along the army's left flank. Crawford assigned one of his brigades to remain at Little Round Top to aid other members of the fifth corps per General Sykes' orders, while the Brandywines with McCandless' brigade of only 1,400 men prepared to charge the Confederate troops approaching Plum Run across the Wheatfield. As soon as members of the regular army were pushed back and off the field, Crawford grabbed the flag of the First Reserves from its bearer and led the charge under fire down the hill to push back the rebel advance. Adding an element of absurdity to an otherwise heroic scene, the flag bearer from whom Crawford had grabbed the regimental colors ran awkwardly alongside Crawford hanging on to the general, refusing to neglect his duty to protect the flag in his care.[22]

The charge took the Brandywines to a low stone wall at the bottom of the hill where they remained all night. As dawn broke, Mott and his men maintained their cover behind the wall taking cover amidst rebel sharpshooters while an artillery duel took place above their heads. At three o'clock in the afternoon, Mott led his men in an advance across the field to some nearby woods. Once under cover, the Brandywines, along with two companies of the Bucktail Regiment began skirmishing.

Mott lost two of his men during the fighting and several were wounded. On the fourth of July, the Brandywines' role in the battle concluded. By noon, he pulled the men to the rear. Though exhausted and famished, the odor rising from the dead on the battlefield overwhelmed his appetite. "[I] could not eat of the daintiest dish," Mott remarked.[23] In his official report of the Brigade's actions during the battle, Colonel McCandless concluded, "I cannot close this report without calling special attention to the gallantry displayed by both officers and men of this command who were fortunate enough to enter the field when our left was overpowered and the enemy was boldly advancing on the key of our position."[24] The Union army was ultimately victorious at Gettysburg driving the Confederates out of Pennsylvania. Lee's plan had failed. As he retreated back into Maryland, Lee could only suspect that the tide had turned in his enemy's favor.

Following the battle, Mott led the Brandywines during a series of grueling marches in hot pursuit of Confederate forces. Some days they averaged a leisurely five to ten miles and other days brought painful advances of up to twenty-four miles.[25] By the end of July, the enthusiasm the Brandywines felt for their triumphant march south began to wane as their rations diminished. They withstood the physical rigors of their march, but they could not ignore the emptiness in their stomachs. Irritable and "devilishly hungry," as Mott described them, several of the men resorted to killing pigs and sheep and scouring the countryside for produce. By the end of the month, General Crawford could hardly pass by the men without hearing complaints about the lack of rations. The men of the second regiment who marched with the Brandywines began to yell "crackers!" at the General whenever they saw him, perhaps fearing that all other protests had gone unnoticed.[26]

The heat only compounded the situation as the year progressed into August. Several men suffered from heat stroke while others, including Mott, broke rank to sit in the shade to cool down whenever they passed any trees.[27] Looking around the camp one night, Mott readily noted the effects of the recent fighting and marching on the men:

Every man's face wears a stern and fixed expression. Cheyney and I attend Guard Mounting as spectators. We like to look at the men's faces when the sergeants come to the front to report. They look like men cut out of bronze. Faces perfectly expressionless and turned nearly black with the sun's rays. Indeed, they look like what they are – veterans.[28]

Mott had also quickly developed a disdain for the Reserves' commanding officer, General Crawford. To be fair, the McCalls of the world who could do no wrong were few and far between. The fact that Crawford occupied a post that had been McCall's automatically engendered a negative bias towards the general. But for Mott, such cynicism of authority and a rejection of blind loyalty would become a defining characteristic of his personality. On September 28, General Meade ordered a troop review in front of a visiting general from Mexico named Cortes.[29] The review was a spectacular failure because, according to Mott,

The stupid asses that command us did not tell us there was to be a review and we went out under the impression that we were going on the route so we did not dress in full uniform and carried our haversacks. The movements and ceremonies were badly performed on account of the cattle who are our commanding officers.[30]

Crawford was admittedly ill-prepared for his command. A graduate of the University of Pennsylvania School of Medicine, Crawford had entered the army twelve years earlier as an assistant surgeon. The attack on Fort Sumter had compelled Crawford to move into a command role, but given his training as a medical officer, he lacked much of the command abilities of his peers. Moreover, when he first took command of the Reserves in May of 1863 before the Battle of Gettysburg, he had just returned to active duty after an eight-month convalescence for a gunshot wound to his thigh he sustained at Antietam. If Mott knew of Crawford's injury and recognized the parallels in their experiences, it did nothing to endear him to the young captain. But what disdain

Mott felt towards Crawford paled in comparison to the hatred he felt towards another former superior officer who had recently appeared in the local news back home.

A few days after Crawford's botched troop review, Mott received a letter from his brother Frank in West Chester informing that a speech was to be given in West Chester by Colonel R. Biddle Roberts, the unpopular former commanding officer of the First Regiment. The mere mention of Roberts' name ignited Mott's wrath and he responded to his brother with a scathing diatribe against the kind of person he felt Roberts to be:

"I write this note for the express purpose of requesting you to give the hound the cut direct if you have such an opportunity and an insult coming from you would not be at all out of place for he has never done anything else towards me but heap insult after insult on me both by word and deed. I believe as firmly that it was through his serpent-tongued influence with Governor Curtin that I was cheated out of my promotion as I do that the sun will shine tomorrow. And yet when he comes to West Chester to make a political speech he can with his two-faced guile laud the ... skies and perhaps say something in my favor. What makes him do this? Is it through feelings of affection he cherishes for his old companions in arms? No. It is because he knows it will please the people and thus make him popular. This man Roberts is this day the most perfidious black-hearted and malignant-natured man I ever knew. You can form no conception of his character. If he ever takes a dislike to a man he will ruin him if it is for years to come. While he is plotting and planning, he will smile and smile and be a villain and pretend to be a friend as he did with me last winter. If I were at home I would be sorely tempted to chastise the damned scoundrel on the street. I hate him. Every bone in his accursed carcass and every ounce of his carrion flesh and if I get a chance I will repay him in such a way that he will not soon forget the donor!

P.S. ... I will tell you of one of Roberts' refined habits when he was with the regt. It was a daily occurrence for him to get beastly drunk and while in that condition he would, in plain terms, beshit his breeches. This is an absolute fact... He is a man without Religion, honor or principle. He is a mass of selfish-ness... No wonder the country totters when such men as he sit in high places and although I would vote for Curtin, damn him, I say, for having such men for advisors!"[31]

Though he only ever hinted at the reason he detested Roberts, Mott suspected that Roberts had somehow used his influence to deny Mott the promotions he had applied for a couple of years earlier.

When autumn arrived, things began to slow down. At Rappahan-nock Station, the Brandywines made camp, received standard rations, and began to reflect on issues beyond their immediate conditions including the war, the state of the country, their families, plans for a draft back home, and their annoyance over the rowdiness of the men in the second regiment who seemed to get drunk every night.[32] Recreation also resumed among the men. Some used their leisure time to gamble while others just enjoyed some quiet reading. Mott spent much of his days sitting beneath the shade of a tree with a book in his hands and passed his evenings around the fires telling jokes and having a good time with his men.[33]

On October 19, after subsequent marching, Mott arrived at a pain-fully familiar. Over a year had passed since the Second Battle of Bull Run on August 30, 1862, but for Mott, the scene would be forever burned into his memory. The current state of the battlefield left little to the imagination when considering the carnage that had taken place the year before. Scattered human remains littered the field in every direction. In most cases, no graves had been dug, but rather piles of dirt hastily spread over the bodies. A year's worth of agricultural produc-tion and exposure to the elements however had exposed a great many skeletons. The Brandywines reverently attempted to cover the remains closest to their tents, but this was a small number compared to the total amount of dead in the area.[34]

On the evening of their arrival at the site, Mott joined two of his men, George Mercer, and Joseph Darlington, on a walk of the field to remember that day. They charted on the landscape exactly where they were during the battle and tried to find the grave of Thomas Nields, the first casualty among the Brandywine Guards. Plowing in the vicinity of where Nields fell had so obliterated the graves and jumbled the remains that it was impossible for them to distinguish their comrade.[35] "Graves are thick all around us," Mott noted in his diary. "It is both affecting and interesting to visit these scenes of past trials and danger and makes one feel thankful that he has been spared."[36] Mott soon found the ditch he had crawled into after he was shot, which was a grim reminder that he nearly wasn't spared.[37] He still believed the Union was assured a victory and doubted whether the South could last another year, but gone was the bravado of 1861 when battle was an abstract proving ground for glory and honor. As Mott lay on the old battlefield sleeping beside comrades who would never again wake, his enthusiasm for glory on the battlefield tempered into a sober optimism of eventual victory.

Back home Mott's family continued to struggle with his absence. With less than a year of Mott's term left they grew more and more eager to have him home. One day, as Mott's mother stepped outside her house she was taken by surprise to see Mott there snacking on a large ginger cake with preserves. The state was in the midst of a gubernatorial election and some of the soldiers were allowed to return home to vote. Ann ordered a hearty meal prepared in honor of Mott's visit and the reunion of the entire family. Then Ann woke up. As her mind readjusted to reality, her heart sank for she realized Mott's return was only a dream. "I do wish it was reality," Ann wrote to her son about her dream, "We are counting the months. I never wanted to see you so badly in my life.[38] The same melancholy overtaking Ann, quickly began affecting the rest of the family. "O Mott, we do talk and think so much about you," Susan had written him several weeks earlier. "There is no real engagement here while you are away enduring such hardships."[39] Susan could not countenance enjoying leisure time knowing her nephew was in harm's way.

Mott continued to march with his men well into the end of November. Rumors abounded about a great battle to come and Mott's nerves were on edge. At three o'clock in the morning on November

26, Mott arose to conditions "dark as pitch and cold as charity."[40] For eighteen miles, he marched through difficult conditions as they entered an area known as the Wilderness where the troops were known to struggle to maneuver. "I don't wonder that Hooker was defeated at Chancellorsville," Mott remarked upon observing the landscape. "This whole country is covered with timber. There is no cleared places except the roads...it is well named the Wilderness."[41] Though he did not know it at the time, his description offered an eerie foreshadowing of a return five months later.

As the men marched towards Gordonsville the next day, the Brandywines came upon a large contingent of worn Union soldiers crowding the road ahead. Their horses carried dead troops slung over the saddles and the sounds of enemy shelling were too close for comfort. Mott feared it was an ominous sign and he braced for a potential fight. "I fear there will be a great battle tomorrow. I hope the Lord will spare my life," Mott recorded in his diary.[42]

The following day brought more posturing, but no action yet. The Confederates held a strong position along a small mountain range ahead of the Union forces. Mott prayed that their commanders would not order an attack. "If we have to storm their position tomorrow, there will be a great slaughter," Mott remarked. "God protect us in the hour of peril...I stuck my head in a cracker box, covered up under the blanket, said my prayers and went to sleep expecting to go into battle the next morning."[43]

At half past one in the morning of the 30th, Mott was roused by the regimental adjutant with orders to report Colonel William Talley, their regimental commander, who was assembling all the captains of the regiment. When each of the captains arrived at Talley's tent, the Colonel instructed them to quietly wake the men, have them build small fires, make coffee, pile the knapsacks, and be ready to march by three o'clock in the morning.[44] Mott returned to his company and carried out his orders. For hours, they expected that the order to storm the Confederate position would follow. "[T]he ascent is steep and high and the creek impassable," Mott observed. Nevertheless, "we had all made up our minds to do our duty, trusting to God for the rest."[45] As far as Mott was concerned it was a suicide mission. Much to his relief the order never came.

By December, the early morning marches had become something of a cruel routine while winter quarters remained elusive. Mott was so exhausted that at one point he actually fell asleep on his feet during a march and had to be nudged awake by a passing soldier from the Second Regiment.[46] These movements were probably "the result of drunkenness," Mott supposed. "[We] were not rested but three times and then only for a few minutes...Halted at 4 and after the usual battalion drill had been gone through with, they magnanimously permitted us to bivouac."[47]

When the Brandywines were finally ordered into Winter quarters, they set up their tents and chimneys in a small wood and prepared for a long stay. On Christmas day, however, Mott learned they would be ordered to break camp and move on to Bristoe Station. Within a couple of days, he was on the move again marching through the harshest and muddiest conditions yet. For three days, Mott devoted his diary entries to reflect what he saw as a great injustice:

We left our good quarters, marched to Bristoe through the rain, encamped on a hill in mud ankle deep where there was no wood and the rain pouring down in torrents. I pitched our tent, but the ground was so muddy and wet that we had to sit up all night and burn pork to keep up the fire. Crawford ought to be shot for moving us. We left the best quarters we ever had.[48]

Men wallowing in the mud like swine. We are having an awful time. Someone should be punished for this.[49]

Men still wallowing in mud. The ground is bottomless. They are suffering. We curse loud and bitterly...firewood is very scarce. The damned hounds.[50]

When they finally arrived at Bristoe Station at the beginning of January, the Brandywines set up their winter quarters for the third and final time. Given how often they had been moved from winter quarters in the last month Mott did not hold his breath that they were settled, but they would in fact remain at the Station comfortably for the next four months.

***

A commotion in camp drew Mott from his tent as he saw his men gathered around what appeared to be a scuffle. As Mott neared the fray, he saw that the men were drawn up in two parallel lines and were egging on one of their comrades to run between them the full length of the lines. The soldier dashed through the narrow passage between the men while those in line began to beat him in turn until he emerged from the other side playfully swearing and smarting from the experience. "How they did thresh the one whose turn it was to run through," Mott remarked with amusement. "He would come out rubbing himself and exclaiming!"[51]

The absurdity of running a gauntlet to amuse themselves reflected the general lack of things to do during their long winter stay at Bristoe Station. For Mott life had become so mundane that he began to run out of things to record in the diary he was intent on keeping. "I wash every week now for the purpose of keeping the lice under," Mott wrote on February day before reconsidering the necessity of preserving such a fact for posterity. "This is surely a nice subject for a gentleman in the 19th century to write about in a diary," Mott remarked.[52]

When not keeping on top of his personal hygiene habits, Mott passed the time reading everything in sight, devouring at least eight books in three months. Dickens, Thackeray, and Sand among others kept him company and he frequently exchanged titles with others to keep his supply going.[53] For Mott, books were his lifeline to sanity. Without anything to read, he cursed the war and wished it to end simply so he would be freed of his boredom.[54] When he needed amusement, Mott could always count on the Brandywines for a diversion. Whether a game of checkers or a hand of cards, there was always someone at hand.

On quiet nights, the regimental band serenaded the men as they rested in camp. However, sometimes the sight of them joking around "making fools" of themselves kept him sufficiently entertained. "I never in my life have seen as droll men as our Company tonight. I thought I would laugh myself sick [at] Hammond and Cochran patting and dancing [the] hula," Mott recalled.[55]

Although the general atmosphere of Bristoe Station tended towards leisure, as an officer in the Reserves, Mott could not escape the military bureaucracy. The army required all officers in the volunteer reserves to attend a weekly school of tactics with lessons to study in between. "What folly this is," Mott ranted about his schooling. "It will be pleasant for me to recite [with] vigor to [Major] Kauffman and Col. Stewart both. What humiliation."[56] Mott felt it beneath him to attend school and the idea of going before his superiors to present his homework was infantilizing to him. The mere thought of school could put him in a foul mood and inspire angry swear-laden diatribes in his tent wishing for his time in the army to be over.[57] Mott avoided discussing school as often as he could and he rarely bothered to prepare for his lessons. April 11 marked the first time he took the time to learn his lesson since the tactical school began that February.[58]

Not all of Mott's administrative duties annoyed him. Official disciplinary boards, such as courts martial, had been largely suspended during the campaigning the previous summer and autumn. Winter quarters allowed the army to get caught up. As one of the officers selected to serve on the court martial board, Mott oversaw and adjudicated on cases throughout the Pennsylvania Reserves on matters going back as far as Gettysburg the previous summer.[59] The board typically dealt with cases of desertion, absence without leave (AWOL), and conduct "prejudicial to good order and military discipline,"[60] though a few dealt with cases of petty theft. The sentencing also followed a typical scheme. Generally, those found guilty of the charges levied against them were required to forfeit pay for a specified length of time, extend their length of service and/or perform hard labor for a specified duration.

As instructive and interesting as Mott found it, it could get awkward when any of his own men appeared on the docket. A few of the Brandywines came before the board for minor infractions that were settled with temporary docks in pay and public reprimands in front of the regiment. However, one Brandywine, Myers Chalfant, objected to being tried by a board that included his own commanding officer when he was brought up on charges of conduct prejudicial to good order and military discipline. In fact, Chalfant desired Mott to serve as a character witness on his behalf and was meant to be the first witness called for the prosecution. It placed Mott in an awkward position because he believed Chalfant to be guilty.[61] Mott had little choice but to inform the judge that were he called to testify, he would have to support the prosecution."[62] If the incident led to any bad blood between Chalfant and his captain, neither said. In general, however, there did not seem to be any lasting hard feelings between Mott and those under his command whom he tried.

***

Mott and the Brandywines finally broke winter camp at the end of April. On May 4, after marching all day, Mott spotted Generals Ulysses S. Grant, George Gordon Meade, and several other high-ranking generals gathered in a council of war. "It was a famous scene to see these generals deliberating as the troops filed by, Mott recalled."[63] He had only a month of service left in his term, but he feared the meeting portended some difficult days before his duty would be done.

Grant had achieved great success in the Western theater, but now in the spring of 1864, he believed it was time to strike at the heart of the Confederacy. Previous commanders had not pressed their advantages and Grant did not want to make the same mistake. Confederate rations were short, manpower diminished, and morale was low. Grant believed the time was ripe for a bold and decisive action to take Richmond, Lee, and the Confederate army to finally end the war.

Grant began consolidating his forces in March, calling troops away from their positions in other areas of the confederacy that no longer held any strategic value. For Grant, occupation of land meant nothing if the enemy still roamed free. By the beginning of May, Grant had decided to cross the Rapidan River and maneuver around Lee with enough speed to force him to leave his entrenchments around Richmond and meet the superior Union forces in open battle. Virginia's geography, however, did not complement the time sensitivity of Grant's plan. Mott and the Brandywines were positioned on General Meade's left flank, which faced only two options under Grant's plan for crossing the Rapidan relative to Lee's position. Upriver offered greater maneuverability and better protection for Washington D.C., but it also meant a loss of communication with the right side of the army and a dependence on railroads for supplies which would necessitate diverting manpower to protect the line.[64] Crossing downriver, on the other hand, allowed Meade to exploit the more stable waterways for supplies and maintain communication with General Butler on the army's right. But this route meant navigating the Wilderness, the densely wooded area with narrow roads that offered virtually no room to maneuver. If a battle broke out before the Union army could clear the woods, the fallout would be catastrophic. The plan required precision timing on Meade's part to reach the open fields on the opposite side before Lee could mobilize his forces to engage them. But fortune favored the bold, Grant reasoned, and after careful consideration, he decided that if Meade could get through the Wilderness in time, the downriver option would prove the most effective. Grant and Meade had hoped to clear the Wilderness by the evening on May 4, but their supply lines bogged them down. The delay gave Lee the time he needed to adjust his lines and engage Meade's army in the worst of all possible places.

On May 5, Mott led his men in line of battle, aware of some skirmishing to their left. Being so close to mustering out, Mott struggled with his nerves more than usual.[65] It was not long before he realized he had reason to feel so uneasy. General Crawford, the division commander, had spotted a small detachment of Confederate troops, which he took for advance scouts. To his dismay, he soon realized they were the first troops of a large attacking force. The Brandywines made for another position fast to evade capture.[66]

Rest proved elusive that evening. To the south, Mott could see infantry fighting which had begun in the woods of the Wilderness. Shells exploded amongst the trees, igniting the woods in front of them. This was no field of battle. It had become a fiery inferno that consumed those unlucky enough to have been caught in its midst. Mott could not ignore the "cries and groans of the wounded" as he tried to prepare his evening meal and get the rest that would not come.[67]

Shortly after seven o'clock in the evening, the powers that be cut short Mott's repast and ordered his men to fall in and advance. After marching for five miles, the Brandywines suddenly found themselves between their own lines and those of their enemy. Mott became infuriated when he realized his superiors had mistakenly sent them in the wrong direction. Remarkably, no one in the company was wounded and they made their escape. By one o'clock in the morning, Mott returned with his men where they were permitted to rest for the night, but his ire had not abated. Believing that the entire division could have been captured during this superfluous evening advance, Mott roundly blamed General Crawford for the march. "[Crawford] is more contemptible every day," Mott confided in his diary. "He rode in rear of the column tonight."[68] He would have given anything for General McCall to be back at his post.

By May 7th, the Reserves occupied a small gorge near the creek and served once more in a support capacity for the Bucktail's 2nd and 6th regiment skirmishers. Although other units in the 1st Regiment had suffered some losses, Mott's company was spared any casualties. That evening, they stood braced for an expected charge against their position, but it never came. Someone in the union lines started to shout at the rebels, which the entire Union line for at least a mile took up. "The rebels took it up in answer," Mott reminisced, "and there were these two great armies lying in line of battle about defiance at each other."[69]

At 11:30 pm on the night of the 7th, the Brandywines marched along the plank road until eight o'clock the next morning, when they engaged in battle briefly before taking refuge in some nearby woods. At noon, they joined the third brigade in a charge but encountered heavy resistance from a Confederate battery, which wounded Col. William McCandless, the Brigade commander. Miraculously, when the Brandywines were relieved in the early afternoon, they could still count their full complement, but their exhaustion was profound. They had marched all night and engaged in battle throughout the day on very little food, often through a knee-deep swamp in scorching heat. The day finally ended with a charge on a well-defended enemy position on the crest of a hill obscured by pine trees. For nearly an hour, the Brandywines fought this uphill battle with their division until they could no longer stand it. When the regiment to their left retreated, Mott had no other choice but to withdraw and join them.[70]

The Brandywines enjoyed a temporary reprieve on May 9th, though the sounds of battles and skirmishes filled the air surrounding them creating a rest that was anything but restful. Confederate sharpshooters harassed them frequently striking perilously close to their heads, signaling to Mott that the battle would not end anytime soon. "I suppose we will be in action tomorrow. The Lord preserve us in our hour of danger," Mott prayed.[71]

Mott roused his men at midnight to dig a new line of rifle pits. Finishing at daybreak, the Brandywines rested for a few more hours before the day's engagements began. Like the day before, when the Brandywines were not skirmishing, they laid flat on the ground for hours at a time, leaving as small a target for the Confederate sharpshooters as they could. In the early afternoon, after managing to regroup with the 2nd Regiment in a nearby wood, Mott led his men in yet another ill-fated advance. The Confederates let loose a barrage so intense that many broke and ran. Mott attempted in vain to rally the men, but they had no choice but to take cover in some nearby rifle pits where they continued to be harassed by enemy artillery for another two hours.[72]

Around two o'clock in the afternoon, the 1st, 2nd, and 6th regiments attempted another advance to the front to join the rest of the division. A neighboring brigade took the lead and began a charge, cheered on by the Brandywines and the rest of their brigade, but no amount of cheering could master the overwhelming firepower of the Confederates. Many of the Union soldiers, including the Brandywines broke and ran. Taking stock of the situation, Mott counted his company among the very lucky. The Brandywines suffered but two significant injuries, and no fatalities. Mott reluctantly reported to the hospital tent himself to calm his rattled nerves. "We were never under such a heavy fire, human nature could not stand it...I never felt so mean in all my life as I did when at the hospital, but I was perfectly exhausted to such a degree that my nerves were shaken."[73]

Mott returned from the hospital the following morning and took command of a picket, noting a relative and welcome quiet along the line as a soft rain fell during the day. He remained on picket duty all day and well into the evening. At nine o'clock the next morning, General Crawford ordered his division to storm the same, well-fortified hilltop enemy works that had almost gotten them killed two days earlier. Once again the Brandywines and their comrades came under such heavy fire that some ran, others hid and laid down, and no one listened to Crawford's futile attempts to prod his men onward. "Crawford was balked in his ambitious and bloody schemes," Mott seethed later that night. "Again the blood of the slain will cry aloud on him for vengeance."[74] That night, sleep eluded Mott. "I had not a wink of sleep last night," Mott wrote the next day. "I was so sleepy that I staggered around like a drunken man. My, what we have to endure for our country,"[75] Given the extreme state of fatigue throughout the company, Mott feared that the Confederates might try to take them by surprise as they slept. "Every sound awakened me," Mott commented. "Rain fell again last night. I am very much exhausted. I wish the fighting would cease."[76]

Over the next week, the Brandywines endured only occasional skirmishing. In fact, a mutual ceasefire was temporarily struck near their part of the line and their camp lay in sight of the rebel encampment. Some men exchanged papers or conversations with the soldiers on the other side- a behavior that never ceased to astonish Mott. "What a singular spectacle is here presented to view two armies lying within rifle shot of each other's pickets on terms of amity and tomorrow each will perhaps try to kill as many of the opposing army as he can."[77]

By the evening of May 29, the Brandywines were likely in relatively good spirits. For most of them, only one more day remained before they would be leaving the front to be mustered out in Washington on June 4. However, when Mott settled down for the night, he felt uneasy about the day to come. The sound of cannonading and gunfire in the distance tempered what optimism Mott might have felt. "I dislike the sound of musketry," Mott confessed in his diary. "I fear it portends battle."[78] The next day, as Mott marched with his men to a small, run-down building known as Bethesda Church, he would learn how right he was to fear battle.

The Brandywines briefly joined the 1st Brigade under Colonel Martin D. Hardin who were slowly setting up defensive works on the nearby Tinsley farm. As most of the Brigade consisted of Pennsylvania Reserves on their last day of frontline duty like the Brandywines, their efforts in setting up proper defensive works proved less than exemplary.[79] With most of Hardin's brigade remaining occupied on the farm, the Brandywines' regiment crossed an open field with the 13th regiment into a thicket of woods to wait for the rest of the brigade to advance from the farm. Unbeknownst to them, there was a silently growing Confederate presence in the area and suddenly came under attack by forces under Confederate General Robert Rodes.[80] The Brandywines opened fire from the cover of the trees, but the Confederate forces were too numerous. With their flank compromised, they made a hasty retreat. Stopping at a small house near some more woods, the Brandywines attempted to throw up some defensive works, but the enemy descended upon them before they could establish a defensive position.[81] "We all had to run for our lives," Mott recalled. "As we ran across the open ground, they poured into us hotly."[82] During the retreat, a sharp pain struck Mott in the leg. Lt. Brinton Parke and Sgt. Philip Price saw Mott stumble and ran to aid their captain. Hoisting Mott to his feet, Parke and Price brought Mott to the rear. Once out of range, Mott quickly examined his leg. Having flashbacks to Second Bull Run, Mott breathed a sigh of relief to discover his leg was only badly bruised. The bullet that struck him was mostly spent.

Back at the Tinsley Farm, a brigade of North Carolina infantry outflanked the lounging, unsuspecting Reserves and easily surmounted their paltry defenses, sending the brigade fleeing for their lives. Hearing word of this rout, Crawford immediately sent his other two brigades, under Colonels J. Howard Kitching and Joseph W. Fisher to assist. Kitching's brigade arrived first but Hardin's retreating men took them by surprise. Before Kitching's men could open fire, they were caught in the attack and fled as well.[83] Despite the confused mass of fleeing Union troops, Kitching managed to rally enough men to cover the retreat and allow the Division to regroup near the Bowles farm.[84] General Gouverneur Warren, the Union corps commander, rallied troops and artillery near the Bowles and Armstrong Farms to the north and positioned Crawford's three brigades in a large crescent over a shallow ridge, in a small hollow surrounded by trees. Fisher's brigade threw up much more effective defenses than the ones constructed at the Tinsley farm and the unit of Kitching's men that stayed behind to cover the retreat fell back and joined the line.[85] Mott and the Brandywines joined the formation in the center of the crescent, covered by a series of slave huts near the house. As the Union troops regrouped and attempted to salvage the debacle that had occurred over the previous hour, the swarm of Confederates surrounding the church steadily grew. However, the Union troops now occupied a strong defensive position.

After a brief artillery duel, which resulted in setting the Bowles house on fire, a brigade from Virginia massed and charged Crawford's crescent. The division held its fire until the Confederates got closer at which point the Union troops opened fire en masse, decimating the Confederate lines. The Confederates continued their advance despite being mowed down in wave after wave of attack.[86] The rebels also inexplicably charged the artillery, the close range of which literally ripped men apart, showering succeeding waves of Confederates with the blood and flesh of the unfortunate souls who preceded them. In the early evening, the surviving Confederates surrendered. With the battle concluded Mott properly took in the field before him. It was strewn with Confederate dead, dismembered body parts, and some soldiers so fully destroyed by close-range cannon fire that nothing remained but indiscernible masses of flesh.[87] The horror of the battle left Mott shaken. "I never saw men worse mangled than the dead on this field of Bethesda Church," Mott remarked. "Some of them were literally torn to pieces."[88] It was a gruesome finale to three years of war.

The day after the battle, on May 31, Mott prepared the Brandywines to leave the front. About two hundred Confederate soldiers had been captured the day before and the army made their escort to Washington the final duty of the departing Reserves whose terms were expiring. As packs were readied, prisoners prepared, and the camp was broken up, Mott stopped briefly to watch a woman who lived in the obliterated Bowles house nearby scurry about frantically trying to salvage whatever belongings she could. "It was a pitiful sight to see the women and children fleeing from their homes for their lives leaving everything to the mercy of the soldiers," Mott observed. "The [Bowles] house where we are now was burned yesterday by a shell exploding in it. The family was in it at the time. The woman was almost crazy this morning trying to carry away a trunk. War, war, horrible war."[89] As he considered the scene feeling a swell of pity for the woman, Mott noticed a few of his men approaching with a body. Benjamin Jenkins, one of the company's sergeants, had been killed during the retreat the previous day. "They carried [Jenkins] in, made a rough coffin and dug his grave under an old oak tree by the roadside," Mott recorded in his diary.

I sent over for his brother, postponing the burial till he arrived. [At] 8:15 a.m. we...finished burying poor Ben. His brother was here. I never saw anyone so much grieved in all my life as Johnny was. He cried and sobbed as though his heart would break. They were so affectionate towards each other. We laid him under an oak tree, his companions were grouped around the grave as we laid him down in his last sleep, the wind singing a requiem to the dead soldier.[90]

Mott found Jenkins' death difficult to take. To be cut down on the eve of returning home was a cruel twist of fate and the loss affected all the Brandywines greatly.

Around four o'clock in the afternoon, Mott led his men to the rear along with the other Reserves whose terms were expiring. Not all the Brandywines were going home with them. Some chose to re-enlist for a bounty while others who had joined the company after June 4, 1861, still had additional time left on their service. They would be transferred to the 190th regiment in the Veteran's Corps to see the rest of the war through. Mott made his goodbyes to those remaining behind and began to march away from the front as the band played "Home Again."[91]

Mott arrived in Washington D.C. on the fourth of June, exactly three years to the day of his muster into Pennsylvania state service. After unloading the prisoners, he proceeded to Harrisburg the next day to be mustered out of state service and officially return to civilian life. As the train progressed through the Pennsylvania countryside towards West Chester, Mott reflected on how much more he appreciated life after his experience in war. "How beautiful the country looks after coming home from Virginia. I appreciate the beauties of nature more than I ever did. We received a perfect ovation from the people of Maryland. As the train passed along, women and children, old men and boys waved their hats and cheered us."[92]

5

Prospects

On June 8, 1864, a rail car carrying Mott and the Brandywine Guards slowly chugged into the train depot on Market Street in West Chester. Mott and the Brandywines had fantasized about this moment before leaving Camp Wayne three years earlier. The send-off they received had been lavish- bands played, a parade followed them through the streets, and citizens from all over the county, beamed with pride as they showered them with cheers and adoration. It exhilarated them. They had not yet met the enemy, but already they felt like the Union's avenging angels, overwhelmed by thoughts of the heroic deeds they believed lay before them. Many of them had looked forward in anticipation of a grand, victorious homecoming. The war had shattered the bravado. These were changed men. Weary and battle-worn, Mott telegrammed his brother ahead of his arrival that "Co. A would prefer coming to West Chester without a public reception. The men are all tired and deserve to get to their homes."[1] These exalted heroes hardly wanted to be acknowledged at all.

For the citizens of Chester County, such a quiet homecoming simply would not do. In the early days of June, West Chester was a buzz with excitement as word reached them that their boys were coming home. Like everyone else in town, Mott's family tracked his movements through the papers in great anticipation. Frank reached out to his family and social contacts in Harrisburg and Philadelphia to be informed the minute they spotted Mott.[2] As the day of the Brandywines' arrival approached, citizens from throughout the county traveled to West Chester to greet their returning war heroes. The local ladies' society quickly planned for a large fanfare. "Our lady friends immediately set to work to prepare for their arrival," West Chester's Village Record reported. "And when ladies once make up their mind to do a thing, they do it, and in no mean way, either, and before you could say 'presto, change!' everything was nearly completed."[3] Pulling into the station to the roar of cannon fire, Mott immediately realized their quiet reception was not to be had.

Mott stepped out onto the platform to the sight of throngs of cheering citizens rushing down Market Street to meet them eager to find their long-absent loved ones in the crowd. Wending his way through the crowd, Mott likely found his Aunt Susan and Frank. Mott never wrote of his family reunion, but his mother and sisters may have made the trip from Springfield. The emotional reunion was a balm for the soul. As mothers, fathers, and other family members embraced on the platform, cadets from the Pennsylvania and Wyers Military Academies arrived and told Mott they wished to formally escort his men into town. Unable to refuse, Mott ordered his men to fall in line and shoulder their arms for one last march.[4]

As Mott led his men up the rising slope of Market Street towards the courthouse, he saw a large arch festooned with flags and flowers suspended across the street emblazoned with the words "Welcome home!" in large letters. Flanking the arch on either side were the names of the many engagements the company had seen- Mechanicsville, Gaines' Mills, Malvern Hill, Charles City Crossroads, South Mountain, Second Bull Run, Antietam, Fredericksburg, Gettysburg, Wilderness, Spottsylvania, and Bethesda Church. They were a solemn reminder of some difficult times. They came to a halt beneath the arch. Cheering citizens showered them with bouquets of flowers as men, women, and children crowded every inch of sidewalk, perched on the low wall and yard around the courthouse, and hung out of windows in the surrounding buildings- a sort of 1860s version of a ticker-tape parade.[5]

Dr. Wilmer Worthington, a prominent West Chester native and sitting state senator, greeted Mott before delivering a moving speech to the assembled crowd lauding the bravery, sacrifice, and honor the company had exhibited during their service. Following Worthington, General McCall stepped forward to greet the men. He was a welcome sight indeed. No other superior officer engendered the loyalty and devotion as McCall had and It was only fitting he be there to congratulate Mott and his men on their return. McCall kept his remarks brief but expressed his sincere pride in them all. His former bodyguards had acquitted themselves well.

After all the remarks were complete, Mott led his men to the Normal School at the south end of town where the ladies who organized the homecoming had prepared a reception in their honor. Personally waited on by two ladies each at a table resplendent with food and flowers, the ravenous Guards devoured the bounty in front of them mustering just enough manners so as not to offend the onlookers. "Had they only been sent to that table, without so many bright eyes on them, they could have made better time and made a better exhibition of how they eat down on the Potomac,"[6] observed the *Village Record.* Fresh coffee and a dessert of strawberries in cream concluded the feast.

The feast was not without its solemnity. At one end of the flag-and-flower- covered room lay a large, green wreath lined with the black crepe of mourning. At its center appeared a list featuring the names of all the Brandywines who had been lost in the war. It was yet another grim reminder for Mott of the ordeal through which they had all just survived, though the men memorialized on the wreath had not been so lucky. As the men finished eating, some of the ladies presented Mott with a large bouquet of flowers as Captain of the company. Mott stood, accepted the flowers graciously and offered some brief words of gratitude and appreciation for all the town had done for them upon their return.

At the conclusion of the meal, Mott stepped outside the building where some of the crowds were still assembled. Though it had been a much bigger reception than Mott initially felt he and his men were ready for, it was nonetheless a moving day. In thanks to the ladies of West Chester who had treated them so kindly, the Guards gave them "three cheers—and a tiger," for their efforts.[7] As the crowds dispersed, Mott bid farewell to the other Brandywines as they each made their way home. For three years, they were rarely separated, now they would all, Mott included, have to find their own way in the world. But they would be forever connected to them through what had become a defining event in all of their lives.

***

In the days and months that followed, the return to normalcy was likely surreal. West Chester, physically untouched by the war, must have appeared an odd foil to the battle-scarred countryside and shelled-out towns of the South that had been the backdrop of Mott's life for the better part of the last three years. No longer were his day's activities dictated by other people. There was no one telling him what to do and when to do it. Now he could go wherever he chose, eat whatever he wanted, and slept whenever he felt tired. A warm bed replaced a rifle blanket on the ground and home-cooked meals replaced the bland army diet of hard tack and bad coffee on which he had subsisted. Rumors of impending battles and troop movements no longer needed to occupy his thoughts. The only rumors swirling now were about who was flirting with whom down at Everhart Grove. Life, in general, had been consistent and prescribed, if somewhat tedious, in the army, but now his fate was once again in his hands.

Mott's return to normal life was complicated by the fact that the war was not yet over. It would be another year before Lee would surrender to Grant at Appomattox, thus bringing an end to the bloodiest conflict ever seen on American soil. During that time, several of Mott's duties as captain continued. He reconciled company returns for the army and counseled those formerly under his command who still looked to him for influence and advice. In July, Mott received a letter from one of his former men, Thomas J. Maloney, since made a Captain in the 108th US regiment who had taken command of a company of Black soldiers. Maloney sought a character reference from Mott regarding his conduct in camp and "in the face of the enemy" for the benefit of determining his rank in the regiment. Maloney also pointed out as an aside that Mott would appreciate the fact that he had "the best-drilled company in the regiment and I intend to keep it so," a nod to the example Mott had set for Maloney in the Brandywine Guards.[8] Family members of the Brandywines who did not survive the war relied on Mott to sort out back pay owed to the men from the state. In November, Catherine Jenkins, mother of Private Benjamin Jenkins who had been killed at Bethesda Church the day before the company left the front lines, wrote to Mott in an attempt to enlist his help in obtaining a bounty for her son.[9] Despite now enjoying all the creature comforts of his family's home, Mott still had one foot in the army.

Acutely aware of the conflict still underway, Mott kept in touch with some of the Guards who had accepted the bounty to continue their service in the 190th Veteran Regiment. He still felt a great sense of concern, if not responsibility, for the boys despite the fact they were no longer under his command. James Mooney, a former sergeant in the Brandywine Guards, became a link to the twelve men who had extended their service. Mott sent Mooney several copies of his photograph to give to the Brandywines he still had contact with and Mooney kept Mott apprised of their movements. Mooney did not always have good news. Three of his former men had not been heard from after Bethesda Church.[10] Unbeknownst to Mooney, they had been captured at that last battle and sent to Libby Prison in Virginia. One passed away in prison, while the other two were transferred and incarcerated in the infamous Andersonville Prison in Georgia. Both miraculously survived their imprisonment, but at the time of Mooney's letter, their fate remained a mystery. Mooney did, however, have some bad news to deliver to Mott regarding another former Brandywine:

I am sorry to inform you that Lewis M. Woodward was killed. He was shot while on picket on the 20th of June. He was shot through the head with a minie ball. Poor boy, he never spoke after he was hit. I had his body carried and buried. We buried him [in] an orchard at the foot of an apple tree.[11]

The news troubled Mott as he cared deeply for his men. In a sense, Mott would never stop being their captain.

Little more than a month after Mott's return home, the front lines of battle were once more encroaching into Maryland and President Lincoln had sent out a call for additional troops. Given Pennsylvania's proximity to the front lines of the fighting, Governor Curtin echoed the President's call most emphatically. Though discharged from the army, Mott lost none of his commitment to serving the Union. He joined his brother Frank and twelve other leading citizens of Chester County, including General McCall, General Galusha Pennypacker, Colonel Henry Guss, and State Senator Worthington on a committee to prepare an address to the county amplifying Lincoln's and Curtin's calls for volunteers. On July 10th at the courthouse in West Chester, the committee hosted a "war meeting," which they advertised in the *Village Record* under the bold heading "TO ARMS! TO ARMS! Chester County to the Rescue."[12] Several members of the committee spoke to the assembled crowd, appealing to their patriotism and encouraging young men in the county to enlist. Flowery language and inspirational oratory dominated the addresses, but the most moving speeches were the most reserved delivered by the most revered. Henry Guss, colonel of the 97th Infantry demurred to speak at length claiming it was "not in his line of business" to make speeches. Instead, he simply discussed his knowledge of the war having been a participant and that, by example, his son was raising a new volunteer artillery company.[13] General McCall also spoke just briefly, acknowledging that the patriotic speeches of the previous committee members had been sufficient, adding simply that "it is the duty of every loyal citizen to assist in this important work. Volunteers ought to be raised at once and sent to the front."[14]

When not answering war correspondence, filling out old company returns, or recruiting volunteers on behalf of the army, Mott returned to Everhart Grove to avail himself of the social pleasures of a young man settling back into civilian life. Several of his friends, James Good, Hampton Hildeburn, and Tom Dillingham, eagerly welcomed him back and he spent much of his first summer home fraternizing and flirting with many of the young women of West Chester. In particular, one Becky Stevenson caught Mott's eye, engaging in a "heavy flirtation" with her all summer.[15] After the previous three years, it felt like paradise. Yet Mott's newfound life of leisure belied an ongoing struggle stewing in his mind. He was now twenty-six years old. Mott had to face his future and decide what he would with his life. Did he flirt with Miss Stevenson to relive the carefree romantic entanglements of his youth or should he be considering a more serious courtship to settle down? Likewise, how should he support himself? He planned to invest in property to generate some independent wealth but relying on a passive income merely to support a life of leisure would not suit Mott's restless soul. He needed direction. He needed purpose.

Mott did not lack opportunity. With his education and standing in the community, any number of occupational paths—business, law, public service—were open to him. His brother Frank was a prominent member of the county bar and the family had many influential friends in local, state and even federal government. He would have a vested interest in at least one shop and apartment building in Philadelphia and several farms throughout the county that he rented to tenant farmers making him a man of property.[16] As late as February 1865, a friend in Philadelphia wrote Mott a letter addressing him as Mott Hooton, Esq., a tongue-in-cheek salutation perhaps suggesting Mott had intimated to people that he would, in fact, pursue a life in law.[17] However, less than two months after his return, Mott began writing friends and former comrades seeking their advice about the prospect of re-entering the army. His friend Bill Bowen out in Nebraska, who had himself re-enlisted and was serving as the 1st Lieutenant of Company D, 1st Battalion of the Nebraska Cavalry, greatly supported the idea and offered a more impassioned argument in favor of the army than anyone.[18]

A man revealed: rare image of Mott clean-shaven
Courtesy of Decker Landry

"First, let me congratulate you upon your safe exodus from the field of Mars. Now you have the glorious privilege, denied by many, of re-enlisting."[19] As far as Bowen was concerned, the nation remained in a fragile state and the country needed people like Mott to fight for it:

It certainly was very honorable to have gone into the war three years ago, but I cannot but think it moreso now...those who cooly calculate the risks and then go are indeed brave as those who camped at Valley Forge or desperately fought at Brandywine.

The jeering, saying the country is in an awful state, is becoming but too correct. Gigantic armies now in the field, huge calls for more in the future. And in the past, almost a generation have laid down and died. And the end is not yet. Our currency is almost useless. Our foreign friends not very friendly. And our domestic northern foes [peace advocates and southern sympathizers living in the north] daily gaining numbers and audacity. Surely, Mott, our entire day and generation must be devoted to this work and happy be if the end be even thus attained.[20]

Like many still concerned with the ongoing war between the states, Bowen assumed Mott's inquiry regarded re-enlistment as a volunteer for the war, but Mott's ambition was greater. He had no desire to simply repeat the temporary volunteer service he had just completed to see out the duration of the war. He sought a position as a career officer in the regular army. The realities of obtaining such a commission, however, would not be so easy. Mott soon turned to Emmor Cope, one of his former Sergeants who was still serving in the army as a captain and aide de camp to General Gouverneur Warren of the 5th Army Corps. Mott asked Cope about the prospects of a staff commission, but Cope informed him there were currently no openings. And while more than willing to do whatever he could for Mott, Cope did not want to get Mott's hopes up. "I think, Captain, the chance of my small influence affecting anything in your cause would be slim," he wrote.[21]

Word eventually got back to Mott's family that he had been making inquiries about joining the army and they actively discouraged him

Help from a friend: Captain Emmor B. Cope (Presumed)
Courtesy of the Pennsylvania Reserve Volunteer Corps Historical Society
(PRVCHS)

from pursuing the idea. They had nearly lost him on more than one occasion during the war and missed him terribly. They had only just gotten him back. His mother, not wanting to endure further separation from him particularly for a position that could put him in harm's way, told him that he should settle down and become a lawyer like his brother. Frank had influences and plenty of resources, so Mott could easily be admitted to the bar with little expense. "Everyone" always said he would be good at it, she wrote to him.[22] But it wasn't just his family that attempted to persuade him to forget the army and find some civilian occupation. Aside from the lack of current staff openings, Cope warned Mott about the difficulty he had endured trying to secure such a position himself and told Mott frankly, "I am surprised at your getting tired of your citizenship so soon. If I were you and could get into business at home, I would not entertain a thought of the army for a single moment."[23]

For a time, at least, Mott let the matter drop and resolved to go into some kind of business. Given his correspondence with Cope, short of attending West Point or some other military academy first, virtually any other occupation would be easier to establish than obtaining an army commission as a civilian, albeit one with military experience. Not everyone encouraged the path of least resistance for Mott. When he learned that Mott had decided to give up on the military, Bowen expressed disappointment in the choice. "Your letter is not at hand at this moment, but I remember you stated therein your wish to engage in some business," Bowen wrote. "I regret this, for I had hoped you would again enter the army, but if it is your desire, I will help you if I can."[24] But the truth is Mott never let go of his military ambition. In a letter that October from another former Brandywine, Luther Mendenhall asks Mott if he will be re-entering the army, suggesting that his friends knew the possibility that a life in the army was still on the table.[25] When the government bestowed upon Mott the honorary rank of brevet Major in 1865 for gallant and meritorious service in the Wilderness campaign, the recognition became a further affirmation of the difference he felt he could make as a leader in service of his country.

The military undoubtedly held a lot of appeal for Mott. His time as captain of the Brandywine Guards gave him purpose and drive. As a man who valued duty, loyalty, and honor above all else, Mott took his role very seriously. As 2nd Lieutenant, he had taken it upon himself to drill the company when he felt Captain Nields had neglected them. Even his detractors during the company election had admitted that he genuinely cared about the company and wanted to make them the most effective unit possible.[26] Even now, with his time done, he remained devoted to his men still in the field. If Cope's dissuasion went unheeded it was not for naivete on Mott's part. After what he had experienced in the war, the carnage he had witnessed, and the physical sacrifices he made having been severely wounded, he held no allusions about the dangerous reality a military life could bring. Despite his family's wishes and his own hemming and hawing about his future, the fact is he solicited more advice from friends about pursuing a career in the regular army than any other occupational path open to him. And his family should not have been surprised by it. Rumors flittered about as early as 1863, nearly a year before his service in the Volunteers was finished, that Mott was considering permanently joining the army. "It is reported here that you are going into the regular army. I have been asked several times. You were the subject of conversation at the Ladies Aid the other day and that was the report," Mott's mother wrote him. "I told them I thought it was not true as you had not said anything about it to me."[27] Despite her doubt about the rumors, as the concerned mother she felt compelled to preemptively dissuade Mott from the idea. "Mott, I think it must be a dog's life. Weigh the matter well before you do it, you would never be at home."[28] Mott might have remembered the pride his family had expressed over his service during the war, his aunt going so far as to suggest that not having served would have been a mark of cowardice and shame.[29] But Mott's enlistment had been in furtherance of a noble cause. Now the war was over, and the Union's goals were achieved. In the absence of any kind of moral imperative, they could not see why one would voluntarily subject themselves to a life of hardship and danger when one had the privilege of so many other professional opportunities available to him.

Yet Mott persisted, writing to Captain Cope again in late 1864, determined to forge ahead, despite Cope's previous warnings about the difficulties in pursuing such a course. In his response, Cope reiterated his doubt that his influence would count for much but offered to do whatever he could. In the end, however, Cope suggested that an application in person would go much farther than the word of a fellow officer.

I think if you went to refrain in person to General Hancock, or to the Secretary of War with any simple statement of when you had served, it would be the best recommendation you could offer. You know that my influence in the matter would not be worth a snap and my name would but serve to swell the list. However, I have always contended that the appearance of the man is three-fourths and I think you would take. I am willing to serve you any way in my power and will give you authority to add my name to your list.[30]

Although he doubted his own influence, Cope stopped offering opinions and instead proffered practical advice on a path forward in acknowledgment of the fact that Mott's mind was clearly made up.

Mott took at least some of Cope's advice to heart realizing that any recommendations he solicited would have to come from individuals of a higher profile and influence than a solitary Captain serving as an Aide de Camp. And higher he went. Mott obtained letters of recommendation from several high-ranking officers, including four generals and two colonels.[31] Colonel William McCandless, Mott's brigade commander considered his service a credit to himself and the government.[32] Colonel William Cooper Talley perhaps knew Mott best having commanded his regiment. In his recommendation to the War Department, he offered high praise for Mott. "I considered him one of my best officers," he wrote, and believe he would make an excellent regimental commander."[33]

The generals whose recommendations he sought were both those he knew well either through direct service or his family's social circles. Not surprisingly, George McCall offered a glowing reference:

I take great pleasure in introducing to your favorable notice my young friend Captain Mott Hooton late of A Company 1ˢᵗ Regt. Penna. Reserves. Whilst I was in command of the Reserves, his company constituted my bodyguard and I had therefore constant opportunity to observe his perfect temperance, diligence, intelligence, and soldier-like qualities whilst in battle. No one was more cool and brave...I have known M Hooton personally for ten years and I can fully vouch for his high moral character.[34]

McCall's successor as commander of the Pennsylvania Reserves, General Truman Seymour, was the only non-Pennsylvanian amongst his advocates. Though he only commanded the Reserves for a short while, he thought highly of Mott writing that he was "always known to me as an officer of good conduct and deserving character...I believe he will be all that you could desire."[35] He shared his recommendation with Mott, appending the note, "with best wishes of your old commander."[36] Not surprisingly, Mott did not seek out a recommendation from General Samuel Crawford, the third and final commander of the Reserves whom Mott detested.

His remaining two advocates had less knowledge of Mott as a soldier, but were prominent social connections whose names alone was believed could attract attention to Mott's application.[37] The first, Major General John G. Parke, was a graduate of the United States Military Academy and one-time member of the Army Corps of Engineers. During the war, Parke was appointed Brigadier General of Volunteers and spent most of the war attached to the 9ᵗʰ Corps as Chief of Staff for General Ambrose Burnside and later as the Corps' commanding officer. Parke also happened to be a native of Chester County, Pennsylvania having been born and raised in Coatesville. No doubt this connection helped in securing a recommendation from the General.

The second recommendation Mott received came with an even

Top brass recommendations (top row L to R): Generals Meade &
McCall; (bottom row L to R): Generals Seymour, and Parke

*Meade: National Portrait Gallery, Smithsonian Institution, McCall: National
Portrait Gallery, Smithsonian Institution, Frederick Hill Meserve Collection; Parke
and Seymour: Library of Congress*

higher profile: Major General George Gordon Meade. Like Parke, Meade was a West Point graduate. Before the Civil War broke out, he saw service in Florida in the Second Seminole War and also fought in the Mexican-American War. However, he is best remembered for commanding the Army of the Potomac during the Battle of Gettysburg, the engagement that turned the tide of war in the Union's favor and stopped a Confederate invasion of the North. The Army of the Potomac had seen several commanders come and go, but Meade saw it through to the end of the war, working closely with Ulysses S. Grant when the latter was named the commander of all Union armies. Meade is among the most recognizable names in Civil War history, just as it was in his own day. To receive a personal recommendation from such a figure was a boon to Mott. Uriah Painter, a well-known journalist and war correspondent from Chester County, was so impressed by these two endorsements that he told Mott's brother that the younger Hooton could have been made Major on them alone.[38] Here too the family's connections in Philadelphia society likely played a role in making this happen. Meade grew up in Philadelphia and would reside there after the war for the remainder of his life. The Hootons, particularly Frank, likely traveled in the same social circles. Moreover, later correspondence between Mott and Col. George Meade, General Meade's son, suggests there may have been a stronger, personal connection between the Hootons and the Meades.[39]

The Civil War officially ended within three months of Cope's letter in April 1865, but Mott's long-term ambitions in the military were never about the current conflict. Indeed, he likely did not even receive his endorsements until after Robert E. Lee surrendered at Appomattox Court House. Although the recommendations would not garner the rank of Major as Painter imagined they should, they certainly got Mott's foot in the door of a significantly reduced post-Civil War army.

***

On July 4th, 1865, committees of soldiers from Chester and Delaware Counties hosted a grand reunion of soldiers at the Brandywine Battlefield in Chadds Ford. Trains carrying veterans and their families descended upon the area from every direction while others made the trek by horse and carriage. The picnic-style event featured a plethora of speakers including General McCall, Col. Samuel Thomas of Governor Curtin's staff, and Mott's brother, Frank. The soldiers, who numbered nearly three thousand by one estimate, were all encouraged to wear their uniforms with a sprig of laurel on their left breast.[40] It had been less than three months since Lee's surrender and spirits were high. With the danger of war passed and victory for their side achieved, soldiers circulated among the crowd unfettered by military discipline or regulations and exhibited a pride for a job well done and an unbridled optimism for the future. No formal military parade or drill was asked of them. This day was for their enjoyment and enjoy it they did. The attendees enjoyed an abundance of food and the soldiers and young ladies danced into the early evening. "The meeting was characterized by entire harmony and unrestricted cheerfulness on the part of the immense throngs who had gathered on this memorable occasion," the Village Record reported a few days later.[41] For most of the men, this would be the last time they donned their uniforms, their duty done and their promise to their country fulfilled. For Mott, however, this happy occasion marked just the beginning of his military career. By the following summer, Mott would find himself out west, a First Lieutenant in the Regular Army of the United States.

6

Into the West

"Why the Devil don't you write a fellow?" Hildeburn wrote to Mott in September 1866. "Here I have been waiting ever since the seventh of last August...to hear from you...I can't stand that from an old friend like you. But never mind. I won't be angry with you if like a good boy you answer this one right away."[1] One of Mott's more colorful friends from home, Hildeburn was several years Mott's junior living a life of leisure. Croquet in the mornings at the Grove with riding parties and picnics in the afternoons. He attended over a dozen parties in town over the summer and for a solid two months attended the young ladies at the Grove every day without fail. Mott had known some of that life himself the previous year, about which Hildeburn did not fail to remind him. But much had changed in the course of a year and given that his own summer included two weeks of marching over one hundred forty miles through "rain and black mud" in the Dakota territory, Mott could be forgiven his less than prompt replies.[2]

Mott's arduous first summer in the Regular Army began on April 16—his twenty-eighth birthday—when he reported for basic training at Governor's Island off the coast of Manhattan. Though originally commissioned second Lieutenant, subsequent promotions from the time of his acceptance to his arrival for service left an opening for a first

"

lieutenancy in the 13th Infantry, which he was granted on his first day. Though commissioned below the rank he held with the volunteers during the war, and not at all what some back home believed he deserved based on the caliber of recommendations he had received, Mott was simply thankful to have received a commission at all.

Mott had joined an army in flux as Congress grappled with determining the appropriate scale of a standing peacetime army. During the war, many officers had been artificially raised in rank due to a want of officers. General Meade was a captain before the needs of the government appointed him General. But when the conflict ended, mass demobilization of volunteer soldiers meant the army had no need for so many ranking individuals, nor could it sustain them. Many officers who had commanded entire divisions suddenly reverted to their pre-war ranks.

When General Lee surrendered to General Grant in April of 1865, the federal army was, by some estimates, as many as two million strong.[3] The vast majority of that number were federalized state troops and volunteers whose service expired at the close of the war. Further, members of a growing Peace Movement in the 1860s put considerable pressure on Congress to greatly reduce the force of the regular army and reign in military spending now that the immediate threat of open rebellion had been quelled. This mindset, however, belied the state of the union in the aftermath of the war. Open rebellion in the southern states may have been subdued, but the government still relied on a considerable occupation to enforce its Reconstruction policies. In addition, there was still the matter of the vast western territories where hostilities between white settlers and Native American nations continued to run hot. There were voices at the other extreme that sought to take advantage of this vast army while the government had access to it in order to quickly "pacify" the West once and for all.[4]

General Grant recommended that Congress set the post-war troop limit at 80,000 strong. It was a far cry from the number of men in the field during the war, but vastly larger than the pre-war standing army of 18,000. Congress balked at Grant's ambitious request but agreed in

1866 to set the standing army at 54,000—still three times the size of the antebellum military.[5] The army send much of this force to focus on Reconstruction, but the rest, which included Mott, were dispatched to the west to enforce the government's plan for pacifying the frontier for white settlement.

Mott's training at Governor's Island lasted only days before he received orders to join a detachment of recruits bound for Fort Leavenworth in Kansas, where the 13th Infantry was stationed.[6] As he made his way west from New York, Mott would quickly realize that service at a western fort would look very different from anything he had experienced before.

Western strategy in the post-war years differed somewhat from pre-war strategy. Before the Civil War, the goal of the army was simply to protect settlers on the overland trails headed for the west coast, which they achieved through a system of forts and outposts. However, in 1862, in an effort to encourage Western migration, the United States government passed the Homestead Act. The act essentially granted one hundred sixty acres of land to any head of a family who staked a claim and remained on the land for at least five years. Now, instead of passing through Native American land to reach places like California and Oregon, settlers were putting down roots anywhere and everywhere in between. Naturally, this caused problems given the fact that these lands were already occupied by a myriad of Native tribes, many of whom had already been displaced from their ancestral lands a generation or more earlier. In response, the government devised the reservation system, which established large territories of land specifically closed to home-steaders for the sole use of Native Americans. Although the official establishment of the reservation system did not occur until 1868, the idea was not without precedent. The displacement of thousands of Creek, Seminole, and other indigenous nations had established "Indian Territory," present-day Oklahoma, by way of the infamously brutal Trail of Tears prosecuted by the federal government following the discovery of gold in Georgia in 1828 and the passage of the Indian Re-moval Act of 1830. That this had now become a widespread, standard policy created a hotbed of conflict, particularly in the Southwest and across the Great Plains.

The task of managing this new reservation system fell to the Bureau of Indian Affairs. To that end, the Bureau created various Indian Agencies to oversee the reservations, which were run by agents stationed near military posts. These agent posts served as disbursement points for aid, such as food and other goods, intended to support the Natives living on the reservations. Not surprisingly, many Native American nations resisted being forced onto land earmarked by the government, particularly as the land was assigned without respect to differences or tensions between nations, which only fueled the fires of resistance. The challenge for the army became less about protecting the Indian Agents and maintaining peace on the reservations, and more about forcing tribes who refused to comply with the policy onto the reservations. As a result, the government greatly expanded the fort system throughout the West and developed a military organization of territories west of the Mississippi to better administer the lands and facilitate these mass-relocation efforts.[7]

The federal government in Washington divided all the land in the United States west of the Mississippi into two divisions: The Division of the Pacific and the Division of the Missouri. Each division was then subdivided into a series of Departments. The Division of the Pacific included two Departments: The Department of California (made up of present-day California, Arizona, and part of New Mexico) and the Department of the Columbia (including present-day Oregon, Washington, and Idaho). The Division was commanded by Major General Henry Halleck, whose Headquarters was located at the Presidio of San Francisco.

The Division of the Missouri, on the other hand, was much larger and contained four Departments. The Department of the Missouri included the areas of Colorado, Kansas, Missouri, and the remaining portion of New Mexico; the Department of Arkansas included Arkansas and Oklahoma (or "Indian Territory"); the Department of Dakota, which included Minnesota, part of Montana, and much of the Dakotas;

and finally the Department of the Platte contained the remainder of Montana, Dakota, Nebraska, and Utah. The famous Union Lieutenant General William Tecumseh Sherman commanded this Division.

Troops moved frequently throughout the West as supply wagons and new recruits required escort from one fort to the next or as old forts were abandoned and new forts established. It was against this backdrop that Mott arrived at Fort Leavenworth to join his regiment. Mott used his brief time at Leavenworth to get his bearings and become familiar with his new comrades. Mott subsequently traveled to Fort Firesteel, also known as Fort James, on the James River in the Dakota Territory, with his company.[8] A steamboat took Mott part of the way, but upon reaching Sioux City, Iowa, the companies disembarked to complete the remainder of the journey overland to the James River. Continuously pelted with rain, Mott struggled over muddy terrain for two weeks to reach their destination some one hundred forty miles from Sioux City.[9]

Fort Firesteel was a short-lived fort on the James River in modern-day South Dakota near the junction with Firesteel Creek. Captain Benjamin King of the 6th Iowa Cavalry built the wood and stone fort less than a year prior under orders by General Alfred Sully for the protection of the local Dakota settlements from Lakota aggression. King and his troops still occupied the site when the companies of the thirteenth regiment arrived to relieve them. Mott served as commissary and Quartermaster of the fort until October when the army decided to abandon the post. Mott helped pack up what remained of the property's provisions in an ox train and traveled the seventy miles to their next post, Fort Randall on the Missouri River.

***

In the spring of 1867, during a reorganization of the army, Mott transferred to the 31st infantry regiment, which was tasked with establishing a new fort on the Missouri River in between the more westerly Fort Buford at the confluence of the Missouri and Yellowstone Rivers and Fort Totten established along Devil's Lake to the east. Collectively,

Buford, Totten, and the new fort would protect the Middle District of the Department of Dakota. Situated near the confluence of Douglas Creek and the Missouri River as the latter shifts course sharply towards the west, the new post, christened Fort Stevenson, stood less than twenty miles east of Fort Berthold, where the 31st Regiment had been temporarily stationed.[10] Berthold was originally established as a civilian fur trading post purchased by the American Fur Company in 1862. It was never intended to be a permanent military post, but since the end of the Civil War, Berthold had housed a military garrison. With the orders to construct the new post downriver, the Army abandoned Berthold and it reverted to its previous role as a private fur trading post. Colonel Joseph N. G. Whistler commanded the 31st regiment and brought his troops to the new site to begin construction on the post in June 1867.

Several hundred miles downriver at Fort Randall, Mott readied his belongings for his departure to the Stevenson construction site. Boarding a steamboat on the Missouri River, Mott set out to join his new regiment, but the annual spring rise had not yet occurred in some parts of the river, leaving Mott and all the other troops with him stranded in shallow water for several days to await the rising water level.[11] Mott and the other passengers had no other choice but to bide their time and disembark occasionally to hunt. One Sunday evening, a young boy clad in little more than rags followed the hunting party back to the boat and climbed aboard. Soaked from head to toe from having swum across the river, he had become separated from his companion after they were attacked by a band of Native Americans.

That evening, Mott assembled a small team of soldiers and took a boat to the opposite side of the river in search of the boy's friend, but finding nothing as darkness fell, he called off the search for the night. Resuming the search the next morning, Mott came upon the boy's ill-fated companion and it was a grizzly sight. "[We] found the man lying with his head in the water dead, shot with bullets and shot through the heart with an arrow. I brought his body back and buried it with the honors of war in the woods nearby."[12] Within a few days the water level rose, and the ship resumed course toward its destination.

Mott had expected to see some semblance of a fort when he arrived at Stevenson, but the construction was severely behind schedule and very little had been done. The site had been surveyed and measured to determine the best elevation and location and while plans had been drafted for all buildings and fortifications, the distance of available resources hampered the speed of the actual construction. The nearest source of stone for the masonry foundations was a series of bluffs about two miles away. Only when the stone had been quarried and delivered to the site could the civilian stonemasons begin the task of cutting the stone to the appropriate size.[13]

While preparations for the foundations were underway, another contingent of soldiers was detached to obtain wood for the lumber- not an easy task given the barren, wind-swept landscape of the Great Plains. The only trees suitable for the purpose were situated on the opposite side of the wide, fast-moving water of the Missouri River. A small unit established a camp among the trees with several ox carts to guard the resource while soldiers felled the trees, removing all the branches by hand. Once prepped, the logs had to be chained to a wagon and dragged to the edge of the river where they were lashed to each other, about a dozen at a time, and pulled by long boat across the river like a giant raft. Upon arrival at the opposite bank, soldiers separated the logs, chained them to wagons, and dragged them uphill to the construction site where a steam-powered sawmill cut the logs into usable building lumber. By mid-August, about four to five hundred trees had been felled, many of which had been transported across the river, but just a fraction of them had been milled. Only the framing for the storehouse had begun in earnest. Meanwhile, at a brickyard established below the camp, a third contingent worked making adobe bricks to supplement the stone and lumber.

With only about two hundred twenty soldiers and forty civilians on site, nearly the entire garrison found itself occupied primarily with the building of the fort. Between guarding cattle, cutting trees, escorting wagons, making adobe, hauling stone, and constructing buildings, there was virtually no activity to suggest the site was actually a military outpost, with the exception of a small, rotating guard duty.[14] Compounding the delays was the fact that a scarcity of officers throughout the district left administration shorthanded at Stevenson. Mott was one of only four first lieutenants reporting for duty in the district out of a full complement of ten. In total, among the three posts of the district, sixteen out of thirty-five officers were absent for one reason or another —leave, illness, or detached on other duties like recruiting or court martial adjudication.[15]

On August 19th, Mott saluted the arrival of his new commanding officer, Colonel Regis de Trobriand who had arrived to relieve Colonel Whistler and take command of the district intending to make Stevenson his headquarters. If Mott detected an heir of nobility about his new commander, there was good reason for it. Born in 1816 in Tours, France, Philippe Regis Denis de Keredern de Trobriand grew up in the orbit of the Royal French court of Charles X. His father, Baron Joseph de Keredern de Trobriand had served in Napoleon's army, but subsequently swore allegiance to the monarchy after the Bourbon Restoration in 1814. Like most of the men in his family going back generations, Philippe was destined for military service until Louis Philippe, Duke of Orleans overthrew his cousin Charles in the July Revolution of 1830. The elder de Trobriand resigned his commission in protest, which effectively excluded his son from service as well.

Regis de Trobriand, having dropped the name Philippe in objection to the usurper King, attended the College of Saint-Louis. He studied law and devoted his time to writing novels and poetry. At twenty-five, he sailed for New York where he became active among the local social elite. While in the United States, he married Mary Mason Jones, the daughter of a wealthy American banker before returning to Europe. After briefly taking up residence in Venice near the exiled Bourbon court, the couple returned to New York in 1847.

European nobility on the Plains: Regis de Trobriand
Library of Congress

When the Civil War broke out, de Trobriand felt called to the destiny that had been denied him in France. He became a naturalized citizen and was given command of the 55th New York Volunteer Infantry, a regiment composed primarily of French immigrants known also as the *Gardes de Lafayette*. He commanded Troops in numerous engagements, most notably Gettysburg, Petersburg, and the Appomattox campaign. By the time the war ended, he had achieved the rank of Brigadier General with a further brevet promotion to Major General.

In 1867, after a brief return to Paris to write a book about his experiences with the Army of the Potomac, Ulysses S. Grant appointed him a Colonel in the Regular Army. Placed in command of the 31st infantry, he was ordered to assume his command at Fort Stevenson upon his return from France.

Like Mott, when de Trobriand arrived at the post, he was dismayed at the lack of progress. In place of barracks, as none had yet been built, the officers situated their tents on a small ridge facing the river. The tents of the rank and file then ran down the slope perpendicular to the officers' tents.[16] Despite the flurry of activity and hard work going on at the site, almost no fortifications had been built. Just a single palisade stood having been erected in response to a minor skirmish that had occurred earlier in the summer. In actuality, it served little real purpose. The paltry defense was "less an effective protection against Indian hostiles than as a means of inspiring the officer's wives with a sense of constant security," the colonel noted.[17]

The idiosyncrasies of the climate on the Great Plains compounded the struggle that Mott and the soldiers faced in constructing the fort. It could get beastly hot in the summer, with little natural shade for relief and when a storm rolled in, it rarely left any rain to cool things down. On the contrary, the open flat land contributed to the formation of horrendous windstorms, some of which were so strong that on one occasion, the entire camp was almost blown away into the river. "The furniture was upset, the dishes were broken, and a sheet iron stove was rolled up to the foot of the plateau," de Trobriand noted in his journal.[18] Moreover, these storms often kicked up terrible whirlwinds of dust owing to the utter lack of rain that accompanied the storm.

Despite its hardships, the location was a spot to behold. Except for a series of low hills to the north, much of the land continued as far as the eye could see. The immensity of the landscape, while impressive, made the prospect of attack difficult to counter owing to the lack of available cover. "Against personal dangers, the protection of the government is a myth," opined de Trobriand. "The only real protection [on the Plains] is a steady heart and a good carbine."[19]

The largest resistance to white settlement and westward expansion in the Dakota territory came from the Lakota. Consisting of seven bands or sub-tribes, including the Hunkpapa, Oglala, Mnikowoju, Sicangu, Sihasapa, Itazipcho, and Oohenunpa, the Lakota nation aggressively fought the threat to their way of life that the reservation system represented. The Hunkpapa under Sitting Bull and the Oglala under Crazy Horse were particularly active in the territory frustrating the federal government's efforts to displace them from their lands, but they rarely approached Fort Stevenson. The predominant nations near Stevenson were traditional enemies of the Lakota and by and large peaceable. The Hidatsa, Arikara, and Mandan tribes, known collectively as the Three Affiliated Tribes, had united in the 1830s after being nearly wiped out by smallpox. In 1862, they established a village called Like-a-Fishhook outside the old Fort Berthold trading post.[20] A month after arriving at Fort Stevenson, Colonel de Trobriand decided to undertake a diplomatic mission to Berthold to meet with the Three Affiliate Tribes.

On the morning of September 21, 1867, de Trobriand selected Mott and two other officers—Major John Vincent Furey and Assistant Surgeon Washington Matthews—to accompany him. Two orderly sergeants and one of the post's mixed-race scouts, Charley MacDonald, joined the officers to help ensure a safe journey to the fort. The route to Berthold across the plains, though only two hours distant by wagon, was bisected by a barren stretch of badlands—a dry, barren terrain of sterile, clay and soft, highly-eroded rock, arranged in a variety of stratified geological formations of plateaus, ravines, and canyons.[21] The striking contrast between the terrain of these badlands and the plains left an unsettling impression on the group. "It grips the soul much more than it pleases the eye," de Trobriand remarked.[22]

The collection of ravines and rocky outcrops put Mott on alert as he realized the potential for an ambush from any number of directions. However, except for a lone red fox, they encountered no other life. Passing through the badlands and back on the prairie once more, they neared their destination. The approach to Fort Berthold offered yet another contrast to Fort Stevenson, namely that the fort was intact and complete. Its sightlines were excellent for detecting approaching danger and its position by the river not only provided additional protection but was deep enough to allow steamboats to land.[23]

The fort itself boasted a simple, yet effective design. The defensive wall featured block forts at two corners with small openings for launching defensive volleys from a covered position. A continuous, upper walkway along the ramparts offered added defense and protection. The interior compound consisted of a series of square buildings surrounding an inner courtyard, the only access to which was achieved via a single pair of large wooden doors that could be barred internally."[24] Passing near the village of the three tribes, located not far outside the fort's walls, the officers' wagon finally arrived at the large gates of Berthold.

Their arrival had been announced in the village and a large gathering of the indigenous people crowded the entrance to get a look at the officers. Crow's Breast, Chief of the Hidatsa, approached Mott and the other officers in welcome.[25] Tall and strong, Crow's breast was about fifty years old, but there was nary a gray hair on his head. Standing in the courtyard "fanning himself gently with an eagle wing embellished with sweet grass," Crow's Breast cut an impressive figure. Sporting jewelry and other ornamental embellishments, the only detraction from his stately appearance was the simple straw hat he wore on his head.[26] The greeting between the Chief and the Colonel was brief, there being no interpreter present, and amounted to little more than shaking hands "silently and with great gravity."[27]

Berthold itself was occupied primarily by the fur traders of the

American Fur Company, as it had been before the 31st had taken up a garrison there a few years prior. Most of the traders were French Canadian by birth, or of mixed Indian and French Canadian descent. Indeed, the prevalence of the French Canadian influence in these parts of the Dakota Territory no doubt contributed to the army's decision to post a French colonel to the district. De Trobriand's native tongue would come in handy on the northern plains. Gustave Cagnat, leader of the trading post, was a native of France, a fact which pleased de Trobriand and frustrated Mott who often found himself out of the loop while the Colonel preferred to speak the trader in French. As leader of the post, Cagnat had four rooms to himself on one side of the fort, two of which he offered to Mott and the others in the party to share along with a pair of sheets and pillows with which to make their beds. Cagnat temporarily converted his office into a dining room and bedroom for the colonel.[28]

As soon as the pleasantries and basic orientation of the fort concluded, Mott accompanied the Colonel on a visit to the village of the three tribes. Situated just outside the walls of the fort, the village consisted of an assortment of large, earth-covered dome-shaped lodges grouped together in an irregular pattern.[29] The circular interiors of the lodges were all alike, the focal point being the hearth in the center of the dwelling. A single opening at the top of the dome brought in light and allowed smoke to escape. Beds lined the perimeter, leaving most of the interior space open for movement and entertaining visitors.[30]

They stopped first at the lodge belonging to Pierre Garreau, a mixed-race trader and interpreter over sixty years of age, who lived with the tribes. Garreau spoke each of the languages of the three tribes as well as French, but very little English. Yet again Mott and his other companions could only stand by awkwardly as their Colonel conducted all of their greetings.

After a brief tour around the village, the men returned to the fort to dine, where they found White Shield, chief of the Arikara nation, waiting to be presented to the Colonel.[31] White Shield presented a more modest appearance. Advancing in years, the chief dispensed with the ornamentations of his Hidatsa counterpart. Partially covered with a blanket slung over one shoulder, his bare chest and exposed arm displayed colorful blue, white, and red body paint.[32]

As it was with Crow's Breast, the greeting was similarly brief and silent. Mott retired to his room to share a quick dinner of buffalo, "prairie chicken," and wild duck with his companions. Capping his meal with a quick pipe smoke, Mott returned to the village with the Colonel's entourage for an evening of entertainment put on by the Arikara.

Escorted to one of the larger lodges used for social gatherings, Mott sat on one of the few available benches reserved for the use of the Arikara's distinguished visitors. Meanwhile, the remainder of the audience, almost all Arikara, took up available spots along the perimeter of the lodge and around the doorway.[33] The performance began with vocal music and chants followed by traditional dancing around the central fire in the lodge. One Arikara manipulated the size of the fire, removing or adding wood to regulate the lighting for dramatic effect. Following the dancing, the Arikara put on a magic show of sorts not dissimilar to the illusions and sleight of hand practiced by white magicians and entertainers. They demonstrated the illusion of smashing a gourd under a blanket, only to make it reappear completely intact; one performer made it appear as if he could partially impale himself with an ear of corn through his stomach; and one woman wore a heavy collar with no apparent means of support.

Mott had never expected his first major encounter with Native Americans to be so relatable. When he first learned he was to be sent West with the army, Mott had harbored the same prejudices against the country's indigenous populations as most white Americans, namely that Native Americans were a monolithic group of aggressive, sub-human savages without the capacity for human compassion.[34] Indeed, up until this point, Mott's only experience with any indigenous group had been minor skirmishes near the forts or the violent aftermath of ambushes against white settlers. Sitting in the Arikara lodge

Unexpected nobility: Crow's Breast (far left) with Lean Wolf of the Hidatsa; White Shield of the Arikara (Right)

Crow's Breast & Lean Wolf: Yale University Library; White Shield: Library of Congress

surrounded by families enjoying entertainment not entirely dissimilar in concept to stage acts found back east, his beliefs began to moderate. Mott would later express a fascination with the diversity of human life as he experienced more of the world. The beginnings of that nuanced understanding of life may have started here on the Plains amidst the Arikara.

Such cultural appreciation did not extend to Mott's Colonel whose aristocratic European sensibilities were so unimpressed by the show that he could not be bothered to watch the entire performance. Obliged to follow his commanding officer, Mott exited the lodge and headed back to the fort, an early morning hunt being the excuse the Colonel gave for his premature departure. In truth, de Trobriand had written off the artistic performance in pejorative terms as an unsophisticated display barely worthy of entertaining a child. Indeed, he likened a prop used in one of the illusions as sounding like "the toy dogs that amuse children."[35] These shows were common occurrences, so the performance may not have been put on solely for the benefit of the visiting officers. Still, as honored guests, their exit would not have gone unnoticed.

The next morning, Mott and his companion slept in and were slow to eat breakfast. While it was true that a hunt had been planned, clearly the hasty retreat the night before was not for the benefit of an early rise. It was at least midday before they started out and after about an hour in the blazing sun, with little to show for their efforts, the group gave up the hunt. The Colonel attempted to salvage their outing with a pleasure ride on horseback, but the heat made the ride anything but pleasurable. The men eventually abandoned the venture and returned to the fort for dinner.[36]

During their meal, the chiefs of the three tribes—Crow's Breast of the Hidatsa, White Shield of the Arikara, and Red Cow of the Mandan—along with a contingent of each of their tribes' influential figures, arrived to discuss the need for additional support by the US Government. While the chiefs and their warriors sat along the floor against one wall, the Colonel, assuming a position of power, remained at the table with Pierre Garreau at his side as interpreter. Mott, Major Furey, and Dr. Matthews each held a position at the table as well, but when it became clear that Garreau could only interpret the native languages to the Colonel in French, Mott, and the others excused themselves preferring to blend into the background among the warriors gathered near the entrance than to sit awkwardly mute in front of everyone not having the faintest idea what anyone was saying.[37]

The meeting opened with the passing of the Peace Pipe. The crux of the nearly two-hour-long meeting concerned the chiefs' worries about having enough gunpowder to get through the winter, both for hunting to build a winter supply of food and for protection from the belligerent Lakota. They also reminded the Colonel that they had done everything the United States government had asked of them at the cost of their own strength and ability to defend themselves. Afterward, de Trobriand reconvened with Mott and the others offering an exceedingly self-congratulatory report, praising his negotiating skills and relating how he won the great affection of the three tribes by seeming to authorize an overly-generous ration of supplies on the spot, despite the fact that the Government was already committed to providing the amount the tribes requested. Conveniently, as the entire meeting took place in French and the indigenous languages, neither Mott nor any of the other officers could confirm or deny de Trobriand's account of the proceedings. Whether or not they viewed the Colonel affectionately as their savior as de Trobriand would have his readers believe, the Three Tribes had their demands met.[38]

The next day, Mott returned with the party to Fort Stevenson where construction of the fort continued at a snail's pace. The building took months and as the year moved towards its end, Mott discovered that the biggest danger he would face at Stevenson would not be Lakota raiding, but the harsh Dakota winter. With no completed barracks, the only shelter available were small tents erected over crudely-dug holes in the ground with "rude fireplaces."[39] As December wore on, the officers' barracks became a priority. By the 20th enough of the barracks were complete for Mott and the other officers to take shelter in relatively increased comfort. It was tight quarters, but they couldn't complain particularly as the next week rolled on.

Mott spent an enjoyable Christmas with the surgeon major, Dr. Charles C. Gray, and his wife whom he had befriended upon his first arrival at the post. Major Furey and later Colonel de Trobriand joined them. The following week, Mother Nature unleashed her fury, which Mott still recalled decades later.

...a terrific blizzard began which raged with such violence for eight days that during that time a person could not go out of doors, and during that time I was not in my company quarters, it being impossible to get there. Our log cabins were covered over with snow so that the men broke the windows when they tried to dig the snow away, and it was necessary to tunnel in some places to get into the officer's quarters.[40]

The brutality of that winter continued to harass the men. Some of the quarters that were finished began to have leaks and structural problems because the mud-plaster roofs had been constructed too late in the season to have properly set in the summer heat. The cold weather caused cracking and losses that needed to be patched, but not before entire rooms were blanketed with a fine layer of snow forced in through every small hole and crack by the violent wind. The cattle, too, suffered greatly and were nearly feared lost as no one could get to them. Access to firewood presented an additional challenge as the massive snow drifts kept the inhabitants captive. Even if some could manage to squeeze out through a window or a hastily dug trench from a door there was no way to get to fresh wood and transport it back. This not only challenged everyone's ability to keep warm, but it also made preparing food extremely difficult. For eight days, the residents of the fort fought an uphill battle, digging out trenches only to have them fill back in within hours. By the last day of this incredible storm, the cabins had been buried such that not a shimmer of light penetrated their rooms. Mott likely agreed with the Colonel who was starting to believe he understood what it must be like to be buried alive.

And in the night, in the death-like unbroken silence, in pitch blackness where not a ray of light penetrates, I began to think of all those on whom a tomb had closed while living, and especially the inhabitants of Pompeii, its terrible secrets kept by death for eighteen centuries. They were buried in cinders as I am in snow. But cinders and snow, what a difference!...What's the use in getting up?[41]

The storm eventually abated, but it was a rude introduction to a Dakota winter. Hunting became near impossible due to the immobilization the snow had caused, compounded by the otherwise lack of game. The scarcity of all but the basest provisions of salt pork and salt fish over the harsh winter led to problems with malnutrition. By the onset of Spring, Mott reckoned nearly eighty members of his company had come down with scurvy, a Vitamin C deficiency characterized

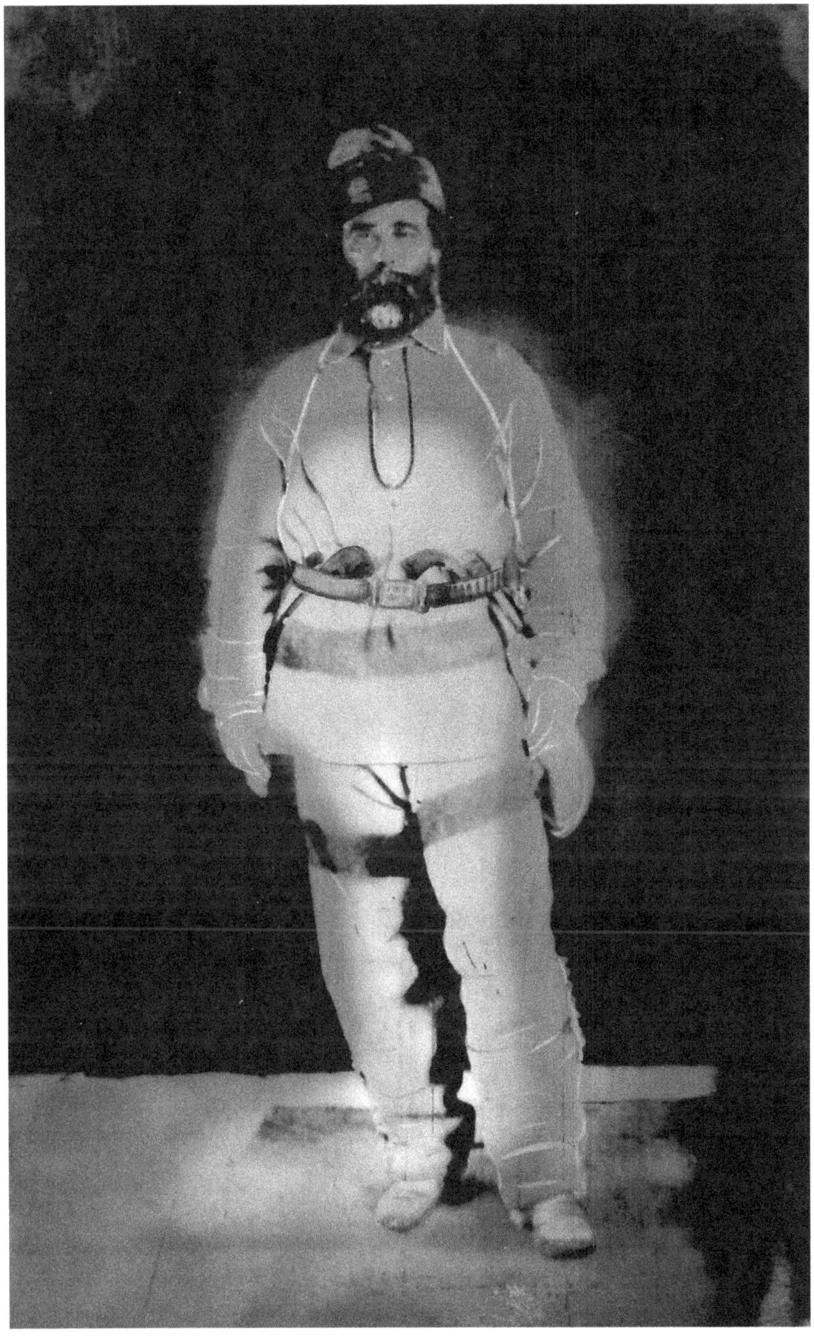

Keeping warm in animal skins, Mott unfinished ambrotype
Courtesy of Ed & Faye Max

by bleeding gums, extreme muscle weakness, tooth loss, bruising, and general exhaustion.[42] Moreover, many of the rank and file, whose cabins were not yet complete, were suffering the effects of exposure. They endured the cold and snow sleeping on the ground in small three or four-foot-deep dugouts covered over with tents. While their fires burned, their accommodations warmed up to an almost unbearable heat, but without the fires, they froze.

While most of the sick made a full recovery, two officers died in early April of complications from scurvy. Mott presided over the funeral as the men were buried next to one another with military honors:

A detachment of twelve armed men and forty others unarmed accompanied and followed the wagon carrying the two coffins. The officers brought up the rear, in full dress and unarmed. When the bodies were lowered into the two graves, Lieutenant Hooton, officer of the day, read the funeral service, a sergeant threw the shovelful of earth at the proper moment, 'earth to earth, dust to dust'; three volleys were fired, and while the fatigue party filled in the graves, everyone hurried back to his lodging, for the weather was very cold...we shivered in our overcoats.[43]

As 1868 progressed, Mott heard reports of hostile activity along the trails, though the Lakota generally refrained from direct assaults on the Fort. In May, a small contingent of Hunkpapa Lakota attempted to capture some horses and cattle belonging to the Arikara. Some soldiers who happened to be hunting nearby heard the commotion and moved to intervene. Back at the fort, Mott and the other soldiers could hear skirmish. Colonel de Trobriand at once dispatched Lieutenant George S. Ward and a contingent of twenty-five men to determine the cause of the commotion. Faced with the hunting party and the arrival of Ward's men, the Hunkpapa withdrew, but they ran into the army's Arikara scouts who engaged the raiders. The Hunkpapa were able to make their escape, but not before shooting a horse out from underneath one of the soldiers, who fell from his dead mount unconscious. In the midst of the fighting, Ward's men were unable to reach the fallen man to rescue him. When the soldiers returned to the Fort and reported what happened, Mott mobilized his company to go rescue the fallen soldier, or at least to recover his body if the Hunkpapa had killed him. No sooner had Mott left the fort when they spotted the man, walking toward them, very much alive, but stripped of all his clothes and weapons, save a loin cloth.[44]

Later that month, two couriers en route to Fort Totten were surrounded and taken before Sitting Bull, chief of the Hunkpapa and one of the most formidable resistance fighters on the Great Plains. Fearing for their lives, the couriers did not identify themselves as employees of the United States Army but said simply they were private citizens headed to St. Joseph to hunt. As their audience before Sitting Bull progressed, they noticed some of the other Lakota warriors wearing familiar accouterments. One of the warriors who ambushed them rode a horse that looked eerily familiar to them. Charley MacDonald, the scout who had accompanied the Colonel, Mott, and the other officers to Fort Berthold the previous year, and another courier, Joe Hamlin, had recently gone missing, and the couriers recognized their captor's mount as MacDonald's. Their clothes and weapons were stripped of them and Sitting Bull gave one of them an overcoat to wear. This too was familiar having belonged to Hamlin. If the men had hoped that MacDonald and Hamlin had merely been robbed, the two bullet holes in the coat's chest disabused them of that notion. As if noting the recognition on the couriers' faces, Sitting Bull proceeded to tell him of two men and a soldier they had recently killed from a passing convoy. One of the warriors took credit for shooting one of the men straight through with an arrow. As he was gloating over the kill, the couriers saw that he was holding MacDonald's carbine and they spotted several items of clothing belonging to the two ill-fated scouts among the assembled warriors. Sitting Bull himself was wearing MacDonald's watch chain.

With night falling, Sitting Bull decided to let the two couriers go, despite his warriors' desire to kill them. The two men ran off, half-naked, back towards Fort Stevenson. They were fortunate not only that

Sitting Bull had let them go, but that he did so before the Sioux found their dispatches, which would have identified them as official army employees.[45]

When the two couriers finally made it back to Stevenson, hungry and exhausted, but otherwise in good condition, the garrison mourned the loss of the MacDonald, Hamlin, and the lost soldier. MacDonald left behind a wife and three children. Angry over the deaths of his men and frustrated by his inability to do anything about it, Colonel de Trobriand cursed Sitting Bull in his journal.

...Dakota has become the theater of his depredations and killings. It is a nice game, the government leaving us in our posts without cavalry, without horses, and absolutely powerless to pursue and punish him...[Sitting Bull's] fierceness is masked by a good-natured manner and a conversation abounding in good humor. To judge by appearances one would believe him to be the most harmless of the redskins. In reality, he is a ferocious beast who seems to be laughing when he is showing his teeth.[46]

With Sitting Bull now known to be active between Stevenson and Totten, the Colonel could not risk sending any more couriers into those parts for some time. For the next few months, communication between the two posts was virtually non-existent.

Towards the end of the summer, a group of Hunkpapa attacked Fort Buford and captured a herd of cattle. Mott assumed command of a detachment of soldiers assigned to escort replacement cattle to the fort, approximately one hundred eighty miles west of Fort Stevenson where the Missouri and Yellowstone Rivers meet. The detachment consisted of seventy-two men in addition to the wagoners, a guide, and four native scouts. Intelligence reports revealed growing activity of the Lakota in the vicinity of Fort Berthold, so de Trobriand also sent his assistant surgeon in case they ran into trouble and suffered wounded.[47]

Mott successfully delivered the cattle without incident at the end of October and received orders not to return to Stevenson. His detachment would remain at Buford indefinitely. As he settled in, Mott took

Custer's favorite scout: Bloody Knife
Library of Congress

up the position of post treasurer and presided over the swearing-in ceremony for Bloody Knife, an Arikara scout, who would go on to work closely with George Armstrong Custer.[48]

Fort Buford was an even more remote location than Fort Stevenson, and less stable. During the winter, it was not unheard of for Lakota war parties to fire into the barrack windows. The mail was also unreliable because the only route between Buford and Stevenson through which the mail would come was fraught with danger. "Every mail that we got was brought by prairie scouts, who were paid $150 for the round trip from Fort Stevenson, about 180 miles distant, and they nearly always had a fight at some point on the route."[49]

With the arrival of Spring in 1869, the army transferred Mott to the 22nd Infantry as a result of another army reorganization. It would be his home unit for the next twenty-seven years. Boarding a boat, Mott traveled to Fort Sully to join his new regiment where he remained for the next year.

In February 1870, Mott took command of a unit traveling to Fort Randall, about two hundred fifty miles south of Fort Sully under orders to lead a band of new recruits back up to Sully. With six mule wagons in tow, Mott arrived at the post without incident. After a few days respite at Randall, Mott assembled the new recruits—about two hundred in total—crossed the Missouri River and began their march north back to Fort Sully. Not a day into their journey, a terrible blizzard rolled in. Faced with blistering cold and poor visibility, Mott ordered the men to strike camp to wait out the storm. He could only wait so long. When the storm showed no signs of letting up, he knew he had no other option than to risk forging ahead. For the next two weeks, Mott led his men on an arduous trek through knee-deep snow and a succession of worsening blizzards. It was a rude introduction to military life on the plains and cracks began to show amongst the men. Many of the recruits buckled under the inhospitable weather conditions. Mott did all he could to maintain morale and keep the unit going, but some of them would still "give up in despair and lie down in the snow." Not being one to give up so easily, Mott halted the train whenever he noticed a soldier falling behind. He ordered the struggling soldiers brought up to one of the wagons and disarmed them for their safety, stowing the weapons and equipment in other wagons to see them through.[50]

By the time Mott arrived at Fort Sully, the recruits had already endured an ordeal worthy of veteran soldiers. Mott was commended for maintaining his composure and delivering all his men safely to the fort, the trip took a toll on him. When the spring of 1870 finally came, Mott requested a five-month leave of absence to return home to West Chester.

Upon Mott's return, he received orders to report to his regiment at the Crow Creek Agency, Dakota Territory. The Captain under whom he served frustrated Mott immediately. No sooner had he arrived back with his unit than he requested a transfer. Mott did not elaborate on the nature of the conflict with his Captain nor did he name this officer in any of his extant letters, but it was quite likely Captain William H. French, Jr., the Indian Agent for Crow Creek. Whatever the reason for not getting on, the speed at which he sought transfer suggests the situation was unbearable for him. The previous year, his friend Bill Bowen, who had so pushed Mott to rejoin the army after the war, suddenly changed his tune telling his friend to get out and take to farming instead as reductions occurring in the army meant there would be little room for promotion. "Better wear out than rust out," Bowen wrote.[51] Mott's current situation may have brought that advice back to mind, but his situation did provide ammunition to Mott's family to encourage him to quit and come home.

Mott's five-month return and subsequent absence rekindled the struggle his family faced in adjusting to his new life far from home. Ann, Mott's mother, continued to hope that Mott might leave the service and return to West Chester and take up the law, a subject she allowed herself to press whenever Mott made any complaint. She felt particularly emboldened to such a suggestion knowing how much Mott suffered under this new Captain.

It must be horrible to be under such a Capt almost too much to bear...Frank was talking about you the other day. He thought you might study law. How would you like to try it? I see no use in living away from all as you are unless you can better yourself. I do hope you will resign if you are not contented as you can live at home. As well as others, we often wish you were here.[52]

Christmas proved to be an especially hard time for Mott's family. During the first year of their separation with Mott out west, Ann couldn't bear the thought of celebrating Christmas in West Chester without her son. "She says she cares very little about going to W. C. [for] Christmas as you will be absent, but Aunt Sue insists upon it," Mott's sister, Sallie, wrote to Mott. "Mott, it will seem very strange not to have you there."[53] Of all his siblings, Sallie was perhaps dearest to Mott. The two shared a close bond, particularly more so in their later years, but even in their younger days, Sallie adored her big brother. Although raised in separate households, their separation affected her no less. "I dreamed you were home the other night," she wrote just prior to the Christmas of 1866, "Mott, I wish you a very Merry Christmas and a happy new year, for I expect it will be Christmas when you get this. I think you might come home and see us. It seems a perfect age since you left...write soon. You don't know how we miss you..."[54] The family even used Mott's old dog, Reb, to emphasize the want of his presence. "Reb is lying at my feet While I write," Mott's Aunt Susan informed him, "[He] has just had his beef. Mort Jefferis came up on the next step the other day, Reb at the window, he thought it was you. He fairly howled [and] cried to get out."[55] Familiar and seemingly innocuous noises, like water running in the bathroom, would catch Reb's attention causing him to look longingly for Mott. "He thought it was you," Susan wrote.[56]

For all of the inducements to leave the army and the sadness that his mother, sister—and dog—expressed in his absence, none felt the separation as acutely as Susan. Without a husband or children of her own and having lost her father several years before, Susan lived in West Chester alone. Though Frank and other family members still lived nearby and she remained the social butterfly, her heart grew heavy without Mott near to her. She never shied away from being honest with him about how she felt:

You don't know how much we all talk about you. That sweet dream as you say, but a sweet reality that will soon come around again and I said before, Mott, you are too dearly loved to be so far away. I do miss you so much. I strain my eyes to see your form in my room and your photo I look at it every little while. I have it by my side in a book. It is life-like.[57]

Like her sister, Susan was not above prodding Mott to leave the service when the time seemed right. She, too, took advantage of Mott's frustrations with his Captain to encourage him home,

I am truly sorry that you will not have an exchange and I know you are disappointed and how it must chafe your spirit to be under the command of such an ignorant [louse] and have to respect the rank of the profession, but with utter contempt for the individual, but if there is no certainty of a change, come home to us and look around for something else and leave that place. I should be so glad for you and I to be together somewhere and Mamma and the girls would so much.[58]

Passages like these, so sweet and somber, punctuate many of Susan's letters and appear as brief, momentary tangents within the mundane discussions of town life or securing provisions. Just after Mott returned to the army from his leave, Susan started talking about buying a new saddle for Mott asking after the condition of the rest of his belongings which she had shipped to him at his post. As if trying to maintain her composure, but finally giving in she suddenly changed the subject. "I do hope, dear, you will be comfortable in the new quarters and try and bear patiently this separation as I am trying to do, for I never missed you so much in my life for it is anything but home here for me."[59] For all Susan's heartache and momentary lapses into sentimentality, she tried to keep a brave face. "...but never mind," Susan continued, "...How can anyone feel sad these glorious days? The mornings are perfectly lovely with those clear blue skies."[60] Then again, even talk of the weather could trigger her longing to see her nephew again, "Aunt Em called to me after we came home to look at the lovely sunset. I thought it might be you were gazing at it too, Mott."[61] But through her sadness also lay the maternal protectiveness and fear for his well-being as the mother figure she was. "O don't have a rifle, Mott. You may forget and stray too far from the post and meet those treacherous Red Skins. I hope you may be changed to some less dangerous post sometime."[62]

In general, Susan's letters at this time followed a similar pattern. A mixture of jovial social gossip and melancholy reflections of the changing times, one almost gets a sense that Susan was beginning to feel her own mortality in frequently sharing news of the various deaths that had occurred around town. Since the passing of Tommy Rhoads, her brother-in-law, she would sombrely report on the appearance of black crepe on people's doors signaling someone had died and relating the sorry state of their grief-stricken family members. In one particularly sedate letter, Susan devotes the first third of her content to two people who had recently passed.

I have just come from seeing Everhart's poor girls. They are grieving so much at the loss of their mother and I do not think they will have their father long, he is looking badly. She was the sweetest looking in Death I ever saw and such a very small hand and foot. Mott, she always thought much of you, always asking about you. Mr. Mendenhall was stricken down a week ago with Apoplexy and died yesterday, so there are many changes happening around us.[63]

In her late 60s by this point, Susan, the oldest of her siblings and about seventeen years the senior of Mott's mother, had begun to feel the passage of time more acutely, both for herself and her friends and relations. Her brother-in-law, Thomas Rhoads, married to her sister Emily and brother to Mott's stepfather Maris Rhoads, had passed away likely of consumption in late 1866. She also noticed her brother advancing in age as well. "Poor Uncle Frank," she remarked. "He is looking old. What a life he has had."[64]

To be sure, while Susan exhibited more introspective and melancholy tendencies in the late 1860s and early 1870s in corresponding with Mott, she still discussed fun and joyous events too. She continued to send him news about births and marriages while her insatiable appetite for cheeky town gossip had not diminished. "You remarked in your last if you were me...you would not have much to do with the Penrose[s].

Have you heard anything? If so, tell me," Susan eagerly inquired of Mott regarding Frank's new in-laws.[65]

***

Undaunted by his family's petition to quit the army, Mott nevertheless continued to press for a transfer going so far as to write Simon Cameron, former Secretary of War under President Lincoln and then US Senator from Pennsylvania. By October, all hope of a transfer had vanished as Cameron replied that Mott could only effect a transfer if he found a replacement, which he could not.[66] Thinking creatively, Mott decided to take advantage of another aspect of military service that would at least solve the immediate problem of distancing himself from his captain. Mott applied for and was granted a two-year recruiting duty assignment in the northeast.

Established as early as 1822 in order to encourage capable young men to enlist, the United States Recruiting Command served a vital function a military that relied almost solely on volunteerism, resorting to conscription only when necessary during times of war. In order to seek out new recruits, the command, then as today, relied on a rotating cadre of soldiers serving two or three years detached from their unit to travel throughout a region essentially selling the idea of joining the military to young, capable men who wished to serve their country or lacked other opportunities. The recruiting soldiers, in turn, could enjoy a respite from the dangers and rigors of military life for a couple of years. By the end of 1870, Mott received his turn. He left his post on the Plains and made his way to a small island for military training off the coast of Manhattan.

***

Nestled in the heart of New York harbor off the southern tip of Manhattan, Governors Island developed after the Revolution as a strategic defensive fortification as part of the federal system of coastal defense. Several fortifications were built on the island during the early nineteenth century. Fort Jay, later renamed Fort Columbus for the bulk of the century, occupied a prominent spot towards the north of the island surrounded by a thick, granite five-star-pointed wall. Castle Williams, a crescent-shaped fortification built between 1809 and 1811 stood right on the northwest shore. By Mott's day, the island's defensive fortifications had long become all but obsolete, however, it remained an important location for army recruitment and training. During the Civil War, the island played host to a prison for captured Confederate soldiers and Union deserters but afterward returned to its peacetime role as a training center for new recruits. Mott, himself, had started his regular army career here just four and a half years earlier.

When Mott reported for duty in January 1871, the island was still reeling from an outbreak of Yellow Fever that had struck the population the previous autumn. The island had been under quarantine until a transfer of sick soldiers to an alternative quarantined hospital on Staten Island helped to abate the epidemic.[67] One of the first tasks undertaken shortly after Mott's arrival was to tear down the series of wooden buildings unfortunately dubbed "Rotten Row," where the sick soldiers had all been housed—likely not the way Mott would have liked to have started his two years on the island, but it was preferable to an active epidemic.

Although Fort Columbus on the Island served as Mott's official home base for his two-year assignment, the actual recruiting took place throughout the region. His official duties took him throughout the region, primarily New England, in search of new recruits, spending time in New York City, Boston, and New Haven, Connecticut, where he became the object of affection for a young, twenty-two-year-old socialite.

7

A Confirmed Bachelor

In 1895, in the small town of Anaconda, Montana, the local paper ran a profile of Mott in honor of him serving as the first commander of nearby Fort Harrison. The unnamed author wrote admiringly of the officer and his many accomplishments but couldn't help but remark on his marital status. "Unfortunately for some good woman, if not for himself, the major is a bachelor. This is remarkable since he has always been extremely popular with the ladies."[1] Whoever wrote the article clearly had some personal knowledge of Mott, but it's clear the nature of Mott's bachelorhood was as vexing to his contemporaries as it is to those looking for evidence of romantic entanglements in the historic record. Mott enjoyed the company of women and he earned a reputation as a flirt, but the modesty he practiced in every other area of his life applied especially so in matters of the heart. He wrote nothing of his thoughts on marriage or any of the women with whom he was associated, however, those in Mott's orbit were less inclined to be so tight-lipped about his dalliances when they knew about them. But perhaps the most telling, if tantalizingly vague, attachment Mott may have had is chronicled in a small handful of brief letters from his days as a thirty-three-year-old Lieutenant of the 22nd Infantry, when he became one in a long line of men stricken by the charms of Miss Justine Henrietta Ingersoll of New Haven, Connecticut.

Mott met Justine and her family in New Haven in 1871 during his travels throughout New England to recruit for the Army. Born in 1849, Justine came from a prominent aristocratic family. Her father, Charles R. Ingersoll, was a well-known figure in Connecticut state politics who would be elected governor just a couple of years later. Her uncle, Colin Macrae Ingersoll served in the US House of Representatives before the Civil War. Her maternal grandfather, Admiral Francis Gregory, had an illustrious career in the Navy suppressing piracy and serving in multiple wars including the War of 1812, the Mexican War in the 1840s, and the Civil War, coming out of retirement to advise the Union Navy to do so. Justine spent a childhood wanting for nothing. Nicknamed 'Tiny,' a moniker by which she would be known throughout her life, visited her grandfather, Admiral Gregory, in Boston and was even fawned over by the famous transcendentalists Ralph Waldo Emerson and Henry David Thoreau.[2] In later years, the *New York Herald* would call her "one of the most blue blooded aristocrats in the country" and a leader of "fashionable society."[3] If Mott ever told his brother of Justine, Frank would have undoubtedly pressured him to pursue a relationship vigorously in order to secure a connection to such a notable lineage. When Mott met her, however, she was a young woman of twenty-two and despite her privilege, she had not yet made such a name for herself. Mott never wrote of his meeting with Justine, but within the first six months of his new tour of duty, he had become a familiar and popular face amongst her family.

In the late summer of 1871, from her parent's vacation home in Plymouth, New Hampshire just south of the White Mountain National Forest, Justine wrote to Mott imploring him to visit on the pretense of official business at nearby Mount Washington. "When I announced to the Beach and Ingersoll families that you thought of stopping on your 'way to Mt. Washington,' they gave three cheers on the spot."[4] None anticipated his visit more than Justine.

I am quite sure that if you come prepared to just do nothing all day long but lie flat on your back in the hay and watch the shadows come and go on the mountain sides and leave your good clothes and manners at home and above all martyr yourself to my cause, you will have a good time.[5]

The wistfully pastoral scene combined with a deliberate invitation to drop formality and "martyr" himself to her achieved the desired effect. Mott traveled to see Justine and her family in New Hampshire. Staying nearby for propriety, he sent her a bouquet and escorted her to social engagements. "My only regret is that I cannot send you a few words that will be half as acceptable to your eyes as your lovely flowers were to mine. Since I cannot, please take for them a thousand thanks and believe me, your friend, Justine Ingersoll."[6]

Mott returned to his station in September while the Ingersoll's spent their last week in the mountains. Justine lamented the end of the season "We turn our faces homeward on the 8th. The dreary dining room with its deserted tables makes me wish it were sooner,"[7] Justine confided to Mott. As autumn wore on, their relationship, whatever it may have been, suddenly ended. "I have made up my mind that you and I must not meet again, simply because it's best that we should not. I think that you must know this too," Justine declared in a hastily written letter one Wednesday evening. "And so I send you these few words of farewell. Do not be angry with me, but believe that I am trying to do what I believe to be right and to make myself worthy of being your most true friend, Justine."[8]

The nature of the relationship between Mott and Justine was as vague and mysterious as its quick conclusion. None of Mott's correspondence to her survives and Justine's letters to him are brief and few. During Mott's time in New England, Dr. Gray, one of his Fort Stevenson friends, teased Mott by asking after "Mrs. Hooton." We can only wonder to whom Gray was referring, but given its timing, Justine is a plausible candidate.[9] What precipitated Justine's "Dear John" letter to Mott likewise remains enigmatic. She insinuated that it should have come as no surprise to Mott and that he was likely in agreement with her but left it at that. Interestingly, Justine's initial invitation to Mott to join her in New Hampshire followed a letter from Mott regarding an unspecified previous encounter. Though the letter has not survived, it projected an attitude of suspicion that frustrated Justine and prompted her to liken Mott to a Greek cynic philosopher.

Your letter came to me last eve'g. It is needless, I think, to tell you how many times I thank you... even tho' you did it in such a half grudging style that I could not help but see what a mistrusting old Diogenes you were and what an utter shame you thought me. Will you never have faith in me? A woman, you know, is always what a man believes her to be.[10]

Although she closed her letter "...and believe me, I know you won't, that I am always your friend," the otherwise jovial nature of the letter, including the invitation to join her in New Hampshire, calls into question the seriousness of her rebukes.[11]

There could of course have been other explanations for their interactions aside from romantic attachment. Although an eleven-year age gap would hardly have disqualified a relationship in 1871, it is possible Mott was simply a friend of the family, and Justine, smitten by a dashing young Lieutenant in uniform, harbored an unrequited crush on him that Mott simply humored. Still, Mott held on to these letters until his death, fifty years later. They could have been sent home for safekeeping with other correspondence where they simply sat forgotten amidst a pile of papers, but it could also suggest they meant something to him to keep. In a documented life otherwise devoid of any hint of serious romantic entanglements, these letters stand out in tone and content. Whether or not Justine was ever a serious challenge to Mott's bachelorhood, in his keeping of her letters there was likely something about her that Mott cherished.

***

That Justine's letters should be so unique is interesting in and of itself. The evidence supporting the existence of any sort of serious love life for Mott is notable for its general absence, though the possible explanations for this are many and varied. He may have been too focused on his career, which was not always conducive to family life. It was hardly unusual for officers in the field to be married, but Mott had glimpsed such a life in the army through numerous friends and colleagues with whom he served, like Dr. Gray whose own wife had accompanied him to Fort Stevenson. It was neither an easy life for the soldier, nor the spouse. Colonel Whistler, the preceding post commander at Stevenson, struggled when his three young children approached the age where they had outgrown the level of education available on the frontier. For the benefit of his children, Whistler and his wife made the difficult decision to separate the family. The Colonel continued in his post while his wife accompanied their children to a more stable, sedentary environment. Such situations were common and there were few alternatives available to soldiers who wanted to keep their families together. The officer could seek out a permanent staff position back east or in a city, but such jobs were extremely limited and intensely competitive. On the other hand, as seemed to be more often the case, the officer could leave the service altogether after a few years having earned enough to settle and establish his family elsewhere.

While the practical concerns for family stability occupied the minds of married soldiers, some in the army saw married life as a frustrating liability to the army itself. Marriage amongst staff officers was tolerated best, but for the rank and file, the army preferred bachelors who were less likely to seek discharge to support a family. At Fort Lewis in Colorado, one officer referred to the challenges of married soldiers leaving the service as a growing "evil" in the military.[12] There were logistical concerns for soldiers with families as well. Providing suitable accommodation became a problem, with often soldiers constructing their own quarters, which were often of questionable habitability.[13]

Whether or not Mott shared the prejudices of some regarding the liability of a married soldier, he had certainly observed the general difficulties of juggling married life with army life through the trials and tribulations of his married colleagues. A year after transferring to Fort Buford, Lieutenant Stevens Norvell, with whom Mott had served at Stevenson, wrote Mott a letter relating the various separations that were to take place once spring arrived and the waterways opened up again for travel. Several army wives were to head back east, including the wife of his friend, Dr. Gray. The one spouse who remained did so only because her husband would soon be detached on recruiting duty, leaving the territory. The separations grew harder in tragedy. Lieutenant Foster Parsons, another colleague of Mott's, sent his wife home to her family to deliver their expected baby. Shortly thereafter, Parsons received the news that his wife had fallen ill and their baby had died. From his distant post, there was nothing Parsons could do but grieve alone. "Parsons is in a bad way," was all Norvell could write to Mott of the distraught Lieutenant.[14]

Mott witnessed for himself the pain that military wives could suffer owing to the heightened dangers the profession could bring. Less than six months into his service during the Civil War, Mott was present when the newlywed wife of a fallen surgeon of the 1st Pennsylvania Cavalry arrived to visit her husband, whom she had been erroneously told had been only slightly wounded. "When I saw her I suppose she had just been informed of the [mistake]. She was held up by two men screaming and groaning in the most pitiful manner. All the men were looking in deep sympathy, poor thing. I pitied her very much."[15] Given his determination to make his career in the army, it is not hard to see that Mott might make the decision not to subject a wife and children to the hardships of the life he had freely chosen. Then again, Mott may have simply not been inclined to marriage. After all, he had grown up in an environment in which an aversion marriage bore some precedent. His Uncle John had died a bachelor in his thirties. Susan never married, nor would his sister, Sallie.

Though never seriously attached to anyone, Mott's life was not without romantic pursuits, even if only casually. During his convalescence in West Chester following the Second Battle of Bull Run, Mott engaged in a "violent flirtation" with Miss Flory Ebbs.[16] When several members of Mott's family, including his mother, informed him the next year that his brother had been calling on Miss Ebbs frequently, sending her flowers in Mott's absence, they tacitly acknowledged it as moving in on Mott's territory. "All's fair in love and war," Mott's cousin, Sallie Rogers, wrote him.[17]

During the summer of 1865 Mott frequently joined his friends at Everhart Grove to socialize with the young ladies. Shortly after Mott entered the regular army, his friend, Hildeburn, the man of leisure who had chided Mott for neglecting his correspondence, claimed to have been inspired by Mott's popularity with the ladies as he spent his summer trying to live up to the same standards.

I go down to the Grove to play croquet with the fair ones- almost every afternoon I go down and sit in the Grove and talk with them- and every evening I go down to the boarding house and flirt and dance with them, following your illustrious example of last summer.[18]

It was a reputation Mott had earned with more than one of his friends. James Good, another close acquaintance of Mott's in West Chester pitied Mott for the social deprivation he imagined Mott was experiencing in the West. "knowing your social disposition, I am afraid you feel the want of society at Fort James- especially that of the other sex," Good wrote.[19]

Mott's infatuation when last at home was one Becky Stevenson, a local West Chester woman. He took her out for walks and flirted with her down at the Grove that summer before going west. Both Good and Hildeburn made specific reference to Miss Stevenson in their letters to Mott the following year having recognized the special esteem in which Mott held her. Hildeburn in particular, acknowledged Stevenson in his letters, passing on her regards and noting, "Beckie[sic] very often speaks to me about you and always in the best terms such as 'oh he was such a nice and jolly fellow,' 'Poor Captain. I wish he was here this summer,' etc. etc. No doubt she remembers with pleasure the heavy flirtation she had with you last summer."[20] One of Mott's cheekier friends, Hildeburn went on to compliment Mott on his eye, writing, "I think myself, Beck is a very nice little piece- got quite a good 'el-e-gy.' [she] knows it and is fond of showing it. I often tell her to do so too. Of course, she scolds me and calls me impudent but at the same time is very well pleased."[21] Any relationship Mott and Becky enjoyed ended in 1865 and it is unlikely it was ever serious.

Mott had no shortage of admirers around West Chester. In June 1863, just a few months after Mott had returned to active duty from being injured, Linda Washington, a friend of Mott's cousin Sallie Rogers, expressed to Sallie her disappointment about missing Mott when he was still at home. As a consolation, Miss Washington requested a copy of Mott's photograph. "She is looking beautifully this spring," Sallie added suggestively.[22] Mott's reputation among the ladies in town and his fondness for flirting were well known to his cousin. Although she enjoyed passing on the sentiments of an admirer, Sallie urged Mott to practice discretion. "Be careful with some persons...[that] are very nice to look at. Try her well for I would not have you love anyone not worthy of you. Plenty of time for you. I waited a good while and could not have gotten a better husband that you know."[23]

Linda Washington was by far the only young woman asking after Mott during the 1860s. Fanny Jacobs and Emma Jefferis, both West Chester society women, sent their regards to him while Ettie Pierce, who had nursed Mott during his convalescence, vowed to Mott's mother to "wait until he comes home and not engage myself to anyone."[24] Even his Aunt Susan remarked on the playful buzz of admiration for her nephew that had resurfaced thanks to his five-month furlough in the summer of 1870. "I heard the other day that you were engaged to Miss Bennes and to Ettie. I laughed," she wrote in October to Mott at the Crow Creek Indian Agency. "I expect you will have quite a time answering all the girls' letters this winter."[25] The following year, while on recruiting duty in New York City, Mott had served as an escort to one of his West Chester townsfolk, Fannie Bemis, who wrote to him hoping to find time to travel to the city to "avail" herself of Mott's kindness once again. The two had bonded over their professed love of music. "I suppose you have plenty of opportunities of having good music in New York and are no longer in the state of musical famine of which you complained when here."[26]

Another enigmatic figure that surfaced in the 1870s was a woman named Carrie. A close friend of the family, Carrie became a fixture in their lives, spending winters in West Chester.[27] Though not romantically associated, Carrie and Mott were close correspondents who filled their letters to each other with playful, familial banter. In one letter to Mott, she masqueraded as his grandmother, referring to him as her "dear little boy." She kept up the grandmother pretense, playfully scolding Mott on his "bad habits" as only a grandmother would,

...your old grandmother, although loving you dearly, cannot shut her eyes to your many faults and trusts her boy will be much improved when next he visits his friends. Indeed, my liking for you is an unexplained mystery unless taken on the same principle that grandmothers in storybooks always prefer those scapegrace grandsons- who run off to sea and cause them any amount of trouble to their well-behaved brothers.[28]

She committed to the charade throughout, ending her letter with "remember you are always 'grandmuzzer's darling.'" The joke amused the family, particularly Susan who felt a soft spot for Carrie. "Carrie met [Sallie and Annie] and told them she had written many pages to you," Susan wrote, "sending her likeness and [acting] as a grandmother. It must have been spicy, no doubt...Ain't she full of fun? I like her so much."[29] The family continued to mention Carrie frequently in letters to Mott.

The banter and teasing typified their correspondence. Carrie would pretend to reprimand Mott for his bad habits and occasional "insolence" while Mott ribbed her on her abilities in keeping house,

Mott, I have been working like a Trojan today cleaning house...Young man, I can see the incredulous smile with which you will read the above, and with my

spiritual ear hear you utter the one word, 'preserving.' But whether you believe it or not, I have been working hard. I washed a doz. windows, packed away all the winter clothing, helped with the churning and did lots of other things. So, my dear skeptic, even you must admit that I have been industrious.[30]

The affection with which she referred to Mott was reciprocated. He addressed her as "little friend," commenting on her "lily white hands" and paid her additional compliments that made her demur and protest as if flattered into embarrassment. "Now, while I am very well pleased to have you think all those nice things about me, truth compels me to add that it must be conjecture with you or perhaps you have made a mistake in the person. One thing is certain, I never gave you proof of either of those qualities and very much doubt whether I possess them."[31] As much as Carrie seemed to miss his company, so too did Mott idealize their time together in his imagination. "My dear Mott, how poetical you have grown," Carrie wrote to him in the spring of 1871, "The description of the enjoyment we would experience playing croquet while birds were caroling over our heads, etc. was quite...quite...words fail me."[32] She too, reveled wistfully in the enjoyment the two had had together, After taking a pleasure ride one day with a friend, her mind turned to Mott.

...we took a drive over the same road you and I traveled once upon a time, when John Woodward was so exhausted and the woods which were then green are now so beautiful in their autumn tints, that a drive through them reminds one of some enchanted fairy scene. But Mott, I beg pardon for troubling you with my tedious description which you no doubt think romantic nonsense and said for effect.[33]

Despite these idylls and flirtations, their affection for each other remained strictly platonic. If there were potential for more, neither seemed to be under the misapprehension that a sustainable relationship would blossom between them. In the very letter in which she mentions being left speechless by Mott's poetics, she tells him about the dilemmas of her social calendar, in particular surrounding the visitation of "a little fellow" in the city who had written her on several occasions attempting to arrange a time for a weekend visit.[34] That this "little fellow" is necessarily a suitor cannot be conjectured by this letter, but if he were, it would not be the first time Carrie was so open with Mott about her desire for male companionship. In the "grandmother" letter, she told Mott how she regretted having passed up an opportunity to go into the city with friends after hearing of the presence of a Mr. Kilgore "who by all accounts is a regular heart-smasher. You can imagine how bitterly I repented of my refusal to accompany them when I learned of this last fact, for at present I am ready to exclaim with Cleopatra, 'I have no men to govern in this world that makes my only woe.'"[35] Likewise, Carrie, who was just as aware of Mott's reputation as his cousin Sallie, fully expected Mott to continue his fraternization with other women, even counseling him to take care about whom he pursued. "Don't flirt with other men's wives, even if they are handsome and wink at you," She warned. "Promise this or I will give my heart to...anyone else that asks for it and will be just as cross and disagreeable as I can be when you come home. How do you like that, Mister Mott?"[36] Mott enjoyed the back and forth. Although her role in Mott's life remains shrouded in mystery, it is clear she was important to him. In writing his family he would frequently ask after her and send his regards to her when writing home.

When Mott joined the regular army and went west, it did not take long for his flirtatiousness to become well-known amongst his colleagues. On New Year's Day, 1870, a comrade from Fort Buford named Marselis, wrote to Mott at Fort Sully to give him the various sundry news of the goings on at his old fort, making particular reference to a Captain Throckmorton and his family who had stopped by the garrison. "The Capt. has three most amiable daughters that delight us with accomplishments both vocal and instrumental, even as I write this I hear the most beautiful piano and more heavenly voices engaged with "Make Me No Gaudy Chaplet." Oh! Perfectly grand. You should be here, old fel to participate."[37] Another friend from Mott's days at Fort

Stevenson, Lieutenant Oskaloosa Smith, wrote to Mott from his post in Indiana in 1872 to let him know about how nice the Indiana ladies were and how well Mott would do with them if he were a Captain.[38]

As the years progressed, evidence of romantic attachments fade and Mott's lifelong bachelorhood became all but a foregone conclusion. Mott never directly expressed regret on this front, but he at least thought about the path not taken. In one postscript to his mother written later in 1876, Mott writes almost bitterly, "Do not give my regards to anyone for they are all engaged."[39] The following year, during a brief stint stationed in Wilkes-Barre, Pennsylvania, Mott told his mother how he missed being among civil society and expressed surprise that at the ripe old age of thirty-nine, there may have been hope for him still if it were in the cards. "I leave Wilkes-Barre with many regrets for I have had a great deal of amusement in society with the pretty girls. And although I am pretty old, it doesn't seem to make much difference. It is strange that men don't grow old as women do. If I were a woman I would be quite out of date."[40]

***

Whatever Mott's reasoning for not marrying, the speculative evidence of relationships stops after Justine. As for Miss Ingersoll, she lived out her life as a free spirit, in some ways not dissimilar to Mott. She gained a reputation as a great beauty and had no shortage of suitors. Even one-time presidential candidate Samuel Tilden, whose hotly contested election race against Rutherford Hayes rocked the nation, once sought her hand late in his life.[41] A few years after her time with Mott, Justine came close to marrying after she fell in love with a student at Yale. When her parents expressed their disapproval of the gentleman, she and her beau decided to elope. However, with license in hand, Justine backed out at the last minute, unable to go through with it. From that moment on she became a confirmed spinster, though it did not stop society men from pursuing her. One gentleman had proposed marriage so many times by telegraph, she finally wired back stating simply "Oh, shut up."[42]

Though she never married or had children of her own, she kept a ward who became the closest thing to a son she would ever have. One night while walking through Providence, Rhode Island, she heard a young boy playing violin near a tenement building.[43] The thirteen-year-old boy had recently moved to the United States from Kyiv with his parents. Though he had come from a musical background and already displayed prodigious talent in his native country, the boy's parents had little money to fund his formal musical training. Justine took him in and paid for his admittance and education at the Yale School of Music. Within four years, the boy was performing with the first violins in the Boston Symphony. The young violinist, Nikolai Sokoloff, went on to have a famed career as a performer and conductor of orchestras throughout the United States and abroad and founded the Cleveland Symphony Orchestra in Ohio.[44] During the Great Depression, the United States government tapped him to lead their Federal Music Project, one of President Franklin Roosevelt's New Deal programs that employed musicians to teach music to the public.[45]

That Justine would take in a young promising musician is not so surprising given her general passion for the performing arts. She frequently organized operas and music concerts in New Haven and New York featuring prominent local musicians and vocalists. In the 1890s she formed a small opera company that specialized in staging the works of Gilbert and Sullivan performed by local amateurs. Having bankrolled the whole company and the productions herself, one paper commented "Miss Ingersoll's hobby is an expensive one, but she can afford it."[46] She was not, however, merely a wealthy patron supporting artistic endeavors out of class obligation. She was often on the program as a performer herself. Respected as an "elocutionist," Justine recited great works of poetry and literature to atmospheric background music at these concerts. Her recitations were greatly admired, and other artists sought out her tutelage.[47]

In addition to being a well-read, well-spoken performing artist,

Justine also became a published author of some note. Several short stories found space in prominent magazines such as the *Atlantic Monthly* and she also published several books, including *My Salad Days* and *Chronicles of Teapot Town*, the latter being a literary sketch of Connecticut life and society.[48] But it was an unusual infatuation with monkeys in her later years that made her an unorthodox and eccentric member of her community.

When a traveling circus passed through New Haven one day, she learned that one of their orangutans had taken ill and faced euthanasia. She interjected and requested to care for it at her home where she succeeded in nursing the primate back to health. From then on devoted her life to the care of monkeys.[49] She wrote informational pieces in leading national magazines and fostered a relationship with the Smithsonian Institute in Washington, D.C. to which she gifted several monkeys for the National Zoo.[50] The marmoset became her species of choice and she kept a small group of them at her home. With names like "Lottery" and "Simeon Sly," the small brood of monkeys were her pride and joy once writing in a magazine article, "when life is empty and existence a horrid bore, I can only say, get a Marmoset!!"[51] Though serious in her passion for the creatures, the eccentricity of it proved too much for her father the former governor, who finally gave her an ultimatum. She either had to let the monkeys go or leave herself. She chose the latter and moved with her little companions to Westville, a suburb of New Haven.[52] By one account, the conflict led to an estrangement between father and daughter over the issue.[53]

Justine passed away of cancer in Boston on August 27, 1909, at the age of sixty with her protégé, Sokoloff at her side.[54] One obituary that ran in the *Chicago Daily Tribune* a few days later, featured a sketch of Justine. It depicted a quintessential Edwardian lady- beautiful and elegant, slender in profile, and wearing a large, fashionable hat. The archetype was broken only by the cadre of small monkeys crawling about her person.

***

Justine Ingersoll with her beloved marmosets
Chicago Daily Tribune, August 30, 1909

Though making no moves towards establishing a family of his own, on October 22, 1872, Mott became an uncle for the first time when Frank's wife Anna gave birth to a little girl, Mary Penrose Hooton, or May as she became known in the family. It was a happy occurrence for the family, which was sorely needed just a month after suffering a terrible loss.

8

Expedition and Insurrection

The tall, rounded marble headstone bore a modest inscription:

Sacred to the memory of
SUSAN CARPENTER
Died September 22, 1872
Aged 70 Years

A design consistent with that of her father and brother buried beside her, the simple monument did little justice to the memory of a woman who had been one of the most important people in Mott's life. Susan had suffered a debilitating stroke earlier that summer. Mott had quickly secured leave from his recruiting post in New York and journeyed home to West Chester to find his beloved Aunt virtually incapacitated. After a brief stay, Mott returned to New York, where his mother Ann continued to update him on Susan's condition.

On August 5, Mott received a long-awaited promotion to Captain. At the conclusion of his recruiting duty, he was to return to the 22nd infantry and assume command of one of its companies. It was a moment of pride tempered by concerns for his aunt. As summer moved into autumn, Susan continued to decline. "Aunt Sue is no better than when you left, in fact more helpless," Ann wrote. "We have to feed her, she lets everything fall. [The doctor] called today, thinks she will never be any better. Can't understand anything she says. She is getting cross and more nervous—don't like me to leave her."[1] Within a few weeks, Susan was dead.

Susan had once written to Mott in a moment of wistful reverie an image of her and her boys in a not-too-distant future which she yearned for. "Dear Mott, how I wish we three were together again as of old. Frank, you, and I, until you get married, which I hope to see some time when you are both able for it takes so much to embark on that nowadays."[2] Susan would never see that day for Mott, but she had only ever been proud of him and his brother. "There is light ahead," she wrote him in 1870 following his return to the West after Frank's marriage, "I feel it so. You have, both of [you], been sunshine ever on my path and it must not be darkness now with you left to me."[3]

There are no accounts of Susan's funeral, but given her social nature and her many friends in both West Chester and Philadelphia, it must have been a substantial procession. The loss hit both Mott and his brother hard. They had lost their father, but they never really knew him. For all intents and purposes, Susan's death was the death of a parent, and a beloved one at that.

Susan made Frank and Mott co-executors of her estate. For the next several months, Mott worked with his brother to settle their aunt's affairs from afar. As the winter of 1873 turned to Spring, Mott completed his two years of recruiting duty and returned to his regiment, then stationed at Fort Randall in the Dakota territory. If he thought he would ease back into life on the plains, he would find himself sorely mistaken. Grief-stricken and with new command responsibilities as Captain, Mott was about to embark on a grueling overland journey thanks to a wealthy Philadelphia businessman and his single-minded determination to bring rail travel to the northern plains.

***

During the Civil War, a shortage of manpower in the regular army had precipitated the call throughout the North for volunteer companies like Mott's. However, Lincoln faced an additional shortage which proved more difficult to reconcile. When the Union defeat at First Bull Run in July 1861 made it clear that the war would not be the short, 3-month affair Lincoln and his administration had hoped, the President knew he would need money, and lots of it.

Enter Jay Cooke. A native of Sandusky, Ohio, Cooke left home at the age of fifteen to work for a dry goods firm in St. Louis, Missouri. When the firm went belly-up in the Panic of 1837, Cooke's brother-in-law invited the young man to join his new transportation business in Philadelphia, which provided passage between Philadelphia and Pittsburgh via several modes of transportation, including rail.[4] Cooke performed many odd jobs at the firm before that company too went bankrupt and Cooke secured a position clerking for Enoch Clark, a prominent banker in the city. Cooke quickly gained a reputation as a hard worker with a keen mind for finance and business operations. By the time Cooke turned twenty-two, Clark made him a partner and eventual successor when Clark died in 1856.[5]

At the start of the war, Cooke opened his own banking house, Jay Cook & Co. As a staunch abolitionist, Cooke was determined to contribute to the war effort, believing it his God-given destiny to do so. He became connected with the Lincoln administration through his brother, Henry, who was close with Lincoln's treasury secretary, Salmon P. Chase. Lincoln had found himself in a financial quandary. The President desperately needed to raise money but did not want to raise taxes or print money to do so. Instead, the administration elected to fund the war through the sale of bonds and turned to Cooke, who turned out to be very good at it. Over the entire course of the war, the Union raised billions of dollars, much of it thanks to Cooke who earned the reputation as the financier and, indeed, the savior of the Union.[6]

Cooke was not just a banker. He was also a speculator specializing in transportation infrastructure thanks both to his experience with his brother-in-law's transport company in the 1830s and subsequent investments with Clark's banking house. After the war, Cooke began taking great interest in the American Northwest. Montana had experienced a gold rush in 1862, which influenced the efforts of the Northern Pacific Railroad company to establish a northern transcontinental rail route to parallel the more southerly First Transcontinental Railroad which would be completed in 1869 at Promontory Summit, Utah. By the end of the decade, after purchasing large tracts of land in Minnesota, Cooke officially decided to invest in the Northern Pacific Railroad believing, once again, that God had chosen him to make the railroad possible.[7] In 1870, Cooke financially contributed to an exploration of the area that would become Yellowstone National Park. The breathtaking geography and natural features of this area astounded the American public. This not only convinced the United States government to protect the area as a natural park but also provided Cooke with an additional value proposition for the railroad—tourism.[8]

Before the railroad could be built, a series of engineering surveys were required to plot the course of the railroad and clear the land. That the railroad route would cross the Yellowstone River Basin through Lakota, Arapaho, and Cheyenne land did not particularly concern the company, but it did mean that the surveyors required military protection.[9] Expedition and construction surveys began along the route in 1871 and 1872 both from the west and the east, but it was not until 1873, under military escort, that the final survey would see the road completely mapped out.

In contrast to the 1871 and 1872 surveys, the 1873 expedition would be the most ambitious undertaking yet. Cooke and the executives of the Northern Pacific determined to achieve two major objectives. First, they would complete the overland survey of the Yellowstone River, finally connecting the eastern portion of the line with the western portion, providing a single continuous route for the line between Puget Sound and Lake Superior. The company's second objective was to finish the surveying of the Musselshell River left incomplete the previous year and hopefully find a shortcut to the main line from Bismarck.[10]

The army had its own objectives. General Philip Sheridan, commander of the Division of the Missouri saw this expedition as a punitive opportunity to subdue the Lakota and Cheyenne who for years had stymied the federal government's attempts to "pacify" the northern Plains. Sheridan requested a contingent of nearly two thousand men to go with the surveying party, not just for the protection of the Northern Pacific's civilian crew, but to reconnoiter a location for a new fort along the way.[11] Colonel David S. Stanley, veteran commander of the 1872 expedition, once more assumed command. His personal life in shambles and struggling with alcoholism, Stanley accepted the command reluctantly on the promise of a transfer back east upon completion of the survey where he could settle down and patch up a rocky relationship with his wife, who had been struggling with life in the west.[12]

Stanley's force consisted of detachments from the 8th, 9th, 17th, and 22nd Infantry regiments, the latter being the regiment to which Mott belonged. Despite the robust force, Sheridan would take no chances. Should the expedition run into trouble with the Lakota, Sheridan wanted a detachment of cavalry at hand to pursue Sitting Bull and his allies if the opportunity presented itself. The infantry would not have been able to leave the survey team. Sheridan specifically requested a transfer of the 7th Cavalry to the Department of Dakota under the command of a man whose name would become legendary: Lt. Col. George Armstrong Custer.

Custer served as a General in the Union Army during the Civil War. A gifted cavalryman and military tactician, he was also an insufferable hothead with an ego the size of the plains themselves. Like many high-ranking officers, at the end of the war he was demoted to the rank of Lieutenant Colonel in the Regular Army. Before his transfer to the Dakotas for the expedition, Custer had been languishing in a dull, obscure post in Kentucky with little opportunity for advancement and even fewer opportunities to burnish his ego. This was no accident. Custer often bristled at authority and had made many enemies. In

David S. Stanley (Left) & George A. Custer (Right)
Library of Congress

particular, he crossed President Ulysses S. Grant who was not inclined to do Custer any favors. Despite his personal feelings about Custer, Grant approved the transfer for the expedition. Frustrated with peacetime service, Custer readily accepted the new mission and assumed command of the 7th Cavalry and ranked second in command of the expedition overall behind Stanley.[13]

When Mott left his recruiting post in April of 1873, he met his regiment at Fort Randall on the Missouri. In June, he traveled to Fort Rice, one of the two forts where Stanley was massing his troops and supplies in preparation for the long journey ahead. Mott encountered a flurry of activity at the fort. Between Fort Abraham Lincoln, where the Northern Pacific surveyors gathered with a protection force, and the troops at Fort Rice, the total force under Stanley consisted of 1451 soldiers, 79 officers—including Mott—two artillery squads, 353 civilians including scouts, sutlers, hunters, cattle herders, a scientific corps (consisting of geologists, zoologists, and artists), a smattering of officers' servants, and a few private citizens who had joined the expedition "for adventure."[14] To support this large force, about 2,321 mules and horses were employed hauling some 275 wagons and ambulances to carry supplies and care for the injured and sick along the way. Once stretched out along the trail, the column extended several miles.[15]

The Northern Pacific had, to a large extent, pre-determined the route. On June 16, the engineers and surveyors of the Northern Pacific set out from Fort Abraham Lincoln with their military escort. Four days later, Stanley departed Fort Rice to intercept the survey crew and make for Glendive in eastern Montana. The two parties would meet and make for Glendive in eastern Montana. The plan called for the column to ferry across the Yellowstone River and begin surveying along the northern bank of the Yellowstone until they reached Pompey's Pillar, a rock formation in south central Montana approximately 25 miles northeast of Billings notable for its many Native American petroglyphs and an inscription by William Clark of Lewis and Clark fame, made during his survey of the valley in 1806. After reaching Pompey's Pillar, the force planned to leave the Yellowstone and travel north across the divide to meet the Musselshell River, which they would follow east to begin their return journey. After a few days, the column would turn south along the Porcupine River, bringing them back to the Yellowstone, from whence they would retrace their steps returning to Glendive and ending the journey at Fort Abraham Lincoln in Dakota Territory. The journey would last several months.

Mott departed Fort Rice with the column as planned on June 20, but the expedition got off to a rocky start. Rain fell in torrents and pelted Mott and his men heavily for fourteen of the first seventeen days and turned the prairie into a virtual swamp. Mott spent as much time digging wagons out of the mud as he did marching. At night, Mott slept very little as the mosquitoes ravaged them all adding to their overall discomfort. During the day, the attack alarm sounded frequently, causing the column to circle the wagons into a defensive formation only to discover there was no real threat. Each time this occurred it took the column nearly an hour to put itself back into marching formation which contributed to the delay. Mott supposed the Lakota were teasing them, but between the mud, mosquitoes, and sleep deprivation, it did nothing to ease the fraying nerves and short tempers of the men.[16]

The engineering team that left Fort Abraham Lincoln likewise struggled at the outset. Having left four days earlier, they quickly encountered a hostile band of Hunkpapa Lakota warriors. The attacking force was eventually repelled and the men escaped with few casualties, but on the 24th, about a week into their journey to meet Stanley's column, the skies opened up, unleashing damaging hail upon the crew. The maelstrom caused animals to bolt, crashing and damaging wagons. Meanwhile, the men sought cover wherever they could find it, fleeing to a large copse of trees nearby. Many were badly hurt and everyone found themselves covered with large welts and bruises. So severe was the hail, it killed antelope grazing on the plains as well as a large dog accompanying the survey party.[17]

Already weary from a difficult march, Mott caught his first glimpse of the surveying team on July 5. After the rendezvous, the expedition force continued onwards to Glendive where it remained for nearly two weeks, ferrying troops, wagons, and supplies across the Yellowstone aboard the steamer *Key West*. Once on the north bank of the Yellowstone, Mott began his journey with the survey team along the river toward Pompey's pillar. The road was slow going, but relatively uneventful until August 4th when the Lakota, who had likely been watching the party, finally made themselves known.

It was one of the hottest days the team had yet endured. "...the thermometer was 114 in the shade," Mott wrote in his memoir. "The command could not descend the bad land path which led down [to] the river bottom before seven o'clock in the evening, and the men were frantic for water and the water in sight at the time."[18] Stanley sent Custer and two companies of his cavalry ahead to scout. About ten miles down the path, Custer and his men dismounted to rest and let their horses graze when a half dozen Lakota approached on horseback. Custer and his men mounted their horses to meet them. Custer proceeded cautiously, suspecting the small party of warriors to be a decoy meant to distract from a larger force. Suddenly, several hundred warriors descended on the soldiers from the nearby woods in which they had been hiding. The war party consisted of Sitting Bull's Hunkpapa Lakota under the command of Gall and Rain-in-the-Face; Oglala Lakota under the command of Crazy Horse; and a contingent of Mnikowoju Lakota and their allies, the Cheyenne.

Custer successfully routed the Lakota and Cheyenne war party, pursuing them for several miles, though never catching them. During the battle, Dr. John Honsinger, a veterinarian with the 7th Cavalry, was killed along with Augustus Baliran, one of the sutlers. Another soldier, John Ball, was also killed having been caught unaware at a nearby spring separated from his company. Honsinger and Baliran were buried, but Ball's body would not be discovered until the column passed by the area on their return the next month.[19]

Emboldened by the Lakota and Cheyenne aggression, Stanley sent Custer ahead to try to locate Sitting Bull's village but the Hunkpapa leader had anticipated a reprisal by the army. By the time Custer located the village, everyone had fled. As the rest of the column caught up, Mott saw evidence of the Lakotas' escape. It looked "as if the ground had been harrowed for many yards in width; indeed, it resembled a trail made by the exodus of a nation, which we followed for several days to the mouth of the Big Horn, where the Indians were assembled in force."[20]

Custer followed the trail to a crossing on the Yellowstone where the Lakota had crossed the river. Custer made camp on the riverbank determined to cross in the morning and continue his pursuit, not expecting the Lakota would come to him. The next day, a large contingent of warriors returned, attacking Custer from the opposite side of the river and swimming across to meet the cavalry head-on. A few miles behind, Mott could hear the commotion of the battle. Stanley rode ahead with his artillery and three companies of infantry to provide Custer's aid but were themselves ambushed. Stanley nearly lost his entire artillery to the Lakota before finally repelling the warriors. Two hours later, Stanley arrived within sight of the battle where the infantry successfully beat back the Lakota. Spotting Sitting Bull and a large party of Lakota on a bluff across the river watching the action, Stanley directed his artillery to fire on his position, sending Sitting Bull and his people into retreat.

Custer pursued the war party for several hours before returning to the main column. Casualties on the army's side included the death of John Tuttle, one of Custer's best marksmen, and the severe wounding of Charles Braden, whose thigh was shattered by an enemy bullet. Several other minor injuries were reported on the Army's side. The casualties for the Lakota were difficult to determine, but deaths were similarly light. Some estimates suggest about four dead and another thirty-six or so wounded.[21]

The column reached Pompey's Pillar, the western terminus of their journey, on the 15th of August. The next day, a small party of Lakota came upon a large contingent of soldiers bathing in the river. Riding out from the opposite bank, the Lakota fired on the unsuspecting troops. No one was hurt, but "there was a scampering of naked men" as they all ran from the river to get out of range. The incident inspired more laughter, and perhaps some hurt pride on the part of the vulnerable bathers, than ire. Stanley noted the event in his report as merely a "ludicrous incident."[22]

The remaining challenges for the expedition involved geography more than Lakota or Cheyenne hostility. The land between the Yellowstone and the Musselshell was virtually barren with poor-quality grass for the animals and only the occasional pool created by recent rainfall as their sole source of water. Reaching the Musselshell, Stanley turned his column east to begin their return journey. The survey team had completed their objectives. By reaching Pompey's pillar, they connected their route with the western line giving the Northern Pacific a clear path to Puget Sound on the Pacific. As the group came to the end of the Musselshell, the engineers accomplished their second goal by completing the survey of this river as well. The land, while seemingly fertile, had been overgrazed by buffalo. To provide enough for the animals, Stanley split the column. He ordered Custer and six companies of cavalry to escort the survey party back to the stockade at Glendive. Mott joined

Stanley and the rest of the column on a more southerly route to the stockade along the Porcupine River where they knew the land could better support the train. Mott arrived back at the Yellowstone with the men in three days and arrived at the ferry crossing opposite Glendive on September 9. It took four days to ferry the column back over the Yellowstone, at which point the troops proceeded to Fort Abraham Lincoln in Dakota Territory, finally reaching the post nine days later on September 23rd.

The expedition lasted ninety-five days, made camp seventy-seven times, and according to the official report covered approximately 935 miles (averaging 13 1/7 miles per day). Due to an unreliable odometer, Stanley conceded that the actual distance traveled may have been longer.[23] Mott estimated the distance to have been about 1,200 miles.[24] Regardless of the exact mileage, it had been an arduous and exhausting trip. Between eighty and ninety mules died, most along the divide between the river where water was scarce and grazing was poor. They abandoned about twelve wagons for lack of animals to haul them.

Stanley supplemented his report with his general observations of the landscape, recommendations for founding a new post along the Tongue River, advice on the available game for hunting, and the kinds of provisions most likely needed for a post in that part of the country. The expedition had also yielded a promising invention for transporting wounded over long distances. Braden, the officer who had been shot in the thigh, had suffered greatly being jostled about along the road in one of the wagons. To remedy the issue, the men constructed for him a litter by suspending a stretcher bed across the front and rear axles of an old spring wagon, an ingenious innovation which provided a smoother ride for the injured man. "This is the easiest conveyance I have ever seen for a wounded man," Stanley wrote, "I recommend the invention to the Medical Department."[25]

Custer's self-serving reports sensationalized the hostilities during the expedition and captivated the American people. They did much to advance Custer's reputation as an American hero but severely damaged the confidence of investors in the Northern Pacific Railroad who suddenly became skeptical that a rail line through such a seemingly hostile country could ever be successful.[26] Reports of additional skirmishes and hostilities in the region fueled that fear. By autumn, the Northern Pacific Railroad had gone bankrupt and a financial panic the likes of which had never been seen before gripped the nation. Although numerous factors went into the Panic of 1873 including the devaluation of silver-based currency, but the failures of the Northern Pacific and other railroads in which the federal government and the country's large banking houses had heavily invested, were key contributors to an economic depression that would slog on for nearly the rest of the decade.

The summer following the expedition, Mott led his company to Fort Porter, New York in the Department of the Lakes. The government had been closely watching a tense situation in Louisiana where the contested gubernatorial election the previous year threatened to boil over into outright insurrection against the Republican state government. By September, violence erupted in New Orleans and Mott traveled to the city to face down a paramilitary white supremacist organization called the White League.

***

Like many southern states, Louisiana bristled under the Reconstruction policies of the Republican-dominated federal government. Following the Civil War, the South experienced an influx of so-called radical Republicans from the North who had come to hold office and bend Southern legislatures to embrace enfranchisement for Black citizens and enforce rights granted to freedmen as a result of the Confederate surrender at Appomattox. Pejoratively nicknamed "carpetbaggers," these northern Republican politicians relied heavily on a military presence for stability.

In 1872, Vermont-born William Pitt Kellogg decided to run on the Republican ticket for Governor of Louisiana against John McEnery, the Democratic candidate. Though a New England native, Kellogg lived much of his early adult life as a lawyer in Illinois, where he became acquaintances with Abraham Lincoln, then a fellow colleague of the bar. When Lincoln became president in 1861, he appointed Kellogg Chief Justice of the Nebraska Territory. Kellogg served briefly in the army during the Civil War but returned to the Nebraska bench in 1862 when his ill health prohibited him from further military service. When the Civil War finally ended, Lincoln offered Kellogg a position as the customs collector for the port of New Orleans just days before John Wilkes Booth shot and killed the president at Ford's theater. Kellogg accepted and moved south earning him the dubious honor of being one of the earliest carpetbaggers in Louisiana. After three years in his post, Kellogg successfully ran for federal office and represented Louisiana in the United States Senate. After four years in the senate, Kellogg turned his eyes to the governorship of his adopted state. The campaign was bitter and when the votes were cast, the results were inconclusive. Two separate partisan elections returning boards emerged, each declaring their candidate the winner. There had been a schism amongst the Republican party in Louisiana over an accommodations bill for equal access to public facilities by people of color. The previous governor, Henry Warmoth, had appointed the State Returning Board, which sided with McEnery, despite Warmouth himself being a Republican. The opposing returning board arose in defense of Kellogg claiming that the Democrats had engaged in voter fraud and suppressed the Black vote through voter intimidation. Neither candidate conceded to the other. Kellogg and McEnery both declared victory and set up rival administrations until the spring of 1873 when President Grant interceded to declare Kellogg the victor.

Unsurprisingly, McEnery and the Democrats would not accept what they viewed as a usurpation of power by Kellogg and the Radical Republicans. Even before Grant had officially declared Kellogg the rightful governor, a mob of angry whites including members of the Ku Klux Klan and the White League, both white supremacist organizations, murdered over one hundred Black men at Colfax Courthouse in Grant Parish in retribution. The White League was primarily composed of former Confederate soldiers, had formed the organization with the expressed purpose of intimidating Black voters and removing Republicans from office throughout the south, frequently resorting to violence to do so. Several Republican officials and Black citizens were murdered by members of the White League in Coushatta, Louisiana in August 1874 and an attempt was made in New Orleans to unseat Governor Kellogg by force. This attempted coup amounted to little more than a disorganized mob. The Republican-controlled Metropolitan police force quickly suppressed the aggressors.

On September 14th the White League once more descended upon New Orleans. Thousands of armed insurgents entered the city and, learning from the previous failure, mounted a far more organized attack. Clashing with the Metropolitan police forces on Canal Street, the insurgents drove back the Republican forces while Kellogg and other Republican officials barricaded themselves in the Customs House. The Battle of Liberty Place, as it became known, was a decisive, but ultimately short-lived victory for the White League. When federal forces arrived to suppress the insurrection, the White League quickly surrendered in exchange for immunity from prosecution. Though nominally restored to power, Kellogg would never have total control over the state.

The initial federal forces ended the immediate conflict, but the situation remained extremely unstable. The following month, Mott led his company, along with other units of the 22nd Infantry to occupy New Orleans. With Mott and his troops in the city, the White League dared not take up arms again, but Mott did not fail that tensions still ran high to notice during the six months he spent there. The Democrats operated a shadow government of sorts at the Odd Fellows Hall under the nominal leadership of Francis T. Nicholls a lawyer and former confederate officer.

Mott spent nearly six months in New Orleans overseeing an uneasy peace. The situation remained quiet while Mott remained in the city, but he knew the issues underpinning the unrest had not gone away simply because of his presence. He could not see any scenario in which Washington could restore stability without the military and still see its reconstruction policies enforced. When another unit arrived in the city to relieve Mott and his men to return to Fort Porter in April 1875, Mott likely wondered if he would be back.[27]

The White League Insurrection signaled the impending end of Reconstruction in Louisiana. Kellogg remained in power only so long as the army was present to protect him. He had lost control over many parts of the state and in 1876 he left the governorship to run once again for Senate, a position he subsequently won. The gubernatorial contest that year bore a striking similarity to the Kellogg-McEnery race of 1872. Once again, the results were contested between Republican Stephen Packard and Democrat Nicholls, with Packard coming out victorious. However, unlike Kellogg who was able to hold on to power thanks to Presidential intercession, Packard's term would be cut short just three and a half months later to be replaced by his rival Nicholls as a result thanks to the fall out of a bitter presidential election the same year.

The 1876 Presidential contest between Samuel J. Tilden and Rutherford B. Hayes was one of the most contested and controversial elections in United States history. Tilden, the Democrat, won the popular vote, but the electoral votes in several states, including Louisiana, were disputed. The two parties came to an informal agreement whereby the Democrats conceded the White House to Hayes, so long as he agreed to several terms including an end to military occupation of the southern states where troops were still present. He also had to promise a hands-off approach where African-American rights were concerned within southern states. Known as the Compromise of 1877, this agreement effectively ended Reconstruction in the south. Hayes kept his word and pulled the military out of the south. Without the army there to secure their power, many of the office-holding Republicans resigned effectively ceding control over southern legislatures to their Democratic rivals who would re-institute policies wherever they could to disenfranchise Black citizens and revive the ethos of the Confederacy in all but name.

Mott had little patience for the political climate, which from his distant perspective on the plains, he deemed utterly out of touch with the realities of the country. At the time of the election, Mott was camped at Glendive in Montana and wrote home about how little he cared for the political situation in Washington.

I don't care three tosses of a copper who is elected President. They are all scoundrels together and I am inclined to think that the Republicans are the worst. At all events, they have ruined the country...If there is another civil war, it will not be between North and South but it will be right in the North among the people and if it does happen I will expatriate myself for such a country would not be worth fighting for. All their parading of minute men and boys in blue and all that is simply to get up a furor so they can ride into office.[28]

Interestingly, though he had fought a war to preserve the union and bring an end to the enslavement of other humans, Mott believed giving African-Americans the vote was a bridge too far and had ruined the South. Mott was never zealous in his politics, so it was uncharacteristic of him to parrot the sentiment of a southern Democrat. To see such subversive signs of Confederate ideology gaining influence and power once more throughout the South, slowly invalidating what the Union had achieved should not have sat well with him. Then again, the Union stance on civil rights was more complicated than being pro or anti-slavery. To many northerners, slavery and racial inequality were mutually exclusive ideas. Just because they didn't think Black Americans should be owned didn't mean they thought they were equal to whites as a rule. And while Mott did not support Tilden any more than Hayes, his comment about northern Republicans exploiting "the boys in blue" in order to "ride into office" suggests he disagreed with the carpet-bagging practice of the Radical Republicans taking control of southern legislatures. Whatever his reasonings, his cynical point of view was in keeping with his personality. He had already experienced the follies of government both during the war and in the West. He had become far too jaded to react to the situation in any other way. Perhaps not surprisingly then, shortly after his return to Fort Porter, Mott decided to take a break from the United States altogether and spend the better part of the year traveling through Europe, Egypt, and the Holy Land.

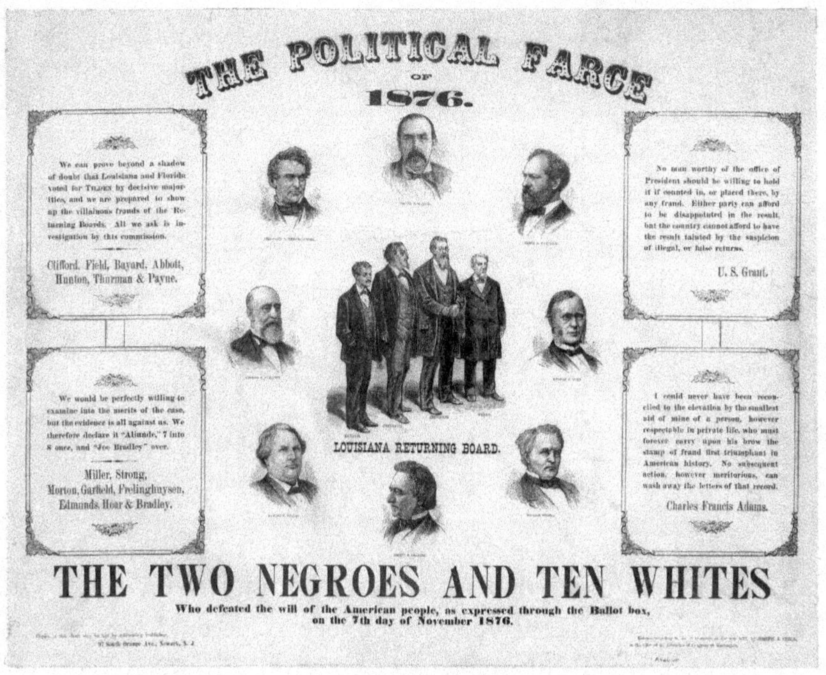

Mott's disgust: the Election of 1876
Library of Congress

9

Wanderlust

"I...looked into the crater which is a bottomless pit filled with stormy vapor...with sharp pinnacles of rock. You could hear strange and awful sounds there like sighs and groans of the damned. It was the grandest sight I ever witnessed."[1] Mott's reflections as he stared into the abyssal caldera of Mount Vesuvius above Pompeii in Italy epitomized the romanticism of nineteenth-century travel. It vividly recalls a famous early nineteenth-century painting by Caspar David Friedrich entitled *Wanderer Above the Sea of Fog*. The piece depicts a dapper young hiker with windswept dirty-blond hair in a dark frock coat leaning on a walking stick. His back is to the viewer as he stands upon the top of a rocky outcropping peering out into an expansive landscape obscured by a thick layer of fog permeated occasionally by rocky projections and shrouded hills in the distance. Occupying a central position within the painting, the man is at once a dominant presence, yet also seemingly insignificant in the context of the setting. Had the painting not been over fifty years old at the time, one could have almost imagined Mott's experience at the top of Vesuvius might have provided the inspiration for Friedrich's work.

Historians of tourism have tied nineteenth-century travel to the Romanticism movement that produced works like *Wanderer Above the*

Sea of Fog.[2] A key element of the movement involved expressing the natural world through literature, music, and art in an attempt to capture and experience the sublime.[3] Travel became a means by which to discover the sublime in reality. In particular, the advent of mountaineering as a sport and the proliferation of climbing clubs in the nineteenth century reflected the belief that the ascent to the summit of a mountain represented the most profound connection with nature. For Mott, the appreciation for the wonder and power of nature he felt while peering down into the fuming crater of Vesuvius was, in essence, his own encounter with the sublime.

Mott's motivations to travel likely stemmed from the same restlessness that drove him into the transient lifestyle of military life on the frontier. For the past nine years, since joining the regular army, Mott had rarely settled in one place for more than a year. He had seen great swaths of his country—from the vast stretches of the Great Plains and the sophistication of polite New England society to cities like New Orleans in the Deep South struggling through the tensions of Radical Reconstruction. But the duty and danger that accompanied his exposure to new places in the army did not slake his thirst for adventure. There was a whole world waiting to be experienced, and preferably through circumstances not involving being shot at or keeping the peace.

Several people in Mott's orbit had seen something of the world, which likely left an impression on Mott. General McCall had traveled abroad, doing so at a time when trans-Atlantic voyages were even more challenging than it would be for Mott. Perhaps the old soldier had regaled Mott, then an impressionable young man, of his adventures across the ocean. However, McCall was not the only known traveler that Mott knew.

In June of 1863, Mott received a letter from his friend, Thomas "Tom" Stellwagen, husband of Mott's cousin, Annie Carpenter.[4] The son of Henry S. Stellwagen, a high-ranking naval officer, Tom informed Mott that he had taken a clerkship position under his father who had been given command of the *U.S.S. Constellation*, then on assignment in the Mediterranean. Heading first to England, arriving in Liverpool and

In Mott's footsteps: 19th-century traveler looking down into the crater of Mount Vesuvius
Library of Congress

traveling south to London, Tom and his father planned to rendezvous with the *Constellation* via Paris and Genoa. "What do you think of my trip?" Tom asked Mott, closing his letter promising upon his return that he would "try and explain the wonders."[5] At the time, Mott had been back in service barely three months after his recovery from Second Bull Run. The Civil War raging hot as ever, Mott may well have envied Tom.[6]

It is hard to examine the last few years of Mott's life and not understand that he might act on his harbored desire to travel in 1875. He had lost arguably the closest person in his life just a couple of years earlier, his life on the plains was transient as ever—the Yellowstone Expedition being particularly rigorous. His time in New Orleans might have offered him some semblance of society, but tensions in the city no doubt made it anything but an enjoyable post. He certainly never wrote fondly of the assignment. Moreover, there was a growing suspicion that his brother, Frank may have been mishandling Mott's money and business affairs back home. The extent of Frank's financial mismanagement would not be known to Mott until after his return, but tensions were beginning to rise between the brothers. The time for a break was a long time in coming and home was not where Mott would find his respite.

✳✳✳

Trans-Atlantic travel was not unheard of in 1875, but to do so for pleasure was a relatively new concept. Within Europe itself, prior to the Napoleonic Wars, travel had been generally restricted to only the very wealthy. The landed elite would send their children on what became known as "the Grand Tour," a kind of rite of passage for adolescents. Sent abroad with tutors—part teacher, part chaperone—the privileged youth were expected to gain a practical education about the political realities of the world and receive exposure to new languages and cultures.[7] Of course, much like young adults entering college today and tasting freedom for the first time, the scholastic goals of the Grand Tour often took a back seat to the hedonistic nature of a young adult out in the world unfettered by the parental restrictions of childhood. Ineffectual tutors could be given the slip as their young charges learned less and partied more.[8]

As the Napoleonic Wars in the early 19th Century compromised the safety of the European continent, the Grand Tour all but died. However, by the mid-nineteenth century, advances in transportation technology, such as railways and steam-powered ocean vessels, provided faster and cheaper access to distant locations, while an increase in disposable income among the burgeoning middle class allowed more people to take advantage of that increased access. Leisure travel was on the rise.

When Mott sailed abroad in 1875, trans-Atlantic travel by steamship was still a relatively new means of travel, having only become more commonplace within Mott's lifetime. Trans-Atlantic departures were still novel enough to be found in the papers. On July 4th, Mott boarded the *Britannic* of the White Star Line.[9] The ship Mott would return home on—the *SS Scythia*—was similar to the *Britannic* and offers some insight into how he would have traveled. Constructed in 1874 by J & G Thomson in Glasgow and commanded by Captain W. H. P. Harris, the *Scythia* of the Cunard Line was operated by the British and North American Royal Mail Steam Packet Company for its New York City to Liverpool service.[10] Like many of the trans-Atlantic steamships at this time, the *Scythia* did not rely solely on steam. In fact, except for a large funnel or smokestack standing in the center of the ship, it resembled an old sailing vessel complete with a full complement of masts. Relying primarily on wind power, the steam engine provided important supplementation during times of calm or windless conditions, which ensured a continuous, uninterrupted journey. They greatly reduced the time it took to cross the ocean to little more than a week.[11]

Mott enjoyed relative comfort during his crossing. Ships such as the *Britannic* and *Scythia* offered a wide variety of food—all kinds of fish, meats, fruits, and vegetables, and several kinds of desserts. His accommodations may still have been relatively spartan, particularly when compared with the luxurious first and second-class amenities on larger ocean liners in the ensuing decades. Still, for an army man accustomed to sleeping in tents on the ground or in drafty log cabins, Mott found himself quite comfortably set up.

Mott arrived in England in late summer and spent his first couple of months touring Western Europe where the art, the architecture, the history, everything was a source of wonder. "I wish you could have seen the jewels at the Opera House in Paris the other night," Mott wrote to his mother, "The scenery and costumes were magnificent and the building is the finest in the world. The interior is a mass of gilding and crimson velvet."[12] It was a sight the grandeur of which he had never seen in the United States.

Mott sought out as much high culture as he could in Europe and with so many options it was difficult to choose. In Berlin, he planned to attend the Opera to see *Lohengrin* but changed his mind to see a concert featuring all-female musicians. The setting was more intimate — eating, drinking, and smoking around small tables as the musicians performed. "It looked funny to see twenty or thirty girls playing on violins and bass viols and they played just as well as men could have done."[13] A few days later, he attended another concert featuring works by Beethoven and Rossini. In Dresden, Mott visited an art gallery to view works by "the old masters," and took in an orchestra performance at a local Catholic church.[14] Mott was no stranger to highbrow culture. He had attended concerts and stage performances in New York City during his two years of recruiting duty and the voracious appetite for literature he exhibited to cope with the day-to-day tedium of camp life during the Civil War indicate a man of well-rounded intellect. None of it compared with experiencing such art at its source in the grandest halls of Europe.

Although he attended performances almost nightly, they were ultimately a relaxing complement to an otherwise active day of sightseeing. He dined in style, visited famous museums, and marveled at the trappings of royalty, including Charlottenburg Palace in Prussia where he viewed the tombs of King Frederick William III and other Prussian royalty. Yet for all his admiration of the cultural products of his Western

European heritage, Mott struggled to appreciate the people. The most he could say of the French was that they were "not very good looking" while the Germans were to him "the homeliest people you ever saw and badly dressed," with bizarre table habits.[15] "The men here comb their heads with pocket combs in the dining room of Hotels and Restaurants before they sit down. What do you think of that for manners? They pick their teeth at the table continuously and sometimes stick the toothpick upright in a piece of bread!"[18] Mott consistently judged most harshly those to whom he was ethnically closest.

In southern Europe along the Mediterranean, the people and landscapes utterly captivated his imagination.

The blue sea is splashing all the time and the Island of Capri looks like an immense animal asleep in the bay. There is a grotto on the island which you enter in a boat through a small hole in the rock. It is called the blue grotto on account of the color of the water which is a beautiful blue which is reflected against the sides and top.[19]

In Italy, Mott felt like a fish out of water. The landscapes, the architecture, and the people appeared more exotic. Not once did Mott discuss the natural beauty of England, Germany, or France the way he discussed the natural landscapes of Italy. On the contrary, it rained so much during his time in Germany he could not wait to rid himself of the climate.

Later that December, Mott visited Pompeii, one of the famous Roman towns destroyed by the eruption of Mount Vesuvius. "They are gradually uncovering it and there you see the streets and houses almost as they were before the Christian era. There were frescoes on all the walls and the colors are as bright as when they were put on. They have found the bodies of several persons lying as they were overtaken by the eruption."[18] And no excursion on his journey equaled his climb to the summit of Mount Vesuvius that followed. Mott first laid eyes on the dormant volcano when he arrived in Naples. "On all sides except the sea," Mott wrote about Naples, "you can see the summits shining in glory through the soft blue haze of the Italian atmosphere and Vesuvius is smoking night and day, threatening destruction to all around it."[19]

Mott spent two weeks in Naples before traveling to Rome where he stayed through Christmas. The marketplaces in the streets of Naples were a source of fascination for Mott. "The streets are jammed with people and vehicles and animals of all kinds, beggars and gentleman, deformed creatures and lovely women...and donkeys. The donkeys bray, the people shout at each other and gesticulate with real southern vehemence."[20] He found the people far more attractive than his northern European brethren as well. "The Italians are the finest looking and most agreeable people I have seen," Mott concluded as he discovered a particular attraction to the Italian ladies.[21] "Naples is the gayest place," Mott had determined. "Carriages roll by with beautiful women bobbling on the cushions with their eyes half closed expecting to be admired by the officers and other loungers in the pack when the band is playing afternoons."[22]

In the new year, he continued eastward towards the Adriatic to catch a ship bound for the Greek island of Corfu, The countryside continued to captivate him along the way,

The entire country is a forest of olive trees all twisted and gnarled and the buildings as white as lime with flat tile roof and surrounded with white walls. Every now and then you see the pinnacle of a mountain crowned with a white village and a picturesque square church tower in bold relief. The fields were filled with groups of men and women sometimes fifty or more together hoeing up the ground and in other places we saw large flocks of sheep with their wild looking shepherds clad in sheep skins (I should think the sheep would be suspicious of them). They always have their large white intelligent-looking dogs standing around the flock. I was glad when we reached the Adriatic and saw the blue water and the white sails and the picturesque towns on the shore.[23]

Heading southeast from Rome to the port city of Brindisi, Mott's admiration for the country only grew. "I don't wonder that the Bourbours [sic] were loath to give up this country," he remarked.[24]

The crossing to Corfu off the coast of the Grecian mainland took about four hours in the middle of the night. When Mott awoke early the next morning, he walked onto the deck to see the Ionian Archipelago, in which Corfu is situated, stretched out in front of him. Arriving at the shore, he spied a Turkish Man of War in the distance across the straight near the Albanian mainland. As he disembarked and walked into the city of Corfu, the streets did not make a favorable first impression.

We came ashore in a tub called a boat and then a man shouldered our baggage and we went under an archway and up a narrow, dirty, stinking street through a crowd of people in strange garments to our hotel. The streets are all dark, narrow, paved with small cobblestones and there are stairs and steps everywhere to break one's neck on.[25]

Adding to the cacophony of the street noise, the garrison band played throughout the afternoon a kind of "barbaric music, such as you might expect to hear here."[26] Mott did not elaborate on whether "barbaric" in his eyes meant simply "foreign" or if it was a pejorative judgment. One evening he climbed to the top of a large promontory to visit the site of an old fortress built by the Venetians in the sixteenth century and took in the stunning view. As the sun set, illuminating the "snow-tipped mountains of Albania" in the distance, Mott stopped to appreciate the "magnificent panorama of mountains and blue water with an English war ship and small craft in the harbor."[27] Although a Greek possession, a fairly large Albanian population resided on the island that particularly caught Mott's eye. "There were groups of Albanians here and there posturing and striding about with the lofty poise and natural grace of free mountaineers," Mott wrote from Corfu in January, 1876.[28] "They are the finest looking men that I have ever seen. They wear their hair and mustaches long, red cap on the head, sheep skin cloak, tight leggings to their handsome legs, short linen petticoats, starched and crimped habit tight to the body and a red sash."[29] Mott departed Corfu at midnight on February 1, 1876. Leaving Europe behind him, he sailed for three days across the Mediterranean bound for Egypt.

Mott's time in Europe had not been all fun. In July of 1875 shortly after he left the US, Duncan, Sherman, and Company, a New York banking firm in which Mott had much of his money, failed with over $5 million in liabilities.[30] The failure left Mott virtually penniless while abroad causing his family much anxiety and prompting Frank to raise funds to wire. Mott's financial relationship with the bank and the full extent of the damage to his overall personal wealth was not revealed, but it did not ruin him. His arrangements for the next few legs of his trip had already been made, and so his more immediate concern was his inability to secure souvenirs for the family. He wanted to purchase a bracelet for his sister Annie, while in Paris, but resigned himself to purchasing it on his return. In any case, whatever he had seemed to be enough for him to get by without greatly detracting from his experiences and, for the next phase of his trip, much of his expenses were already covered in a package tour of Egypt and the Holy Land offered by the iconic Thomas Cook & Son.

Credited as the pioneer in the development of the leisure tourism industry, Thomas Cook & Son began in 1845 by organizing travel to temperance rallies throughout Britain. Their business model proved so successful, they soon expanded services to include arranging trips to areas of interest throughout Britain and the European continent.[31] By 1870, they began to lose market share in Europe as more and more service providers for tourists (hotels, transportation services, etc.) started cutting out middlemen like travel agents in favor of interacting with travelers directly. To stay relevant, the company looked further afield, expanding travel options to more exotic places where independent travelers would be hard-pressed to make their own arrangements. Egypt became the first such trip that Thomas Cook & Son offered.[32]

The rise of interest in Egyptology following the Napoleonic Wars had captured the imaginations of Westerners and by the middle of the nineteenth century, Muhammad Ali, then the khedive, or autonomous ruler, of Egypt had opened the country to Western travelers. The British influence in Egypt, owing to the construction of the Suez Canal, made the country an enticing destination for creating a vertically-integrated tourism business in which transportation and accommodation were all controlled directly by Cook & Son as a single commodity to be purchased as a worry-free package by their customers.[33]

In 1869, Cook & Son offered their first all-inclusive package tour which included Egypt and Palestine, or more generally the Holy Lands. The tours began in Cairo and traveled by steamship up the Nile as far as the Aswan dam before returning to Cairo. From there, the tour took travelers by horseback across the Sinai Peninsula and into the Holy Lands. Owing to the lack of amenities on this leg of the journey, tourists were required to sleep in tents, but here too, the company took care of establishing the camps and setting up the tents in advance, making the trip as easy as possible. Thomas Cook's General Baptist beginnings as a service for getting the faithful to temperance rallies influenced his attitude towards tourism in the Holy Land. While the Egyptian experience focused on the marvels of the ruins of ancient temples and tombs of the great Pharaohs, their curated tour of the Holy Land represented a kind of pilgrimage, bringing travelers to the divine source of their faith.[34]

Mott never discussed his specific travel arrangements, but he would not have had many alternatives to a Cook tour as the Khedive of Egypt had granted Cook a virtual monopoly on commercial steamer transportation on the Nile from Cairo to the Sudanese border.[35] Moreover, the itinerary of his travels in the region so closely mirrored the route offered by Cook, it is unlikely Mott traveled any other way.

Unlike his experience in Europe, Mott had little opportunity to interact with the local population in Egypt. Cook's tours were specifically designed to insulate travelers from the locals as an added benefit to the firm's wealthy clientele seeking to experience exotic locales without the stress of negotiating their own culture shock.[36] Mott was not of that ilk. His predilection for observing every population of people he encountered suffered as a result and his letters are uncharacteristically devoid of any thoughts about the Egyptian people. However, the compromise was necessary in order to experience the wonders of the nation.

As Mott sailed down the Nile, the natural beauty of the country unfolded before him. The grandeur of the ancient ruins made up for the relentlessly oppressive heat of the desert. "There are sufficient temples and gates still standing to give you an idea of its former greatness," Mott recalled of his visit to Thebes.[37] In particular, the Temple of Karnak left the greatest impression for its sheer size and for the imagery carved into the walls.

The greatest of the temples, that of Karnak, is 1180 feet long and it is a mile and a half around the outer circuit of its gates. The lintel stones of the doorways are 40 ft. long. In the grand hall, there is a central avenue of 12 columns 62 ft. high and 11 ft. 6 in. in diameter and 22 other columns 42 ft. 5 in. high and 28 ft. in circumference. The caps of these were colored and still retain a good deal of coloring. On the walls of these temples, there are pictures of wars cut in stone and in some of them there are prisoners being brought before the King of Egypt and you can see from their expression that they are Jews.[38]

Mott studied the carvings and hieroglyphs attempting to make sense of their ancient religion. "The ancient Egyptians used to grope around for Gods to worship and among other things they worshipped bulls and hawks."[39] Though not a particularly nuanced understanding of the religion of Ancient Egypt, it captivated him as he soaked in the sight of rows of tombs of "sacred bulls" made out of whole blocks of granite.

Mott remained in Cairo for a couple of days before setting off by rail for Port Said on the coast. A storm delayed his crossing for a few days, but when the skies finally cleared, he journeyed overnight towards Palestine across the Mediterranean, boarding a smaller boat to reach land after sighting the coast the next morning. Mott's group landed at the city of Jaffa, where they took breakfast, navigated the "usual narrow dirt streets crowded with Turks, camels, and asses" and visited the house where Simon the Tanner was said to have lived in biblical times.[40]

Mott's stay in Jaffa was brief. At noon, he and his tour party had mounted up and began their overland excursions through Palestine by horse, making camp that night at Ramleh. As Mott continued his journey the next day, he began to recognize many famous locations from the Bible almost anywhere he looked, "[we] passed over the plain of Aijalon where the Lord commanded the sun and the moon to stand still so that Joshua might destroy his enemies...passed the village of Kiriath Jearim whence David took the Ark to Jerusalem and we crossed the brook where he was said to have selected the stones with which he killed Goliath."[41] The approach to Jerusalem was less enticing. "We rode along over the most gloomy rocky scenery I have ever [seen] and came on Jerusalem suddenly about 4 o'clock. The first view is disappointing as you see a number of new buildings which are beside the gates."[42] Mott did not stay in the city. Instead, the tour operators had arranged to have tents pitched outside the city upon their arrival.

After a quick break to wash up after his journey, Mott ventured into the city to explore. Winding down the "narrow and dirty" streets, groups of lepers and beggars threw themselves at his feet looking for charity. Mott's initial sojourn into the city was brief. The next morning, the tour embarked on a three-day circular excursion from Jerusalem south to Bethlehem, then east toward the Dead Sea and the Jordan River before turning north towards Jericho and back west to Jerusalem. Not surprisingly, Cook's tour of the Holy Land focused on visiting some of the holiest places in Christianity. The road to Bethlehem included a stop at the tomb of Rachel, the biblical matriarch and wife of Jacob, as well as Solomon's Pools, three ancient reservoirs constructed by the biblical king for whom they are named. Bethlehem, the birthplace of Christ, inspired awe and emotion amongst the pilgrims who gathered there. "There is a church erected over what they point out as the place where He was born and the manger. These places are below the floor and they have candles burning and a soldier on guard to keep the different Christian sects from fighting. This is the oldest Christian church in the world about 1300 years. The roof is made from the cedars of Lebanon."[43]

Leaving Bethlehem, Mott journeyed onward to the Dead Sea, known for its heavy salt content, and later to Mount Nebo "where Moses saw the Promised Land."[44] By mid-day, Mott and his party reached the banks of the Jordan where they paused to take lunch. While his companions ate, Mott walked down to the river where Christ was baptized and collected some water in a small vial. He learned that his sister, Annie had given birth to a son while Mott was still in Egypt and the proud uncle intended the water for his nephew's baptism.[45] That evening, the tour group camped their final night of the excursion near Jericho, the biblical city known for its famed walls brought down by the trumpets of Joshua's Israelite army.

Mott returned to Jerusalem the next day, where the approach from the east presented a far more favorable view than the route that had brought them to the city previously. "We had a splendid view of [the city] from the Mount of Olives [from] where we returned. It contains a great many domes and is surrounded by a wall with great gates and towers."[46] Mott finally had time to really tour the city, seeing all of the "sacred places" including the ruins of the Jewish Temple, the Wailing Wall, and an arch from the bridge "which Solomon threw across from Mount Zion to Mount Moriah"[47] The following day, he went to the Church of the Holy Sepulcher, built over the spot where Christ was supposed to have been crucified.

At this point in his travels, Mott had seen a very many sacred places and yet he took them in with the same detached fascination that he viewed the great temples and tombs in Egypt. For many, this leg of Cook's tour was a deeply moving spiritual experience, but Mott harbored a certain ambivalence to religion. Though not an atheist—he still ascribed some significance to Christianity as he had thought to bottle the water of the Jordan for his nephew's christening—he struggled to encounter the divine despite being immersed in the holiest of places in Christendom. "I experienced a good deal of emotion although I did not believe it to be divine," Mott confided to his mother after his visit to the Holy Sepulcher.[48] Mott was not one to blindly accept many of these locations for what they were presented as. He cynically acknowledged there were conflicting ideas regarding the site of the Holy Sepulcher, "It is built over what they say is the place where He was crucified and buried and a great many other things such as the place where they found the three crosses so that really nobody knows anything about it."[49] As Mott looked upon the assembled pilgrims reflecting on the metaphysical, Mott remained focused on the physical. "There were a number of Russian pilgrims there today going about from one chapel to another chanting with candles in their hands," he observed. However, the church was "ornamented in the most wretched taste with glass lamps and gewgaws" of the Greek orthodox Catholics who operated it.[50]

On March 14, Mott bade farewell to Jerusalem and resumed his tour through Palestine, heading north towards Beirut, Lebanon stopping along the way to see "nearly every place in Bible history in Palestine."[51] They traveled to Tiberius on the Sea of Galilee, on to Nazareth where Christ lived, a castle built by King Herod of Judea, and Damascus, "a beautiful place embowered in olive trees with the mountains towering behind it." In Damascus, just like everywhere else, the appearance and customs of the people intrigued Mott. "Everything is oriental here. You see no carriages nor European costumes. The people all use horses and asses and camels and wear the turban and loose trousers and long robe to the feet."[52]

Mott arrived in Beirut on April 5 and set out by boat on a six-day journey into the Mediterranean, around the south side of Turkey, and up through the Grecian archipelago towards Constantinople through the Dardanelles and across the Sea of Marmara. "It was a delightful sail among these islands, it was like being on a lake," Mott wrote home. "We were so close to them and occasionally we would stop at a town to take on cargo and then we would go ashore to see the place."[53] Constantinople was unlike anything Mott had ever seen. Far more exotic than the great cities of Europe, and larger and more bustling than the cities in Egypt and Palestine, Constantinople offered a stunning view for Mott when he awoke in the wee hours of the morning on April 11. Leaving his cabin just before dawn, Mott clambered up to the deck to see the city before sunrise. "...the moon was shining on the minarets of the great mosques and the cypress trees in the seraglio looked dark in the moonlight. It was a splendid night to see this great city..."[54] As the steamer arrived, Mott and everyone else on the ship were delayed in disembarking in order to let a Pasha, a high-ranking Ottoman official, and his "half dozen wives and children" go ashore.[55]

Mott spent four days in Constantinople where he marveled at the sites, the architecture, the natural landscape of the city, and, of course, the people. "I saw the Sultan go to prayers in great state riding a splendid grey horse covered with gold strappings surrounded by dignitaries and soldiers in all ranks [who] all shouted in Arabic 'God bless you' or something like it..."[56] The splendor of the Sultan and his entourage, however, could not compare to a performance of the Howling Dervishes. An ascetic order of Muslims who had taken a vow of poverty, Dervishes are well known for their unusual ceremonies. In particular, the hypnotic spinning of the Whirling Dervishes, with their long skirts that fan out as they spin continually with their eyes closed, was a more popular site for Western tourists. The constant spinning was intended to place the Dervish into a trance to bring them closer to God. Mott, however, witnessed a ceremony of the Howling Dervishes. This ceremony involved a group of Dervishes, led by a chief Dervish, in a series of chants and grunting, gradually increasing their movements in wilder, more frenetic movements swaying forward and backward, often until participants lost consciousness. Like with the Whirling Dervishes, the intent was to enter a trance-like state of ecstasy. Mott likened their howling to that of the Methodists back in the United States.[57] Another component of the ceremony involved the healing of the sick by the laying on of feet by the chief dervish. "They finish the performance by the chief man standing on the prostrate body of an infant and then walking over the prostrate forms of men and a lot of girls about 5 or 6 years of age."[58] How the chief Dervish accomplished this without injuring the children Mott did not describe, but it was one of the strangest sights he had ever seen.

Mott boarded his steamer once more on the fifteenth of April, leaving Constantinople across the Sea of Marmara and back to Europe. It would take another several weeks to get back to the port in England where he would board a ship back to the United States. Mott sailed to Athens, Greece where he spent five days, then on to Florence, Italy for another few days before retracing his steps back through Paris, London, and Liverpool where he boarded the *SS Scythia* bound for New York City. "I have seen so many places and queer people and strange things that when I attempt to write I get them confused in my mind," Mott wrote to his mother after leaving Turkey.[59] Over the last seven-plus months, Mott had experienced a wide breadth of cultures, landscapes, and histories. It was an eye-opening experience and no doubt contributed to his continued appreciation for the many diverse ways humans around the world understood and navigated their world. Despite being away from home for more than half a year, he would have stayed longer if he could. Driven to experience more, Mott immediately began saving up for another, more ambitious trip a few years later to the opposite side of the world.

10

Peril at Clear Creek

Colonel Nelson Miles paced anxiously around the cantonment on the Tongue River. The supply train from Glendive had not yet arrived. His men scanned the horizon as far they could see, but there was no trace of the wagons or soldiers that had been expected twenty-four hours earlier. The situation on the Plains was as precarious as ever in this autumn of 1876 and Miles was concerned that the absence of the wagons portended a grim fate for the men charged with leading it to the small outpost. When the two scouts he had sent out did not return, Miles feared the worst. Assembling a large contingent of the 5th Infantry, Miles set out to investigate the apparent disappearance of his supply train and its military escort which included among its complement Captain Hooton of the 22nd Infantry.

Mott had returned from his sojourn through Europe and the Holy Land, several months earlier. Landing in New York City, he arrived home to a country in shock. Colonel Custer and over 260 members of his seventh cavalry, alongside whom Mott had participated in the 1873 Yellowstone expedition, had been killed at the Battle of Little Bighorn at the end of June. It was the largest military loss since the Civil War and the news had shaken the American public. In Philadelphia, the Centennial Exposition was in full swing commemorating the one-hundredth anniversary of the United States of America, an event made more significant by the fact that just over a decade earlier, it hadn't looked like the country would make it to such a milestone still intact. Yet, Custer's defeat had cast a pall on the various anniversary events.

The Battle of Little Bighorn, or the Battle of Greasy Grass as the Lakota refer to it, has become an iconic event in the history of the American West. In truth, however, it was one in a series of engagements from March 1876 through the following May 1877 known collectively as the Great Sioux War in which the long-held tensions between the United States Government and the Western Lakota Sioux would finally come to a head. For several years, poor enforcement and outright violations of treaties by white settlers and the United States government led Chief Crazy Horse of the Oglala Lakota and Sitting Bull, one of the most revered and respected leaders of the Hunkpapa Lakota nation, to encourage thousands of Lakota and their allies, to leave the reservations and resume their traditional, nomadic way of life.

The Treaty of Fort Laramie in 1868 had promised vast swaths of land along the northern Plains to the Lakota, Cheyenne, and numerous other tribes on the Plains. But in the intervening years, the Lakota endured multiple encroachments onto and through that land, whenever it proved convenient for the United States government to do so. The surveys in the early 1870s for the Northern Pacific Railroad—including the 1873 expedition that Mott had joined—placed the proposed path through the Powder River region in the Yellowstone Valley, an area that had been promised to the Indigenous People of the area as hunting grounds by the Treaty. However, the catalyzing event that led to an all-out war on the Lakota and their Cheyenne allies was an enticing discovery in the Black Hills in 1874. As part of the 1868 treaty, the Federal Government had granted the Lakota sovereignty over the Black Hills, a sacred region for them. When Custer led an expedition into the Black Hills to identify a suitable place for a new fort and to evaluate the mineral resources of the land, he discovered a commodity that the government had not anticipated: gold. When word reached eastward that the expedition had discovered the valuable element, thousands of prospectors and miners still reeling from the Panic of 1873, fled to the Black Hills in droves to seek their fortunes.[1]

That the expedition into sacred land had happened at all angered the Lakota, but the illegal migration of these miners brazenly violated the Fort Laramie Treaty. The army struggled to remove the trespassing miners and protect them from the Lakota who were outraged by the violation of their rights, the desecration of their sacred land, and the scaring away of the buffalo upon which the tribes of the northern Plains depended for survival. The army could not stem the tide of emigration and so the US Government proposed buying the Black Hills, a proposition the Lakota nation roundly refused.[2] For the Lakota—and indeed all the Indigenous People of the northern Plains—this was yet another existential threat to their very way of life. For the United States government, however, this was simply a geopolitical challenge to be negotiated. In light of the Lakota refusal, by November 1875, in a meeting at the White House, President Grant decided that instead of using military forces to control white emigration into territory promised to the Lakota, it was time to do with the Lakota and Cheyenne what had been done with other Native Americans throughout the rest of the country: redraw the boundaries of the reservation, force the Lakota onto it, and open the land in both the Black Hills and the Yellowstone Valley to the inevitable tide of American expansion.[3]

In early 1876, the Bureau of Indian Affairs instructed all Lakota and Cheyenne people in the Black Hills and Yellowstone Valley to relocate to the Great Sioux Reservation, which had been set aside for them. Given an unrealistic January 31 deadline to comply, many of the nations' people spread out throughout the region had not even heard the orders by the end of January. Not that the deadline really mattered. The Lakota and Cheyenne would not sacrifice their way of life. Stymied by the resistance, Indian Affairs turned to the War Department for help and Generals Sherman and Sheridan answered by mobilizing the army in the northern Plains to force the Lakota and Cheyenne to submit.[4]

Sheridan's strategy was one of total war. He did not wait for the Spring thaw to move against the Native Americans. Instead, he directed

General George Crook to dispatch his forces north from Fort Fetterman in Wyoming Territory to attack the Lakota and their allies by surprise as they lay in their winter camp near the Powder River. About four hundred soldiers were sent out under Colonel Joseph J. Reynolds. When they came upon what they believed to be a Lakota village, they attacked but underestimated the resistance they encountered. Although the village was eventually destroyed, the bulk of the villagers escaped, which for the army resulted in a strategic loss. Moreover, the village turned out to be Cheyenne, not Lakota. The Northern Cheyenne and Lakota had been allies before, but nothing did more to solidify that relationship against the United States Army than this attack.[5]

In June, Crook escalated the offensive. To surround the rogue Lakota and Cheyenne, Crook devised a three-pronged movement. He would mobilize his forces north from Fetterman, while Col. John Gibbon would lead his troops at Fort Shaw in western Montana eastward leaving General Alfred Terry to march west from Fort Abraham Lincoln in Dakota Territory with the goal of meeting in the middle. The 7th Cavalry under Custer was assigned to Terry who ordered Custer to ride ahead anticipating he would join with Crook's forces from the South. Little did Terry or Custer know, Crook had encountered resistance at the Rosebud River, which delayed his march north as he awaited supplies and reinforcements. Meanwhile, Custer spied an enormous herd of horses in the distance grazing in the hills beyond an obscured valley. The herd belied the presence of a Lakota village in the vicinity. But something was amiss. The head of horses on the hill numbered in the thousands, far more than would accompany a typical Lakota village of three or four hundred people. Custer sent scouts out to lay eyes on the village and when they returned, they confirmed the uncommon enormity of the village saying it was one of the largest they had ever seen. However, Custer still believed he had enough manpower to subdue them. According to records from the local Indian Agents, there should not have been more than eight hundred or so hostile forces total in the region. Custer continued to lie in wait for reinforcements from the surrounding area, but when he learned that a small group of scouts of

The Hunkpapa freedom fighter: Tatanka Iyotake (Sitting Bull)
Library of Congress

unknown tribal affiliation had come across one of the cavalry's former campsites where supplies had been left, Custer assumed his presence would soon be known to the Lakota. It forced his hand and he moved up his attack so as not to lose the element of surprise.[6] As he approached the village, the full scope of his mistake presented itself. The records of the Indian Agents were grossly inaccurate as they had not taken into account the scores of Native Americans who had unofficially left their reservations to join Crazy Horse and Sitting Bull. The 7th Cavalry had landed directly in the middle of thousands of Hunkpapa, Oglala, and Mnikowoju alongside their Cheyenne allies who had assembled for mutual protection and a resumption of their way of life in defiance of the US government. Custer paid for his mistake with his life and the lives of all his men.

The Lakota and Cheyenne celebrated a great victory, but Sitting Bull and Crazy Horse knew the reprisals would be hard and swift. The scale of humiliation for the United States government emboldened the military to retaliate with full force, while the papers wove a tale of bravery and sacrifice around Custer, enshrining him amongst the martyred heroes of the nation and galvanizing popular support against the "savage" Native Americans responsible for the massacre. What had not been disclosed was Custer's intended strategy to round up and capture as many non-combatants—women, children, and the elderly—to use as hostages, knowing from experience that the warriors would lay down their arms and surrender before putting their families in danger. Indeed, many such non-combatants perished during the conflict, but to humanize Native Americans in the eyes of American public opinion would have been counterproductive to US interests in the region.

With the events of the Sioux War escalating, following the massacre of Custer and his men, Mott resumed command of Company K of the 22nd Infantry, under Lieutenant Colonel Elwell Otis, at Sault St. Marie, Michigan along the Great Lakes. Only three weeks older than Mott, Otis began his military career, as so many others, in the Civil War. A Marylander by birth but a New Yorker by transplant, Otis had originally intended a career in law. He graduated from the University of Rochester and briefly moved to Massachusetts to attend Harvard Law School. After graduating from Harvard in 1860, Otis returned to New York and had only recently established his law practice in Rochester when the war broke out. In 1862, Otis joined the 140th New York Volunteer Infantry and fought in several battles with the Army of the Potomac, including Chancellorsville and Gettysburg. In late 1863, he was promoted to Lieutenant colonel of his regiment and led troops in several more engagements until becoming severely wounded at the Battle of Peeble's Farm in the fall of 1864. The injury kept him out of the rest of the war, but when he recovered, he joined the regular army where, unlike many of his counterparts, he retained his rank of Lieutenant colonel and became attached to the 22nd Infantry.

Upon Mott's arrival in Michigan, Otis called an audience with Mott and the commanders of five other companies of the 22nd giving them orders to join General Alfred Terry's forces in Montana. Mott assembled his men and sailed across Lakes Huron and Superior, thence by rail to Fort Abraham Lincoln along the Missouri River near Bismarck in Dakota Territory. After a brief respite at the fort, Mott proceeded to rendezvous with Terry in Montana.

Leaving Fort Abraham Lincoln, Mott traveled up the Missouri River towards the Big Horn River passing by Forts Stevenson and Buford where he had spent the early years of his career.[7] It was a nostalgic trip for Mott who never thought he would see either place again. He stopped briefly at Fort Stevenson to post a letter to his mother, which was an unusual feeling. "It seems strange that I should mail a letter there, a place which I never expected to see again."[8] The personnel at the fort were entirely different and Colonel de Trobriand had since moved on to a different assignment, but Mott felt a certain sentimentality about the first fort at which he spent any great length of time as an officer. After a brief stop at his old Stevenson haunt, Mott continued to the mouth of the Rosebud, where he joined General Terry's army. Once reunited with Terry, the entire command moved up the Rosebud

Determined to supply the Tongue Cantonment: Elwell Otis
Library of Congress

to rendezvous with General Crook's army before moving on toward the mouth of the Powder River.

***

Mott's role in the Great Sioux War focused less on realizing Philip Sheridan's desire to subdue the Lakota and more on achieving a second goal for Sheridan—establishing a permanent military presence in the Yellowstone Valley. Toward that end, Congress granted Sheridan two hundred thousand dollars for the purpose of establishing two new forts.[9] One of the forts, named Fort Custer in honor of the fallen cavalryman, would sit at the confluence of the Bighorn and Little Bighorn Rivers. The site for the second was situated further east along the Yellowstone at the junction of the Tongue River. Although it would later be christened Fort Keogh, in 1876 it was no more than a small outpost known only as the Tongue River Cantonment.

The army chose Colonel Nelson A. Miles, commander of the fifth infantry, to establish the Tongue River post. Nearly a year and a half Mott's junior, Miles had made a name for himself during the Civil War as a volunteer in the Massachusetts Infantry. Despite no formal military education—he was working as a clerk in a crockery store when the war broke out—he participated in most of the major engagements of the Army of the Potomac. He was wounded four times and earned the Medal of Honor for bravery at the Battle of Chancellorsville in 1863. By the end of the war, Miles had risen in rank to major general of volunteers while still in his mid-20s. After the war, Miles joined the regular army in which he was granted the commission of colonel and sent west to prosecute the Federal Government's reservation policies. Just prior to being stationed at the cantonment on the Tongue River, he led troops against the tribes of the southern plains—the Kiowa, Comanche, Arapaho, and Southern Cheyenne—successfully forcing them onto reservations within the Indian Territory of modern-day Oklahoma. Now, the army hoped Miles could achieve the same success against the Lakota and Northern Cheyenne along the northern Plains. Miles conducted the war against the Lakota from his new position on the Tongue River, but the small remote outpost needed regular support from a nearby post. The nearest option was a similarly small post at Glendive.

By September 1876, with the water level in the Yellowstone too low for supply steamers to move upriver, Colonel Otis ordered four companies of the 22nd Infantry, including Mott's, plus two companies from the 17th Infantry to settle at the Glendive Cantonment, a familiar place for Mott who had visited there three years earlier during the 1873 Yellowstone Expedition. Though only the beginning of September, Mott reckoned they would spend the winter there. "I think the campaign is over till next summer," he wrote to his mother. "We have been too strong for the Indians and they have avoided us all the time. The red devils always do that."[10] The anti-Indian, or at least anti-Lakota, sentiment running fervently among the American public had caught up with him.

Glendive was never intended to house six companies of infantry and so the men spent much of their energy that September constructing new log cabins in preparation for the winter. The strategic importance of the Glendive camp rested in its location on the Yellowstone between Fort Buford in Dakota Territory and the new Tongue River Cantonment. With the water too low to transport supplies via river, all provisions funneled through Glendive and overland to the Tongue River. For much of the month of September, units not assigned to building winter cabins made routine trips to the cantonment with wagon trains of supplies to support Miles' forces. Mott made several such trips, about three in a month, escorting about one hundred wagons at a time, none of which proved particularly eventful.[11]

By the beginning of October, Mott felt settled at Glendive. "I am accepting a cabin already. We may have some ladies here as several of our officers are talking about bringing out their wives."[12] Mott welcomed the proposed infusion of the feminine presence at the camp, but it also further signaled a level of semi-permanence in their position.

Glendive bored Mott. Not even the odd hunting excursion could satisfy him. Instead, Mott busied himself with matters back home.

Though having no children of his own, as a doting Uncle he took an interest in his baby nephew Maris even offering child-rearing advice for Annie, which included a curious suggestion to put him in a barrel to "keep the air from blowing on" him. He also sought his family's opinions on the contentious Tilden-Hayes presidential election. "I suppose you are in the midst of a political hurly-burly with all its vaporings and slanders and lies," Mott wrote to his mother, "contemptible business generally."[13] By contrast, the biggest controversy Mott faced thus far was concern over the sanitary condition of his food. He fired his cook, "a fat Dutchman who I suspected of not washing his hands."[14] With the exception of the occasional supply trip to the Tongue River, Mott did not expect the monotony of the Glendive camp to change any time soon. However, as they moved into the second week of October, one of Mott's supply trips would become anything but routine.

On October 10, Mott and his small company were assigned as part of the escort for that day's supply wagons to the Tongue River. Mott reported to Captain Charles Miner of the 22nd whom Otis had placed in command of the escort consisting of Mott's Company K and two additional companies of the 22nd with one of the 17th—about one hundred sixty men in total—to guard a supply train of about ninety-four wagons and one ambulance.[15] Colonel Otis had received intelligence from Major Marcus Reno at Fort Abraham Lincoln that a large band of Lakota warriors was amassing potentially to capture this train.[16] Undaunted, but on their guard, the train set out at noon for Colonel Miles' command on the Tongue just as they had numerous times before. The overland route followed the north bank of the Yellowstone River and required periodic fordings of the various tributaries that flowed into it, the first of which being Spring Creek, about fourteen miles from Glendive. Camped along the banks of the Spring Creek for the night, a single shot rang out near the picket line between ten and eleven o'clock. Already at a heightened state of alert, the men readied for an attack, but it turned out to be a lone warrior who retreated amidst brief retaliatory fire.

Shortly after three o'clock in the morning, however, the men were awoken by a series of shots being fired at them from the darkness of the prairie. The sparks of musket fire shone through the darkness in the distance. The soldiers did not return fire, opting instead to save the ammunition rather than shoot blindly into the dark. Still, it made for a harrowing night as they could hear the sound of the bullets passing by and in some cases striking the ground perilously close to them before the attack ceased on its own.[17] When morning came, Mott discovered the real target of the attack. Several mules had been injured and over fifty of them had broken free from their corral and fled. This greatly weakened the train, but nonetheless, after a hasty breakfast, Captain Miner ordered the train onward. No sooner had they begun their march when the rear guard of the train under Captain Malcolm McArthur came under a surprise attack by a group of Lakota who had been hiding in a nearby ravine. McArthur's men successfully repulsed the attack, but throughout the morning, more such surprise attacks occurred targeting different parts of the escort. Given the loss of so many teams of mules and the steadily increasing enemy force, Captain Miner realized they would never make it to Miles' cantonment in their current condition. He ordered the train to turn around and fight their way back to Glendive. The Lakota broke off their attack seeing the retreat as a victory.[18] The train arrived back at Glendive that night at about nine o'clock.

Frustrated by the attacks and determined to get the needed supplies to the Tongue River camp, Colonel Otis regrouped and planned for another attempt a couple of days later. This time, Otis would personally command the train. In addition to the four companies detailed as escorts during the first attempt, Otis added an additional regiment of infantry from the 17th under Captain Louis Sanger. Otis also ordered three Gatling guns to accompany the train as well. On October 14, the train, consisting of eighty-six wagons and about one hundred eighty-five men, left Glendive about ten o'clock in the morning.[19]

The first day went without incident and the train camped for the night about twelve miles from Glendive. Much like as happened during the first attempt, that evening a couple of warriors approached the picket line but were quickly repulsed. The next morning, Otis organized the train to move in four lines, surrounded on all four sides by soldiers. Company H of the 22nd was placed at the front as the advance guard with Company C of the 17th taking up the right and left advance flank. Company G of the 22nd covered the right rear flank as its counterpart, Company G of the 17th, occupied the left rear flank. Mott and his Lieutenant, William Kell, took Company K of the 22nd to the train's rear.[20]

Upon reaching Spring Creek, where the train had been previously beset by attacking Lakota warriors, Otis sent two of his scouts ahead to a high bluff to watch for any hostile forces while the wagon train forded the creek. Almost immediately, the scouts encountered a band of Lakota. Retreating to the wagon train, Otis sent out skirmishers from his advance guard to meet the force and take the bluff, allowing the train to safely cross the creek. Once up onto the flat plain, three beleaguered scouts approached them. They had come from Colonel Miles to ascertain the fate of the overdue wagon train unaware of the delay caused by the first failed attempt to make the journey. The scouts warned Otis of a hostile force of warriors in the area. They had been attacked, lost their horses, and taken refuge in some woods near the river. A fourth scout had been with them but was killed in the attack. As the train made its way to the next crossing at Clear Creek, they came upon the deceased scout and stopped to bury him on the prairie.[21]

The crossing at Clear Creek presented a difficult challenge. It ran through a deep ravine, which meant placing the train in a vulnerable position as it descended to the water, crossed it, and climbed to the other side. The Lakota understood their strategic advantage and two hundred warriors gathered on a ridge to the left to show it. When Mott spotted them, he knew the crossing would not be easy. With a series of signal fires burning on the horizon in front of them, the troops knew there were still more warriors on the way, the rising smoke advertising their position.[22] Otis repeated the strategy he had employed at Spring Creek. Under the cover of Gatling fire, Otis sent out his advance guard. Company H, along with Captain Sanger's Company G of the 17th crossed the creek and charged up to the ridge to drive back the warriors. Although they succeeded in repelling the Lakota, the warriors set fire to the dry prairie grass before retreating. "The smoke was blinding and the heat intolerable," wrote Lieutenant Alfred Sharpe of Company H, the train's advance guard, "but rushing onward and upward, we gained the crest and again drove the villains before us. Panting and exhausted, the men sank down completely overcome. But we had cleared the way, and we soon saw the long, white train of wagons climbing the hill."[23] Unlike the previous crossing, however, the Lakota persisted in their attack, particularly as their numbers steadily increased on all sides, called to the area by the signal fires and the burning prairie.

From his vantage point from the bluff, Lieutenant Sharpe watched as the entire train and escort became surrounded by Lakota warriors, large numbers of whom were bearing down most heavily on the rear – Mott's position. "[T]here were several hundred Indians charging up furiously around us through the smoke trying to find a weak place, but in vain. Our deadly rifles were too much for them" Mott wrote home proudly. "My company and Major Sanger of the 17th Infantry were in the rear and we would 'fall back' as the train moved on once after a run to secure another position...At the top of the hill, they turned and whipped their horses, ran as fast as they could go while we were pouring a storm of bullets into them. Gave them such a lesson that they left us to go into camp unmolested."[24]

Mott's recollection of the event exhibited an uncharacteristic bravado. When writing about the dangers of battle, he typically approached it with a calm solemnity not seen here. He may have been expressing confidence merely for the benefit of his anxious family or perhaps the monotony of his service enhanced the feeling of adrenaline of the event. In truth, Mott's position was far more precarious than he admitted to his mother, so much so that he would later receive a brevet promotion for his actions in this encounter.

Mott's tactics as rear guard in many ways mirrored the advance guard. To give the train some breathing space and buy it time to advance as it ascended the valley after crossing the creek, Mott and his company charged down the hill back towards the creek, away from the advancing train, to repulse the warriors approaching from the rear.

Once the train had advanced and the attacking force pushed back, the guard had to retreat quickly back into formation with the train. When the attacking Lakota regrouped to make another attempt, Mott repeated the charge-repulse-retreat tactic. Mott's timing required precision. If he ordered his retreats too soon, the train would not have sufficient time to progress. If he held off too long and allowed too much distance to grow between his men and the train, the gap would leave him vulnerable to being outflanked and surrounded, cut off from the rest of the troops. The Lakota concentrated much of their assault on Mott hoping he would slip up and leave the train's rear vulnerable for too long. Mott continued to buy the train more time as he advanced and retreated, but the number of warriors bearing down on his position only grew – and his ammunition was running out. From his vantage point on the ridge above the train, Lieutenant Sharpe of the advance guard witnessed the danger Mott was in.

Down in the valley, the reverberations of the musketry was deafening. As the train slowly climbed the hill and the rear guard – Company K, 22nd Infantry, Capt. Hooton and Lt. Kell – descended into the valley, the Indians closing in on them in great numbers. A report came that their ammunition was failing and another thousand rounds were sent back to them. Major Sanger [of the 17th] then turned back to the relief of Capt. Hooton as he was in imminent danger of being cut off.[25]

Sharpe's account restored the harrowing details Mott had conveniently omitted in his personal correspondence. As the train cleared the valley, the fighting subsided. Miraculously, the wagon train made camp at nightfall having sustained few injuries among its escort, but the state of the surrounding area disabused them of any notion that they could relax. "That night the camp was in a blaze of light from the burning prairie," Mott described in his letter home.[26] Lieutenant Sharpe, offered an even more detailed description of the aftermath, "The scene reminded me of the rhetorical description we so often read of Napoleon's smoking wake," he wrote. "We left blackened, desolate waste behind us.

Perhaps our little conflict of a single day may not compare with his mighty struggles, but it was enough for about 180 men to attend to," he wrote. In addition, Sharpe reflected on his perceptions of the nature of the fighting they had all just endured, comparing it to the tactics of "civilized warfare," writing "fighting a civilized enemy is perhaps rough work, but battling with fiends incarnate, highway robbers and midnight assassins, 'shapes hot from Tartarus,' together with fire, smoke, hunger, and thirst and the horrible fate of the captive at the stake in prospect is quite a different mode of warfare."[27] A product of his time, Sharpe's epithets were perhaps an unfair disparagement of the Lakota. After all, had he participated in the Battle of the Wilderness during the Civil War as Mott had, so he had witnessed first-hand the kind of fire and smoke a "civilized enemy" could employ in a battle.

The following morning, the wagon train proceeded on in the same formation as the previous day – the trains divided into four columns, surrounded by troops. Except for a few random potshots intended to harass the soldiers, the Lakota maintained their distance but were never out of sight. As the train moved uneasily onward, the warriors gathered on hills in the distance, closely watching and occasionally "haranguing" Otis' men.[28] The soldiers crossed Bad Route Creek without incident and as they approached Cedar Creek, Otis spotted a white cloth on a stake pitched in the trail in front of them.

Otis sent one of his scouts forward to investigate. Attached to the stake was a letter from Sitting Bull ordering the wagon train to drop some rations and ammunition for them and leave the area because they were scaring away the buffalo. "I want to know what you are doing traveling on this road," the letter said. "You scare all the buffalo away. I want to hunt on the place. I want you to turn back from here. If you don't I will fight you again. I want you to leave what you have got here, and turn back from here. I am your friend, Sitting Bull." The Hunkpapa leader likely dictated the note to John Bruguier, a mixed-blood Frenchman known to camp with the Lakota. Otis was unmoved by the letter. He instructed one of his scouts to proceed ahead of them and inform the Lakota war party gathered in the distance that they would be taking the train to the Tongue River and if Sitting Bull wanted a fight, Otis would be happy to oblige.[29]

Shortly thereafter, a pair of warriors bearing a white flag of truce approached the wagon train. Otis allowed them to come forward into their lines and discovered that they had been sent out from the Standing Rock Agency Reservation to implore Sitting Bull to return to the reservation. The Hunkpapa leader had, of course, refused, but Sitting Bull instead proposed negotiating with Colonel Otis out on the prairie, away from his lines. Otis balked at the idea and told the two messengers that he would gladly talk with Sitting Bull, but under no condition would he leave his lines.

Sitting Bull was as apprehensive to trust going behind Otis' lines as Otis had been with the idea of meeting Sitting Bull on his terms. Instead, he sent three warriors as his surrogates under a flag of truce to Otis. The Colonel agreed to talk with them. The men who spoke on behalf of Sitting Bull reiterated their concerns that Otis and his men were scaring away all the buffalo. They asked again for rations and more ammunition for hunting. Otis did not have the authority to negotiate any kind of terms with Sitting Bull and told his representatives that their chief should appear before Colonel Miles at the Tongue River cantonment if they wanted to negotiate. Otis' job was simply to get their supplies through to the Tongue and that was what he intended to do. The Lakota representatives informed the Colonel that they would move on to trade at Fort Peck in northern Montana and then route to the Tongue River camp. Otis refused the Lakotas' request for ammunition, but as a sign of good faith, he left some rations of bread and bacon for them on the trail.[30] During the negotiations, Mott kept a watchful eye on the horizon for any sign of attack by the Lakota gathered along the surrounding hills. It was an impressive, if ominous, sight. "When the chiefs and Col. Otis were talking, the warriors were drawn up in line like soldiers a half mile to the rear and there was a larger number grouped on top of a hill all in showy blankets," Mott recalled. "It was very picturesque."[31] After depositing the rations in the trail, the train continued, receiving no further resistance from the Lakota.

On October 17, the column spotted a large force advancing toward them from the west. It was Colonel Miles and troops of the 5th Infantry who had set out from the Tongue River the previous day in search of them. Relieved at finding the men safe, albeit weary, Miles stopped to debrief Otis before moving on in pursuit of the Lakota who had attacked the train. Mott finally arrived at the Tongue River with the supply train a couple of days later. With the supplies delivered, on October 21, the escort cautiously and uneasily traveled back to Glendive without incident.

Mott continued to serve at the Glendive cantonment for the remainder of the year, continuing to escort supplies to the Tongue River and back. He would not encounter any more attacks by the Lakota on his subsequent journeys, but as winter set in, the passage became no less harrowing. "Christmas week I was on the march from Glendive to Tongue River when the cold was most bitter, and when I arrived at Tongue River I found that the thermometer had been for several days more than 50 degrees below zero."[32] The severe cold and frequent snow made the supply runs extremely challenging and it wore Mott down.

From September 1876 to early February 1877, Mott participated in a total of six marches between Glendive and the Tongue River Cantonment. Mott reckoned the total distance traveled back and forth during that time amounted to about 1,350 miles. Despite the hard marches, he never wanted for sustenance, informing his mother in early February that he weighed 168 pounds, a condition rather unusual for him. "I was never so fat as I am now," he wrote.[33]

With the arrival of spring and the rising of the Yellowstone, the army disbanded the Glendive cantonment. Mott briefly relocated his company to the camp on the Tongue River, but after several weeks, the army ordered him back to Fort Abraham Lincoln in Dakota Territory along the Missouri River near Bismarck. En route, Mott picked up the trail of Lame Deer, leader of the Mnikowoju, an ally of Sitting Bull, tracking him to Rainy Butte in Dakota Territory. By the time Mott arrived, however, Lame Deer and his band had already fled, and the trail had run cold.

Mott's role in the principal campaigns of the Great Sioux War ended with his march back to Abraham Lincoln, but the conflict continued well into the summer. Colonel Miles continued to aggressively pursue Sitting Bull and his allies until the Hunkpapa leader escaped into Canada with a large contingent of his followers. Most of the remaining Lakota and Cheyenne surrendered at official army posts and submitted to relocation on one of their reservations. The scarcity of buffalo in Canada would eventually influence Sitting Bull to return to the United States and move onto the Standing Rock reservation with his people five years later. His submission and the surrender of his allies, including Crazy Horse, the Oglala Lakota chief, who would later be killed during an attempted escape from capture, effectively marked the end of the war and of the Lakota's active resistance. The Federal Government could declare they had finally secured the northern Plains while the establishment of Fort Custer and Fort Keogh, the latter being the Tongue River cantonment, did much to instill confidence in white settlers who began moving into the area in increasing numbers.

Within a few days of Mott's arrival at Fort Abraham Lincoln, reports reached him of massive labor unrest across several states back east. With the situation rapidly deteriorating, President Hayes called in the army to support the overwhelmed local militias and police forces. Mott, as part of the troop deployment, assembled his company and headed for Chicago.

11

Fires of Unrest

Mott peered out the window of his room with a heavy heart. It was a late September day and he had just sat down at his desk in the stately Wyoming Valley Hotel to compose one last letter to his mother before assembling his troops to lead them out of the city, bound for Fort Brady near Sault St. Marie in Michigan. The people of Wilkes-Barre had charmed him and Mott lamented having to leave the social scene to return to the drudgery of fort life. "I leave Wilkes-Barre with many regrets for I have had a great deal of amusement in society with the pretty girls," Mott wrote to his mother on hotel stationery.[1] After several years of hard duty on the Plains, Mott's time in Wilkes-Barre, Pennsylvania exposed a weariness in the thirty-nine-year-old Captain who had fully come to realize his want of society. But Mott had not come to Wilkes-Barre for restoration. That Mott found his wants so well fulfilled in the small Pennsylvania city belied the irony that Mott had come here to keep the peace in a city embroiled in labor unrest.

The Panic of 1873, and the so-called "Long Depression" that followed, had been precipitated in large part by the financial failures in the railroad industry—most notably the Jay Cooke-financed Northern Pacific for which Mott had participated in the Yellowstone Expedition four years earlier. As a result of this downturn, railroad workers suffered multiple wage cuts and poor working conditions at the hands of railroad companies across the nation. What small proto-unions or "brotherhoods" that existed to support rail workers were largely disorganized, sometimes illegal, and negatively perceived by the general population. Compounding the fact that workers' representation was so ineffective, high unemployment as a result of the depression meant that labor supply outstripped demand for rail work. This gave employees little leverage and few options for redress as they were easily replaceable.

In 1877, public perception of labor rights was beginning to shift in their favor as most of the major rail companies in the country coordinated a joint ten percent wage cut on all rail workers. This was a devastating setback for workers who were already struggling to get by after several previous pay decreases. With limited choices, workers throughout the country ceased working.

The employees of the B&O Railroad in Martinsburg, West Virginia were the first to go on strike in July. The state called in local militias to quell the protests which had begun to include not only rail workers, but also farmers angered by rising freight costs and other tradesmen fed up with what they perceived as massive corruption in the industry. In solidarity, members of the public at large eventually joined in, and even members of the militias who had been called in to break the strike either defected or simply refused to respond. It quickly became clear that the situation could not be brought under control by local authorities.

Strikes spread like wildfire in over a dozen cities across Pennsylvania, New York, Maryland, Missouri, and Illinois. For three weeks chaos reigned as many of the strikes escalated from a mere work stoppage to violence. Recognizing that local forces were failing to contain the strikes and feeling pressure from state governors and railroad executives to act, President Hayes dispatched federal troops to the cities in turmoil to break the strikes and end the upheaval by force.

Mott arrived first in Chicago. The strikes in the midwestern metropolis had begun several days later than in cities like Baltimore and Pittsburgh. This delay likely contributed to the relatively short duration of the city's riots. It also gave local officials more time to prepare—stocking muskets, readying artillery, and calling up police and militia. On July 24th, workers at the Michigan Central Railroad stopped work after executives refused their demand for a reinstatement of their full wages. The work stoppages spread to other rail companies in the city as laborers in other industries were induced to do the same in solidarity. Despite a few small clashes with police, the initial demonstrations remained peaceful.

The work stoppages continued the next day as workers in more companies outside the rail industry shuttered their doors to join the strike. Police responding to strikers at the Chicago, Burlington, and Quincy roadhouse later that day fired into the crowd after people started throwing stones at them. The police action killed three and injured several more.

By July 26th, additional detachments of federal troops entered the city, which was quickly devolving into chaos as tens of thousands of strikers and protesters hurled stones and other projectiles at police officers. At the Halstead Street Viaduct, an assembled mob assaulted police, even firing pistols, which set off a violent exchange of fire in an event that would become known as the "Battle of the Viaduct." Units of cavalry and regular infantry intervened to quickly disperse the strikers and end the battle. By the end of the 27th, the remaining unrest had been put down and the strike was over. In total, about thirty strikers were killed with many more wounded over the course of the previous few days. For all their efforts, the laborers saw none of their demands met.

With order restored in Chicago, Mott left the city to assist with suppressing the unrest that continued in Pennsylvania. The Keystone State had experienced perhaps the worst violence during the 1877 strikes, particularly in Pittsburgh as it was such a large industrial center and a hub for several rail companies. Mott led his unit to Wilkes-Barre, a small town southwest of Scranton, to assist the local militia and National Guardsmen who were continuing to break strikes throughout the region.

For all the unrest, violence, destruction, and loss of life, nothing changed for workers in the immediate aftermath of the strikes. Wages were not restored and many workers who had prominently participated were fired and quickly replaced. In the long term, however, the strikes catalyzed a nascent labor movement. Though violent strikes would still occur periodically throughout the rest of the century, the events of 1877 emphasized the need for a strong, nationalized labor movement that could lobby the federal government in support of workers' rights and effectively negotiate with employers without resorting to violence. The strikes had also shifted public perception in favor of unionization, making such organizations more palatable overall. Four years later, in 1881, Samuel Gompers would create the Federation of Trades of North America, which would evolve into the American Federation of Labor in 1886. For the rail workers, Eugene V. Debs would emerge as an important leader in labor relations in 1893 when he established the influential American Railway Union.

* * *

Order was quickly restored in Wilkes-Barre and the city remained quiet while troops were present, so much so it felt almost for Mott almost like being on leave. Initially, he camped with his men at a racetrack on the outskirts of town. Their regimental band entertained them, while curious townspeople came out to see them. Mott eventually moved to a room in the grand Wyoming Valley Hotel where he slept in a comfort he hadn't experienced since his time in Europe a few years earlier.[2] Mott also happened to run into "a good many old friends of the [Civil] War."[3] Captain Wilson Matlack of the National Guard's Washington Troop may have been one such acquaintance. Matlack was deployed to Pittsburgh during the riots and may well have been part of the National Guard contingent in Wilkes-Barre as well. Matlack had formerly served as a corporal in the Brandywine Guards under Mott.

In September, Mott received orders to lead his men to Fort Brady near Sault St. Marie, Michigan. He did not welcome the news. Situated in the northeast of Michigan's Upper Peninsula, Mott characterized the post as a "hateful hole."[4] He requested leave hoping to visit New York and spend some time at home in West Chester but was denied. Wilkes-Barre notwithstanding, the last few years had been strenuous for Mott and he had nearly lost his life at Clear Creek. Mott was exhausted and felt his unit had been overworked given the "arduous service" they had just come through in comparison with four other companies of the 22nd which "have not done anything for years."[5] That Mott could not now have a break did not improve his opinion of Fort Brady. On the contrary, all he could do was think longingly of the comfort and pleasantness of Wilkes-Barre. "There was such nice society there and they were so polite to me," he remarked.[6]

Mott would remain at his "hateful hole" of a post for the next year and a half. Militarily, Fort Brady was quiet. But what Mott lacked in action in the field he made up for in a war of letters with his brother. Suspicions of financial mismanagement grew into a vicious battle that would very nearly see the siblings permanently estranged.

12

Cain and Abel

"Mott's home! Mott's home!" cried John Carpenter as he dashed up-stairs. John's father, Frank stared at his son in disbelief. It was late 1863, the Civil War raged on with no end in sight and Frank believed his nephew to still be at the front. No sooner did John return downstairs to greet his cousin properly than he embarrassingly realized his mistake. It was not Mott who had come to their door but his older brother, Frank Hooton, come to pay a visit to his eponymous uncle.[1] The mistake amused the whole family but surprised no one. Mott and his older brother bore a striking resemblance to one another. Born just a year and a half apart, the two Hooton brothers were often mistaken for one another at first glance even amongst family. "He does look so much like you," Mott's mother wrote to Mott.[2] The next day, Mott's cousin, Annie Stellwagen, John Carpenter's sister, wrote to Mott stating very much the same thing, having seen Frank in Philadelphia recently. It was a familiar trope for Mott, who jokingly demurred saying with character-istic self-deprecation, "I guess if [Frank] were to see me, he would not think it much of a compliment...My hair and whiskers stand all ways for Sunday and to crown the whole, I have not washed nor changed shirts, drawers, nor stockings for a month."[3]

Frank wore a beard while in the military but shaved it off upon his return, leaving the thick handlebar mustache he would sport for the rest of his life. Contrary to photographic evidence from this period in his life, Mott likewise preferred this look. The big, bushy beard that appears in his several portraits during the Civil War was the exception rather than the rule. He revived the beard at least once more during his regular army career, but for the people who knew him well, it represented a surprising break from the norm. For their cousin John to have so quickly mistaken the brothers, he had clearly associated a mustache and a clean-shaven jawline with Mott. In fact, the beard was not always a welcome sight amongst his friends. In early 1864, having recently received a copy of Mott's portrait, Mott's friend Bill Bowen wrote to him, shocked to see what he described as an "ambush" of hair on his friend's face. Not only did Bowen disapprove of the look, he believed it a liability if Mott had ever hoped of advancing in the military.

Your vignette is admirably correct, Captain Hooton, but presents much more hair than I suppose a line officer of the first Pennsylvania Reserves would wear. I certainly cannot wonder at your not being promoted while you remain in such an ambush. Get your hair trimmed down to 'the short warrior cut' and shave all but your upper lip and a short military ear whisker, and I'll warrant you your Majority in a month's time.[4]

Although an inordinate number of Mott's extant photographs from his younger years seem to have been taken during those few occasions when he wore the beard, there is at least one portrait of Mott as a young man with just a mustache, which, when compared to a photograph of Frank at a similar age, clearly shows the resemblance that struck family and friends alike.

Despite their physical similarities, the two brothers could not have been more different. On the eve of the Civil War, Frank was already an established lawyer and member of the bar with designs on elected office as District Attorney. The twenty-three-year-old Mott was not engaged in any particular line of work. After the war, Frank settled down to life in West Chester where he sought to make a name for himself,

A striking resemblance: Frank (Left, Detail) & Mott (Right)
Frank: Courtesy of the Chester County History Center, West Chester, PA; Mott: Courtesy of The Civil War Museum of Philadelphia and The Union League Legacy Foundation

while Mott exemplified everything unsettled, living transiently on the Plains and traveling the world. Frank aspired to a higher social rank and married into the Penrose family, one of Philadelphia's oldest and most prominent families. Mott remained a confirmed bachelor. Frank had political ambitions and fancied himself an influential figure in local politics. Mott had little patience for politics and even less so for politicians. Frank was a stalwart member of the Church of the Holy Trinity Episcopal Church on High Street in West Chester, while Mott's views on religion were ambivalent at best. Frank was an inventor and businessman, always looking for the next opportunity to be successful. Mott was more intellectual, a quiet observer of human nature who would sooner experience the cultures of different people around the world than strike it rich—an aspiration he gladly left to his brother.

Focus and ambition drove Frank to be a man of status, respectability, and influence, in both his professional and social lives. He read law and was admitted to the county bar in 1857 at the age of twenty. Within two years, he set his sights on the role of district attorney for Chester County. His bid for the election was unsuccessful at the time, but twice more he campaigned, eventually securing a single term in 1867. Frank used his professional credentials as a springboard to become active in politics and in 1868 he served as the presidential elector for the district helping to install Ulysses S. Grant in the White House.

In the early 1870s, Frank saw his political star begin to rise when he was nominated for auditor general of Pennsylvania. His bid did not pass the primaries, but he continued to serve the Republican party, being named chair of the Chester County Republican Committee in 1876, 1877, and 1878. In 1879, his reputation and notoriety garnered a large boost when he became chairman of the Republican committee at the state level. Under his tenure, the Republican party saw the largest victories in the state since the election of President Grant.[5] He ran for Clerk of the United States House of Representatives in 1881, hoping to ride his success with the state party into national politics, but was defeated.[6] Instead he would devote most of his political career in support of others.

During the Civil War, Frank served as the county's first draft commissioner in 1862. That fall, concurrent with his second failed bid for District Attorney, the 175th PA Regiment elected him as their Lieutenant Colonel. The regiment served in North Carolina and briefly in Maryland during the Peninsula campaigns. He served for only one year and mustered out with the regiment in the fall of 1863, but not before receiving a promotion to Colonel just one month shy of the end of his service. Despite having only served as a colonel for a month, Frank continued to use the rank for the rest of his life, which only added to his social capital. This was a common practice that would not have been held against him, but it is ironic that he should spend one year in military service and for a lifetime reap the benefits and prestige that a

Colonelcy bestowed when it would take his brother, a career military man, almost forty years to attain the same rank.[7]

Frank frequently spent time in Philadelphia and was no stranger to its upper echelons. He was a friend of Isaac Wayne MacVeagh, a Yale-educated lawyer and prominent member of the Chester County bar. In 1866, Frank traveled to New York City where he attended the extravagant wedding of MacVeagh to his second wife, Virginia Cameron, daughter of President Lincoln's Secretary of War, Simon Cameron. Among his many accomplishments, MacVeagh served as the Chester County district attorney, went on to establish a prominent Philadelphia-based law firm, was appointed United States Ambassador to Italy and Turkey, and served as the U.S. Attorney General under Presidents James Garfield and Chester Arthur. MacVeagh's brother, Charles, would later serve as the Secretary of the Treasury under President Taft. As a good friend, Frank would remain a staunch political supporter of MacVeagh.

During his bachelorhood in the latter half of the 1860s, Frank had a reputation as a ladies' man, much like his little brother. He had been engaged in 1862 to a woman named Jennie, but the couple called off the engagement shortly before Frank entered the army. By all accounts, it was the best decision he ever made. Sallie Rogers, a cousin of Mott and Frank, wrote to Mott that "[Jennie] has no heart. She didn't love him. Your mamma was so happy."[8] After the war, Frank was seen about town with several ladies, including Flory Ebbs, with whom Mott had flirted during his convalescence from his Bull Run injury.[9] At one point, Frank even went out to Pittsburgh after a lady, causing his Aunt Sarah Carpenter to remark that "all the girls are crazy about him."[10] When he finally settled down he hit the social jackpot by marrying Anna Rowan Penrose Ralston, daughter of John Rowan Penrose, a prominent Philadelphia shipping merchant from an equally prominent family.

One of the oldest families in Philadelphia, the Penroses descended from Cornish stock and gained their fortune in the shipbuilding trade. Bartholomew Penrose, the progenitor of the family in America, was a one-time partner of such luminaries as William Penn and James Logan.

Anna's great grandfather, Thomas Penrose Jr., served on the Committee of Correspondence in 1774, a body composed of forty-three of Philadelphia's most influential citizens responsible for assembling the First Continental Congress at Carpenter's Hall. Thomas and his wife, Ann, were even present at George Washington's presidential inaugural ball. Anna's grandfather, Charles Penrose, amassed a large fortune in the shipbuilding industry. He went on to serve as a port warden for Philadelphia and superintendent of the Philadelphia Naval Yard in 1812, having been asked to take on the role by William Jones, Secretary of the United States Navy and personal friend of Charles. By any measure, Anna had an enviable pedigree.

Anna married John C. Ralston in 1859. After seven years of marriage and one child – a daughter also named Anna – Ralston passed away and Frank likely met Anna through the prominent Philadelphia connections he had already built. By early twenty-first century standards, the Hootons and the Carpenters would have been considered very securely middle or upper-middle class. But despite their means, it was likely inferior to the level of wealth and breeding of the company Frank kept in the city. If this were ever a source of self-consciousness for Frank, his marriage to Anna Penrose would certainly have legitimized his presence among Philadelphia's social elite.

When Frank and Anna married on June 20, 1870, they settled in West Chester. Mott supported his brother's marriage outwardly and served as a groomsman in the wedding. Privately, however, he disapproved of the match, tantalizing his gossip-loving Aunt Susan shortly after the wedding by cryptically telling her that he would have nothing to do with the Penroses.[11] Much to Susan's chagrin, he did not specify his objection, but from subsequent off-hand remarks Mott would later make, he viewed them as a family of rich, disingenuous snobs referring to them as "an Episcopalian worldly lot of people" and sarcastically opining, "what a nice thing it is to belong to a family like the Penroses who have money...One might as well be dead as to be poor."[12] Mott did not hold his sister-in-law in particularly high esteem and he had no patience for the air of entitled selfishness he believed she exuded.

An entitled niece: Mary "May" Hooton in her younger years (Detail)
Courtesy of the Chester County History Center, West Chester, PA

In 1872, Anna gave birth to a girl, Mary, whom the family called May. She was the only child the couple would have and, as if genetically bred into her, May grew up with the same sense of snobbish entitlement that Mott could never stomach in her mother. "Anna and May are a shabby lot," Mott would later confide to his sister Sallie. "Especially Anna. She is mean and contemptible and selfish. She never gives me any of her big talk. She knows better. I like May a great deal better than her mother."[13] While he seemed to have tolerated his niece more than his sister-in-law, it was not exactly a ringing endorsement.

So Frank was an accomplished lawyer and socialite married to a socially respectable woman, but he was never one to rest on his laurels. In addition to his legal and political exploits, Frank fancied himself an entrepreneur. He speculated in property, owning a few large farms in Chester County, and published several books throughout his career. His *General and Special Road Laws of Pennsylvania* published in 1869 followed by his *Supervisor's Guide: A Manual of the Road Laws of Pennsylvania* in 1872 established Frank as an expert in all legal and regulatory matters of the state's roadways. Years later, in 1900, a keen interest in the Revolutionary War led him to sit on the "Committee of the Baptism of the American Flag in Battle" through which he authored a report entitled: *The Battle of Brandywine: With Its Lines of Battle.*

Frank also harbored an inventive streak, filing two patents in the 1870s. His first patent, granted in 1871 was an "Improvement in Preserving Fruits and Vegetables." It described a method of preserving perishable items, such as meats, fruits, and vegetables, in barrels or containers buried in what he referred to as dry, "air-slaked" lime. The lime, he contended, acted as an absorbent of oxygen and other off-gases that contributed to decomposition, keeping items from decay. Using such a highly caustic material as lime for food preservation meant that the food had to first be placed in a porous jar or container of some sort unless it had thick rinds, in which case it could come in direct contact with the lime.[14] He advertised the rights to manufacture it in a local paper, *The Jeffersonian.* He charged $2.50 for household use in cities and towns, $5.00 for farmers, and between $10-$16 for grocers and fruiters.[15]

His second patent, granted in 1875, was an "improvement in apparatus for lighting and heating houses." Used in gas lamps, the invention consisted of an elevated reservoir of oil attached to a saturated wick that ran through the tube and supplied oil to a secondary wick in the burner, separated with a cut-off valve. The improvement was designed to provide a uniform and steady supply of oil to the wick, without the danger of flooding it, risking explosion.[16] Dubbed "the Hooton lamp" by the local West Chester newspaper that announced the patent, it is unknown if it was ever commercialized.[17] Interestingly enough, the pursuit of safety in heating and lighting a home may have been a preoccupation of Frank's. Sixteen years later, in 1891, when the borough of West Chester installed above-ground wires to electrify the town, Frank circulated what he called an "anti-death" petition to convince the Borough to bury the lines. He believed that live electrical wires exposed to the elements, whether insulated or not, would electrically charge the whole town in inclement weather, turning every wet building and sidewalk into an immense conductor of a deadly current.[18] It was a fear many people shared.

In 1894, another local paper promoted two culinary innovations Frank explored in his earlier years claiming they would have made his name a "household word" if only his law practice hadn't taken up so much of his time. The first, ice cream pie, involved encasing ice cream within a pie dough crust and baking it just long enough to bake the crust without melting the ice cream. The method is difficult to imagine and the paper anticipated a confused reaction by its readers. "Now, don't laugh," the author wrote. "There are hundreds of people right here in West Chester who would delight in an ice cream pie."[19] Frank's second innovation was perhaps even more bizarre: cooked butter. In this concoction, one placed a pound of butter on a spit and spun it quickly over a light heat all while pouring flour on it to form a solid crust without melting the butter. The article doesn't specify how the cooked butter was intended to be used in a meal, merely that it was "one of the needs of the housewife for a good dinner."[20] Sadly, the paper lamented that because of Frank's law practice, these ideas were "lost to the world."[21]

***

The exact nature of the relationship between the brothers is difficult to discern before the mid-1870s. What little correspondence exists between the two men during these years shows only the most basic elements of brotherly affection and is instead comprised mostly of army news and current political affairs. This is hardly indicative of how they felt about each other but given the stark differences in the men they turned out to be, they didn't share a lot in common.

Despite the differences in their personalities, they were at least on good terms. They looked out for each other and helped each other when they could. In the fall of 1862 when Frank first contemplated going into the army after a failed bid for district attorney, Mott offered his advice on the best way to go about joining. "I would advise you to try and [get] a commission in the line for it is no fun being a Private in this army," Mott wrote. "It is, like all armies, a despotism."[22] Frank likewise did his best on numerous occasions to use what political and social influence he was gaining in West Chester and Philadelphia to help advance Mott's career in the army.

That Mott also depended on his brother to help in managing his finances, particularly where his own property was concerned, suggests a high level of trust between them. In the 1870s, Mott owned a one-quarter interest in a store and tenant building on 3rd Street in Philadelphia and he owned at least two farms in Chester County that he leased out to tenant farmers. The extra income provided Mott with additional financial comfort and likely made his voyages abroad possible, but his transient lifestyle in the army was not conducive to effective business management and so he entrusted his older brother with the task of managing his non-military business affairs at his direction. Indeed, Frank took charge of much of the family's financial matters as the resident, educated, white-collar professional that he was. In the waning years of the decade, however, that trust was irrevocably damaged and Mott nearly disowned his brother.

In the mid-1870s, Mott started to suspect that Frank had landed in financial trouble. The nature of Frank's indebtedness is not clear, but it was enough to shake Mott's confidence in his brother's ability to manage money. In 1874, when the army sent him to New Orleans to assist in the peacekeeping efforts following the failed White League Insurrection, Mott stopped in West Chester en route to see his brother and examine his accounts for himself. Taken aback by Mott's impromptu visit, Frank could not produce the account book, claiming he had mislaid it. Instead, he offered to recall from memory all of the money of Mott's he had ever had. The incident did little to bolster Mott's confidence in Frank, but he let the matter drop as the amount Frank recalled squared with Mott's expectations.

Over the next few years, Mott allowed Frank to continue to manage his money, but he never quite trusted him. He began to ask that transaction receipts and certificates of deposit for any business be provided directly to him through Charles Muirhead, the family accountant, or Washington Townsend, Mott's attorney. He similarly advised his mother never to take Frank's word alone when asking about accounts. On one occasion in 1877, Mott sought to sell the two farms he owned in Chester County to settle some of his debts and to raise some money to embark on another large international trip. He directed Frank to have the properties sold at auction but also wrote to his mother to ensure that Maris, Mott's stepfather, would be present to witness the sale and the amount the properties sold for. He also wanted her to make it abundantly clear to Frank that the proceeds of the sale would go towards a bond intended for Maris and Maris alone.[23]

In 1878, frustrated by the way his business was being handled back home, Mott entrusted his cousin, Carpenter "Carp" Rhoads, with $1000 to deposit on his behalf. When he did not receive confirmation that the deposit had occurred, Mott became concerned. "I wonder if I will ever have my business arranged satisfactorily," Mott complained. Meanwhile, Frank's financial problems continued to deteriorate. Although he kept the circumstances to himself, Frank was buckling under the weight of crippling debt. He had little money to his name and what real estate assets he owned could not provide him with sufficient collateral. He owed far more money on his properties than they were worth. Given his brother's situation, Mott suspected Frank was to blame for the lack of accounting and Carp's failure thus far to account for the $1,000 deposit. "What a bad man Frank is and I could let him rot in a poor house before I would give him one cent. I perfectly detest him. He's such a liar and a scoundrel."[24] By that summer, Mott considered his brother ruined and advised his mother not to give him any money to pay his debts unless he was faced with imprisonment, which would bring disgrace to the entire family. "He might just as well be sold out now as at any other time for he is a ruined man," Mott declared. "We may have to support him, but I shall never pay his debts."[25]

A few days later, Frank wrote to Mott asking if he could have the $1,000 in Carp's care to settle his debts and be done with his troubles. The request revealed Frank's awareness of the missing money but suggested he had no further knowledge of it to suspect that it wasn't still in Carp's possession. Mott's anger cooled and he agreed to let Frank have the money. Frank approached Carp to secure the funds only to discover the reason why Mott had never been given any confirmation regarding its deposition. Over half of it was gone.

John Carpenter Rhoads, known in the family as Carp, was Mott and Frank's first cousin. He was the son of their Uncle Tommy and Aunt Em. Carp had a hand in managing the family's 3rd Street property in Philadelphia, which consisted of a store on the ground floor and three additional floors of rented rooms. The property was jointly owned by Mott's immediate family in equal shares. Carp owned no part of it but was involved in the running of it. When Frank approached Carp about the money, his cousin claimed he had to use a portion of the money—approximately $550 of it—to pay the mortgage. Upon further investigation, Frank discovered that Carp had also collected an advance from all the tenants, charged the family a $100 fee to do so, and granted a few of the tenants unauthorized discounts on their rent. Carp also brought up a bill for $200 for the cost of repairing a pipe in the basement, not realizing that Frank had already been quoted less than $100 to do so. Frank suspected that Carp had pocketed the difference.

Mott believed Frank regarding the conduct of their cousin, perhaps in part because Mott's mother had already been questioning Carp's integrity on her own. "Your surmise about Carp is correct," Mott wrote to his mother in early July 1878. "He is a liar and a scoundrel. He has been living on you, your rent, and my thousand dollars."[26] Curiously, Frank asked Mott not to write to Carp about any of it and let him handle it. Carp must have been desperately poor to have acted as he had, Frank reasoned, and that any note from Mott indicating that his treachery had become known would cause nothing but anguish and accomplish nothing.[27] It was ironic advice coming from Frank, who arguably had the most to lose by Carp's actions. After all, he had depended on that money to stay financially solvent himself. Frank may have simply not wanted Mott to get Carp's version of events so as not to get caught in a lie. But, if Carp was as hard up as he claimed, perhaps Frank genuinely felt sorry for him. Given his own circumstances, if anyone could be sympathetic to a man who had fallen on financially hard times, it would have been Frank. Whatever the reason, Mott acquiesced and did not contact his cousin, but it did not prevent him from continuing to believe Carp was a scoundrel and a "miserable wretch." However, if Frank thought the Carp affair would take some of the heat off of him, he was sorely mistaken.

The portion of the $1000 Frank obtained from Carp gave him a stay of execution from his creditors, but it far from solved his indebtedness altogether. In a turn towards victimhood in explaining his financial woes, Frank began to reveal the real causes of his money problems as he saw them. The first hit to his personal wealth followed a $6,050 judgment brought against him via Mott's lawyer Washington Townsend likely concerning a property transaction between the brothers. Frank suggested that Mott could not appreciate the devastating effect the judgment had had on both his reputation and financial stability. "It was as disastrous to my career here as a businessman as it would have been to you in the army had someone filed charges against you for conduct unbecoming an officer and a gentleman."[28] Frank was very careful to not directly blame his brother for his ruination. "I don't suppose for one minute you would have done anything to break me up," Frank wrote to Mott, "I have told everybody that you would be as slow to break me up as I would be to disgrace you in the army."[29] It was a calculated strategy. Frank knew that to compare his plight with the disgrace of being accused of an offense worthy of court martial and perhaps a dishonorable discharge from the army would strike a nerve with his brother who valued his integrity, honor, and proper military conduct above all else. Instead, Frank explicitly deflected blame onto Mott's lawyer, Washington Townsend, suggesting that the lawyer, in a stroke of political vengeance, had purposefully manipulated Mott into bringing the judgment up at a time when he knew it would destroy Frank's standing in the community. Frank had earlier opposed Townsend's bid for congress in favor of his friend, Wayne McVeagh, and therefore believed Townsend must have harbored some bitterness towards him. Whether his goal was to plant a seed of distrust in Mott against his lawyer or if he believed Townsend to be so vindictive, Frank nonetheless noted that Townsend undoubtedly "rejoiced at the humbling of a dangerous opponent."[30]

Though Frank had outwardly absolved his brother of culpability in his troubles, Mott read the accusation between the lines. Mott may have let Carp off of the hook, but his suspicions surrounding his brother remained. He still wanted to know why Frank had never given him an account of his financial troubles earlier. Less than a month passed before Mott continued to hound his brother for information, frustrated over the delays, excuses, and obfuscations. Finally, on July 24, 1878, Frank wrote Mott a lengthy letter which, in Frank's eyes, finally went to the heart of the matter. All of his financial misfortune stemmed not from poor business deals, but from the last will and testament of their beloved Aunt Susan.

In the spring of 1870, Susan approached Frank with the suggestion of purchasing a home that was for sale on Miner Street in West Chester. He was not yet married and did not have the money, but she said she would take out a $2000 mortgage on her share of the store in Philadel-phia and loan it to him to buy the property. Instead of making Frank pay her back, Susan told him she would take it out of his inheritance when she passed. Frank agreed to the terms and acknowledged that he would receive $2000 less than Mott in the will.[31] Frank proceeded with the purchase of the house on the verbal understanding that Susan would be allowed to live there, paying $100 per month, while Frank furnished the house and paid all the household bills. He also agreed to leave a room available for Mott whenever he came back into town.

When Susan died two years later, her will had indeed been updated to reflect the extra $2000 granted to Mott. Frank was shocked to discover, however, that Susan also left Mott an additional $1000 in the codicils of the will. What's more, the family claimed that the $2000 loan for the house still had to be paid back and that the extra money allotted to Mott in the will did not qualify as forgiveness of the loan. "I knew that was the end of me unless something else turned up," Frank wrote to Mott.[32] Frank felt sorely used by his family, writing "I never had any genuine ambition after that. I felt that in some unaccountable measure my whole family had turned against me."[33] Despite his grievances, Frank maintained a self-righteous commitment to his honor, empha-sizing that despite the inequity of the situation and what it meant for his own solvency, he resolved to pay his debts:

I have nothing to say. No offer to make. Nothing. I simply know that never, in any way, shape, or form did I ever, either by night or day, waking or sleeping, try to induce or in any way agree to accept from Aunt Susan one cent more than she was to give you. Never. I have always dealt with perfect fairness with everybody. In politics, religion, business, and everything else. I have never taken advantage of anybody. I have always tried to have my word as good as my bond. And always endeavored to pay every man, every cent I owed him.[34]

By contrast, Frank accused Mott of taking advantage of his brother's kindness only to turn his back on him, reminding Mott who had bailed him out of his financial distress while in Europe. "…I worked night and day to raise money and send it to you," Frank recalled. "Your condition prevented me from sleeping at nights. When your letters came, the only thanks you gave me were curses."[35]

Typical of Frank's defense, his explanations were crafted labyrinths of facts and figures all leading to the inescapable conclusion that he had been wronged. He had been stewing over the issue for quite some time and his frustration and sense of betrayal were palpable. Through his eyes, so many of his accomplishments—his books, his inventions, his law practice, and his political aspirations—were all feeble attempts at repairing the damage to his reputation and livelihood caused by Susan's will and Mott's apathy.

Mott was unmoved. Frank's candor only enraged him further. The idea that his brother would play "the injured man" and squabble about money over the grave of the woman who raised them offended Mott deeply. Whether or not the will was unjustly inequitable, interpreted improperly, or updated inaccurately to reflect any verbal agreements which may or may not have been made, the idea that Frank could blame the entire ruination of his personal economy on their aunt's will stoked Mott's considerable temper. "After I had given him a thousand dollars he turned around and had the cheek to write me that letter. I despise him. He is a liar," Mott wrote to his mother two months later.[36] Mott did not believe a word of Frank's martyrdom and had become convinced that his brother would say and do anything to keep his head above water, even if that meant bringing his whole family down with him. Concerned for his mother and stepfather, who still depended on Frank for financial management, Mott spent the next year trying to protect them from Frank's wheeling and dealing. By the end of 1878, Maris' health was beginning to fail and Mott feared Frank might try to take advantage of his mother's emotional vulnerability during that trying time.

I have been thinking a good deal about your affairs and I fear that Frank will get all of your property eventually unless something is done to prevent it. You will take notice in reading his letter which I sent you yesterday that he considers himself an injured man and I know he will take everything he can get his hands on. He will go on running into debt as long as your property lasts.[37]

Mott began regularly warning his mother not to trust her oldest son and to only work through impartial, third parties for any transactions. He even took steps to purchase Maris' share in the Philadelphia store to ensure Frank would not try to go after it.

The trials and tribulations surrounding Susan's will continued the following year when Mott received a notice stating that a collateral inheritance tax on the estate amounting to $400 had never been paid. An annoyed, yet jaded Mott claimed to have paid it seven years earlier, but suspected his brother simply stole it to pay off some other debt declaring matter-of-factly to his mother "I believe he would rob if he had the chance without being discovered."[38] Still, it was the last straw for Mott. In June 1879, Mott wrote to his brother saying they were "quits forever." "I shall never cross his threshold except in case of mortal illness or death," Mott vowed to his mother, "and if he gives me any more trouble about the property I shall denounce him in West Chester as a scoundrel. Think of him cheating his own brother over the very grave of his aunt."[39]

Things only got worse in late August 1879 when yet another statement regarding Susan's will arrived in the mail from Townsend showing an outstanding indebtedness of $5,397.47 against the estate. The amount was disclosed in the will, but Mott believed he had already paid his half of that bill many years prior. He asked Townsend to investigate the matter and if necessary, file suit against Frank for the money. Mott refused to pay the bill a second time and had had enough of dealing with his brother.

He is the greatest scoundrel I have ever known. I shall never darken his doors again as long as I live. If he had been an honest man, I would have had sufficient money to support me out of the army instead of tramping about at my time of life (forty-two years of age) and living in a tent. I hope to see him destitute! How I do hate him! I could almost put him to death. Such a liar![40]

Mott had always had a quick temper, but the fire in this particular letter reveals a man at the end of his rope in more ways than one. He had been encamped in tents all autumn in Animas, Colorado overseeing the construction of a new post in an area more remote than any previous assignment and his nerves were already frayed. Mott's charge that Frank's actions had somehow trapped him in the army stemmed more from anger than reality. It is difficult to believe he would have had no means or opportunity to leave and take up a different line of work had he so desired, even accounting for the financial struggles Frank had dragged him into. Nevertheless, whether Frank deserved such harsh words, he cannot be entirely absolved of Mott's ire.

In the ensuing years, Frank's troubles followed him as he continued to make one bad deal after another, desperately robbing Peter to pay Paul for his debts. In early 1884, Frank's own mother told him that he had earned a bad name in West Chester. The allegation cut Frank deeply and only fueled his feelings of betrayal. He wrote his mother a similar letter to the one he had sent Mott years earlier laying out once again his claim that Susan's will was the source of all his problems. His explanation proved no more effective with his mother than it had with his brother. It must have been heartbreaking for Ann to witness the unraveling of her eldest son and the rift it had caused between her boys, but she held firm. Within three days, Ann ordered her son to hand over power of attorney and any other documents related to her personal business to her son-in-law, Morton Chase. Four days later, Frank wrote another long note to his mother defending his actions regarding a litany of business transactions that had gone sour recently. He defended the legality of a transaction with his cousin John which ended up in court; claimed he was cheated out of money he had borrowed from Collins West, husband of his paternal Aunt Rebecca, which made him unable to repay his uncle; he made a passing reference to an indebtedness to Matthew Quay, political ally and future US Senator from Pennsylvania, which he evaded by calling it a private matter that he would not discuss; and once again he reiterated his objections to his aunt's will.[41] Frank even owed his mother money, which he claimed he was attempting to raise by any means necessary, including selling some mill machinery he owned, but first, he had to raise enough money to save his house:

I owe $224 interest on my house on the 1ˢᵗ of next April. If I cannot pay that interest I will be sold out of house and home and then Anna and May will have to go to Anna's mother I presume and, well the Lord knows where I will go. I don't know, but I am going to try and raise that $224 and save my house. If I can get through this summer I will be all right.[42]

The letter is a testament to Frank's sorry situation but did little to convince him of reconsidering any personal responsibility in his situation. He continued to claim that his misfortunes were the fault of others while clinging to the righteous resolution that he would always pay his debts. Frank did, however, allow himself a little freedom to expose the depths of his pain. "This is what I do not understand- and never have understood," Frank declared.

I cannot see how you could back [Mott] up in taking away from me all of Aunt Susan's money. And I cannot see why. If I make an error in giving him the account I did, there should be anything wrong in his seeing it or in trying to see it.[43]

The family's seeming lack of support truly hurt Frank. His financial woes had been a tangled web for the better part of a decade and everything he did to try to help himself got him further and further into debt, but the loss of his family's faith in him perhaps stung the worst.

As the years went on, Frank earned a measure of forgiveness from his family. The relationship between the brothers had been strained and Mott continued to keep him at arms-length where his finances were concerned, but he did not abandon Frank. The insults and insinuations regarding Frank's integrity that came out of Mott's rage-induced tirades were perhaps a little unfair, though characteristic of Mott's flashing hot temper and rush to character judgments. Frank never set out to pursue anything intentionally illegal or unethical. The mere fact that his schemes and plans continuously fell apart and that to his genuine surprise, people perceived his actions to be utterly wrong suggests that he was not a calculating fiend carefully plotting ways of getting rich at the expense of other people. The complete transparency of his questionable business dealings illustrates a certain naiveté. When the bottom inevitably fell out, his wallet was not the only thing to be injured. These failures seriously damaged his pride and, in his embarrassment, he desperately clung to any excuse that could help him save face and preserve his own good name. His long, defensive, letters to his family were the result. They are carefully crafted narratives that make him appear blameless with a logic that can't quite be followed. They are at once vague in circumstance yet flush with minutiae to confuse and exhaust the reader into simply assuming the veracity of their author rather than trying to unravel the labyrinthian situation for themselves. Frank simply could not admit to his family and friends that his misfortunes were of his own doing. He probably could not admit it to himself. The genuine sense of hurt and frustration that hover between the lines of his correspondence show a man who truly believed the world was against him. Mott was wrong to say Frank "played" the injured man. Frank truly believed he was an injured man.

Frank was a man motivated by success—materially, professionally, and socially. He might have made a very good, stable living simply as a town lawyer, but it just was not enough. When he ran for district attorney, he had only been a practicing lawyer for two years. His brief tenure in the army granted him an impressive rank he could leverage for his whole life. Even his marriage, if one believes Mott's cynical take on it, was a way of elevating his social status. Frank may have genuinely loved Anna, but the implications of marrying into a family like the Penroses could not have been lost on him. His political activities, his publications, his property speculation, and his inventions and patents all show his drive to do more and to be more. In that, he was a product of his time.

Frank's ambition represented the epitome of the late 19th century middle-class entrepreneur. Advice manuals about business during this time lauded the virtues of the entrepreneur and even went so far as to suggest that to remain in one position without constantly striving for more signaled a personal failure almost as severe as financial bankruptcy. What's more, middle-class men like Frank during the so-called Gilded Age enshrined their very masculinity in their ability to successfully pursue a plethora of diverse business enterprises. Whether or not Frank ever read such advice manuals, the values they extolled would have been an internalized part of the societal discourse with which he was associated. For nineteenth-century men like Frank, wheeling and dealing was a way of life.[44] When their deals worked, they felt unstoppable as if they had reached the epitome of manhood. This idea of the self-made man was a persistent voice in American society made famous in rags-to-riches stories like those of Horatio Alger. Nearly all of Alger's works follow the same formula of a young boy from very humble beginnings who, through moral fortitude, hard work, and determination, grows up to become a successful pinnacle of middle-class respectability. However, much like many Americans in the twenty-first century struggle with a barrage of unattainable cultural prescriptions of the ideal life, the belief in the self-made man narrative in the nineteenth century was similarly unrealistic. When men like Frank fell on hard times, it was a blow not only to their wallets but to their very identity as men.

Frank always attributed his financial troubles to forces beyond his control, namely the unfair treatment he claimed to have received in regard to his Aunt Susan's will, but he may also have been a victim of the economic climate at the time. The Panic of 1873 and the subsequent depression primarily affected the banking and industrial sectors, but, as with any integrated economy, the systemic downturn led to a decrease in property value. Frank owned several properties during this time on which he owed more money than they were worth. It was often his inability to liquidate his mortgaged property that prevented him from paying his debts, compounding the implications of his business speculation failures.

Many men who struggled to keep their heads above water at this time began to realize that hard work and ambition did not necessarily guarantee success and, by extension, failure did not necessarily indicate a flawed personal character, regardless of the prevailing cultural ideas to the contrary. Men cut down by the financial panics of 1873 and 1893 or who had otherwise fallen on hard times, wrote sincere letters to some of the wealthiest businessmen in the country, such as Andrew Carnegie, J.P. Morgan, and John D. Rockefeller, asking for their help in securing employment. These begging letters poured in by the tens of thousands, though the majority of them went unanswered. The letters were remarkably formulaic in structure. They asked not for charity, but for gainful employment. In so doing, they sought to emphasize their personal integrity and character as a way to reassure their prospective employer that their current condition was a function of forces beyond their control, as opposed to an inherent deficiency in their character, and that given the opportunity, they could be successful, productive members of society.[45]

Frank's letters to his family share many of the same attributes as these begging letters. Though not written as a means of securing employment, his letters were designed to defend his character and reputation in light of his utter failure. Whether or not Frank blamed any one person or just an unfortunate series of events, he continually emphasized that the fault was not his. Still, while Frank believed himself to be the victim of circumstance, his penchant for naively getting involved in ethically questionable business deals does not exonerate him of the hand he played in his own fate. He got caught up in the societal expectations of the Gilded Age middle-class entrepreneur. He may also have suffered from the same restless spirit that plagued his brother, though in his case, he channeled that energy into business and deal-making rather than wanderlust and adventure. Whatever his motivations, Frank never quite learned his lesson. His never-ending quest to acquire material wealth and social prestige continued to severely cloud his judgment. The next time he found himself in trouble it would cost him more than money. It would cost him his freedom.

In 1888, a young man named James Neely engaged Frank to write his will. His father, Robert Neely had amassed a sizeable estate from many years as a banker and a director of the National Bank of Chester County. When the elder Neely died in 1884, he bequeathed his entire estate to his son James to be held in trust until James' twenty-first birthday. When James finally took possession of his inheritance in 1888, he squandered nearly half of it before going to see Frank, though what remained was still a sizeable amount.

Frank sat his new client down to learn more about potential beneficiaries and the intended disposition of the estate but was quickly taken aback to discover that Neely intended to leave the bulk of his remaining fortune, nearly $70,000—or nearly $2 million in early twenty-first-century money—to Frank. It was a highly unusual arrangement, particularly since Frank and Neely had no personal relationship with one another apart from Frank perhaps being an acquaintance of his father as a prominent citizen of the town.[46] There is no record of the subsequent exchange, but if Frank protested, the lure of getting back on top financially likely drowned out any qualms he may have felt.

There is no evidence to suggest Neely was ill or that he knew he was not long for the world when he had Frank draft his will, but on May 25th, 1889, James Neely passed away in Philadelphia at just twenty-two years of age. Frank, as an article in the *Times* noted, had finally become a "man of property."[47] Papers in both Philadelphia and Pittsburgh carried the story of the unusual bequest and it generated a fair bit of chatter around West Chester.[48] Though Frank had inherited a large sum of money for 1889, there was more to the will than was left to the lawyer. Frank had not just been made beneficiary in the will, he was also its executor and so it was his duty to see to it that all debts against the estate were paid and that the other beneficiaries noted in the will received their bequests. Under the terms of the will, some small donations were left to the West Chester Library and the Episcopal church, while $15,000 was to be held in trust for others. One-third of that sum was to be held in trust for a man by the name of John Steiner for the remainder of his life and then to his grandchildren. For the remaining 10,000 dollars, the will directed Frank to invest it on behalf of Ellen

Bleloch, Neely's significant other. The will granted Ellen the proceeds of the investment for the rest of her life and on her decease, half the principal amount was to be donated to charities of Ellen's choice and the other half to her heirs. Had Frank left well enough alone, he would have been well set, but his quest for wealth and prestige bordered on addiction. What Neely had told Frank about Miss Bleloch inspired a scheme in Frank's mind to buy out her bequest. The arrangement would be his undoing.

Born Ellen Virginia Jones in 1863, Bleloch had gained a reputation in her late teens and early twenties for being "addicted to habits of intemperance."[49] In other words, she was an alcoholic. In 1884, she met and married Henry Bleloch. Henry was well aware of Ellen's "habits," but believed marriage could reform her. He was wrong. After only a few weeks of marriage, Henry left her to seek his fortunes in the West, convinced that Ellen would not change her ways. Three years later, Ellen met James Neely, then only nineteen years old and five years her junior. The two formed an intimate relationship and lived together in the home of her mother, Anna Jones.[50] The fact that Anna would allow for such a living arrangement, particularly at that time, is curious. That Neely had to live with the Joneses at all was additionally odd as evidenced by the level of wealth reflected in his estate only two years later. Nevertheless, Ellen told her mother she had every intention of marrying James as soon as she could get a divorce from Henry.

Neely was also aware of Ellen's addiction. Locking up his financial bequest to her in a life trust to be administered by Frank was his way of saving her from herself. He knew that given $10,000 outright, she would squander it to fund her bad habits. Allowing her instead to live off the investment proceeds of her bequest at least assured her a source of income for the rest of her life even if she never reformed. It was a noble gesture if only Neely had chosen a more scrupulous man to manage it. In April 1890, after Neely had died, Frank approached Ellen and offered to pay her $2,000 cash for her life interest in the half of the inheritance designated for her heirs. For any clear-thinking individual, it was a shoddy deal—trading $5,000 for $2,000—but, guided by her alcoholism,

Ellen accepted the deal. Her mind focused on the instant gratification the lump sum could give her over the much smaller, though stable income stream spread out over the course of her life. In September of the following year, Frank proposed to buy the interest in the other half of the inheritance – the sum designated for charitable donation – for an additional 1,000 dollars. Once more Ellen agreed.[51]

Shortly after Neely's death, Ellen's estranged husband returned and attempted to patch up his marriage. Henry had never met Frank and it is unlikely that he knew the particulars of his wife's inheritance, or at least the transactions giving it all away to Frank. Nevertheless, the reunion was short-lived. Henry found he still could not stomach his wife's poor habits and left her once again.

Frank felt on top of the world. The debts that had plagued him for the past decade were solved and he had great plans for his newfound wealth. He purchased an old homestead in Honeybrook in northwestern Chester County formerly owned by the Suplee family and went about turning the home into a hotel. He even purchased an expensive hack to transport guests from the local train station to the hotel.[52] He sank much of his money into the venture, but there was one thing he hadn't counted on. At only twenty-eight years old, Ellen Bleloch died.

Within days of her passing, Ellen's death notice in the local papers identified her as the husband of the late James Neely, a legal impossibility as her marriage to Henry Bleloch, though estranged, had never been officially dissolved. After learning that Frank had been involved in Neely's will, Henry wrote to Frank at once to inform him of the illegitimacy of the reported marriage between his wife and James Neely. Henry's only goal in writing Frank was for the benefit of other potential beneficiaries of Neely who might have more legitimate claims as his heirs. There was no way for him to know at that point that he had any stake whatsoever in anything bequeathed to his late wife. Frank, on the other hand, became nervous. He didn't want to take any chances that the arrangements he made with Ellen could be challenged by members of her own family, particularly as he had already spent so much of it on his debts and the hotel. He needed to get this newly resurfaced husband, her closest heir, to validate the transactions and secure the inheritance for himself. Frank wrote to Bleloch, thanking him for bringing the matter to his attention and asking that he travel to West Chester as soon as possible to meet with him. Bleloch obliged and arrived in West Chester from Philadelphia on the evening of November 6, 1891.

The meeting with Frank left Bleloch somewhat bewildered. When he arrived at Frank's office, the lawyer immediately showed him the two assignments between Ellen Bleloch and himself detailing the transactions which passed the rights of her inheritance to him. Frank then called on a colleague, R. T. Cornwell, to come to the office as an impartial third party to interview Bleloch and determine if he planned to push any claim to the inheritance. Bleloch, still unaware he held any right to the bequest, simply stated that he had not decided to explore any potential claims to any inheritance. On the contrary, the marriage had so disgraced the Bleloch family that the young man's parents considered any inheritance of Ellen's from Neely "the price of adultery" and didn't want their son to have anything to do with it. Although it seemed unlikely that Bleloch would contest Frank's purchase of Ellen's inheritance, Frank left nothing to chance. He casually informed Bleloch of an Act of Assembly from 1855 declaring that if a man unjustly deserted his wife, he forfeited any rights of inheritance he might otherwise have claimed on her estate. Bleloch had left Ellen not once, but twice. Frank likely knew that the circumstances of Bleloch's desertion would be seen as justifiable under the law and not subject to the 1855 Act, but he was clearly trying the case before Bleloch knew there was one.[53]

Blinded by his anger towards his in-laws for enabling adultery and Influenced by his parents who considered any inherited assets from Ellen to be tainted, Bleloch signed an agreement that Frank had drawn up, officially abandoning any possible claims he or Ellen's family had to his wife's inheritance. The agreement effectively acknowledged Frank as the lawful owner of Ellen's bequest for use however he saw fit. Frank breathed a sigh of relief and believed the matter was closed.

Later that month, Bleloch learned the true nature of Ellen's inheritance. He discovered that he did have a very solid claim to the money that neither Frank nor his impartial colleague Cornwell had made suitably clear. Although he still wanted nothing to do with the money, Bleloch had moderated his opinions regarding Ellen's family. Bleloch made a new agreement assigning his rights to Anna, Ellen's mother, and in so doing denied the legitimacy of the agreement he had signed with Frank on the grounds that he was not provided adequate knowledge of the situation to have made an informed decision.[54]

With Frank standing by his arrangement with Ellen and refusing to hand over the money, Anna Jones took him to court. The judge ruled that Frank could not have any title to the inheritance since Ellen did not own full title to the money herself. The money bequeathed to Ellen was limited as a life interest, meaning she only held title to the proceeds of the invested money while she lived. Under the provisions of Neely's will, the money was not Ellen's to direct as part of her estate, it instead would transfer to the next of kin, in this case, her husband or, barring his refusal to accept it, her family. As such, Frank had only purchased Ellen's rights to the earned dividends on the invested money only so long as they were hers to manage. Her death nullified that arrangement.[55]

Frank likely realized the legal limitations on Ellen's ability to sell her rights indefinitely, otherwise, there would have been no reason for him to induce Bleloch to relinquish his rights, and by extension the rights of his in-laws. He knew the receipts and written agreements with Ellen were insufficient by themselves. In an appeal, Frank attempted to mitigate the damage by claiming that the $2000 he had paid Ellen could count as a lump sum payout from the trust account, and thus her family was therefore only entitled to the difference of three thousand dollars rather than the full five thousand, but neither the initial judge nor the appellate judge saw it that way. Moreover, the judges each upheld the challenge to the validity of the agreement that Henry Bleloch had signed at Frank's office that November night. That an agreement had already been written and ready for signing convinced the judges that Frank, as an experienced and shrewd lawyer, perfectly understood the situation and willfully took advantage of Bleloch's naiveté by purposefully withholding information and giving him no time to deliberate. In early 1893, the court ordered Frank to pay Anna Jones the full five thousand dollars owed to her per the stipulations laid out in James Neely's will. The judge ordered the money due by March, but Frank did not pay it. He pleaded with the judge to give him more time admitting that the money was tied up in his real estate. The judge granted the extension so long as he put up a bond as security. Mrs. Jones' lawyer, M. Hampton Todd, agreed to the extension in exchange for the bond. Frank quickly hurried out of the courthouse speaking to no one. Todd, however, spoke with a journalist for *The Times* telling him he understands it takes time to put affairs in order, but was convinced Frank had the money. "We don't want to reflect on him in any way," Todd offered generously, "but he doesn't seem to care much about a court order, does he?"[56] Indeed, one particular report claimed Frank was openly defiant of the order claiming he would "rot in jail" before paying the judgment.[57]

Despite suggestions in the press of open defiance, Frank's refusal to pay the amount awarded to Anna Jones was not borne of principle. He simply no longer had it. After paying his debts, he had sunk the bulk of his money in the Honeybrook property and like many of his earlier financial investments, this one was not providing the return he had hoped. In fact, he had sunk into debt yet again. Todd had originally offered to take a mortgage on the real estate as payment of the judgment, but Frank declined without disclosing that he already owed some $8,000 mortgage on the property and it was facing sheriff's sale after being fought over by multiple creditors. The remaining portion of the property, he had "sold" to his wife to protect it from sale by the Sheriff hoping he would be able to use that portion to pay the judgment.[58]

Months went by and still Frank could not produce the money. Mrs. Jones' lawyer began to do some investigating of his own and discovered the dismal state of Frank's affairs. Todd appealed to the court to bring him back before the judge when he realized the money would never materialize. On August 2, Frank went back before the orphans' court to respond to Todd's findings. He had no choice but to admit that what Todd had learned was true. With no other option, the judge charged

Frank with contempt and committed him to Moyamensing prison until he either produced the money or gamble that an appeal to the court of common pleas would find him an insolvent debtor and clear him of the obligation. However, if he failed in the latter case, he risked being charged with embezzlement.[59]

Most of Frank's acquaintances believed his circumstances to be the tragic result of an honest miscalculation rather than deliberate chicanery. Frank was "careless about his affairs and that he often overlooked the small details of his transactions," an unnamed source close to Frank reported to the local paper.[60] As the lawyer for the plaintiff, Todd offered a more suspicious opinion of Frank several months later telling the *Daily Local News* that "I do not know much about Colonel Hooton's affairs, but I think they are somewhat complicated. There are a number of executions against him, but these could have been fixed and the matter between him and Mrs. Jones settled."[61] Todd goes on to note that much of Frank's property had been put in his wife's name as a deliberate attempt to protect those assets from his creditors. Todd felt no sympathy for the financially struggling man. "Colonel Hooton has no one to blame but himself for his present position. He was given ample time to turn over the funds entrusted to his care and I think that nothing but stubbornness prevents him from doing it now."[62]

Whether willful or naive, the result was the same — Frank's reputation in the community was all but ruined. A man who had so carefully crafted his life to be a figure of class and distinction now sat in prison, hopelessly in debt. An article in *The Times* reminded the reader of his great success as chairman of the Republican State Committee over which he presided amidst one of the largest victories ever seen in the state for the Republicans. "This made Hooton temporarily a big man," *The Times* wrote, "but he soon relapsed into obscurity."[63]

No doubt Frank considered himself the injured party or the victim of circumstance as he always had, but he could count himself lucky that public opinion would show him mercy.

The troubled lawyer: Francis C. Hooton in his later years (Detail)
Courtesy of the Chester County History Center, West Chester, PA

On August 2, 1893, the *Daily Local News* devoted a considerable amount of space (nearly three columns) to his case. Entitled "Colonel Hooton's Troubles," the piece paints the picture of a tragic hero fallen from grace. Opening with a sympathetic exposition of his current predicament, the author establishes Frank as a generous and big-hearted man who had demonstrated his kindness to people many times over during his legal career. In the political arena, the article recounts the nearly unprecedented majority with which he won the chairmanship of the Republican party in 1879, dubbing him the "Honest Farmer." Statements from several of his friends follow and while they all admit to his flawed business acumen, they nevertheless emphasize his virtues as a decent and honest man who was simply a victim of his naivete.[64]

Frank remained in Moyamensing for a few weeks, being released on August 25, 1893. He settled with Todd, Anna Jones' lawyer via a mortgage bond on the portion of the Honeybrook farm listed in his wife's name. The judge in the case subsequently suspended the charges of contempt of court for not paying when so ordered. His confinement had been hard on him and the more cynical reports of the case suggested that it was those conditions that broke what they saw as Frank's calculated stalemate with the court. "His fortitude did not sustain his courage," one paper remarked when learning of the eventual deal struck with Todd.[65] Friends and acquaintances, however, appeared to stick by him as a large retinue attended the arrival of the train that brought Frank home from prison, "I feel somewhat weak after my incarceration," Frank told well-wishers after his release. "I had not been used to living on soup and boiled rice, but I will be all right in a day or so."[66]

Neither Mott nor the rest of his family addressed the events surrounding the Neely/Bleloch case and Frank's subsequent imprisonment, but it likely came as little surprise. They certainly did not come to his rescue, despite Mott declaring years earlier that debtors' prison would be one of the few circumstances to break their estrangement. Then again, Frank might not have accepted assistance if it were freely given as the newspapers alluded to the fact that he had turned down offers of help from several of his friends and associates.

Mott had extricated himself from Frank's affairs long before the incident with Neely and Bleloch. It was 1879 when Mott severed the remaining business dealings he had with Frank, though the damage to their relationship would last longer. Shortly before leaving Michigan in the spring of that year, Mott advised his mother to think carefully about entrusting Frank with any future business and suggested she always consult a lawyer.

I want to impress it upon you that... when Frank is in trouble he will say anything and if you are not careful he will ruin you all. He is capable of it...I shall never give him another cent. My conduct towards him in business matters is the same as if he were a stranger. What a miserable man he is. I expect to see the day when Anna will return to her mother's house for he looks to me as if he drank.[67]

Mott would eventually reconcile with Frank, but the damage to the relationship was severe. The aspersions cast towards Frank would continue in Mott's correspondence home. Interestingly, Mott began referring to his brother more formally as Francis in future correspondence, further signaling a certain distance in their fraternal relationship.

In the ensuing months, a new posting came to preoccupy his mind with matters other than his brother's financial mismanagement and his mother's financial protection. Under the command of Major Alfred Hough, Mott left Fort Brady in the spring of 1879 bound for Fort Gibson in the Indian Territory where a specious claim of open land had brought an influx of illegal white settlers to the area. The Boomers, as these invading settlers were nicknamed, threatened the fragile sovereignty of the Native American tribes in the territory.[68] The movement signaled a new chapter in Mott's career as his orders would be less about enforcing the government's displacement of the country's indigenous population and more about managing the white settlers who replaced them.

Tarnished reputation: Frank Hooton's post-scandal political efforts
met with little success
Philadelphia Inquirer, January 12, 1904

13

Paranoia in the Animas Valley

For a small, remote town in the Colorado Rocky Mountains, Pagosa Springs threw a good party. The food was fresh, the drinks plentiful, and the music sweet. As the townspeople invited the officers to dance, Mott looked out over the ball unexpectedly impressed by the warm welcome and caliber of society this backwater village had offered him. It was a pleasant respite from the chill in the November air outside. Suddenly, above the crowd across the room, an argument broke out and a man was thrown down the stairs. Shortly thereafter another gentleman, out of nowhere, discharged his pistol into the air for no apparent reason, or at least not one anyone cared about. None of the villagers batted an eye as they continued to dance while Mott and the other officers stood astonished by the utter lack of response to the violent disruptions. Evidently, the townspeople were used to it. It wasn't a ball in Pagosa Springs if someone wasn't knocked unconscious, Mott supposed. In other posts, Mott would have thumbed his nose at such behavior, but here in the depths of the Animas Valley, he simply shrugged, smiled to himself at the expression of local color, and concluded, "such is life on the frontier."[1] Though the local Coloradan society was a bit rougher than Mott was used to, it was still society, which was more than Mott had experienced since leaving Fort Brady in April. The entire party could have broken out into a brawl and Mott would have preferred it to the summer he had just spent in Kansas in defense of the Indian Territory.

Established in the 1830s, the Indian Territory covered the area that would become the state of Oklahoma. Many of its inhabitants were the descendants of the Choctaw, Cherokee, Chickasaw, Creek, and Seminole who were forcibly relocated there from their ancestral homes in the southeastern United States via the infamously deadly Trail of Tears. Since that time, federal law had forbidden settlement by any non-Native person in the territory unless they were a federal employee or a resident permitted by the Native American nations within the territory. As was the case with virtually every treaty and removal of indigenous peoples throughout the western United States, the law was routinely challenged in Congress. Up until 1879, delegates to Washington from the Nations occupying the territory were able to defeat such calls for white settlement.

In February 1879, a Railroad promoter, Elias Boudinot, ironically himself a Cherokee, identified a large swath of the Indian Territory that he claimed was unassigned to any specific tribe arguing that Creek and Seminole rights to this particular land had been ceded during a subsequent treaty and was therefore open for homesteaders under public domain. Boudinot widely publicized this claim about the so-called Unassigned Lands amounting to some two million acres, which immediately attracted white settlers, nicknamed "Boomers," to occupy the territory without waiting for the federal government to assess the claim.

Mott expected his work at Fort Gibson — expelling the illegal "Boomer" homesteaders from Indian Territory — to last until that fall, but within a couple of months, the army repositioned his unit to focus on suppressing the Boomer Movement from outside the territory. By June of 1879, four companies of the 22nd, including Mott's, moved to relieve the Fourth Cavalry at Coffeyville, Kansas, where they would spend the next four months preventing further Boomers from entering the Indian Territory. It would prove to be one of his least favorite assignments in the army. "All the inhabitants of this place are more or less affected with malaria," Mott observed. "Especially if they are obliged to work in the sun and their constitutions are ruined."[2]

With temperatures north of ninety degrees in the shade, Mott attributed much of his misery at Coffeyville to the brutal climate of the Kansan summer. By early September, sweltering in his tent, even writing a letter expended more effort than Mott could muster. "It is so hot and disagreeable in my tent- that I can't write anymore," he concluded to his mother after composing just three lines.[3] The heat moderated somewhat as the summer wore on, but that did little to assuage his distaste for the region. He would not live in such a place if he were given land there for free.[4]

It wasn't just the climate and business of keeping settlers out of the Indian Territory that frustrated Mott, it was also the general lawlessness of the region. "I am very tired of this nasty [place]...I should have been relieved [of this post] if it had not been for the excitement about robbers," he wrote.

There is a band of about fifty men living one hundred miles south of here and they are liable to appear in any of these frontier towns at any moment...Some of my company were sent out to search for [a] man who had been missing for some time and they found [the] remains of the traveler with a bullet in his head.[5]

Between the heat, surrounding poverty, and the general sickly feeling he experienced, Mott was happy when he received orders to move on from Kansas.

In October 1879, Mott and the four companies of the 22nd stationed at Coffeyville headed west towards Colorado, once more under the command of Major Alfred Hough. The army dispatched them to Fort Lewis, a newly built, remote post in the San Juan mountains of southwestern Colorado as a reassurance to white settlers in the Animas Valley that they would be protected from the Southern Ute, who resided in those parts. The Ute posed little threat to settlers in the valley, but they had been uneasy neighbors for years with tensions simmering just under the surface. When a tribe of Northern Ute revolted against their local Indian Agent further north, white paranoia in the south erupted into all-out panic believing it was only a matter of time before the Southern Ute would do the same.

***

White settlers first arrived in southwestern Colorado's Animas Valley in the early 1870s, attracted by the arable land, quality timber, and, perhaps most importantly, lucrative mining in the San Juan Mountains. Settlement patterns driven by mining moved more quickly than those driven by most other industries, so it wasn't long before several towns were established in the region. Towns sprang up in the mountains as fast as settlers could reach the region. Farmers and ranchers soon followed arriving in droves to set up their own settlements in the valleys below, taking advantage of the region's rich natural resources and profiting from the mutual support the mining towns in the hills offered.[6]

The relationship between the farmers and ranchers of the valley and the miners of the mountains reflected a perfect symbiotic arrangement, or at least it would have been, they thought, were it not for the presence of their Native American neighbors whom they wanted removed. It mattered little to the settlers that the valley had been the ancestral land of the southern Ute nation for generations and that it made up part of their legally protected reservation. Although no outright hostilities had erupted, white settlers believed it was only a matter of time. The settlers felt that the mere existence of the Ute in the region threatened transportation, scared away investors, raised the cost of living, and impeded the progress of agricultural development. The Ute, for their part, resented the presence of settlers on their land. They had taken their land, scared away game, and were destroying the Utes' traditional way of life. The total lack of regard for their rights and the treaties that had been established frustrated the Ute.[7] Meanwhile, the United States government responded by placating its citizens in order to hold on to the valuable mineral resources in the San Juans rather than uphold the treaty they had previously entered into in good faith. In 1873, Washington forced the Ute to sign the Brunot Agreement officially ceding the San Juan mining region to the United States government.[8]

Under the terms of the agreement, the Ute were permitted to roam freely and hunt, but they had officially lost their legal rights to a large portion of the region. This included a series of therapeutic hot springs sacred to the Ute, but now occupied by white settlers through fraudulent land claims and faked discoveries of gold. Just as it had done in the Black Hills of South Dakota and Wyoming, nothing persuaded the government to open up previously protected lands of the Indigenous People like the whisper of gold. President Hayes subsequently established the first military reservation around the springs, making the founding of a small village known as Pagosa Springs possible.[9] Over the next five years, the mere proximity of the Ute, as well as the Navajo to the south, led to a petition for an increased military presence in the Animas Valley. Washington agreed and in October 1878, the army established a new post near Pagosa Springs.[10] Christened Fort Lewis after Lt. Col. William Henry Lewis, a West Point graduate who had been killed in a skirmish with the Cheyenne in Kansas earlier that year, the post was situated in a remote area along the San Juan River. At one hundred forty miles from Fort Garland, the next nearest military post, Lewis was one of the most isolated stations in the country. In the winter, the snow closed off the mountain passes that provided access to the valley, effectively sealing off the garrison from the outside world for months at a time. Mail service, if available at all, ran to the post only once per week.[11]

Captain Wilson Hartz of the 15th Infantry commanded the first garrison to occupy the fort, which consisted of Company I of the 15th and D Troop of the 9th Cavalry, a Black unit. In all, about ninety-two men and six officers comprised the total force at Lewis. Despite the hot springs and beautiful mountain valley setting, Fort Lewis was anything but a glamorous post. The fort's official assignment was peacekeeping throughout the Animas Valley — peace between the settlers and Native Americans; between the Ute and Navajo; and amongst the settlers themselves. It was a mundane task. The fort's location at Pagosa Springs was considered advantageous owing to its position in the region as a gateway to the valley beyond. In truth, its isolation even within the region would have prevented it from being particularly effective in protecting anyone if hostilities had erupted.[12] Instead, the settlers exploited the post as another market for their goods, while the army found itself constantly in the middle of white and Native American complaints. In the waning days of 1879, events in the northern part of the state would cause the uneasy paranoia in the south to boil over into a panic, bringing Mott into the Animas Valley, an area he would come to know very well.

In 1878, a journalist from Ohio named Nathan Meeker was appointed agent of the White River Ute Indian Agency in Northern Colorado. Meeker had no experience dealing with Native Americans but had established the Union Colony in northwestern Colorado several years before. The colony, which grew into the town of Greeley, was designed as a Christian cooperative agricultural commune based in part on the utopian ideals of eighteenth-century French philosopher Charles Fourier and on Meeker's own experiences living in the Trumbull Phalanx, a similar type of commune founded in Ohio. By 1878, with the colony financially failing and Greeley's family calling in his debts, Meeker sought a position with the federal government as the local Indian Agent. Meeker believed he could "civilize" the Ute in the area and force them to abandon their cherished, nomadic way of life as hunter-gatherers by turning them into sedentary farmers.[13]

Meeker's utter disdain for the Ute and their way of life would be his undoing. The Northern Ute of Colorado deeply resented Meeker's forceful efforts to settle them and to impose his religious doctrine upon them. Matters came to a head in September 1879 over a horse-racing track that the Ute used. The horse was an important symbol for the Ute. It represented wealth, status, and the traditional nomadic lifestyle of the nation. The racetrack, therefore, represented a tangible expression of Ute resistance to sedentary life. Meeker targeted the track and ordered it plowed under to make way for farming. The move outraged the Ute who had finally had enough and raised up against the agency. Meeker sent for military aid, but it was too late. The Ute killed Meeker and ten other employees. They also captured several women and children, including Meeker's wife and one of his daughters.[14]

The Government sent troops in response, but en route, the contingent of soldiers from Fort Steele, Wyoming under Major Thomas Thornburgh was attacked at Milk Creek, twenty-five miles north of the agency. Major Thornburgh and several of his men were killed in the attack as the Ute pressed on until reinforcements from Fort D. A. Russell arrived, turning the Ute back and securing their surrender. Ouray, a Northern Ute Chief not involved in the attack, agreed to help the United States government secure the release of the hostages that had been taken, but the uprising had sealed the Utes' fate.[15] Banished from Colorado by the subsequent Ute Removal Act, they were removed and sent to a reservation in eastern Utah. Despite the loss of life, the attack in many ways played right into the hands of Coloradans. Just the year before, they had elected a governor, Frederick Pitkin, who had run on a platform of Ute removal, citing many of the imagined and exaggerated claims of danger and violence that the Ute presence supposedly represented to Colorado's settlers. Though largely unfounded, such claims gained credibility after the Meeker Massacre, particularly in the southern part of the state along the Animas Valley.

The Southern Ute who resided in the area were in no way affiliated with the Northern Ute of the White River Agency, but that mattered little to the already fearful and paranoid farmers and miners of the settlements throughout the valley and mountains. At one point, one man rode into the town of Howardsville frantically declaring that the citizens of nearby Silverton had all been massacred in their sleep. A group of townsmen, all too willing to believe the panic-stricken rider, assembled a party to go to Silverton to bear witness to the carnage. However, upon arrival in the town, nothing was amiss. It was early morning and the citizens of Silverton were found to still be sleeping peacefully in their homes. Though the rumor of the attack on Silverton proved unfounded, the ordeal was indicative of the level of fear among white residents of southern Colorado. Thankfully this had been a false alarm, they thought, but what of next time? The cries for additional troops in the Animas Valley continued and the settlers wanted the government to remove the Southern Ute as they had done their northern brethren.[16]

Following the paranoia stemming from the Meeker Massacre further north, the federal government eventually acquiesced to the pleading of the citizens of the Animas Valley in early October. Mott's company was one of four from the 22nd to march for Colorado under Major Hough. Upon arrival at Fort Lewis near Pagosa Springs, Hough held a council with the leaders of three of the southern Ute Tribes—the Weeminuche, Mouache, and Capote. The Ute sympathized with the loss of life in the northern Ute uprising and assured Major Hough that they had no connection with their northern brethren. They vowed that they would not move north to aid them in any way and said the settlers had nothing to fear from them. However, the influx of troops into the Animas Valley greatly concerned the southern Ute, who feared they would suffer the same fate as their northern counterparts despite their innocence. Hough assured the Ute leaders that the increased military presence was merely to ensure that no northern Ute attempted to migrate south into the region. No doubt assurances on both sides did little to allay anyone's fears.[17]

After the council, Hough and his men were ordered to leave Fort Lewis and establish a camp near Animas City where the citizens of the region could tangibly feel the increased presence of the troops. Frustration set in quickly, however, when the troops noticed that the hysteria that had overcome the region the previous month had all but disappeared. Certainly, the settlers wanted the southern Ute gone, but they no longer seemed overly vexed by their continued presence. On the contrary, many local businessmen and entrepreneurs seemed more excited by the new customer base for their various goods and services.[18]

The government likewise acknowledged that tensions had cooled and ordered Hough and his men to stand down and do nothing more than stay in camp while the government conducted its own investigation on conditions in southern Colorado to draw up a new treaty. Mott, who was in camp at Alamosa some 150 miles from Animas, was among those frustrated by the sudden lack of urgency that had brought them to the area in the first place. "What a fraud [the] Interior Department is. Just as we were getting our hands on the Indians they stepped in and stop[ped] all movements and now it is getting too late for we are liable anytime to be caught in a snow shower."[19] Still, their new position proved far superior to their old post in Coffeyville. "I don't know where we shall be stationed this winter, but I should hope to remain here," Mott wrote. "...it is such a healthy climate that all the malaria would be eliminated from our blood. I had a fever today (a slight attack) which I brought with me from Coffeyville."[20]

By November, Mott had already begun to experience some of the impressive snows that would characterize the isolation of this region. Though it was a source of frustration in that it prevented the soldiers from the duty they had been sent there to perform, Mott was glad to be rid of the conditions in Coffeyville. "My health is splendid," Mott wrote to his mother. "I am taking a great deal of exercise on the mountains."[21] The climate excused much of the immediate monotony he felt in camp. Game of all sizes was plentiful and even the local fish proved a superior meal, writing that he "had the finest trout for breakfast I have almost ever tasted."[22]

Isolated though the post was, it was not devoid of society. Mott originally appreciated this perk of the post, setting aside the roughness of the local character as a regional idiosyncrasy. By December, the rough edges of the white settlers and the amusement it offered Mott had grown old. "This is a nasty, muddy place and everybody is sick. It freezes at night and thaws during the day," Mott wrote from Animas City.[23] He enclosed an account of a man he saw dead in the street with a gunshot wound to the back of his head as an example of "the manners of this part of the world."[24] His tolerance for the peculiarities of frontier life in Colorado was waning.

Mott's initial time in Colorado was short-lived and by January he was back in the heat of the southwest. Although his unit was once more assigned to Fort Gibson in the Indian Territory, the only passable way out of the mountains given the heavy snowfall was a nearly 500-mile march due south to Santa Fe. At Santa Fe, they could take the railroad back to Fort Gibson. The next six months found Mott moving with great frequency throughout the Southwest. From Santa Fe, he took his company by rail out to Fort Gibson in the Indian Territory, but shortly thereafter moved on again to San Antonio, Texas, where he remained for several weeks before escorting his men out to Fort Clark.[25]

In the Spring, Mott left his company at Fort Clark to serve Court Martial duty at Fort Ringgold on the Mexican border. His journey to Ringgold had been fraught with flooding which required careful navigating across high waters. At the conclusion of his court martial duties, Mott made his way briefly to Fort Brown along the Rio Grande before returning to Fort Clark outside San Antonio.[26]

Despite the hardships of the Colorado winter and his oft-times contradictory feelings towards the people there, his distaste of extreme heat likely made him wish he had never left. While he did not know it at the time, Mott would return to the Animas Valley. In the meantime, the prospect of spending more time in the southwest encouraged Mott to move up his timetable to take another leave of the army and see more of the world.

14

Captain and the King

The royal transport glided upon the Chao Phyra River north from Bangkok toward Bang Pa-In, the summer residence of the Siamese king. Along the way, subjects gathered at the riverbanks to catch a glimpse of the petite, nineteen-year-old Queen Sunandha Kumariratana, first wife of King Chulalongkorn, and her daughter the infant Princess Kannabhorn Bejaratana. King Chulalongkorn had several wives and numerous concubines, as was tradition for Siamese royalty, but Sunandha Kumariratana was his favorite. She was not only his first queen; she was also his half-sister and he loved her greatly.

Pregnant with the couple's second child, the queen traveled to Bang Pa-In alone where the king would arrive later in the season. Sometime into the journey, the boat began listing and capsized tossing the pregnant queen, her infant daughter, and their entourage into the river. Subjects watched in horror from the riverbanks as their queen and baby princess struggled to stay afloat, but none moved to intervene. To touch a queen as a commoner was an offense punishable by death. No one wanted to test the law to find out if there were exceptions to that rule. In front of many anguished onlookers, Queen Sunandha and her only child sank beneath the surface and died.

Stricken with grief when he found out what had happened to his wife, young daughter, and unborn child, Chulalongkorn demanded the highest honors be shown for the queen and princess. He devised a lavish funeral, the grandeur of which would surpass anything the country had seen before. However, it was the end of May 1880 and the rainy season was just beginning, making it unsuitable for a royal funeral. The king ordered the remains of his wife and daughter preserved and over the next eight months he planned a multi-day event which spared no expense. He invited foreign dignitaries from around the world. High on his guest list was the American consul and his staff, which by March 1881 would include a globe-trotting captain of the 22nd Infantry.

***

By the time Mott arrived at Fort Clark, one hundred twenty miles outside San Antonio, Texas in February 1880, he had wearied of his service. Heavy rains had delayed his arrival and two weeks passed before he had caught sight of the fort. "I am economizing as much as possible to take a long sea voyage in a year from now," he wrote his mother after arriving at Fort Clark. "This is such a bad climate that I should like to get away from it for a while to recuperate and have the malaria eliminated from my system. I have a slight fever every day or two and I feel low spirited a good deal."[1] In truth, Mott had been itching to travel again ever since he arrived in the US from his previous overseas trip in 1876. Within months of his return, Mott informed his mother that he intended to travel again as soon as he could save up enough money.[2] In July 1880, after five months of service at various posts throughout Texas, Mott decided he could no longer wait another year. He applied for a year-long absence at Fort Clark, which his superiors granted.

In support of Mott's application for leave was a special order announced by the War Office in August 1880, which sought to use the travel of military personnel as a form of general foreign military reconnaissance. The order stated:

Hereafter, officers of the army traveling or stopping in foreign countries, whether on duty or leave of absence, will be required to avail themselves of all opportunities properly within their reach for obtaining information of value to the military service of the United States, especially that pertaining to their own arm or branch of the service. They will report fully in writing the result of their observations to the Adjutant General on their return to duty in the United States, if unable to do so earlier.[3]

He planned to take full advantage of the opportunity the Special Order afforded him. Unlike the prescriptive tour of Europe and the Holy Land, Mott decided to take a more free-form circumnavigation of the globe with a particular focus on Asia. With a requested leave of fourteen months, Mott planned to travel west across the Pacific, visiting Russia, Japan, China, and several countries across Southeast Asia, with a final stop in India before making his way home across the Indian Ocean, through the Suez Canal, and along the Mediterranean. However, the conditions Mott wished to escape in order to embark on this journey interfered with his plans.[4]

Diagnosed with "Rio Grande fever," Mott returned first to West Chester to recover his health.[5] While there, family matters delayed his departure further. His stepfather's health was rapidly deteriorating. Ann first informed her son of Maris' unspecified illness in October 1879 when the prognosis did not seem particularly serious. Maris rallied and all believed his health would return.[6] But the recovery was short-lived. Over the course of the following year, Maris slowly declined until he was finally committed to an insane asylum. With Maris on his deathbed, Mott remained in West Chester to help his mother prophylactically settle Maris' affairs, freeing up assets and selling their farm in Springfield to provide Ann with a living once her husband finally died.

Not surprisingly, Frank was not involved. Tensions between the brothers still ran high and without Maris around to look after his mother, Mott worried greatly about his brother taking advantage of his mother's grief, a fact of which he reminded his mother at every opportunity. That fall, Maris died. After the funeral, with Maris' affairs settled and Ann secure in her finances, Mott set sail in October of 1880.

Given his illness and unexpected detour to the east coast, Mott did not wish to delay his travels any further. He reversed the course of his trip and sailed across the Atlantic from New York to England. After a brief stay in the United Kingdom, he boarded a ship and traveled across the Mediterranean, through the Suez Canal, down the Red Sea, and across the Indian Ocean to India. Mott was determined to be less structured in his itinerary than in his previous overseas voyage. There was no package tour or prescribed route. His travels throughout Asia would be largely independent. This time, he would play less the tourist and more the explorer.

Mott stayed in India for three months, yet no correspondence or reporting exists that documents his specific experiences.[7] Apart from a pair of vases he purchased and sent home, Mott's experiences in India remain a mystery. When he finally left the subcontinent, he worked his way across southeast Asia. Crossing into Burma, Mott sailed up the Irrawaddy River to its then capital, Mandalay.[8] Mott entered Burma at a difficult time in its history as European imperialism threatened Burmese self-governance. King Thibaw, the hereditary ruler of Burma, still occupied his throne and ruled from the royal palace in Mandalay, but his control over the country was diminishing. Lower Burma had become a British colony in all but name centered around Yangon. The year Mott arrived, Thibaw began to engage with the French, seeking their help in keeping the British advance at bay. This only increased tensions between the British presence and the Burmese crown. By 1885, just four years after Mott's visit, the British would invade Mandalay as part of the formal annexation of Burma into the empire British empire and the king would be forced to abdicate and flee the country to live in exile in India. Mott never revealed the motives behind his chosen routes, but that he traveled through the still-sovereign Mandalay and not the European-Controlled Yangon is perhaps telling of Mott's desire to see cultures untouched by Western powers. His career was largely predicated on managing the forced imposition of a white, Western culture and ideology on an indigenous population. This trip was designed to get away from all of that. For all his apparent desire to experience new cultures unadulterated, he may have at least sensed some increased anxiety and tension in the capital. By the end of February, Mott left Burma and crossed the border into Siam, present-day Thailand, in early March.

When Mott arrived in Bangkok in March of 1881, the city was bustling with the arrival of foreign dignitaries as well as subjects from throughout the kingdom. A series of pavilions and other lavish-looking buildings were nearing completion in the Sanam Luang, a large, open field just north of the Great Palace normally used as a public park or for various ceremonial purposes. The main building at the center of this new complex of buildings was a Phra Men, a large, lavishly decorated, cross-shaped building intended as a place of cremation for deceased royalty. The Phra-Men resembled a palace in miniature "with wings and pagoda spires and beautiful roofs all covered with gilt paper, and ornaments that sparkled and flashed like gems in the tropical sun."[9] Upon entering the city, Mott sought out John Halderman, the American Consul.

General John Adams Halderman was five years Mott's senior almost to the day. A native of Kentucky, Halderman read law and moved to Kansas in the mid-1850s where he became an active voice in local politics. He served as private secretary to the Governor, sat on the bench of the Probate court, served as mayor of Leavenworth, and held elected office in both chambers of the state legislature. Like Mott, Halderman fought in the Civil War. A staunch abolitionist, he joined the Kansas volunteers with whom he served with distinction and was eventually elevated to major general of the state's forces. After the war, Halderman traveled extensively around the world. In recognition of his education as a lawyer, his service to the Union, and his international travel, President Hayes appointed him as consul to Siam in 1880, followed by a promotion to consul-general by President James Garfield the next year.[10]

Halderman greeted Mott warmly and informed him of the reason for all the activity in the city. The rainy season had ended, and the weather was suitable to cremate the queen and princess who had died the previous May. Mott had arrived just in time to witness the spectacle, but little did he realize that he would be counted among the foreign dignitaries. The king had invited Halderman and his staff to attend the ceremony as his honored guests. As an officer of the United States Army, Halderman asked Mott to join the entourage in an official capacity. It was an honor Mott could not refuse.

The royal funeral, as the king intended, was unlike anything Mott had ever seen. The bodies were placed in a sitting position inside two large urns. Each urn consisted of a plain, copper urn nested inside a larger urn beautifully decorated in gold and jewels. The ceremony, which by some estimates cost as much as a half million dollars—or several million in twenty-first-century terms—lasted for eleven days and consisted of games, tournaments, fireworks, and performances of various kinds.[11] The central event of the ceremony was the great funeral procession from the Wat Pho temple on the south side of the Grand Palace – where the deceased had laid in state in their urns – to the Phra Men grounds north of the Palace. The long procession included the king carried aloft in his sedan, followed by regiments of soldiers dressed in various colors, bands playing dirges, throngs of priests and several large palanquins bearing lavish gifts, relatives of the deceased queen, and of course the golden urns bearing the remains of the deceased royals.

The various pavilions and buildings erected around the Phra Men in the Sanam Luang were intended for the various dignitaries and visiting foreigners who were given places of honor from which to witness the ceremonies. In his report to the State Department in Washington, Halderman noted that he and his staff "had been specially invited by the King to witness these ceremonies, and throughout the same, attended by the foreign minister, they occupied choice positions for comfort and observation."[12] In his report to the State Department, Halderman included a lengthy article describing the ceremony and various buildings that had appeared in a local English-language paper, the *Siam Weekly Advertiser*. Interestingly, the article made note of one traveler in particular: "In making the circuit of the globe, Captain Hooton, of the United States Army, is spending a few days in Siam. During the cremation exercises, he was attached to the staff of General Halderman, the American consul."[13] It is curious that Mott's presence elicited a special mention in the paper, especially considering the throngs of foreign visitors, both official and unofficial, that had descended upon Bangkok.

The afternoon of the funeral procession, after the urns bearing the deceased had arrived at the Phra Men, the King invited all of the foreign consuls and their guests to join him in the Phra Men to witness the placing of the urns on their altars. With the urns in place, the consuls and their staff were escorted into the west hall of the building where they enjoyed a formal audience with the king. Chulalongkorn greeted everyone and thanked them for being a part of the ceremony. That evening, the king made a public appearance to the assembled crowds signaling the beginning of a night of performances of various kinds. Tight-rope walkers, jugglers, and theatrical displays were capped by traditional lion dancing. The king set off an impressive display of fireworks to accompany more dancing performances as he went among his multitude of young children.[14] Mott had a front-row seat to it all.

The cremation itself took place the following evening. The opulent outer urns were removed and the deceased queen and princess were lowered from their altars in their simple inner urns and placed upon the pyres. The King began the cremation ceremony by lighting the pyres while numerous relatives, ministers, and princes followed adding their own candles one by one. As the fires burned, a band played funeral dirges and a group of women employed as official mourners began to wail. Once more, the consuls and their guests were brought forward to have an unobstructed view of the cremation ceremony.

After the official ceremony ended, Mott joined the other foreign dignitaries at the pavilion of Prince Bhanurangsi Savanfwongse, the king's brother, for refreshments and another personal audience with the King. As a token of his thanks, the king ordered presents distributed to those in attendance. For the masses, this typically consisted of limes and hollow nuts filled with silver coins tossed into the crowds. The king's brother handed out such tokens personally to foreigners in attendance, but for the foreign officials, Chulalongkorn himself distributed finer gifts. One foreigner in attendance wrote that "the gifts drawn were almost infinite in their variety and style, and most of them costly. I saw jeweled rings and pins, gold and silver boxes and bottles, vases, trays, cups, teapots, goblets, all of silver and gold."[15]

On the following day, the remains of the queen and princess were processed to the river and placed aboard the royal barge to be taken to Wat Yanawarahm, a temple north of the city where the ashes would be spread. Any remaining bones that had not been entirely consumed by the fire were placed in Gold boxes and brought back to the Phra Men to sit on the altar alongside the remains of other deceased Siamese royalty. For the next three days, performances continued and priests made various "recitations."[16] The ceremonies officially ended after a total of eleven days. The boxes of remains were brought back into the palace and the work of deconstructing the Phra Men and various pavilions on the Sanam Luang began.

Mott oddly never wrote about his time in Siam despite the surrealness of the experience. The few times he referred at all to this second grand voyage of his, neither the funeral nor his honored position during the ceremonies rated so much as a footnote. This omission is all the more curious considering what happened next. After the funeral, General Halderman personally arranged an audience between Mott and the king.[17] As Mott stood before Chulalongkorn, he thanked his majesty for his hospitality with the presentation of a pearl-handled revolver that he had purchased shortly before setting sail on his voyage.[18] The king took great interest in Mott and they spent some time together. Whatever they discussed stayed between the two of them, but the topic of Western military strategy and discipline most certainly entered their conversation. During the remainder of Mott's stay in the country, he saw the king several more times. Chulalongkorn enjoyed his talks with the American captain and Mott likewise felt honored by their acquaintance. One day, shortly before Mott was due to continue his journey, the king requested his presence once more. Chulalongkorn greeted Mott warmly at the palace and laid before the officer a surprising offer.

Friends in high places: King Chulalongkorn of Siam
Library of Congress

Chulalongkorn's father King Mongkut—famously immortalized in Rodgers and Hammerstein's *The King and I*—believed in a Western education for his wives, concubines, and children. He hired an Englishwoman, Anna Leonowens, to provide that instruction. Mongkut took particular interest in Chulalongkorn's education under Leonowens as heir apparent to the throne. As King, Chulalongkorn exhibited the influence of his instruction under Leonowens in continuing his father's efforts to westernize Siam. As Mongkut had done, Chulalongkorn sought out experts from the West in a variety of fields to help him in these efforts from finance and education to the military. In Mott, the king believed he had found the man who could westernize his army. In one of their last meetings, Chulalongkorn asked Mott to resign his commission with the United States Army and remain in Siam to train the Siamese military in the ways of Western warfare and tactics.

The offer came as a shock to Mott, who felt neither worthy nor qualified to take on such a task. He graciously thanked Chulalongkorn for the honor but felt compelled to decline. Though disappointed, the king accepted Mott's answer and bade him farewell. It was the last he would see of the king. Shortly thereafter, Mott left Bangkok and continued his journey.

Mott's silence on these events makes their occurrence difficult to corroborate. That Mott and the king met was confirmed by a Siamese correspondent who noted in an article for the *Army Navy Air Force Journal* that Consul Halderman had personally introduced Mott to Chulalongkorn.[19] Had Halderman known the extent of the interactions between the captain and the monarch, he did not divulge it to the press. However, it is in a brief, undated article from Mott's hometown newspaper, the *Daily Local News,* that the details were revealed. Having heard several companions discussing Bayard Taylor, a prominent statesman, author, and renowned traveler from Chester County, the unidentified author became inspired to write of Mott remarking "we know one of our citizens who has done about as much traveling abroad as any of them, but there are few people aware of it. We allude to Captain Mott Hooton, the old commander of the Brandywine Guards and brother of

Col. F. C. Hooton."[20] While it is difficult to determine the veracity of the article without knowing the author or knowing the source of their information, the facts that appear regarding Mott's previous travel experiences as well as details regarding a subsequent journey through Russia align with things Mott did write about. Additionally, evidence exists, albeit circumstantial, to suggest there was likely some truth in the reports about the King's offer.

In 1881, within months of Mott's departure from Siam, Gerolamo Emilio Gerini, a young Italian graduate of the Royal Military Academy in Modena, arrived in the country and enlisted in the Siamese Army as a lieutenant and instructor. Within six years he would become the General Director of Military Education and become the first director of the Royal Cadet School, effectively assuming the kind of position that Chulalongkorn had envisioned for Mott. Gerini had heard that the Siamese king had been looking for Westerners to join and train his army, which gives plausible context to the king's request of Mott.

Mott's presentation of a recently purchased pearl-handled revolver adds an additional level of intrigue considering that in 1880, the year before Mott left on his voyage, he had indeed purchased a Colt Model 1878 Double Action Army Revolver, which was shipped to him on July 22. Colt also recorded a shipment that July of an unusual Deluxe 3 revolver, engraved and silver plated with pearl stocks.[21] There is no way to determine if that pearl-handled gun shipped by Colt in July was the one Mott purchased, but the coincidence of the purchase combined with the newspaper account is certainly suggestive. Ultimately, the author of the article attributed Mott's gracious decline of the King's request to his substantial modesty, which would have been in character for Mott, but whatever truly transpired between Mott and the king stayed between them.

When Mott left Siam, he continued his journey through southeast Asia stopping briefly in Hong Kong before turning northward into mainland China traveling to Shanghai and eventually to Peking—modern-day Beijing—in the northeast of the country. He remained in the vicinity of Peking for some time exploring ancient temples, the

Great Wall, and Manchuria so much so that he would claim "I have a more thorough knowledge of the country surrounding Pekin [sic] than I have of that surrounding my native city, Philadelphia."[22]

While in China, Mott traveled with a couple of companions, one an unidentified Englishman and Dr. Frank Cowen, an eccentric renaissance man from a prominent western Pennsylvania family.[23] Born in 1844 in Greensburg, Pennsylvania, Cowan gained a reputation as a prankster in his youth, which later resulted in expulsion from Jefferson College. When Pennsylvania elected his father, Edgar Cowan, to the United States Senate in 1861, the younger Cowan moved to Washington D.C. where he obtained a clerkship with the Committee on Patents. During his time in D.C., Cowan studied law and was later admitted to the Westmoreland County bar in Pennsylvania.

In 1867, President Andrew Johnson appointed Cowan as his personal secretary in charge of land patents, a position he held until the end of Johnson's term. Cowan never completely left the prankster days of his youth behind. While secretary to President Johnson, he helped an acquaintance increase the readership of his struggling newspaper by devising a fake story about the discovery of the remains of an eleventh-century Icelandic woman under the Great Falls of the Potomac River, placing the European discovery of America centuries before Columbus sailed the ocean blue. It was not a hoax that caught on very well, but it did sell a lot of papers.[24] Cowan left government life after his time with Johnson and opened a private law practice while also going to medical school on the side. By 1869, Cowan had graduated from Georgetown Medical School and returned home to Greensburg, Pennsylvania. Cowan was never satisfied with a single vocation. He opened a law office and a private medical practice in addition to running a small newspaper, *Frank Cowan's Paper* that covered all things related to western Pennsylvania. Despite an already full professional life of law and medicine, Cowan authored a fair amount of books including poetry, plays, and other works of fiction as well as factual works including everything from the political landscape of the country after the Civil War and accounts of some of his travels abroad to treatises on insects and a biography on the discoverer of Spectrum Analysis. He married Harriet Jack, the daughter of William Jack, a late United States Representative from Pennsylvania. Tragedy struck in 1873 shortly after their marriage when Harriet died in childbirth. Shortly thereafter, their infant son, Jack also passed. Cowan himself fell ill sometime later and embarked on his 1881 voyage around the globe to alleviate the effects of his illness. It was during this trip he met Mott.

When he finally left China, Mott sailed for Japan. In 1881, Japan was in the midst of the Meiji Restoration, a period of imperial consolidation, rapid industrialization, westernization, and social modernization allowing the Japanese people freedom to pursue their own occupations regardless of class or status. While in the country, Mott encountered some Russian travelers who invited him to join them in a trek across their homeland on his way home. Mott had not planned to journey overland on his return trip given the time he lost at the beginning of his leave, which he had already extended by another two months. While in Tokyo, Mott wrote to the Adjutant General's office requesting an additional month to make the journey across Russia, referencing Russia's presence in his initial itinerary and reminding his superiors of the illness he suffered due to his service prior to his trip.[25] The War Department approved the extra month and Mott accepted the invitation.

Departing from Yokohama, Mott, and his Russian companions sailed across the Sea of Japan and landed in Vladivostok northeast of the Korean peninsula. Joined by the governor of Western Siberia, Mott embarked on a trans-Siberian crossing, being the first American military officer to achieve such a feat.[26] Mott and his entourage journeyed 2,000 miles up the Amoor River then overland by tarantass—a four-passenger horse-drawn carriage—for another 1,800 miles. For the next two weeks, Mott sailed up the Yenisei River nearly to the Arctic Circle. The rest of his trip included travel along the Volga River and a visit to Moscow before traveling to St. Petersburg where he boarded a ship home.[27]

When Mott returned from his time abroad, he was dismayed to learn his unit was still stationed at Fort Clark in Texas. Mott spent the next year there facing the same miserable climate he had fled when he went on leave. Yet, in July 1882, Mott's delight at the welcome news that the 22nd would be leaving Texas was tempered by the destination – Fort Lewis, Colorado.

15

⚭

Peacekeeper

The Animas Valley was no less picturesque in 1882 than it had been two years before, but as a military posting, it was no more prestigious either. Paranoid settlers and frustrated Native Americans both turned to the army at Fort Lewis to solve their problems, which were essentially each other. Even amongst themselves, the settlers treated the military as a mediator, despite legislation preventing them from doing so. In 1878, Congress passed the Posse Comitatus Act which curtailed the ability of the military to intervene in civilian affairs. The act was designed to assuage fears of a powerful standing army by limiting military jurisdiction over civil authorities except where situations could not be managed through local law enforcement.[1] In a sense, the army was unrealistically expected to be all things to all people, and in trying to serve everyone, they ultimately satisfied no one. The army could not even satisfy their own as keeping the garrison manned became a constant struggle.

When Mott last served in Colorado, Fort Lewis had been situated near Pagosa Springs. In 1880, just after he had left the first time, the army ordered the post moved further west, closer to Animas City where natural resources were more plentiful and the positioning was deemed more advantageous in keeping the Ute and Navajo in check. Larger than

248

the Pagosa Springs site, the new post, built along the La Plata river southwest of Durango, was designed to house ten units—six regiments of infantry and four of Cavalry. While still a remote area, the new location allowed the government to establish a 50,000-acre military reservation to adequately supply the fort with the necessary amount of natural resources to sustain itself and to provide some insulation from the civilian population.[2]

The complex demographics of the region added to the challenges the army faced in trying to maintain order. Pre-existing tensions between any number of conflicting parties simmered constantly under the surface ready to boil over with just the spread of a rumor. The troops at Fort Lewis had to deftly navigate potential conflicts between the Southern Ute and the Navajo; between white settlers and both of the aforementioned Native American groups; and between white settlers from Colorado and those from northern New Mexico. That several other Native American nations – the Apache to the southeast, Paiute to the west, and additional bands of Ute to the north – were all within reasonable proximity meant the troops had their work cut out for them. Mott and his fellow officers were often caught in the middle. As tax-paying citizens, white settlers expected the army to side with them in every conflict, but the various Native American nations looked to the military to honor the treaties their country had made and check settler incursions onto their land.[3]

The fort itself was generally healthy and with the exceptions of the harsh snow in the winters, the elevation and climate throughout the year made the post more comfortable than many other western forts. Still, with its backwater location and its mission of peacekeeping, recruitment became a persistent problem at Fort Lewis. For recruits with any serious ambition, the post was not attractive, which meant that the recruits that did make it to Lewis were often found lacking. Some deserted the army upon arrival having used the recruitment process simply to score a travel ticket to the west having no intention of serving. Those that did come to serve were often unfit to do so. Typically recruits underwent a physical evaluation before being sent west, however, the exams were inconsistently performed and not always thorough. Shortly before Mott arrived in 1882, for example, a smallpox scare rattled the post after they were informed a week late that a recruit infected with the disease had shipped out potentially exposing all the other recruits who traveled with him. Fortunately, an outbreak never occurred, but the oversight put the entire post in jeopardy. Other recruits showed up with physical or mental debilities that rendered them unable to serve, the frequency of which irritated Mott to the point that he remarked in one report that a "reduction instead of an increase in the force would have been in the interests of the service."[4]

The intensity of the snow in the valley also posed serious challenges for this remote post as it had at the Pagosa Springs site. Nearly every winter, heavy snow rendered the mountain paths impassable for months at a time. Mott's second winter at the post over 1883-1884 was particularly harsh, having been dubbed the "winter of the century" with snow in some places measuring as high as twenty-five feet.[5] This meant that their stockpiles of food and fuel for heat had to be carefully rationed. Mail service could not reach the post and general military administration became all but impossible since the troops were not able to respond to potential conflicts in the region if they couldn't leave the fort. They couldn't rely on garrisons in the field either since many were recalled in advance of winter for fear they would be cut off from the resources they needed to survive. Even the number of troops at the post could decline in the winter since many of those whose service was due to expire during the winter requested an early leave, sometimes months in advance, to avoid being snowed in and unable to get home. Likewise, a greater proportion of leave requests occurred during the winter as well, including Mott who requested his own leave of absence to return to West Chester at one point during his tenure at the fort. Likewise, new recruits, such as they were, could not even reach the post in winter to bolster the garrison's diminished numbers.

The army was in no hurry to reassign the 22nd. Mott would spend the next six years at Fort Lewis, far longer than he had stayed at any one post up to this time. In fact, it was far longer than he had actually lived in any one place since before the Civil War. Mott's six years of peacekeeping duties at Fort Lewis were relatively uneventful as conflicts tended to follow a predictable pattern: rumor and innuendo amongst white settlers engendered paranoia-induced panic leading to incitements of violence in response to an imaginary threat that Mott and the other men would have to quell. In the summer of 1885, local newspapers began inciting violence against all Native Americans in the area, regardless of any actual threat that may have been presented. Lieutenant Colonel Peter Swaine, who commanded the post at this time, frequently received demands for protection following a suspected Native American attack only to discover the issue was overblown. One such "attack" turned out to be a small band of Ute minding their own business and merely spotted in town with weapons on their way to hunt. In some cases, genuine acts of violence occurred, proof in the minds of the settlers of the inherent danger posed by their Native American neighbors until further investigation uncovered clear provocation. One investigation into the death of a white settler on the Mancos River at the hands of the Ute revealed an earlier attack by a group of cowboys who had murdered six Ute—including women and children—in their tepees simply because they had vowed to themselves to "shoot Utes on sight."[6]

For Mott and the other troops at Fort Lewis, the white settlers in the Animas Valley were generally the aggressors, despite the victimhood they presented to the army. They acted on impulse at every rumor, no matter how unfounded and they read scathing editorials in local newspapers laden with lies about Ute barbarity. One local newspaper editor referred to the Ute as "our national pests" and called for their extermination.[7] It led to an impossible situation for Swaine, who had to both placate and reassure the settlers, while also combating hysterical calls by citizens for state troops and local militia whom Swaine knew would shoot first and investigate later. Instead, Swaine had to put on a sort of theater for the local citizenry, making troops visible and letting everyone know the army was well-equipped to handle any outbreaks of violence. Mott was personally ordered to take his men on patrol where

Immortalized in painting: Mott as a captain with the 22nd Infantry, n.d.

Courtesy of Ed & Faye Max

they could "show themselves as much as possible to the settlers to assure them of [their] intention and ability to protect them."[8] Not everyone bought the theatrics. Rumors abounded that the military was ordered to prioritize the protection of the Native Americans in the area over the settlers. Though not an entirely unfair assessment by circumstance given the frequency of white aggression as the source of the immediate conflicts, it was nevertheless another lie that Swaine had to battle. It also served as a clear indication that the citizens in the valley would never be truly placated until not a single Native American remained in the region.[9]

Fortunately, after the tensions of the summer of 1885 reduced back down to a simmer, the cycle of rumor-panic-anger-placation continued less severely. Mott spent time commanding his company in the field in 1886 and assessed the situation to be quiet enough to recommend relieving the troops from field duty for a while. The one incident he was called on to investigate involved a charge of trespassing by some Navajo shepherds, but Mott immediately sided with the Navajo stating that the settler had no cause to complain and that the more prominent settlers, or the "responsible men in the vicinity," as Mott referred to them, were on good terms with the Navajo and wanted to keep it that way.[10]

Between the flare-ups of tensions, Mott and his comrades developed a community of their own at Fort Lewis, not unlike other civilian, rural communities.[11] Though not entirely dissimilar to other Western posts, the availability of religious services and education, the presence of a library and store, as well as other forms of recreation and entertainment became all the more important in this remote place.[12] As with any small community, internal conflicts and tensions existed over time, particularly during the lonely winter months when quarters were tight, heavy snows separated field units from the post for long stretches at a time, and being generally shut in could thin anyone's patience. At such times, community and an active social scene became vital means of survival. Dinners and other festivities occurred frequently, the band played concerts almost weekly, sports games gave troops a healthy outlet for their energy, and the local civilians in Durango were often invited to partake as well so the troops could socialize.[13]

Mott spent the greater part of the 1880s at Fort Lewis, and while his service throughout the decade presented a relative calm, these years proved more trying on a personal level. In February 1882, Mott learned that his four-year-old niece, Susie, and seven-year-old nephew, Maris, had contracted diphtheria. Susie developed croup and on the 24th, her airways became obstructed due to severe laryngitis and she succumbed to the disease. Shortly thereafter, Maris developed a fatal blood clot in his heart as the diphtheria toxin spread through his bloodstream. Just three days after Susie's passing, Maris was gone.[14] The tragedy devastated the family. In the span of a few days, Mott's sister, Annie, and her husband, Mort had lost their family. Mott had been so pleased to hear when they had been born and had even stopped beside the Jordan River to collect water for his nephew's baptism. Now they were both gone.

Annie and Mort managed to carry on and two years later it seemed things were looking up for the family when Annie gave birth to a son, Morton Hazen Chase. Hazen, as he became known to distinguish him from his father, was a happy and healthy baby. Two years after that in 1886, a daughter, Annie E. Chase was brought into the world. But the joy of the growing family was not to last. In 1888, as Mott's time at Fort Lewis drew to a close, he received the news from home. His sister, Annie had developed appendicitis and died.[15] In six years, his brother-in-law, Mort, had lost two children and his wife. Left alone with a four-year-old and two-year-old and not knowing which way to turn, Mort entrusted Annie's mother Ann, and sister, Sallie to look after the children. As a traveling salesman, Mort worked for several different firms, moving at times between Pittsburgh and Philadelphia eventually living in a boarding house and working in a galvanizing business with his brother in the latter city.[16] Despite his best efforts, his success was limited and he relied on his wife's family to help raise and support the children so he could travel for work. But he made sure to visit the children as often as possible during his transits across the state.[17]

Tragic couple: Annie Rhoads Chase & Morton Chase
Courtesy of Clay Chase

The same year Annie died, Mott was finally reassigned and left Fort Lewis. Though often boring, life at Lewis was stable and offered Mott a fair amount of comfort and diversion for a remote western outpost, but it was also a more sedentary existence and not conducive to the kind of distinguishing service that would lead to promotion. Moving to relieve the 5th Infantry at Fort Keogh, the more sedate life would continue taking him to Montana for an even longer period of time.

16

End of the Frontier

At the dawn of the 1890s, the Federal Census Bureau determined that settlement had reached so many corners of the nation that they could no longer demarcate a frontier line. The Census essentially declared the frontier closed. Many United States citizens welcomed the pronouncement as a victory for the nation. Contemporary historians like Frederick Jackson Turner began writing about white western settlement as a closed chapter in American history, arguing that the decades of settling and pioneering the West had profoundly shaped the American character in a way that distinguished Americans from their European kin. Two years into his service at Fort Keogh, Mott did not share the feeling of moral righteousness about the final subjugation of the West having spent nearly his entire career along the ever-shifting "frontier line" managing the fallout of the country's growing pains.

The late 1880s and early 1890s were a particularly difficult time for the various Indigenous Peoples of the northern Plains. The buffalo herds had dwindled and the lands guaranteed to them in the multitude of treaties with the United States government were continually shrinking as Washington continued to cave to pressure by settlers to break the treaties and open reserved land up to white homesteaders. The Dawes Act of 1887 attempted to dissolve tribal affiliations by dividing up Indigenous lands into individual parcels and then offering them to individual Native Americans in exchange for United States citizenship. Outwardly, Congress portrayed the legislation as a benevolent act to lift the Native Americans out of poverty, believing that stability came through property ownership and subsistence farming. The spin belied the real intent of the Act's authors. With the stroke of a pen, they sought to neutralize an enemy through assimilation, turning them into subsistence farmers like the white settlers. Any land left over after allotments was doled out were put up for sale to white settlers, thereby appeasing their constituents eager to push into the open land.

Not everyone in Congress agreed with the idea. The minority report of the House Committee of Indian Affairs acknowledged the idea of allotment for what it was — a land grab for whites — and decried the paternalistic language used to justify the plan arguing "If this were done in the name of Greed, it would be bad enough, but to do it in the name of Humanity…is infinitely worse."[1] Not surprisingly, the Act proved devastating for the Native Americans on the Plains. The allotments provided were not suitable for successful subsistence farming and many resisted this thinly veiled attempt at erasing their culture. By 1890, the Cheyenne, for example, stood on the brink of starvation. Many in the military were at least nominally sympathetic to the Native Americans' plight. Nelson Miles telegrammed General John Schofield in Washington just over a week prior to the Wounded Knee Massacre imploring Congress to make good on the treaties they had made. "The difficult Indian problem cannot be solved permanently at this end of the line. It requires the fulfillment of Congress of the treaty obligations that the Indians were entreated and coerced into signing," Miles wrote. "They signed away a valuable portion of their reservation, and it is now occupied by white people, for which they have received nothing. They understood that ample provision would be made for their support; instead, their supplies have been reduced, and much of the time they have been living on half and two-thirds rations."[2]

**Outraged by Wounded Knee: Nelson Miles rejected the army's
narrative of the massacre**
Library of Congress

Had Mott known what Miles wrote to Schofield, he likely would have agreed with it. Service in the West had changed Mott's perceptions towards the indigenous population. He had come to respect the people of the various nations he encountered not just as formidable enemy combatants, but as people. "When I first went to the Sioux country in Dakota, I had the preconceived idea of all Americans that the Indian is a stupid brute without affection or sense of humor or even very much of a soul," Mott wrote several years later. "But shortly after I had arrived at Fort Fire Steel on the Jim River in Dakota, I was surprised one day to see an Indian about thirty years of age weeping bitterly over the sick bed of his baby."[3] This heartfelt show of emotion surprised Mott and as he continued his encounters with various Native American peoples throughout his career, he came to see them as an "exceedingly amiable, and pleasant-natured people, self-sacrificing, hospitable, and gener- ous."[4] While he had observed from personal experience that America's indigenous people could be "most brutal and cruel when engaged in war," Mott believed it was borne of necessity rather than savagery.[5] When a religious movement emerged in 1889 amongst the Northern Paiute in response to the extreme hardships they were experiencing as a result of Americans "closing" the frontier, Mott sought to understand it where others were determined to suppress it.

Introduced by a Paiute healer named Wovoka, the movement in- volved a blending of Native and Christian ideologies. Wovoka claimed to have had a vision in which Jesus Christ would return to earth to unite and deliver all of America's indigenous people from their plight. The white people would vanish from the land and the indigenous dead would rise again to walk the earth once more in peace and prosperity. To hasten the occurrence of this coming of the Messiah, Wovoka cre- ated a slow, circle performance referred to as the Ghost Dance.

Representatives from various other nations traveled to the Paiute to learn of this ritual and many of them brought it back to their own nations, incorporating the Ghost Dance into their own rituals with slight variations. The Lakota were among those that adopted the Ghost Dance and saw in it the ability to provide a physical defense against white aggression. When performing the dance, Lakota warriors donned "Ghost Shirts" which they believed provided spiritual protection from bullets.

As more and more Native Americans along the plains started to perform the Ghost Dance, white settlers became jittery, assuming the ritual portended an attack. On the Standing Rock Reservation in the Dakota Territory, U.S. officials tried to compel the various chiefs living on the reservation to command their people to stop practicing the Ghost Dance. Among the chiefs living on the reservation was Sitting Bull, whom the military believed had the influence to put an end to the ritual and calm the fears of the settlers. Standing Rock's Indian Agent, James McLaughlin, aggressively approached Sitting Bull supported by an escort of about forty Indian police with the intent of taking Sitting Bull and the other chiefs into custody. Sitting Bull resisted as on-lookers gathered to protest the arrest. As Sitting Bull tried to pull away, an anonymous shot rang out killing one of the police officers. In the ensuing confusion, both sides opened fire resulting in more deaths, including eight protestors and six police officers. When the smoke cleared, Sitting Bull, too, was dead.

The event caused about two hundred of Sitting Bull's Hunkpapa Lakota to flee the Standing Rock reservation to seek safety with Spotted Elk, leader of the Mnikowoju Lakota on the Cheyenne River Reservation directly south of Standing Rock. A few days later, Spotted Elk led his group of Mnikowoju with several dozen Hunkpapa to meet with Red Cloud, a chief of the Oglala Lakota on the Pine Ridge reservation in the southeastern corner of Dakota Territory.

En route to Pine Ridge, a detachment of the 7th Cavalry intercepted Spotted Elk and his group and escorted them to Wounded Knee Creek where they were ordered to go into camp on December 28th, 1890. That night Colonel James Forsyth arrived with the rest of the 7th Cavalry and surrounded the camp. The next morning, with a force of about five hundred soldiers surrounding the camp along with four pieces of artillery, Forsyth ordered a search of the camp to disarm Spotted Elk's group. By contrast, there were approximately 350 Lakota in camp, about 120 of whom were women and children. The exact accounts of what happened next vary slightly, but the result was the same: tragedy.

As the soldiers searched tents and confiscated weapons, one warrior refused. According to some accounts, this warrior was deaf and scuffled with the officer because he had not understood the order. While the soldier tried to disarm the deaf man, another warrior began performing the Ghost Dance and tensions rose. During the scuffle, a shot went off prompting the already jittery troops to open fire on the Lakota. Since most of the Lakota had been disarmed, they offered little resistance and the troops, overtaken by adrenaline, began firing indiscriminately. From outside the camp, the artillery opened fire into the camp with their four Hotchkiss-designed mountain guns. Over sixty soldiers were killed or wounded, perhaps most as the result of friendly fire.

During the fight, women and children fled the camp to seek cover in a nearby ravine, where the soldiers, their adrenaline now coupled with rage, pursued and slaughtered them. It took three days to sort out the dead owing to a blizzard that had blown into the region. When the civilian burial party hired by the army arrived to bury the dead, they found about 84 men, 44 women, and 18 children dead. Four infants were discovered alive still wrapped in shawls against their mothers, some attempting to nurse from their mothers' dead bodies.

When General Miles learned of what happened at Wounded Knee, he was furious. He condemned Colonel Forsyth and relieved him of command. Miles began an Army Court of Inquiry into the event. It was not a formal court martial, however, and despite a reprimand for Forsyth's tactics, the inquiry all but exonerated him. Forsyth, with the support of Stephen Elkins, the Secretary of War, was reinstated to his command believing that the troops had tried to spare non-combatants as best they could. Miles knew better and continued to denigrate Forsyth claiming that the incident at Wounded Knee was a deliberate massacre intentionally prosecuted by Forsyth in order to destroy the Lakota in that camp. Miles' outspoken criticisms of Forsyth fell on deaf ears. Forsyth would go on to eventually achieve the rank of Major General.

Forsyth was not the only individual to benefit from their role in the Massacre. Twenty soldiers involved in the attack were awarded the Congressional Medal of Honor. It was an unusually high number of recipients for such an engagement, even if it had been a legitimate skirmish against only armed combatants. Many of the medals were specifically awarded for having pursued the Lakota who had attempted to run and hide without noting that those they chased were unarmed women and children. A few soldiers were cited for simply rounding up a stampede of pack mules. For the Lakota, the awards were a cruel insult and even into the twenty-first century, they have attempted unsuccessfully to have the medals posthumously revoked. At the time, however, the army officially maintained that they were at war with the Lakota and so the regrettable loss of innocent life was an unfortunate by-product of a battle. All credibility for the army in this matter relied upon the contention that a state of war had existed at the time of the massacre and in the days following they cemented that contention using the murder of a friend and colleague of Mott's to do so.

Lieutenant Edward "Ned" Casey was born in California in 1850 to then Lieutenant Colonel Silas Casey and his wife Abby. Silas Casey was a West Point graduate and veteran of both the Second Seminole War and the Mexican-American War. When the Civil War broke out, he fought for the Union and was eventually promoted to Major General of Volunteers. Ned resolved to follow in his father's footsteps and entered the United States Military Academy at West Point in 1869. Upon graduation in 1873, he joined the 22nd Infantry as a lieutenant where he and Mott first met. Mott and Casey served together in New Orleans during the White League Insurrection and later in the Indian Territory during the Boomer movement. Casey was also with Mott during their movements throughout Texas and their first arrival at Fort Lewis in Colorado in 1879. In 1884, Casey took a position as regimental adjutant for several years, but he reunited with Mott at Fort Keogh in 1888 where he assumed an ill-fated command of the post's Cheyenne scouts.[6]

Over three hundred miles southeast of Fort Keogh, where Mott was stationed at the time of the massacre, Casey led his scouts into the vicinity of the Pine Ridge Reservation. His mission was to surveil a village of Oglala and Sicangu Lakota at No Water in the White Clay Valley not far from where the Wounded Knee massacre occurred. Under the leadership of the Oglala chief, Red Cloud, the Lakota at No Water had refused to submit to the federal government's order that they move onto the reservation. Among the Lakota at No Water was Plenty Horses, a troubled, twenty-one-year-old warrior who had participated in a few brief skirmishes against the 7th Cavalry at Drexel Mission, the day after Wounded Knee. Plenty Horses was educated in the east at an Indian school in Carlisle, Pennsylvania in the 1880s. He resented the school's attempts to assimilate him into white culture and did everything he could to reject their efforts. But, when he returned home, his people regarded him with suspicion. They feared he had become too white to rejoin his people, despite his efforts to shed the yoke of his white education. Caught between two worlds — the white world into which he could never assimilate and the Lakota world that all but rejected him — Plenty Horses fell into a state of anger, frustration, and depression.

One day, Plenty Horses and a small band of Lakota came upon Casey a mile or two outside the No Water camp. Casey had with him a couple of his own scouts. The encounter was cordial enough. The Lakota asked Casey and his scouts to leave the area. Plenty Horses quietly positioned himself behind Casey, his hands slowly gripping the rifle hidden beneath his blanket. As Casey began to turn his horse to leave, Plenty Horses threw aside his blanket, raised his weapon, and fired. The shot ripped through the back of Casey's skull and he fell from his horse. Casey was dead before he hit the ground. The other Lakota warriors were as surprised as Casey's scouts and fled back to the No Water camp with Plenty Horses in tow. Meanwhile, Casey's men returned to their post to inform the commanding officer what had happened. General Miles, who had positioned his forces in strategic locations around the No Water camp to intimidate Lakota into surrendering peacefully, took a measured response to the killing. The last thing he wanted was more bloodshed. Miles restrained himself from ordering a violent reprisal and continued to pressure Red Cloud to submit. Red Cloud, angry at what Plenty Horses had done, surrendered to prevent an attack.

Miles had not forgotten about Casey's killing, but he treated the matter delicately, seeking prosecution only of the one who committed the murder. Plenty Horses had hoped his actions would prove his worth and loyalty to his people, but no one in the camp protested when Miles arrived to arrest him. The killing weakened Red Cloud's credibility and had the potential to turn No Water into another Wounded Knee. Plenty Horse's actions did his Lakota brethren no favors.

Plenty Horses stood trial in federal court in Sioux Falls charged with murder. Although the particulars of the case seemed straightforward, the crux of deciding his guilt came down to whether or not a state of war existed when the killing took place. If it did, Plenty Horses could be acquitted as an enemy combatant. If it did not, then it would be considered a prosecutable murder in cold blood. The problem for the US government was that if they pursued conviction, it would have to rest on the basis that the US was not currently at war, which would undermine its prior justification for Wounded Knee. Despite many in the army wanting to hang Plenty Horses for murder, had his actions been declared so, the army would also then have had to acknowledge that Wounded Knee was, in fact, a massacre. The acquittal of Plenty Horses was a political necessity to maintain the exoneration of Forsyth and the 7th Cavalry. Casey's death was framed as a justifiable killing of a spy on enemy territory and Plenty Horses walked free.

Mott had little patience for such political games. He had known Casey for nearly twenty years and to see his death go unavenged all for the purpose of shielding the government from the uncomfortable optics of Wounded Knee would never sit well with him. In 1909, Plenty Horses died in a railway accident in Boston. Though eighteen years had passed since the death of Casey when Mott read of the accident in the papers, his anger resurfaced and he felt compelled to write about the old injustice. "The wretch who killed [Casey] escaped the gallows through the instrumentality of the Indian Rights Association, who regarded this educated Carlisle Indian murderer as a martyr," Mott remarked.[7]

Caught between worlds: Plenty Horses of the Sicangu
Library of Congress

***

Sitting Bull's death and the fallout from Wounded Knee effectively ended organized Lakota resistance to the United States government and symbolically marked the close of the Indian Wars. Decades of fighting and the need for the fort system had effectively ended. Just two years later, Congress would officially capitulate to settler demands and open the Indian Territory — the last bastion of indigenous American sovereignty — for white settlement transforming the area into the Oklahoma Territory.

It is unlikely that Mott believed that Wounded Knee and its aftermath signaled a neat and tidy end to conflicts between Whites and Native Americans, regardless of what academics or the U.S. Census Bureau declared. Despite all talk of white civilization conquering the frontier and pacifying the Native Americans, Mott did agree that the clash of cultures, for better or worse, had indeed shaped American culture as historian Frederick Jackson Turner posited. "I have become thoroughly convinced that the American character has been radically affected by contact with the American Indian in many respects, especially in regard to oratory," Mott wrote.[8] Mott had grown fond of what he considered the "poetical" way in which many Native Americans expressed themselves through "imagery and figure of speech." In particular, Mott remembered a Blackfoot Chief who stood trial for murder a few years after the events of Wounded Knee while Mott was still serving in Montana. The chief's lawyer, a white man from Helena, had managed to get the chief acquitted. The exonerated Blackfoot chief "arose in that dirty, dingy, ill smelling room with its dirty, dingy, ill smelling people, and made a speech expressing his gratitude...they say it was such a magnificent effort that it penetrated the hide of the average person in the room and all were, probably, natural born Indian haters."[9]

Mott did not assess every effect of their contact with Native Americans to be positive. "We have also been affected in other directions not so beneficially," he wrote. "We have without doubt become a cunning race of people from our intercourse with the Indians, not only in war, but in other respects, but especially in war."[10] Mott had experienced first-hand what it was to be in armed conflict with warriors from many different nations – particularly the Lakota and Cheyenne – but he had come to respect their fighting. "They are not treacherous at all, but full of warlike guile and stratagem," Mott wrote.[11] Far from the savages he once imagined them to be, he saw honor and a strict moral code. In concluding his remarks, he made allusion to the nobility of Cornplanter, a Seneca chief at the Battle of Kanawha, "when his stentorian voice could be heard from one end of his line of battle to the other, which was probably a mile long, shouting to his men to 'be strong,' meaning in his poetical mind, to be brave."[12]

Interestingly, despite having played a role in the subjugation of the country's native populations, Mott did not see the victory as a moral one. He believed the suppression of the Native American was the stifling of a potential for greatness.

After thirty odd years intercourse with the American Indian, I thoroughly believe that if they had had a chance to become civilized by degrees as our ancestors did, they would have developed into the grandest race that ever existed. But he had our abominable civilization of dirty tin cans, bacon rinds and trash thrust down his throat and was surrounded by the scum of the earth called Christians, so that he had no opportunity to become civilized.[13]

Mott's attitudes towards America's indigenous people, while perhaps more progressive than those of the average American in the nineteenth century, should not be overstated. After all, Mott's criticism of his own people and the role they played in subjugating Native Americans was predicated on the fact that he believed them to be uncivilized as they were.

Mott's comments revealed more than a cynical judgment of his people with regard to their treatment of America's indigenous people. That he specifically called out Christians as the "scum of the earth," betrayed an equally cynical attitude where religion was concerned. Mott had begun questioning his faith at least as early as the mid-1870s when he remarked to his mother that he had not experienced any sense of divine emotion at Christ's tomb.[14] However, he had still placed value at that time in collecting water from the River Jordan with which to baptize his nephew, Maris. By this point in his career, his estimation of Christianity, or at least many of the practitioners thereof, had eroded further. He had witnessed many horrors in his life, from the bloody battles of the Civil War to decades of hardship on the Plains. Many of the people he was closest to in life were gone—his Aunt Susan, his sister Annie, a niece and nephew dead as children within days of each other, and even his relationship with his brother, while not entirely severed had been severely strained. Mott never abandoned the idea of faith entirely, but he kept an open mind about how it should be expressed. He dabbled in alternative religious practices including that of Christian Science. A recently-developed metaphysical movement of Christianity founded by Mary Baker Eddy, the Church of Christ, Scientist was based on the precepts that the material world of humanity—with its physicality, illnesses, and death—was but an illusion of the human mind and that only through prayer and a focus on a spiritual reality could the ills of the world be healed.

Whether Mott came to ascribe faithfully to any particular dogma is doubtful.[15] By his retirement, he had no use for church, a fact that prompted admonishment from his cousin Mary Jane when Mott suggested he would not attend church services with them during a proposed visit. "If you do not wish to go to church every day, you had better not come here until after Easter, for you would have to do it as all of us do," Mary Jane wrote. Urging him not to give up on his Christianity she concluded, "and it might be the best thing in the world for you. Who knows? You might want to go somewhere as a missionary."[16] That would not be in Mott's retirement plans.

***

In 1888, several hundred miles away from where the violence at Wounded Knee would occur just a few years later, Mott arrived at

Fort Keogh. It looked very different from the small cantonment on the Tongue River that he had helped supply during the Great Sioux War in 1876. It was on one of those supply runs to Keogh in its early days that had nearly cost Mott his life when he and his men were surrounded by Lakota warriors protecting the rear of the supply train as it crossed Clear Creek. It was fitting then that Mott would be serving at this place two years later when he received a brevet, or honorary, promotion to Major in 1890 for his actions at Clear Creek. The stability of Fort Keogh had also changed. While the primary duties of the post remained the same —escorting supply chains across the northern Plains and protecting the construction crews of the Northern Pacific Railroad, which had somehow managed to survive the depression of the 1870s — peace had largely come to the area by the early 1890s. Mott would find his time at Fort Keogh simpler and more sedentary this time around, not dissimilar to his time at Fort Lewis.

Mott occupied some of his time at Keogh with a pursuit of scholarship. As part of an effort to professionalize the army, General John Schofield, commanding officer of the United States Army, introduced General Order No. 80 in 1891. The order created an "Officer's Lyceum" at all military posts wherein each post commander brought together participating officers every month for six months out of the year to lecture, discuss and give recitations on different scholarly or strategic topics relevant to the military. Officers could also be assigned written essays on a given topic for presentation to the group the following month. The quality of the Lyceum programs varied from one post to the next and was often dependent on the number of officers present, but the goal of the program was to modernize the army by providing professional military education to all officers in the field who, like Mott, never attended a military academy.[17]

By the time General Order 80 was issued, some posts were already holding informal Lyceums as simply another diversion to occupy their time. Mott participated in the Officer's Lyceum at Fort Keogh and in subsequent posts, but it was an activity he had been engaged in for several years. His travels around the world inspired an interest in the comparative study of military tactics of different nations and their historical developments. Among his papers from the 1880s and 1890s are scholarly essays evaluating the influence of skirmish-style American tactical strategy during the Revolutionary and Civil Wars as compared to French and German tactics of the same period.[18] In 1883 he corresponded with and sent some books to a Russian army officer by the name of Captain Chestinsky. The correspondence itself does not survive, but they went through official military channels via Robert Lincoln, the secretary of war and son of the late president. It is possible that Chestinsky was among the party Mott encountered during his Siberian trek and would have been interested to learn more about the Russian military system.[19] In 1888, he translated into English a portion of *Resume of the Principles of the New Tactics by Baron Wechmar, General Major and Brigade Commander, German Army, 1875* from a French edition which he submitted to army administration as a suggestion for improving infantry tactics of the US army for the dispersed order of battle. His work was positively received and forwarded up the ranks to Washington by General Sheridan. The Board of Officers considered his thoughts in their preparation of tactics that year.[20] During his last year with the 22nd Infantry in 1895 while at Fort Pembina, Mott would successfully propose an essay "under the provisions of General Orders No. 80 of 1891," entitled "The Four Epochs in the Development of the Modern Art of War, Commencing with Gustavus Adolphus."[21] That same year the Journal of the Military Service Institution published an article by Mott entitled "Certain Historical Data Regarding Extended Order."[22] General David Stanley, with whom Mott had served during the Yellowstone expedition in the early 1870s would later remark about Mott's intellectual commitments in a commendation writing. Mott was, in Stanley's terms, "a man who improves his knowledge by reading and very extensive travel."[23]

Mott seemed to enjoy his work through the Officer's Lyceum. The last time the army enforced a mandatory education program for volunteer officers during the Civil War, Mott despised it so much he would fly into a rage at the mere thought of it. However, unlike the simpler school of tactics he attended as captain of the Brandywine Guards, the Officer's Lyceum bore a more mature and more intellectual character. And Mott, himself, had matured as well. His purpose in the army was different. He wasn't a single-minded volunteer only interested in fighting for a righteous cause. This was his chosen professional career and his ambition required a broader appreciation for a more well-rounded officer. Besides, given the quietude of many Western posts in this post-Indian Wars era, there were fewer opportunities to exercise the combat side of military service.

When incidents did arise to interrupt the general calm of life at Fort Keogh, they typically involved labor disputes, something Mott would not have expected to encounter being so far from the industrialized east. But in 1892, Mott received orders to travel to Idaho to assist in suppressing a violent labor uprising, not unlike his time in Chicago and Wilkes-Barre during the Great Railroad Strike fifteen years earlier.

Couer d'Alene, Idaho was home to several mining operations mostly focused on lead, silver, and gold. In April of 1892, as a cost-saving measure to offset the higher freight costs charged by the railroads, the mine operators cut worker pay and increased the number of hours laborers were expected to work. The miners were represented by a union, but its demands fell on deaf ears. In response to the general walk out, mine owners decided to replace the workers with non-union labor from as far east as Michigan. They also hired agents from the Pinkerton and Thiel detective agencies to protect the new workers coming to work the mines. Tensions continued to mount until July when hostilities boiled over after a guard killed a Union miner.

On July 10, a large group of armed miners took up a position above the Frisco mine, one of the larger mines in the area that had been returned to full operation employing non-union labor. Much to the miners' surprise, the guards were prepared for them, and what was intended to be merely a show of intimidation turned into a gunfight. The fighting only ceased when the miners destroyed one of the mills with a bundle of dynamite. The guards surrendered and were imprisoned in the union hall. Miners then descended upon the Gem mine. Although a small firefight broke out, the operators of the Gem Mine did not want a repeat of what had just occurred at the Frisco mine and they, too surrendered.

The preparedness of the guards at the Frisco mine confirmed what many of the miners were beginning to suspect already. There was a mole within the union. The local press had published information that could have only come from union meetings and suspicion had fallen on Charles Allison a shoveler at the Gem mines who had taken up the role of secretary of the Gem Miner's Union. Allison was in fact Charles Siringo, an undercover Pinkerton Agent who had indeed been hired by mine operators to infiltrate the union and report on its activities. Immediately following the incident at Frisco, a group of miners went after Siringo, who narrowly escaped his boarding house by sawing a hole in the floor and crawling over a block beneath the wooden boardwalk before surfacing and fleeing to the surrounding hills.

The next evening, a large group of miners descended on a third mine, the Bunker Hill Mine, where they took possession of the ore mill and planted explosives throughout the building. The mine union here also had a mole from the Thiel Detective Agency, but the mine owners were genuinely caught off their guard. Faced with the ultimatum of laying off all their non-union laborers or watching their property explode, the operators conceded to the strikers' demands. In response, the governor declared martial law, deployed the Idaho National Guard and called for federal troops to respond. Military rule over the Coeur d'Alene lasted about four months and the strikers were imprisoned in a small building surrounded by a stockade.

Like much of Mott's work over the last several years, his role in Idaho involved being visible to keep the peace rather than engaging in protracted military action. In the end, it came to very little as the Supreme Court decided that the miners had been illegally imprisoned and ordered them released. The strikers went on to form the Western Federation of Miners, but it would not be the last time unrest would embroil the Coeur d'Alene.

The next year, the United States suffered another financial crash.

Fueled in part by the falling price of silver as well as bankruptcies in the Philadelphia & Reading Railroad and the National Cordage Company —which held a near monopoly on rope in the US—the Panic of 1893 ushered in a four-year depression and nearly unparalleled levels of unemployment. With no social safety net, those who went without work quickly became destitute. Jacob Coxey, a businessman from Ohio, organized the first mass protest march in history to promote a government jobs bill he called the "Good Roads Bill" which would provide needed infrastructure work for the unemployed around the country. A radical idea in the 1890s, it was not be dissimilar in character to the Works Progress Administration of Franklin D. Roosevelt in the 1930s. Inspired by Coxey's ideas, thousands of unemployed Americans descended upon Washington from all corners of the country in the spring of 1894. The press dubbed the horde "Coxey's Army."

Travel to D.C., particularly those from the western-most reaches of the nation, was not always easy, particularly for an unemployed group of people with no money to their names. The northwestern United States was particularly hard hit due to the prevalence of mining and railroad work that the financial crisis had impacted most heavily and the Coxeyites in this region were among the most aggressive. On April 21, 1894, a man named William Hogan led hundreds of marchers in capturing a train belonging to the Northern Pacific Railroad to take them cross country. Since many of the protesters were out-of-work rail workers who were fed up with the rail companies being the seemingly perennial culprit of late nineteenth-century financial panics, there was a certain poetic justice in getting to Washington by hijacking the source of their trouble.

Federal marshalls pursued the train but were frequently stymied in stopping Hogan, in part thanks to sympathetic citizens in towns along the way who helped cover Hogan's tracks. By the time the train entered Montana, federal troops were requested to intercept and stop the hijacked train. Mott served as part of the six-company battalion of the 22nd infantry sent out from Fort Keogh under Lt. Col. John Page, who successfully caught Hogan and his band at Forsyth, Montana. While three of the companies of the Battalion escorted Hogan and the other captured Coxeyites to Helena, Colonel Swaine, commanding officer of Fort Keogh, placed Mott in command of the remaining three companies as a temporary battalion.[24]

Coxey's effort was ultimately unsuccessful. Police in Washington dispersed the crowds and Coxey was arrested while trying to read his proposed bill on the steps of the Capitol, charged with disturbing the landscaping on Congressional grounds. However, the frustration and unrest revealed by the grassroots support of Coxey's Army would continue. In the summer of 1894, just a few months after the incident with Hogan and Coxey's Army, a strike on the Northern Pacific Railroad, precipitated by demonstrations in Chicago, once again brought the attention of the army.

Situated approximately fourteen miles south of Chicago, the small town of Pullman, Illinois was home to the Pullman Palace Car Company, a manufacturer of railroad cars. Pullman was a company town. The company owned all the property and all the stores and other amenities, and the residents were all employees of the company. Feeling the effects of the latest financial crisis, Pullman severely cut the wages of its workforce by about a quarter, while still expecting its employees to spend the same amount on rent and goods purchased in the company's stores. Without a commensurate reduction in other living costs, Pullman's employees were going destitute and hungry in the company's own town. A committee of workers approached the company's executives to demand reinstatement of wages and a redress of living conditions, but Pullman not only denied an audience with them, it also fired them. In response, Pullman workers went on strike in May 1894.

Although the Pullman Company was not itself a railroad company—it only manufactured cars used on the railroads—the strikers appealed to the nascent American Railway Union for help. Founded just the year before by Eugene V. Debs, the ARU had successfully brokered a reinstatement of wages for workers on the Great Northern Railway and so Pullman employees hoped the organization could do the same for them. Debs typically favored negotiation over work stoppage unless such measures failed, but in this case, he supported a boycott of Pullman cars throughout the ARU membership. Workers of rail companies throughout the nation were encouraged to refuse to hook up any Pullman cars to their trains or even to drive trains with Pullmans connected. Given the prevalence of Pullman's cars, the boycott effectively stopped rail lines from running, except for mail trains and a few other essential trains.

Pullman refused to blink. Tensions increased at Pullman and violence broke out. The General Manager's Association, a consortium of railroad executives who managed railroad lines running through Chicago, appealed directly to President Grover Cleveland. The president responded to the GMA's call which infuriated Illinois' governor, John Altgeld, who was annoyed that GMA had not approached him first and believed he could contain the situation with state forces. Altgeld saw Cleveland's unilateral interference as setting a dangerous precedent for violating a state's sovereignty. Cleveland, however, viewed the railroads as an essential resource for national security—the US government depended on them for troop transport, mail delivery, and other essential services—and justified the move on the grounds that actions like strikes that interfered with the railroads violated federal law, specifically the Sherman Anti-Trust Act and the Interstate Commerce Act. Cleveland also used the courts to impose an injunction on the ARU to prevent them from encouraging, enticing, or even communicating with railroad workers with respect to strikes or demonstrations. Debs, who had never sanctioned the violence that broke out, could now not even use his influence to try to calm the situation either.

In Montana, not far from Mott's post at Fort Keogh, the local union working for the Northern Pacific supported the Pullman boycott, but continued working otherwise until they received word that several union members in St. Paul had been fired for following the ARU's recommendations. Montanan workers threatened more than the boycott and vowed a full work stoppage if the jobs of the union members were not reinstated. Representatives of the ARU local chapter in Livingston, Montana attempted to negotiate with the regional Northern Pacific officials, but the rail executives refused. On June 27th, the Northern Pacific in Montana came to a standstill as workers went on a strike that quickly spread throughout the state.[25]

The strikers in Montana had not acted solely out of solidarity. They had their own axe to grind with the railroads. Earlier in the year, workers on the Northern Pacific suffered their own wage reduction and while a strike was averted at the time, the animosity remained. The Pullman boycott became a larger vehicle for redress, adding their own wage reinstatements to the list of demands. This exceeded the national ARU mandate and Debs attempted to convince the Montanans to stay focused only on the boycott for the time being, but his words were not heeded.[26]

The Northern Pacific refused to negotiate with the strikers and by July, taking a note from the General Manager's Association playbook, officials sought legal injunctions against the strikers. The court granted the injunctions and empowered federal marshals to arrest anyone interfering with the operation of the rail lines. Judges from both Montana and Idaho called on US Attorney General, Richard Olney, to dispatch federal troops.

Military commanders in the area were all too ready to suppress the strike. General Wesley Merritt, commander of the Department of Dakota in St. Paul, complained to his superiors in Washington that the disruptions on the Northern Pacific were interfering with supplies, pay, and post throughout the region. President Cleveland approved the deployment of troops to open the lines and resume rail service. General Elwell Otis operating from one end of the line in Seattle and General Merritt operating from the other in St. Paul, dispatched troops to sweep the entire line of "obstructions." The Department of Justice also sent additional U.S. marshals to perform any and all arrests along the way.[27]

The same day that General Merritt mobilized troops from St. Paul, he sent orders to troops in posts throughout the region to occupy rail centers, bridges, and other important junctions.[28] As part of his plan, Merritt ordered Mott to take the three-company battalion he commanded to join a transport on the Northern Pacific Railroad bound for the western boundary of Montana. While en route, he commanded Mott to "furnish such protection as may be necessary to the crew as to secure your progress and remove obstructions offered the train."[29] Although any arrests of individuals impeding the progress of the train would be made by the civil authorities, Merritt authorized Mott to use any force necessary to subdue the offenders.[30] The westbound train Mott was to protect contained a group of Italian laborers—likely non-union strikebreakers brought in as replacements for the rail workers—bound for Livingston, Montana in the southwestern part of the state. Upon arrival at Livingston, Mott was to turn the laborers over to the commanding officer at that location who would take over their protection.[31]

Livingston had become a particularly heated location and just a few days prior to Mott's arrival in the city there had been a tense incident in which an army Captain, misreading the intentions of an assembled crowd, assaulted two people, including the leader of Livingston's chapter of the ARU. The incident further reinforced for the people that military intervention portended despotic oppression. In fact, the strike had been peaceable with virtually no destruction of property until federal troops became involved. Even then, hostilities and violence were sporadic and not serious enough to severely hamper operations on the railroad for any great length of time. What Mott and the other soldiers did not know at the time was that the Northern Pacific, as well as the General Manager's Association in their jurisdiction, purposefully manufactured a bigger crisis by employing Pullman cars on mail trains knowing it would attract federal aid.[32] Mott completed his mission without incident but had he any foreknowledge of the situation in Livingston, he likely felt a certain amount of apprehension as he pulled into the town with his battalion.

As was the case with many of the other labor strikes at the time, the combined might of the corporations and the federal government were insurmountable. With the rail lines occupied and strikers dispersed throughout the state, members of the ARU conceded defeat.

The Northern Pacific offered to reinstate the jobs of any striker who had not been among the "agitators" of the unrest, however, they had to accept the reduced wage the company had set earlier and any members of the American Railway Union had to renounce their membership. With the exception of those in Livingston where the staunchest opposition had been, workers accepted the railway's terms and reapplied.[33] The workers' actions had gained them nothing.

Mott returned to Fort Keogh where he remained until the end of the year. When a fire broke out among the barracks, Mott's unit was transferred to Fort Pembina in North Dakota where he remained until May when another fire broke out there all but destroying the post. The army officially abandoned Pembina in August and Mott transferred to Fort Assiniboine in Montana. In September, Mott led a garrison to a new fort near Helena, called Fort Harrison. Being the first troops garrisoned at the site, Mott and his men received a "royal reception" at the Montana Club from the citizens of Helena.[34] Mott appreciated the welcome, but he was growing weary of his current duty. After nearly twenty-five years as a captain, Mott believed his time for advancement was due.

Mott had gone before a board of examiners while still at Fort Pembina seeking promotion. Although he had been brevetted major in 1890, the title was an honorary one. It offered neither an increase in pay nor additional rights or privileges afforded to the rank, not even the honor of being addressed by it. On May 1st, 1896, Mott finally received the results of the examination. His application was approved and his elevation to the rank of major was official. Accompanying his promotion came orders to return to Fort Assiniboine to assume command of the 25th Infantry Regiment. As Mott bade farewell to his men and departed the unit with which he had served for over twenty-five years, he set his sights toward new priorities. The promotion had offered another step towards providing a more comfortable life for the family back home who now needed his support.

17

New Priorities

His recommendations were glowing. "[An] efficient officer and has always borne an excellent character," wrote Nelson Miles.[1] Elwell Otis commended him for his "attention to duty, for efficiency as an officer, for sobriety and integrity, for courteous demeanor and gentlemanly deportment," whose courage, bravery, and cool head in the face of "overwhelming numbers of hostile Indians intent upon his destruction" at Clear Creek had distinguished him as an important asset to the army.[2] David Stanley remembered him from the third Yellowstone Expedition and reiterated his military capabilities as an officer but noted particularly that he possessed a "bright mind" and was a "man who improves his knowledge by reading and very extensive travel."[3] With such advocacy, it's little wonder that Mott received his promotion to major. Except, that was not the job for which he had sought their recommendations. The real object of Mott's ambition was a desk job in Harrisburg, Pennsylvania.

In 1892, Mott lost his mother. In the wake of Ann's death, Mott became the de facto head of the family. He would have expected Frank, as eldest child, to fill the role, but his brother had a hard enough time tending to his own affairs in order to take care of his own wife and daughter, let alone his extended family. After all it was just one year later that Frank would find himself in Moyamensing prison for being unable to pay the court judgments against him over the Bleloch case. Hazen and Annie, children of Mott and Frank's late sister, still required looking after as their brother-in-law Mort struggled to provide a sufficient living through his traveling sales work.

Mott did not see his status in the family as a burden. Though he never married or had children of his own, Mott firmly believed in the importance of family. The biggest challenge for him was how to be an effective parental figure to his niece and nephew at such a distance, never knowing where he would be at any given time. Hi sister, Sallie, could handle the daily care of the kids, but there was little else Mott could do apart from the financial support he sent back home.

Mott's newfound role as patriarch reordered his priorities. It was this transformation that led Mott in 1894 to apply for a position in Harrisburg on the staff of Robert Pattison, Governor of Pennsylvania. Mott's request of what was essentially a desk job was entirely antithetical to his otherwise restless disposition, but it would have brought him permanently to Harrisburg, less than one hundred miles from Bethlehem, Pennsylvania where he could visit Sallie and the kids with far greater frequency than he could were he still traipsing around the frontier.[4]

Why Mott's bid was ultimately unsuccessful is debatable. It was an election year and Pattison was not standing for reelection. This would have made any late-term appointments tenuous. Mott was also not the ambitious social climber his brother was and he had largely stayed out of political games. Outside of army circles, he was simply not well-known. "Few know his merit and deserts," wrote his former commander General Otis, "with the exception of those who have been long connected with him in military association."[5] Mott's noted modesty may have done him a disservice.

With a position close to home off the table, Mott's next best option was to continue to apply for increases in rank as officer positions became available through retirements or other promotions. He might not be able to provide Hazen and Annie with his regular presence, but the higher up the command structure he could go, the more money he would earn to support them. His promotion to major on May 1, 1896, marked the first step on that journey.

Mott's new command brought him to a unit far different from any unit with which he had previously served. The 25th Infantry was one of the army's so-called Buffalo Soldier regiments—a unit whose rank and file consisted entirely of African American troops. The regiment was created in 1869 as a consolidation of two pre-existing African American regiments—the 39th and 40th regiments. Like every segregated Black regiment at the time, all commissioned officers in the 25th—Lieutenants on up—were white. Everyone else—sergeants, corporals, and privates—were Black. This would not change until 1901. Stationed initially in New Orleans, their role in suppressing the racial violence which plagued the city was not without controversy. The racially divided Reconstruction-era South greatly resented being occupied by Black soldiers.[6]

Along with the 24th Infantry and the 9th and 10th cavalries—also all Black regiments—the Black men of the 25th made up almost ten percent of the U.S. army in the west. However, unlike their white counterparts, their deployments were usually motivated more by race than strategy. After a few years of service in Louisiana attempting to quell racial violence, the government sent the 25th to Texas where they remained for the entire decade of the 1870s. Although active in campaigns against the Apache, Comanche, and Comanchero, one of the primary reasons for keeping them so far south was the bizarre belief that African American physiology made them impervious to the sweltering conditions of the Texan climate. In truth, the soldiers suffered from terrible conditions, occupying old adobe forts abandoned during the Civil War. Poor circulation in the old structures meant that soldiers in the field without permanent shelter actually fared better than their counterparts at the main post.[7]

The 25th continued to face racial discrimination despite being removed from the hotbed of racial tensions further east. Stagecoaches in the area, which they were ordered to ride and protect, often refused to carry them back to their posts once they completed their duty. As white settlers increasingly populated the region throughout the 1870s,

Promoted at last: Mott as Major of the 25th Infantry Regiment
"Buffalo Soldier Regiment" by John Nankivell

the army felt increased pressure to transfer the Black troops elsewhere. By 1880, the army finally caved to popular pressure and transferred the 25th to the Dakota Territory, despite concerns by white officials in the War Department that they would be physiologically incapable of enduring the colder northern climate.[8]

In spite of the War Department's initial, albeit irrational, concerns about African American suitability in Dakota, the soldiers acquitted themselves well. In addition to fatigue duties—cutting logs, laying telegraph lines, etc.—they engaged in community service activities, providing disaster relief to flood-ravaged communities and raising money to support Prudence Crandall Phileo, who had founded the nation's first school for African American girls over fifty years earlier. Even the regimental band gained positive notoriety by giving regular public concerts throughout the region.[9]

By the late 1880s, the regiment moved to Montana where their service was not dissimilar to Mott's, who was still a captain with the 22nd. They responded to the Coeur d'Alene mine workers' unrest in Idaho in 1892 and guarded the trains and mail along the Northern Pacific Railroad during its labor dispute in 1894. By the time Mott joined the regiment as its major in the Spring of 1896, he may have already been familiar with the unit.

Mott admired the Black men under his command and there is no evidence to suggest he felt his was a lesser assignment. The *Chicago Tribune* once quoted him as saying "no white soldier ever showed more tenacity, pluck, and dash than the black men" under his command.[10] His extensive travels had given him a broader perspective than most and in practice, he likely cared little for the color of one's skin provided they followed orders and conducted themselves with honor. Still, his was a segregated army and there is no evidence to suggest he thought it should have been otherwise. If he ever fraternized with his African American subordinates as he might have had his rank-and-file troops been white, Mott never said. The fact is, Mott was joining the regiment at a particularly difficult time in race relations in the United States, which is saying something given the generally dismal state of race relations previously.

During the 1890s, most former Confederate states drafted new constitutions or amendments that effectively disenfranchised African Americans in their states. They instituted new laws like poll taxes, literacy tests and comprehension tests knowing such restrictions would disproportionately affect African Americans. Legislatures did not limit these laws to African Americans, so they did not technically violate the 15th Amendment. After all, such restrictions affected many poor, illiterate whites as well. However, many lawmakers included grandfather clauses in the laws allowing an exception to the restrictions if one's grandfather had the right to vote—something no Black person at the time could claim. This helped to exclude many whites from the additional qualifications and allowed southern governments to target Blacks without doing so explicitly. In addition, segregation laws became commonplace and received constitutional blessing through the U.S. Supreme Court under Plessy v. Ferguson in 1896, the same year Mott joined the 25th. Plessy v. Ferguson essentially allowed institutions to be separated along racial lines, so long as those institutions were equal. In practice, however, separate was never equal. The increased entrenchment and legitimacy of these southern legislatures emboldened instigators of race riots and violence against African Americans. Incidents of racial conflict rose dramatically.

The beginning of the Jim Crow era, in which state and local governments throughout the South passed increasingly oppressive segregation laws, is often associated with the 1890s, but its roots extend back to the contentious presidential election of 1876 between Hayes and Tilden. The compromise that settled the election brought an end to Reconstruction and allowed Southern Democrats to regain their political power. Over the next decade and a half, as the southern democrats started to dominate their legislatures once again, they passed more and more restrictive laws against Blacks.

Mott had witnessed first-hand the early, more militant attempts to restrict Black rights in the South through intimidation and paramilitary insurgency when he was sent to New Orleans to suppress the White League Insurrection. At the time, Mott had decried the 15th Amendment claiming it had ruined the South.[11] Now he was taking command of troops whose rights in vast swaths of the nation were quickly eroding. It is difficult to say if Mott's thoughts on African American suffrage had changed in the twenty years since his time in New Orleans, or in general what his true thoughts on race were. Mott never clearly explained his problem with Black enfranchisement in the first place. Mott liked to be well-informed of the political climate in the country, even if at times it made him want to "expatriate" himself out of the United States, so while he remained mostly silent about his thoughts on his new unit, their standing in the country would not have been lost on him.[12] Whatever his thoughts on race, Mott was committed to the success of his new unit.

Life for the 25th and its new major was quiet in their new post at Fort Assiniboine. Mott spent much of his time instituting improvements in drilling and regulation. The increased focus on tactical training became common throughout the army at this time, but it wasn't something Mott found particularly exciting. About eighteen months into his service with the 25th, he led a detachment of the regiment under orders to occupy the newly built Fort Harrison near Helena, Montana. Life proved little more exciting here, but in truth, there were few posts that would have satisfied him as his long-term ambitions resided outside the army. After just two years as major, Mott resumed his efforts to secure a brigadier generalship so he could maximize his pension and retire to support his family.

Back in West Chester, his brother Frank drummed up as much local support as possible to lobby Washington for his brother's cause. In the Spring of 1898, Frank approached Uriah Hunt Painter, a Chester County native who had made a name for himself during the Civil War as a war correspondent for the Philadelphia Inquirer. By the late 1890s, Painter had become a familiar, if controversial, fixture in Washington, acting as both congressional correspondent and lobbyist for hire. Despite Painter's dubious reputation as both a lobbyist and a member of the press corps, he had a wealth of political connections at his disposal and Frank believed his influence could be instrumental in securing Mott's promotion.[13] Frank reminded Painter that he had consulted the newspaperman thirty years earlier when Mott was applying for a commission in the regular army. "You know all about him," Frank wrote to Painter about Mott. "You probably recollect that he was appointed to the regular army upon the letters of General Meade and General Parke...You told me at the time if I had applied to you, you would have made him Major on those letters."[14] Frank also called on Thomas Butler, another Chester County native and member of the Pennsylvania delegation to the US House of Representatives. Both of Pennsylvania's senators, Matthew Quay—the state's Republican political boss once dubbed the "kingmaker" by President Benjamin Harrison—and Boies Penrose—a Philadelphia native and shirttail relative of Frank's wife—also found Frank knocking on their doors.

Frank succeeded in garnering support. Painter agreed to put in a word for Mott while Butler, Quay, and Penrose all promised to lobby on Mott's behalf. Still, Mott was pessimistic about his chances. He kept abreast of promotions within the army and grew frustrated at the methods the War Department employed in promoting younger staff officers into the limited free slots of brigadier generalships at the expense of much older officers still in the field and more worthy of ascent. "This is the d[amn]dest outfit that we have ever had. They can't find a regular staff officer who can perform his duty and they have to detail company officers to do their work. There's a whole lot of cols. of the army, old men serving here who can't get anything, while these staff officers are promoted over their heads."[15] It didn't help Mott's frustration that while he was trying to conclude his army career, the government was about to send him into another war.

***

Since 1895, Cuba had twice become embroiled in revolution. Territorial subjects of Spain, the native Cubans bristled at the mistreatment they experienced at the hands of their imperial rulers. Matters only escalated when General Valeriano Weyler, the commanding Spanish officer on the island, instituted *reconcentrado*, a brutal policy that rounded up rural populations from the island's interior and placed them in concentration camps among the coastal cities in order to prevent insurgents from hiding amongst remote communities far from the watchful eyes of the Spanish. Between food shortage and disease, conditions in these camps were abysmal. Hundreds of thousands of Cubans died during the years that Weyler's policy remained in effect.[16] The United States was not blind to what was happening in Cuba. Since President Cleveland's second administration, the United States Government had appealed to Spain to end its inhumane policies and reform its rule over Cuba. However, while Cleveland had offered to serve as a mediator between Spain and the Cuban insurgents, U.S. policy was one of strict non-intervention. By the time President William McKinley assumed office in 1897, popular opinion in the US no longer supported the non-interventionist policy. The popular press continued to report on the atrocities occurring in Cuba and the outcry of sympathy and support for the insurgents grew loud and clear. Unofficially, supplies, weapons, and even manpower in some instances, made their way to Cuba. It became harder for McKinley to remain committed to this isolationist stance.

In the late summer of 1898, Spain experienced a change in government after the assassination of its then Prime Minister, Antonio Cánovas del Castillo. The Government under the new Prime Minister, Práxedas Mateo Sagasta, found itself in a similar situation as the McKinley administration. Sagasta wished to avoid conflict with the US, but popular opinion in Spain disagreed. Sagasta was more willing to enact some of the reforms the US demanded. He removed General Weyler from Command, planned to terminate the *reconcentrado* policy, and offered the Cubans limited political autonomy. These concessions only worsened the situation. For the US and the Cubans, half-measures were not good enough. They required full independence. But Sagasta had his own internal tensions to manage. The Spanish military in Cuba resented Weyler's removal and saw relinquishing any sovereignty of the island to the Cubans as a sign of weakness.[17] Growing discontent in the ranks of the Spanish soldiers and officers towards their own government led to riots in the streets of Havana. Soldiers sacked newspaper offices sympathetic to the limited autonomy policy and the stability of the island fell further and further into decay.

With the situation rapidly escalating, the American Consul in Havana appealed to President McKinley to send a warship to Cuba as a show of strength and a symbol of their commitment to protecting both US citizens on the island as well as American investments in the country. In late January 1898, McKinley dispatched the *U.S.S. Maine* of the North Atlantic Squadron from the Dry Tortugas off the Florida Keys and sent it south to the port of Havana.[18] The decision to send the *Maine* over any other ship in the fleet was a deliberate choice as it was not just any warship. Clad in steel, the *U.S.S. Maine* was a new kind of battleship built by the Navy. Gone were the sails and rigging, and in their place a series of smokestacks making the vessel fully steam-powered. The *Maine* represented the unprecedented might of the US Navy.[19] When it arrived the next morning and fired a salute to announce its presence, it had the desired effect. Havana settled, but tensions under the surface remained high.[20]

Outwardly, the Spanish military treated the US naval presence with deference and respect, but no one could fail to see that the *Maine* was not welcome. The uneasy peace lasted only a few weeks. On February 15th, an explosion occurred on the *Maine* and the mighty warship sunk to the bottom of the harbor. Survivors were quickly taken to shore or rescued by other ships. Among the Americans in Cuba to rush to the soldiers' aid was Clara Barton, founder of the American Red Cross, who happened to be in Havana at the time.[21] The sudden explosion immediately propelled the rumor mill into overdrive. Was this a freak accident or had the Spanish planted a mine beneath the ship? Given the epicenter of the explosion towards the front of the ship, many experts believed it was likely an accident, the result of poor-quality coal spontaneously combusting near the forward ammo magazine. That sort of thing had nearly happened on other ships and seemed a plausible excuse.[22] The Unites States launched an intensive investigation, sending divers down to the Maine to ascertain the origin of the explosion and determine if it came from within the ship or below it.

None of that mattered to the American people for whom there was no denying that Spain had deliberately attacked the *Maine*. As the investigation wore on, the possibility of an intentional attack became more credible. Members of the US government quickly jumped on the bandwagon and called for support to go to war. Theodore Roosevelt, then Assistant Secretary of the Navy, was so convinced of Spain's deceit that he took it upon himself to mobilize strategic parts of the Pacific fleet while his boss was out for the afternoon. In the days before the Panama Canal, it would take a long time for the Pacific fleet to sail to Cuba by way of the straits of Magellan south of Chile and Argentina. Roosevelt believed that if war was inevitable, the fleet should begin its journey now.

As the American investigation wore on, the findings appeared to lean more and more toward a mine beneath the ship which had caused the forward magazine to ignite and explode. Although the official findings of the investigation concluded that the *Maine* was attacked, it could not identify the party responsible. McKinley, still wishing to avoid open conflict, hoped that it had been a make-shift bomb planted by a lone dissident and not an act of war by another sovereign power.[23] But the president could no longer deny the outpouring of popular support to go to war, which had grown stronger than ever given the public desire to see the *Maine* avenged.[24]

Despite mounting pressure to go to war with Spain, President McKinley continued to seek out alternatives to open conflict. The Spanish government was equally loath to go to war and so McKinley gave them a way out: provide reparations for the destruction of the *Maine*, end the *reconcentrado* policy, and immediately grant full Cuban independence. Prime Minister Sagasta was still prepared to end the *reconcentrado* policy, but the earlier revolt by his own military made him reticent to take any actions that would be deemed weak and dishonorable to the military leaders on the island.[25] With his back to the wall, Sagasta turned to his allies in Europe for assurance that they would render aid in the event war broke out. None of them would commit, however, without England taking the lead. England, though, supportive of the idea of a joint European coalition to assist, roundly refused to lead it. With Europe at an impasse, Spain found itself alone, awash in sympathy but bereft of aid.

With help from Europe off the table and tenuous control over its own armed forces in Cuba, the best Spain could offer the US was an armistice to cease hostilities, but it would have to be initiated by the insurgents. To save face with its generals, Spain could not be the initiator of a peace proposal. This was unacceptable to the US. The internal optics of Spain's government did not concern McKinley and he wasn't about to compromise the terms simply to engage in Spanish political theater. McKinley had no choice but to give Spain an ultimatum. If they could not agree to the original terms by April 11, McKinley would address Congress and seek authorization to intervene militarily in the Cuban situation. This was already a longer grace period than many in the US wanted, but McKinley justified the delay by noting the need to evacuate all American citizens from the island. Over in the Department of the Navy, assistant secretary Roosevelt was begging to send a squadron to blockade Havana harbor even though no resolution for military intervention had yet been authorized. McKinley denied Roosevelt, but he knew it was a delay of the inevitable.

In the meantime, Spain continued to seek alternatives, including appealing to the Vatican for Papal intervention in brokering an armistice. Here, too, Spain was denied. By April 10th, with time running out, Spain made one last counteroffer. They agreed to an immediate end to the *reconcentrado* policy and arbitration of the *Maine*.[26] On the question of Independence, however, they signaled a willingness to comply, but not on the timetable the US demanded. Instead, they would agree to an armistice proposed by a joint European coalition with eventual Cuban independence to be granted later in the year. That the armistice would occur at the behest of Spain's European allies and not Spain was intended to help the Spanish government save face with its Generals and avoid internal military strife. It was still not good enough.

The next day, with his options exhausted, McKinley traveled to the Capitol and addressed Congress as planned. In his speech, he formally requested authorization to intervene militarily in Cuba to end hostilities and to aid in establishing a stable government on the island. The speech fell short of the expectations of many in Congress. Nowhere in McKinley's speech did he explicitly recognize Cuba's right to self-determination. The phrasing around the establishment of a stable government was viewed as one propped up by the US, effectively annexing Cuba as a territorial holding.[27] It took another week of congressional deliberations and amendments to deliver a resolution that would formally recognize an insurgent Cuban government and explicitly disavow any suggestion of ongoing US control. On April 22, 1898, the North Atlantic squadron arrived at Havana from Key West and established a blockade. The United States was now at war with Spain.[28]

In the lead-up to war, the Navy was not the only branch of the armed forces chomping at the bit to mobilize against Spain. The rumor mill that churned amongst the American public operated just as strongly among the troops of the 25th Infantry in Montana. In late March, Mott and the other staff officers of the 25th officially received word to prepare to move south to the Gulf of Mexico. The regiment was currently deployed across three separate forts in the territory. Staff headquarters along with Companies B, F, G, and H were stationed at Fort Missoula. Companies C and E occupied Fort Assiniboine and Mott commanded companies A and D at Fort Harrison.[29] By early April, it became clear to the whole regiment that they would soon be headed south. They did not know where they would be sent first—Key West, St. Augustine, Dry Tortugas—but it did not matter. Everyone knew their ultimate destination was Cuba. On April 10, the day before McKinley's deadline, Mott assumed command of both the Fort Harrison and Fort Assiniboine contingents of the 25th and lead them under orders to Chickamauga National Park in Georgia. The troops under Mott's command were officially the first army troops in the United States to mobilize in the Spanish-American War.[30]

When the 25th arrived at Chickamauga five days later, they became the talk of the nation. Congress was still deliberating McKinley's resolution, but the sudden troop movement effectively validated the swirling rumors of war. While a few companies broke off and moved ahead toward Tampa, Mott remained with the bulk of the regiment at Chickamauga where the War Department sent units of volunteers to join them. When the volunteers arrived, Mott noticed the army had furnished them with outdated models of Springfield rifles. Mott shook his head in disbelief at what he saw. "The Spaniards are armed with an improved rifle of small caliber and all they have to do is storm off a mile or mile and a half and hail them into eternity," Mott wrote to his brother in exasperation. "There are some of the d[amn]dest fools in the army on the War Board directing the war from Washington."[31]

Mott spent most of his time in Chickamagua putting his men through heavy field drills before moving on to Tampa where they would join the 1[st] and 4[th] Infantries to create the 2[nd] Brigade, 2[nd] Division, 5[th] Corps. Mott continued the relentless drilling of the troops in Tampa in order to acclimate the men to physical exertion in a tropical climate. After all, the climate in Montana, from which the regiment had so recently been stationed, was about as far from the Cuban climate as one could get. It didn't help matters that problems with the supply trains meant that the soldiers were still outfitted with the heavier uniforms designed for the Montana winter. This restricted drilling to either early morning or early evening just after sunset.

By June 6th, war with Spain had been officially declared, the naval blockade of Havana was in place and it was time to mobilize the ground troops. At 6:00 in the evening, Mott and his regiment received orders to strike their tents and make for Port Tampa where they would board a transport bound for Cuba. Their transport, the *Concho*, was a large vessel, but one devoid of the resources to accommodate an entire regiment comfortably. As they set sail for Cuba, Mott fell seriously ill. He had never tolerated the heat well and he blamed the Tampa climate for his current affliction.[32] By the time the *Concho* sailed beyond Key West, it was clear Mott could not continue. He disembarked and his commanding officer ordered him aboard a hospital transport heading back toward the Keys. Back in Key West, Mott lay in hospital for a month. The army doctors cleared him for travel, but not duty. They placed him on extended sick leave and sent him home to West Chester to convalesce.

In Mott's absence, his regiment went on to take an active part in the Battle of El Caney and the fall of Santiago, though they had to fight to get their role recognized. General Chaffee, major general of volunteers, had given all credit to the 12th infantry and downplayed the involvement of the 25th entirely. Numerous staff officers of the 25th submitted letters and testimonials rebutting Chaffee's account of the action. Had Mott been present, there is little doubt he would have strongly added his voice to undoing the injustice, but from his brother's home in West Chester, there was nothing he could do. It was an ironic parallel to the mutiny of the Brandywine Guards during the Civil War. For the second time in his military career, Mott cursed his absence at a time when the honor of his men needed defending.[33]

In late August, Mott's doctors finally cleared him for active duty, but his unit's role in Cuba had already ended. Following the surrender of Santiago da Cuba earlier that month, the 25th boarded the *U.S.S. Comanche* en route for Camp Wikoff on Montauk Point, Long Island.[34] There Mott rejoined his regiment on September 1. Wikoff had become host to thousands of soldiers recently returned from Cuba, many of whom were suffering from tropical diseases brought back with them from the island. Conditions at the camp were abysmal, causing a stir in the national press with accusations of government neglect and mismanagement. One hundred twenty-six soldiers in total would die in camp—equivalent to a third of the amount of overall combat deaths in Cuba. Of course, illness ravaged the army well beyond Camp Wikoff. Over 2,500 soldiers died of disease and other non-combat causes during the war with Spain, while only about 365 soldiers died in battle. Disease was a pervasive problem, but it mattered little where popular opinion was concerned. All they saw were sensational headlines about the specific conditions at Camp Wikoff.[35] Having just regained his health after several months of recovery, Mott did not welcome the conditions which greeted him when he arrived at Montauk Point. He managed to avoid a second illness, but it was a relief when in late September, the army ordered Mott to lead the regiment to its next assignment, Fort Logan, Colorado. On October 3, Companies I, K, L, and M arrived at Fort Logan where Mott established and took command of regimental headquarters. The remaining companies split off to occupy several additional forts throughout neighboring Arizona and New Mexico.

Although Mott missed out on the action in Cuba, he soon got another chance to set foot on the island. In November, his newfound allies in Washington, courtesy of his brother, managed to secure a promotion to lieutenant colonel of the 5th Infantry. It was not the generalship he had sought, but it was a step in the right direction. The 5th Infantry was stationed at Santiago de Cuba, the city his previous regiment had participated in taking. Mott immediately left Colorado and sailed for Cuba to join his new regiment in mid-December. He remained in Santiago de Cuba until April 1899 when he assumed command of the neighboring District of Guantanamo. Nearly a quarter of the district's 28,000 inhabitants resided within the town of Guantanamo. Mott did not oversee any military engagements during his command, but the greater threat of disease once again occupied much of his time. New cases of malaria occurred almost daily. He ordered a sanitary camp placed on Cayo Toro south of town in Guantanamo Bay consisting of three tents, one of which served as accommodation for the guard of the camp. After his illness the previous year, Mott did not welcome the prospect of being struck down yet again with another illness, but it was practically unavoidable. While in command, Mott fell ill with Cuban Fever—a variety of Malaria. Although he was able to recover without going on extended leave, the effects would plague him for months after his recovery. Despite the rampant disease, the death rate among soldiers under Mott's command was surprisingly low. Only three deaths occurred in the district in 1899 due to illness—Delirium Tremens,

Intestinal Obstruction, and Typhoid Fever having taken the lives of three new recruits who had traveled to the island in May of that year.[36] In November, an outbreak of Yellow Fever in the district was traced to a Norwegian vessel that had recently arrived from Santiago. Mott placed the vessel under quarantine, averting a more serious epidemic.

Apart from managing tropical illness among the troops, Mott's time in Guantanamo was otherwise quiet. He lived in a comfortable house that he rented for $48 per month and enjoyed speaking with interesting people and other kindred spirits who had traveled the world as he had. In the smoking room of the transport *Seneca* docked at Caimanera in Guantanamo Bay, Mott met George F. Kennan, a well-known American journalist and founding member of the National Geographic Society, who was known for his travels in Siberia.

Born in 1845 in Norwalk, Ohio, Kennan joined an expedition as a young man to survey a telegraph line across Russia to Europe. His book, *Tent Life in Siberia: An Incredible Account of Adventure, Travel, and Survival* spring boarded his career in journalism. He worked for the Associated Press covering countless stories of national and international importance, but his specialty was in writing and speaking about Russia. Kennan explored many parts of the world including subsequent travels to Russia, where he became an outspoken opponent of the Imperial practice of exiling criminals and political dissidents to Siberia where they were forced into hard labor under debilitating conditions.

Kennan's writings heavily influenced American attitudes towards Russia in the nineteenth century, which earned him the enmity of the Russian government which would have him arrested and deported during a later trip. Kennan did not travel with Mott across Siberia as he was not known to have been in Russia in 1881. His second documented travel did not occur until 1885. Kennan was in Cuba having been hired by *The Outlook* magazine to report on the status of the country in the wake of the war. In noting the number of world travelers and the places they had all visited, Kennan was pleasantly surprised to meet Mott and reminisce over their shared experiences in Russia. "There were three of us who had been in Siberia," Kennan wrote in his article

A Siberian Connection: George F. Kennan in the dress of a Siberian exile
Library of Congress

for *The Outlook*. "Lieutenant-Colonel Hooton and I had crossed it from the Pacific Ocean to St. Petersburg."[37] Mott's penchant for experiencing chance encounters with interesting and prominent people had become a recurring theme in his life.

Mott left Cuba in September when the army ordered him to take command of Fort Sheridan in Illinois. When he arrived with the 5th Infantry at Sheridan, Mott was still suffering the effects of the fever he had contracted in Cuba. By his estimation, it took him about nine months to fully shake the disease.[38] Mott enjoyed his time at Sheridan. "I am delighted with my station," he wrote to his sister Sallie in early 1901. "It is near a fine City in a healthy country."[39] The biggest drama he faced at the post was the abolishment of the canteen, or Post Exchange, which Mott worried would lead the men to seek drink in the local saloons. "The abolishment of the canteen will be the greatest blow at army discipline since the days of Secretary [Redfield] Proctor," Mott is reported to have said. "It will open the way for the post trader again, I fear, and the repetition of an experience of the most unsatisfactory character."[40] To the outside world, the canteen, which sold alcohol, condoned drunkenness. However, advocates for the canteen, claimed the service reduced alcoholism in the ranks by controlling the kind of alcohol available and providing it within a more regulated environment. The Exchange also offered additional benefits for morale and diversion which Mott and other proponents of the canteen believed reduced the need for soldiers to turn to drink. Louis Livingston Seaman, a retired surgeon and Major in the US Volunteers wrote an opinion piece for the *North American Review* in 1903 advocating the reinstatement of the canteen by reiterating its intended purpose:

The purposes of the Post Exchange or Canteen combined the features of a reading-room and recreation-room, a co-operative store and a restaurant. Its primary purpose was to furnish to the troops, at a reasonable price, the articles of ordinary use, wear and consumption, not supplied by the Government, and to afford them means of rational recreation and amusement suitable to their taste and station in life, which, if denied, they would seek outside the limits of camp.[41]

Ever the stickler for discipline and gentlemanly conduct amongst his officers and soldiers, Mott agreed with people like Seaman. He would rather see his men enjoy themselves in a controlled environment than seek such vices unbridled at the saloons in nearby local towns.

Though Mott still fought for what he considered proper administration of the army, with just over a year left in his career, his thoughts were increasingly focused more on home and family. His sister Sallie had taken on the solemn duty of raising their nephew and niece, and Mott was keen to join her in serving as a proxy parent for the children who were quickly approaching adulthood.

18

Uncle Mott

"Now that you are about commencing your career as a collegian, I want to give you some advice," Mott wrote to Hazen in 1900.[1] His nephew had been accepted to Lehigh University in Bethlehem to pursue a degree in mechanical engineering. Though well-educated himself, Mott had little advice to offer on the academic front, but he believed six decades on earth had taught him a thing or two about what it meant to be a good man. "You realize, I suppose, that you have to make your own way in the world, so you must be diligent in your studies and cultivate industrious habits," Mott continued.[2]

Mott specifically counseled his nephew in three areas: personal integrity, physical exercise, and women. Not surprisingly personal integrity, and the dogged defense of it, ranked highest in Mott's estimation of character. "Above all, be manly and learn to box," Mott entreated. "And if anyone insults you, promptly knock him down."[3] Boxing would also help fulfill another important aspect of living a good life. Having spent decades in an extremely physical occupation, Mott likewise believed in the power of exercise to maintain one's health. "If I were you, I would go in for all kinds of athletics...Baseball is a fine game—about the best of all out of door sports."[4]

The children Mott never had: Hazen (Left) & Annie (Right)
Courtesy of Clay Chase

There was a softer, more gentlemanly side to being a man in Mott's estimation. Despite his confirmed bachelorhood, he placed immense value on polite society and the importance of regularly mingling with women. "...cultivate ladies' society," he advised. "Go into society and commence dancing. Whenever a young man shuns the company of decent girls, it is a bad sign and very often goes before or with bad habits."[5] Mott did not elaborate on what "bad habits" he had in mind, but in spending most of his time in forts surrounded by dozens of young, single men with nary a woman in sight save the occasional wife of a superior officer, he may have observed the effects of a want of society in the behavior of his men.

While Mott could offer wisdom and life experiences more readily to Hazen, he did not neglect his niece, Annie, where advice was concerned. As she got older, Mott took a keen interest in making sure she pursued age-appropriate pursuits advising when to stop childish activities like paper dolling.[6] As Annie matured into her adolescence and began going out into society herself, Mott sought to guide her into not making the same mistakes he had with regard to neglecting important social skills like dancing. "You ought to take up dancing again," Mott instructed his fourteen-year-old niece. "A person who cannot dance is like a lost sheep. I know from my own experience."[7]

Mott did not suddenly decide to take an interest in his niece and nephew as they approached maturity. Ever since their mother died and Mort needed financial help to support the kids, Mott felt a paternal responsibility to the children regardless of the miles that separated them. He sent money back home regularly to help them but also imparted advice on the best hygiene regimens and how to stay fit and healthy. He felt a certain connection to Hazen and Annie that he did not share with his brother's daughter, May. He likely recognized the parallels between their upbringing and his own. Mott, too, had lost a parent to illness early in life and largely lived apart from the other. But the most striking similarity between Mott's upbringing and that of Hazen and Annie lay in their day-to-day care. Once again, a pair of young children found themselves in the care of a devoted, maiden aunt, this time in the guise of Mott's sister, Sallie.

Born in 1846, Sallie Rhoads was the first child of Maris and Ann Eliza Rhoads. Mott held a soft spot for his half-sister who grew up in the shadow of their youngest sibling, Annie. Intelligent, beautiful, gregarious, and socially graceful, Annie provided an image that Sallie, despite being five years her senior, could never live up to. While Sallie did not entirely lack these qualities, they simply came easier to Annie and her family noticed. "Annie is like Frank. No trouble to learn," Mott's mother observed. "Poor Sallie. She [takes] after me."[8] Her own self-deprecation notwithstanding, Ann's allusion to Frank's intellect and not Mott's own is perhaps telling of a corresponding comparison of the two brothers as well. Mott had not enjoyed school as a boy. He once confided in Sallie that he could never stand being cooped up in a classroom all day.[9] It also didn't help that Ann was aware of self-confidence issues in her eldest daughter. "Sallie says she intends to improve herself as much as she can," Ann wrote to Mott, "You know she has a very poor opinion of herself. But I hope she will change."[10]

Such comparisons between the two girls were not an isolated event. "You should really hear Sallie and Nan, your sisters, sing," Susan wrote to Mott in 1869. "They are taking lessons. Nan has a natural soprano. The teacher says without cultivation it is lovely."[11] Susan offered a more measured assessment of the elder sister. "Sallie is a fine contralto, which needs cultivation."[12] Mott's mother concurred with Susan regarding her daughter's musical talents. "Annie is a great singer. Sallie is good, but of a different style."[13] Adding insult to injury, Susan also added to her observation that Annie was "a beautiful girl, so natural, unsophisticated and very attractive indeed."[14] She wrote nothing of Sallie's appearance. Notwithstanding their clear admiration for Annie beyond that of her sister, the family loved Sallie. If there were any favoritism between the girls, it was not intentional. "Your mamma is very proud of her four children," Susan told Mott.[15] But the tacit comparisons paint the picture of a golden child who could do no wrong alongside a reliable, if unexceptional, sibling.

Mott felt particularly endeared to Sallie, perhaps seeing something of himself in her. He too was the sibling of a more social, seemingly successful, and ambitious person, while he preferred instead to live life his own way. He harbored a cynical suspicion of those individuals prescribed by society as perfect specimens. In Mott's experience, such superficial qualities often belied some serious character flaws. He need look no further than his own family for validation of his belief. He watched his brother's pursuit of social perfection very nearly lead to his ruination and saw similar failings in Frank's wife and daughter. "Anna and May are a shabby lot, especially Anna," Mott confided to Sallie early in 1901. "She is mean and contemptible and selfish. She never gives me any of her big talk, she knows better. I like May a great deal better than her mother."[16] His more favorable opinion of his niece should not be overstated. It was a low bar to clear. When May became a glove model for Wanamaker's in Philadelphia, Mott derided it as an unhealthy expression of materialism in furtherance of a shallow social

The Rhoads sisters (presumed): Annie (left), Sallie (right)
Courtesy of Decker Landry

ambition, aspiring to a socio-economic class to which she felt entitled despite her father's squandering of the money that would justify that lifestyle. "What do you think of May having her photo in Wanamaker's advertisements?" He asked Sallie. "It is the image of her and you will notice that it is called the Princess May Glove. I think they would do almost anything for money."[17] Given his brother's checkered reputation, Mott was particularly sensitive to the effect of his brother's actions, or those of his household, on the family at large. "Just imagine one of our family doing such a thing," Mott wrote a few weeks later regarding May's modeling. "I expect she gets gloves for nothing," Mott concluded cynically.[18]

Mott's opinions of his brother and his family were no secret, but his relationship with Annie, his youngest sibling, is harder to parse. She pursued a family and aspired to a more traditional life. In the early 1870s, she married Morton Chase. Together, the couple would have four children—Maris Rhoads Chase, named for Annie's father; Susan Carpenter Chase named after their cherished aunt; Morton Hazen Collins Chase, known by Hazen; and Ann Eliza "Annie" Chase, named for Annie's mother. Mott always showed an invested interest in Annie's children, offering advice on child rearing on more than one occasion noting for example when to protect the baby from cold air and to not feed fine sugars that could upset their delicate digestive systems.[19] It was ironic for a bachelor military officer stationed in rural outposts to be so opinionated about raising children, but it showed he cared. The loss of the elder two children to diphtheria and Annie's own passing in the late 80s rocked the family and Mort came to rely on his in-laws for help.

By the latter half of the 1890s, the two people who never had families of their own had become proxy parents. Mott provided financial and moral support from afar while Sallie took responsibility for their day-to-day care at her home. In 1897, at Mott's behest, Sallie moved to the Wyandotte Hotel in Bethlehem, Pennsylvania so the children could attend the Moravian Parochial Day School. It was inexpensive and taught according to German educational traditions, which, for reasons unknown, Mott found to be superior to the American approach.[20]

If Sallie ever worried about raising the kids properly, Mott would not leave her to do it on her own. "I am glad to know that you are keeping up your baths and exercise." Mott wrote approvingly to Annie. "Whenever you have a holiday, you ought to be out of doors all the time like English children, running and racing. That is the only way you can ever be strong and to be strong is to be good looking."[21] He made sure that Sallie kept on top of their health regimen. "Tell Hazen to take cold baths in the morning and at no other time—as cold as he can take—and exercise every day. Annie ought to do the same. If she expects to grow up good-looking, she must bathe and exercise," Mott wrote.[22]

Mott had very clear convictions when it came to healthy living. The idea that a strong constitution made one physically attractive was perhaps as much motivation for Annie to take his advice as much as it contributed to good health. His belief in the benefits of a cold bath was almost dogmatic. "For gracious sake, don't take hot baths, they are the worst thing for catarrh," Mott opined.[23] He also believed in a healthy diet as a cure for most ailments and did not limit his advice to the children. When Sallie wrote Mott concerned that she was suffering heart trouble, Mott, having no medical training, confidently reassured her that it was "caused by dyspepsia," or heartburn, all of which he blamed on diet and her living situation at the Wyandotte. "If you had your own house where you could have what you ought to eat, you would never have anything the matter with you," Mott remarked.[24] To prove his point, he related from experience the case of a sixty-year-old officer at death's door with heart trouble and lung disease who was cured "simply by living on rare beef, broiled, and stale bread."[25]

However, Mott remained cautious and protective when it came to the two surviving legacies of his sister. Once when Hazen was ill, he wrote Sallie very explicit instructions on how to proceed. "Stop all of Hazen's running and jumping till you see a doctor and don't pay any attention to anything that others say about it."[26] Mott was concerned that Hazen could be more easily prone to appendicitis which had taken his mother's life over a decade before. "If there is a scientific, old-practice physician in Bethlehem, see him alone and tell him all about Hazen's mother's disease and ask his advice about exercising."[27] Mott did not elaborate on what he meant by an "old-practice physician," but his cynical nature had clearly extended to the medical profession.

Sallie, Hazen, and Annie were not the only members of the family whose well-being occupied many of Mott's thoughts. He had entrusted another life in his sister's hands—his beloved dog, Malsee. Mott devoted nearly as much space in his correspondence to Malsee as he did his niece and nephew.

Mott had always had dogs. During the Civil War, his dog Reb used to pace around the house desperately awaiting Mott's return, frequently running to the door when someone came calling only to sulk away when it turned out not to be Mott. By the early 1870s, while stationed with the 22nd Infantry out on the Plains, the Greyhound became Mott's breed of choice. He became an avid hunter in the service as it was "the principal amusement" to while away the time.[28] To aid in the chase, the regiment employed primarily foxhounds and greyhounds. As Mott readied to leave for recruiting duty in 1871, General Stanley asked Mott to look into procuring some new puppies to replenish the regiment's pack. As luck would have it, Mott's duties one day took him to Fort Adams in Rhode Island where the 5th Artillery was stationed under Colonel Henry A. DuPont. An avid hunter himself, DuPont had with him a pack of "beautiful greyhounds evidently of noble lineage."[29]

The DuPonts were one of the premier families of Delaware, having earned their wealth from the gunpowder company that their forebear, E. I. DuPont de Nemours had established along the banks of the Brandywine at the turn of the 19th century. By the 20th century, the DuPont company would evolve into a global chemical behemoth known for introducing to the world such products as Nylon, Teflon, and Tyvek, among others.

Colonel DuPont had not followed his kin into the family business. Instead, he went to West Point where he graduated first in his class and served with distinction in the Civil War, earning the Medal of Honor for his role in the Battle of Cedar Creek. He would later leave the army and return to Delaware to become president of the Wilmington and Northern Railroad Company in addition to starting an experimental farm at his Winterthur Estate just outside of Wilmington.

Having grown up just twenty miles north of Wilmington, Mott was likely familiar with the DuPonts. He admitted to feeling a certain presumption in writing to the Colonel without a formal social introduction. He explained that he had spotted DuPont's greyhounds while at Fort Adams on army business. "[I] conjectured that you were a member of the 'brotherhood of hunters' and would pardon one of the brethren for addressing you without an introduction," Mott ventured.[30] Mott explained the mission General Stanley had set him and asked if the colonel would be willing to spare some pups. DuPont graciously provided two or three puppies for Mott to bring back with him to the frontier.[31] From then on, Mott took a keen interest in raising and breeding Greyhounds himself.

In all his years with dogs, none stole his heart so much as Malsee. Mott raised Malsee since her birth at Fort Keogh in 1894. He and his men grew so fond of her, that she became an unofficial mascot of sorts for the 25th Infantry when Mott served as major of that unit. She was of the best pedigree—a direct descendant of Master McGrath, the most famous champion hare courser in Ireland in the late 1860s.[32] By 1898—likely when the 25th was ordered to sail for Cuba during the war with Spain—Mott "retired" Malsee and sent her home for Sallie to look after.

Mott was just as particular about Malsee's care as he was about his niece and nephew. She was only to be fed raw meat—about a pound per day—to keep her from running off and killing chickens.[33] He was also adamant that she should not be spoiled by feeding her scraps from the table as it would create bad habits. "One reason people dislike dogs is because people rob the table to feed them," Mott reasoned.[34] If Sallie ever decided to go away, she either had to take Malsee with her or put

Mott's faithful greyhounds: Malsee (right), Mott with unknown companion (left)
Malsee Courtesy of Clay Chase; cyanotype of Mott & dog (misidentified as Malsee), author's collection

her in the care of only certain people whom Mott knew would care for her according to his wishes.

When Mott returned to the U.S. from Cuba and was stationed at Fort Sheridan, Illinois, he brought with him one of Malsee's sons. Mott loved this dog as well, not least because he was Malsee's. "My dog is exactly like Malsee. The other morning I had found that he had wet the floor, something which he rarely does. I did not say anything to him, but he was so much ashamed that he attracted my attention by rolling his eyes at me wherever I went in a shame-faced way. I then, to tease him, pointed at the place and talked to him about it. He looked as though he would like to sink through the floor."[35]

Malsee's son did not live very long. He died in the fall of 1900, a loss that genuinely pained Mott. "How I miss her son whenever I return from town. I always feel as though he was coming to meet me as he used to last summer. I never had any luck with dogs or money. My dogs always die young."[36] Mott goes on to cite Malsee as the one exception to the rule. Even those under Mott's command felt the dog's absence. "It is strange, but for two nights since he died, there was a loud voice in the fireplace in one of my rooms and the soldiers on guard at night near my quarters say that they see his ghost and that he howls. They believe this for they say he was so near human in his ways."[37]

Mott did not go long before getting a new dog, but his next companion was a far cry from the dog he had just lost and he struggled with his new charge. He was disobedient, unreliable, and hung with a bad crowd. "I am so disgusted with my dog that I shall part with him if I can," Mott wrote his sister. "I never say anything to him and I kicked him around the room the other day. He goes off hunting with a miserable pointer. I despise bird dogs. You ought to see him look at me when he is lying about my room. He knows I am vexed with him."[38]

Malsee's son was a hard act to follow for any dog, not only because he was so special to Mott, but because the whole lineage had captured Mott's heart in the same way. That the guards who claimed to see the dog's ghost remarked that the animal had been so human-like in his ways came as little surprise to Mott. Like her son, Malsee also seemed particularly special. "What a strange dog, Malsee," Mott wrote in a postscript to his sister. "I believe she has a spirit. She knows so much and she never forgets people that have been good to her."[39] Malsee eventually reunited with her master after Mott retired and lived on for another six years, dying in Maine in 1908. After her death, Mott lovingly buried her in a manner consistent with his view that she must have had something akin to a human soul. He placed a small gravestone at the burial site near Windham encircled by a small fence. On the stone, Mott had inscribed:

In Memory of Maslee
General Hooton's Faithful Greyhound
Born in Montana, 1894
Died 1908
With First Regiment at Chickamauga
In Spanish War

The touching tribute to Malsee attracted the attention of the local newspaper, the Kennebec Journal, which ran a short obituary for the dog in 1909 and was picked up and run in papers across the nation seemingly at random.[40]

***

When Mott arrived at Fort Sheridan, Illinois in September 1899, he had planned to end his career there. He was sixty-one years old and ready to leave the service. After the illnesses he had suffered en route to and serving in Cuba, the thought of an additional campaign held little appeal. He liked Fort Sheridan, telling his sister "I hope I shall remain here on account of the climate. It is the finest post I have ever been."[41] But Mott still had one piece of unfinished business—become a brigadier general. Apart from the financial benefit that rank would bring him, he also felt he had earned it. In early 1900, Mott learned of two proposed bills in Congress that would essentially abandon promotions by seniority and instead promote by "selection." The intent was to build a corps of officers who held their positions based on the merit of their capability. Mott, however, believed it would devolve into a popularity contest. Not only did he find it unfair to those, like himself who had put in their dues, but he also feared the advancement of young officers who lacked the experience to be gained on each rung of the command ladder. Such a jump in rank, he feared, would develop an over-inflated sense of self-importance leading to overconfidence, poor judgment, and low morale.

There were only so many officer positions of each rank and having struggled in the past to gain promotions, it is little surprising that at this point in his life after everything he had endured, Mott would rail against such proposals and expect a greater consideration. Given his cynical views of most politicians, he generally preferred to avoid entering the political fray, but the proposed bills irritated him enough that he wrote letters to the military committees of both the United States Senate and House of Representatives urging them to vote against their passage. After laying out several logical arguments about the damage to morale and effectiveness that promotion-by-selection would cause in the armed forces, he concluded with some personal remarks:

I trust that you will pardon the egotism of the following remarks, but this is a matter that comes home to me. I am the third for promotion on the list of Lieutenant Colonels of Infantry. I have been in the military service of the country since eighteen sixty-one constantly, with the exception of a short interval between service in the volunteers and regulars. I have never been on detached service but once when I was detailed on recruiting service. I have spent my life in the wilderness serving with soldiers, and at this late day to have my promotion jeopardized by the passage of such a law as this is hard to bear. To cut a man of my age and [experience]—and nearly all the line officers are about the same in regard to age and experience—out of this long expected promotion would be like cutting out Shylock's pound of flesh, for my service is a part of my life.[42]

Mott was never one to shy away from telling his superiors what he really thought, but this very personal and public display of expressing the emotional impact of these bills was highly out of character and revealed just how much his career meant to him. He had given his life in service to the nation and sacrificed much. In forty years, he had almost never occupied a position that could be considered cushy and so the thought of the government potentially deciding that such experience, commitment, and devotion, provided insufficient grounds for advancement was a slap in the face to him and every other older officer who had put in their dues.

Ironically, as a lieutenant colonel, Mott continued to lobby for promotion to brigadier general, bypassing the rank of colonel and seemingly requesting the very jump in the line that he had so passionately argued against. However, Mott's goal in obtaining the rank of general was to retire, not acquire authority. Upon retirement, Mott's position would be immediately vacated and available to fill. It would neither block nor deny anyone else's promotion or have any effect on the command structure of the army. It would simply recognize Mott for his many years of service and allow him to better provide for himself and his family, or so he reasoned.

Others in Washington found the process of promotions a bit controversial, and indeed, some viewed Mott as having already benefitted from special treatment and believed that officers like he had come to expect advancement for advancement's sake because the army had shown favoritism to any who had fought in the Civil War. One op-ed appearing in the April 14, 1902 edition of the *Times-Democrat*, complained that being a Civil War veteran was cited too often as a reason to continuously "reward" an individual with an increase in rank. After multiple advancements, at what point has the soldier been justly rewarded, they wondered. In Mott's case, he advanced from major to lieutenant colonel and was on the cusp of a full colonelcy all within about five years. While those who cited Mott as an example of the problems in the army's approach to promotions held nothing against him personally and believed him a "deserving officer," nevertheless, the process struck of favoritism to some with the goal of artificially creating openings for handpicked successors.[43]

Others came to Mott's defense. In remarking on the controversy, the author of an article in the *Augusta Chronicle* likewise used Mott as an example to decry the assumption made by opponents of the process that it was all a corrupt system of covetous officers. On the contrary, there were a number of benefits to the system, namely that it incentivized retirement for aging officers who would otherwise hold on as long as possible for a promotion, allowing younger, more energetic officers to fill command positions. But more importantly, there were understandable financial realities that could not be ignored. According to the author of the *Augusta Chronicle* article, army officers could not get life insurance to provide for their final days, except from a few very expensive sources. They were also not permitted to make certain investments or speculations, restricting other avenues for building personal wealth. And lastly, the fact that retired officers received three-quarters of their terminal pay as pension—and that pay was tied to rank—the promotion strategy offered a way to thank old soldiers for their long years of sacrifice and service by helping to provide them with a more comfortable life in their later years.[44] Mott would have been grossly insulted by the article in the *Times-Democrat* if he ever read it. While the author found no fault in Mott, the insinuation that he had not properly earned his promotions, and that he was elevated too quickly, especially having spent a full twenty-four years as a captain before advancing through the higher ranks, would have enraged him as an affront against his honor. The *Augusta Chronicle,* on the other hand, perfectly articulated why Mott worked as hard as he did to receive the advances he sought.

In January 1901, Mott told his sister that he intended to ask Frank to go to Washington on his behalf and use whatever political or social influence he had to secure the promotion. He also arranged for a biographical sketch to run in the Philadelphia Inquirer.[45] Interestingly, the photo he proposed the Inquirer use was not a portrait in full dress uniform, but a more casual image of Mott in his Khaki uniform, perhaps projecting a more realistic representation of his career as a field soldier.[46] Even his brief military memoir from 1899 was likely written more as a resume to convince the powers that be that he was worthy of the rank. Frank succeeded once again in securing the signatures of nearly the entire Pennsylvania delegation in Congress. Senator Boise Penrose promised the recommendation would be delivered to President McKinley personally. Having been down this road before, Mott remained skeptical. "I am not very sanguine about it," he wrote.[47]

McKinley considered the recommendations very carefully, but ultimately decided a promotion to general inappropriate. The efforts did not go entirely unrewarded as the president did elevate him to the rank of colonel less than two and a half years after becoming a lieutenant colonel. Now just one step away from his generalship, Mott decided to stay in the army and continue to bide his time. At his age, he felt he would likely be spared further action and could quietly run out his service until mandated to retire for age the next year. It was a bit of a gamble as the army was currently engaged in securing the Philippines as a United States territory and his first assignment as colonel was to form and take command of the 28th Infantry at the Vancouver Barracks in Washington state, whose position near the Pacific suggested the unit was likely being groomed for the Philippines.

An authentic field officer: Mott as a lieutenant colonel
Courtesy of the Massachusetts Commandery MOLLUS

19

⚜

One Last Mission

He never should have been sent, Mott thought to himself as he looked out on the tropical landscape of Santa Cruz de Malabón. Crossing to the desk in his quarters, he began to compose a letter requesting a transfer back to the United States. He had only been in the Philippines for four days, but at sixty-one years old and five months from retirement, this was not his war.

The insurrection in the Philippines is often considered a continuation of the Spanish-American War. Like Cuba, the native Filipinos were struggling to overthrow Spanish imperial rule and the war with Spain did indeed influence the United States' decision to go there, but it was a separate conflict largely fought between the US and the Filipinos after the Treaty of Paris in December 1898 ended the fighting with Spain. Shortly after it declared war against Spain over Cuba, the United States government ordered the Asiatic Squadron under the command of Commodore George Dewey to sail for the Philippines to eradicate the Spanish fleet stationed in Manila Bay. The US hoped that by defeating the Spanish fleet it could prevent Spain from dispatching reinforcements to Cuba. On May 1, not far from the Cavite naval base on the island of Luzon, Dewey quickly defeated the Spanish squadron.

Like Cuba, the Philippines was a Spanish territory gripped by social unrest as the native population fought to overthrow its colonial rulers. In the 1890s, Spain sought to consolidate what holdings remained of its empire and pull more value out of them. On the archipelago, it meant squeezing and displacing the *Principales*—the de facto ruling Filipino class.[1] As the quality of life for many Filipinos deteriorated through hunger and disease, many of these *Principales* advocated for rebellion. In 1896, a nationalist organization called the *Katipunan* called for a revolution to overthrow the Spanish. Emilio Aguinaldo, a young politician from Luzon came to lead the *Katipuneros* but was not particularly successful in garnering popular support among the people. Aguinaldo was of the *Principale* class and it was no secret that goal of the *Principales*—and thus the *Katipuneros*—was not a free Philippines for Filipinos, but rather a sovereign nation with the *Principales* at its head. The Filipino peasantry was not invested in Aguinaldo's revolution. Without popular support, the movement had little chance of succeeding. Moreover, internal strife developed amongst the *Katipuneros* leaving the *Principales* too disorganized in the mid-1890s to mount a serious opposition to Spanish rule.[2]

The rebels may not have been able to fully overthrow the Spanish, but neither could they be entirely put down. Spain simply did not have the resources to deal with them, particularly as they faced a growing likelihood of war with the United States.[3] In December 1897, the Spanish government reached a truce with Aguinaldo. Under the terms of the truce, Aguinaldo and several of his followers agreed to go into exile in Hong Kong in exchange for what Aguinaldo understood to be extensive reforms and reparations.[4] A few months later, during a trip to Singapore, Aguinaldo met E. Spencer Pratt, the American consul stationed there, who informed him of the impending attack by Dewey against the Spanish fleet at Manila and suggested that it might provide an opportunity for Aguinaldo to return. The *Katipunero* leader interpreted the conversation as a commitment by the United States to recognize Filipino independence and assist the rebels in overthrowing the Spanish, but the consul had made no such promise.[5]

In the Caribbean, the United States supported the removal of the

Spanish in favor of an independent Cuban government, but the situation in the Philippines was a bit more complicated. President McKinley held his cards notoriously close to his chest where the Philippines was concerned and his communications after the fall of the Spanish squadron regarding what would come next for the archipelago were frustratingly vague. Some missives referenced an occupation of the Philippines, which was something Dewey could not accomplish with the manpower at his disposal. Other communique suggested possession of the islands, which seemed to presume annexation. Still, others made it sound as if the United States was concerned with controlling only Manila and its bay. McKinley eventually ordered ground forces sent to the Philippines to occupy territory, but the initial mobilizations were mishandled and disorganized. The US relied heavily on volunteers from state militias to supplement its regular army which was stretched too far and mostly engaged elsewhere. The government couldn't even provide proper ships to take its forces across the Pacific. Instead, they converted commercial vessels into troop transports. These makeshift vessels were ill-equipped to carry three expeditionary forces to the islands. Conditions for the crossing troops were awful.

A few weeks after the defeat of the Spanish fleet in Manila Bay, Aguinaldo returned to the Philippines to take up his revolutionary cause once again, thinking he had the support of the United States. However, the US did not believe the Filipinos were as capable of self-government as the Cuban revolutionaries given their lack of organization and the self-serving goals of the *Principales*.[6] The last thing the US commanders wanted to do was to cooperate with the Filipino insurgents and share a joint occupation. If they removed the Spanish, but could not hand control to the Filipinos, it left no other alternative than the annexation of the archipelago as an overseas territory. By mid-August, the war with Spain over Cuba was all but concluded and the governments signed a peace protocol on the 12th, agreeing to end hostilities and appoint representatives to draft what would become the Treaty of Paris. At the same time, in the Philippines, the Spanish forces in Manila were now besieged behind the walls of the city proper and agreed to negotiate a theatrical surrender to save face once again.

The Spanish had seen the writing on the wall, but Spain worried about the optics of their surrender, just as they had in Cuba. Working through the Belgian Consul, Spanish forces communicated with US commanders and proposed a sham battle of sorts. The US could press their advantage and the Spanish would resist just lightly enough to preserve their dignity in battle before officially surrendering. The proposal was attractive to the US not just because it was essentially a surrender, but because it would allow them to direct the confrontation in such a way as to cut the Filipino insurgents out of the action and ensure that the sole occupation of Manila fell to the US. The Filipinos were already amassing on the outskirts of the city and US troops struggled to keep them at bay.[7]

The First Battle of Manila occurred on August 13, 1898, just a day after the US signed its peace protocol with Spain. As promised, the Spanish resisted mildly, but the American commanders did not appear to have communicated the plan to their troops. The US fought much harder than expected and the Spanish suffered far heavier casualties than they had anticipated. The excessive force angered the Spanish, but there was little they could do. Eventually, they waived the white flag and Manila was taken. Outside of the city, Aguinaldo and his insurgents were not happy to be cut out of the battle.[8]

That December, delegates from Spain, Cuba, and the United States met in Paris to sign the peace treaty officially ending the Spanish-American War. Under the terms of the Treaty, Spain granted independence to Cuba and ceded Puerto Rico, Guam, and the Philippines to the United States. The Filipinos lobbied for their own representation in Paris, but they were denied. President McKinley justified the annexation of these territories as a sort of Manifest Destiny—that it was the United States' obligation to secure the economic advantages that the Philippines brought and in turn raise up the Filipino population into a modern, western civilization, what Rudyard Kipling contemporaneously called the "White Man 's burden." McKinley's plan for his new territories was one of "Benevolent Assimilation," which assumed that popular support for American sovereignty would grow among Filipinos once they were convinced that they were better off being ruled by the US than being independent.[9]

For the United States, the outcome of the war with Spain brought with it an existential pivot in American foreign policy. Though late to the game amongst the Western powers, the various territorial annexations, including territories like the Kingdom of Hawaii whose contemporaneous annexation by the US was unrelated to the Spanish conflict, transformed the United States from a largely isolationist nation into an imperial power in competition with Europe on the global geopolitical stage. However, none of this mattered to Aguinaldo who refused to recognize the annexation, and the Filipinos would not come around and offer the popular support the United States naively expected them to give.

In January 1899, Aguinaldo declared himself President of the First Philippine Republic. The following month, fighting broke out between US troops and the Filipinos on the outskirts of Manila. It marked the second, but this time very real, Battle of Manila and catalyzed over three years of fighting that would spread across the entire Philippine archipelago for control of the nation.

By 1901, when Mott arrived at the Vancouver Barracks to form and take command of the 28th Regiment, the situation in the Philippines had taken on a regional character. Two areas separated by only a few miles might have experienced entirely different levels of fighting.[10] Aguinaldo held little control over insurgent forces in different areas. He had become a symbol of the independence movement rather than its military leader.[11] For several years, the Filipinos engaged in guerrilla warfare, playing the long game in a war of attrition to frustrate and wear down the American forces.

Mott knew his regiment would likely be ordered to the Philippines, but he believed that once he organized the unit and oversaw the training of the men, the army would transfer command to a younger officer for mobilization. In March, Mott received a letter from Washington that said "in so many words" that given his age and impending retirement the following year that he would not be sailing for the Philippines.[12] By November, the army command had either changed its mind or Mott had misinterpreted the March communique as it became clear that he would be setting sail with the 28th. Mott protested on the grounds that he was but five months from retirement, but to no avail. He even attempted to obtain a different assignment. He tried to get Congressman Butler to secure a transfer to the 7th infantry only to be told the War Department was "not disposed to modify" Mott's original orders.[13] He also wrote to the Adjutant General to request command of the Departments of Columbia and California, which would necessitate his staying behind. Through the political connections within Oregon, Senator John Mitchell amplified Mott's request by writing to Secretary of War Elihu Root.[14] Both Mitchell and Mott acknowledged that it would be atypical to grant a departmental command to a colonel, but cited precedent in the recent posting of a colonel to command of a department in Texas. Root was unmoved and responded that the Departments of Columbia and California were too important to have anything less than a general at their head. All requests were denied.

On the 16th, Mott arrived in San Francisco and boarded the transport ship *Grant* bound for Manila.[15] Mott treated this new assignment almost like another of his overseas travels writing home about his impressions of the people and the countryside. After arriving in Manila Bay around the 12th of December, Mott boarded a steamship on the Pasig River to report to General Adna Chaffee, the new military governor of the Philippines, at his headquarters. "We passed old storm walls and fortifications picturesque with the green moss and slime of centuries and went under a beautiful old Spanish bridge with several arches," he wrote to Sallie like a tourist.[16] The following day, he arrived at his post at Santa Cruz de Malabón, today known as Tanza, about twenty-five miles south of Manila. His impression of the area again reads like a travel postcard, belying the military purpose for his presence:

This is a large native village with an old stone church and Spanish barracks

on the little parade ground which is covered with grass. The country is beau-
tiful and picturesque although flat, but the native houses built of leaves and
bamboo are as pretty as toys. The women and children wear bright colors and
the whole thing resembles a play somewhat.[17]

Despite his own innate curiosity and the opportunity to see yet another part of the world, Mott did not want to be there. What Mott and
Chaffee discussed was not recorded, but the colonel likely expressed his
desire to return home at the earliest availability. Within four days, he
officially submitted a request to his superiors for immediate transfer
out of the Philippines.[18]

Mott's experiences during the rest of his time on the archipelago
were quiet. By the time he took command of his post at Santa Cruz de
Malabón, the local resistance leaders in Cavite had long since surrendered, ending much of the hostilities in the district.[19] Cavite had been
the heart of some of the staunchest resistance in southern Luzon.[20] The
resistance movement was supported and aided by Filipino elites and
popular opinion was distinctly anti-American.[21] The army's response
had been to punish the wealthy elites by destroying their property and
isolating the insurgents in the countryside by ordering all civilians and
food supplies into the towns. In many cases, food was simply burned
by the Americans rather than relocated where it could do some good.
Further south, the Americans employed a concentration camp system
like that imposed by the Spanish in Cuba in order to further separate
resistance forces from the general population. It was deeply hypocritical
and publicly unpopular given that the employment of such tactics in
Cuba by Spain had been a key motivation for the American public to
support war in Cuba.[22]

However duplicitous, the tactics were ultimately successful. Though
fighting continued elsewhere, Mott was spared most of it. In February,
after only two months in the country, the army capitulated to his
request and Mott received his eagerly-awaited orders to sail back to the
United States so he could be home in time for retirement on April 16,

1902—his sixty-fourth birthday. On March 1st, Mott boarded a ship and headed home.

Mott arrived in Washington on April 8th upon orders to report to the War Department where he learned that his admirers in Congress had not stopped working towards his advancement. No sooner had Mott been promoted to colonel in 1901 that Representative Thomas Butler along with Senators Matthew Quay and Boise Penrose, all of Pennsylvania, called on President McKinley with yet another petition signed by the entire Pennsylvania delegation to Congress. Even the governor of Pennsylvania, William A. Stone, appended his signature to the list.[23] He also received endorsements from Senator Addison G. Foster of Washington as well as John Mitchell, the Oregonian senator who had previously tried to secure a domestic position for Mott.[24] McKinley agreed to investigate the matter later in the year, but that September, Leon Czolgosz, a Polish-American steel worker and anarchist assassinated McKinley at the Pan-American Exposition in Buffalo, New York. When Theodore Roosevelt succeeded to the White House, Senator Quay visited him and told him of the request he and his colleagues had put before McKinley. Roosevelt told the senator he would consider the matter and act if he believed Mott to be worthy of it, but cautioned the senator that he believed officers should be advanced solely on merit and not seniority or political connections. In fact, Roosevelt was reported as saying the more political connections one had, the less inclined he was to grant a promotion.[25] Quay dropped the matter with nothing else to do but await the president's decision. Mott's record would have to speak for itself.

In early April, with Mott en route home and just a couple of weeks from retirement, it seemed that colonel would be his final rank. But then Congressman Butler heard a rumor that Roosevelt was considering promoting senior colonels in the army to brigadier general upon retirement if they had also served in the Civil War. Mott fell squarely into that category. Though Roosevelt had not yet made his decision regarding the petition to promote Mott, Butler went to the White House to confirm the rumor. Roosevelt corroborated what was circulating

The campaign for General: (top L to R): Senators Matthew Quay &
Boies Penrose; (bottom, L to R): Rep. Thomas Butler, Governor
William Stone

Library of Congress

and Butler informed the president of Mott's eligibility, and requested he be added to the list noting the colonel's time was nearly done.[26] Roosevelt could not deny that Mott met his criteria for this promotion program. The president pulled out a small notecard and quickly scrawled on the front to set the wheels in motion:

Secy Root
How about Col. Mott Hooton for Brig. Gen'l? Please
report to me.

T. Roosevelt[27]

Secretary Root met with the president and quickly jotted his own note to Adjutant Corbin stating, "The President would like to have the Hooton promotion come over as soon as possible so that it can be sent to Senate at once."[28]

On April 14, 1902, on behalf of Elihu Root, Adjutant General Corbin circulated the order that the formal nomination be prepared "at once" to promote Mott to Brigadier General.[29] The next day, April 15, 1902, the day before Mott reached the mandatory age of retirement, the Senate convened a special executive session "for the purpose of confirming the nomination of an army officer to a higher grade."[30] Brigadier General Isaac DeRussy had retired on April 1st, leaving a vacancy among the ranks of the army's Generals, which needed to be filled and several names, including Mott's, had been submitted for consideration of the open positions.[31]

The following day, April 16, 1902, Mott retired after nearly forty years of continuous service to his country. Donning his dress uniform, Mott went to a studio to have his photograph taken. Standing proudly at attention, he looked straight into the camera with medals on his chest, sword at his side, and upon his shoulders, a pair of gold epaulets featuring a single silver star—the insignia of a brigadier general.

Brigadier General Mott Hooton, 1902
Courtesy of Clay Chase

20

General Hooton

The corridors of the White House were a "blaze of glory," festooned with flags and flowers on that mid-February evening in 1904. As President and First Lady Roosevelt descended the stairs with a small retinue of officers and advisers, they made their way to the Blue Room to receive many of their distinguished guests. Soon, the Executive Mansion became filled with hundreds of guests marking the last major social event of the season—a grand reception honoring the men of the Army and Navy. Members of Congress, Justices of the Supreme Court, administration officials, and dignitaries of all kinds circulated amidst the sea of crisply uniformed officers and their escorts. Aside from Roosevelt, two other future presidents were in attendance—Secretary of War William Howard Taft and Dr. Woodrow Wilson, president of Princeton University. But the guest who received the most attention was an eighty-four-year-old woman dressed in simple black silk with a white lace collar and cuffs, the activist and champion of women's suffrage, Susan B. Anthony.[1]

To be surrounded by throngs of some of the nation's most influential people must have been both exciting and a little intimidating for young seventeen-year-old Annie Chase, though she felt reassured escorted by her dapper uncle dressed in the uniform of a brigadier general.[2] It was not the first time Mott had been to the White House. Just a few weeks earlier, he attended a smaller gathering in the East Room to enjoy a concert hosted by the President featuring works by Liszt, Schubert, Chopin, and Bizet among others.[3] The February reception reunited him with many of those who played a role either directly or indirectly in his career. Several of his former commanders were present, including Nelson Miles, with whom he served in the Dakotas in the 1870s, and Adna Chaffee, his superior while in the Philippines. Wesley Merritt had issued many an order to Mott while in the west and Admiral George Dewey had cleared the way for the army's actions in the Philippines. Retired senator and former governor of Louisiana, William Pitt Kellogg could be found in the crowd. Mott had never met Kellogg personally, but it was the White League's insurrection against him that brought Mott to New Orleans in 1874.

Mott did have closer connections in attendance. Isaac Wayne Mac-Veagh, former attorney general under President Garfield and retired ambassador to both Japan and Italy, was a close friend of Mott's brother. Frank had attended MacVeagh's wedding in 1867 when he married the daughter of Lincoln's former Secretary of War, Simon Cameron. Mott also encountered Major William Kell, though when last they met, Kell was a Lieutenant in the 22nd under Mott's command. Kell fought side by side with Mott at Clear Creek in 1876 when they were nearly overwhelmed by the Lakota and he had received a brevet promotion alongside Mott for his service in the battle. Mott and Kell served most closely in the 1870s, but their service continued to parallel each other frequently until the late 1890s.

It's not clear how Mott came by the invitations to these two prestigious events at the White House, but if anyone believed that a quiet, sedentary retirement would suit Mott, they were kidding themselves. Shortly before his retirement, his own family could only speculate how he would fill his days. "What the thunders he will do with himself when he does get out I don't know," Frank confided in Sallie, "but I think he ought to settle down at this place."[4] Frank likely knew his suggestion that Mott should settle down in West Chester was naïve. The fact

General Mott Hooton in full uniform
Courtesy of Clay Chase

that he couldn't even hazard a guess as to where Mott would end up shows how well Frank knew his brother. Still, he believed Mott owed it to the town, and indeed the state, to make his home once more in Chester County given the aid the state's congressional delegation had extended in securing his most recent promotions. "This is his home," Frank declared. "The people of this county are proud of him and all the support I succeeded in getting for him was by reason of him being from here...I would like him to appreciate this and to know he would throw it all away if he lived somewhere else."[5] Mott greatly appreciated all the efforts of his brother and his political connections, but for the first time in nearly forty years, he was free to go and do what he pleased. West Chester would always be his home, but the good General was finished with other people deciding where and how he should conduct his life.

In all his time in the army, Mott had scarcely lived in one place longer than a year or so at a time. Forts Keogh and Lewis, where he spent seven and six years, respectively, had been the exceptions to the rule by far. Though he had grown weary of military life, his aversion to being sedentary did not change. Officially, Mott took up residence in Bethlehem with his sister, Sallie, but within a couple of years, he was eager to travel again.

Later in 1904, Mott wrote to several places in Idaho and Washington state in search of opportunities for a rigorous elk hunt. C. C. Bowman, a guide in the Olympic Mountains, responded that he could accommodate Mott, specifically reassuring the general that the trek would not be easy per the tone of Mott's request.[6] Sixty-four years old or not, Mott's idea of travel was never one of ease and leisure. In 1905, Mott traveled to Washington state where he visited military acquaintances, including Captain John McAdams Webster, a former comrade of the 22nd Infantry and Superintendent of the Coleville Indian Agency at Fort Spokane.[7] Three years later, Mott returned to New Orleans thirty-four years after his previous visit and under vastly different circumstances. Among other diversions in the city, he spent time at the Boston Club, the third

Restless Spirit: Mott (left) visiting Captain John Webster in Washington state, 1905 (Detail)
Courtesy of the Chester County History Center, West Chester, PA

oldest gentleman's club in the United States named for the card game called Boston.

***

When Mott wasn't traveling, he split his time between Bethlehem and West Chester fulfilling obligations to his family. In early 1904, just weeks before the events at the White House, Mott's brother, Frank, died of pneumonia complicated by heart disease. Mott traveled to West Chester for the funeral, staying several weeks to help with his affairs. Interestingly, Mott was not listed among the pallbearers or even the honorary pallbearers.[8] Mott and Frank had always had a complicated relationship and Frank's own scheming and legal troubles irrespective of his familial relations weighed on Mott for the way it reflected generally on them all. Still, Frank had worked on Mott's behalf numerous times to advance his brother's rank over the years and Mott felt great loyalty to his family despite how he may have felt about their actions. Before leaving town to return to Bethlehem after the funeral, Mott took Frank's military sword as a memento.[9] It was a fitting token not only because of Mott's own connection to the military but because it was a symbol of the one part of Frank's life he could truly relate to.

Frank had never regained his reputation after his imprisonment from the Neely debacle in 1893, and it continued to haunt him for several years. In 1896, Judge Hanna, the same judge who had sentenced him to Moyamensing three years earlier, ordered Frank to appear in court to provide money owed to additional heirs of Neely's estate. Once again, Frank did not comply. The judge allowed Frank more time, but by the next year, he was forced to appeal to the Court of Common Pleas to discharge his obligations by declaring him an insolvent debtor.[10]

Frank tried to pick up the pieces and rebuild his name. In 1895, he ran a vigorous campaign for Chester County prothonotary. He drew particular attention to his candidacy through the unique method of canvassing he performed throughout the county. He saddled his horse and rode out to personally greet the electorate. The horse had its advantages. It allowed him to cover more territory in a day and reach more locations inaccessible to other forms of transport, like bicycling. Frank's brief military background engendered a certain authenticity to the move as well. His was the image of the mounted soldier in the field. The optics appealed to a great many in the county who had served, particularly in the cavalry.[11] Frank's campaign officially garnered him the nickname "the lone cavalryman."[12] The novelty of his canvassing helped to make him a serious contender as many felt it showed a genuine effort to reach people. "The Colonel knows every man, woman, child, and goat from the rocky fastness of the Coventries down to the scrub oaks in the Nottinghams, and who their ancestors were," wrote the author of an article in *The Times* of Philadelphia.[13]

Though a viable candidate, the competition was stiff and the people's memory was long. Most everyone in the county knew of Frank's recent financial and legal troubles and while his supporters hoped that voters would see passed it, others cynically saw it as a run of desperation to begin to rebuild his wealth. "He is recognized as needy to an extent as would permit of this office putting him on his financial plus again," the *Times* author acknowledged before appealing to the reader to be understanding. "While the plea of sympathy isn't a good one to use in these days in the work of booming a candidate, those who are acquainted with the Colonel's public and private life will be inclined to think it over carefully and view it in its most generous aspect."[14]

It was not enough. Frank lost his bid in 1895 and though he tried again the following year the field was even more crowded, and he lost out yet again. As the 1890s wore on and a new century dawned, Frank focused his energies on supporting the candidacies of others but eventually ran afoul of the county Republican Committee. He remained steadfastly loyal to Pennsylvania political boss and United States Senator Matthew Quay, even when much of the party within Chester County wanted to distance themselves from him. Quay had been charged with misappropriating funds in 1898 and although he was acquitted, a rift began to form as reformers within the party felt Quay's days of influence should end. Frank stood up for Quay, spoke out against his competitors, and in the few years before his death accused the Pennsylvania state's Republican Committee of cheating and manipulating state electors into voting against Quay. His efforts only led to further alienation and descent into obsolescence. "Colonel Hooton's object of course…is to create feeling against the regular organization," wrote a *Philadelphia Inquirer* columnist in 1903. "But as he is never taken very seriously in matters political, it created nothing but a momentary ripple," the author snidely concluded.[15]

Frank's attempts to support other Republican candidates in the pro-Quay end of the party were met with similar derision. After holding a public meeting in support of the gubernatorial candidacy of Judge Samuel W. Pennypacker, the *Philadelphia Inquirer* reported the event to be "the biggest political fiasco in this section." The meeting was so poorly attended, Frank delayed the proceeding nearly an hour hoping for a rush of latecomers that never occurred. The business concluded quickly. Calling Frank the "Poo Bah" of the meeting, the paper denounced Frank as a "has-been" and ridiculed the event as "a complete farce, an opera bouffe performance and to-night the whole town is in laughter over it..."[16] Ironically, the mocking aimed at Frank was rather unfair. While Chester County may have predominantly favored reform-minded Republicans, the state as a whole reelected Quay to the senate and installed Pennypacker as Governor.

Whatever vindication Frank might have felt by the ultimate success of his candidates, he knew it was no thanks to Chester County or his political stumping. Frank's career was essentially over. Frank had spent his life striving for greatness, but except for the momentary flash of opportunity as chair of the state Republican Committee for Pennsylvania in 1879 and having his name bandied about in serious contention for a state senate seat in the 1880s, he could never quite attain the positions of influence and notoriety of those whose company he kept. While the positions and honors he did achieve in life were certainly respectable, notwithstanding his bankruptcy in the 1890s, he died having never realized the extent of his life's ambitions.

Shortly after Frank's death, Mott returned to West Chester where he remained for several years in his widowed sister-in-law's household. He paid Borough, School, and County taxes from 1904-1908.[17] It was a curious living situation as Mott made no secret of his distaste for Anna as evidenced in his earlier correspondence to Sallie. However, as family, Mott may have felt duty-bound to step in and help his sister-in-law whose own health was faltering. In 1908, he walked his niece, May, down the aisle at her wedding to Thomas Buchanan Gilford, Jr. of New York City. Gilford was May's second marriage and the affair was small, taking place in the parlor of Anna's home on Matlack Street.[18] May moved away with her new husband to live the life of a socialite in New York. Shortly after May's wedding, Mott left West Chester to return to his sister and never looked back.

When Anna Hooton died in December 1915, a bitter dispute ensued over her will that dragged the Hooton name through the mud once again. The conflict led to a court battle, which the local newspaper euphemistically called "one of the liveliest will contests heard here in a long time."[19] According to the will, the bulk of Anna's estate went to May. This included all her property, $1000 in cash, and a trust worth nearly $100,000. Anna bequeathed just five dollars to her eldest daughter, Anna Ralston Jones, whom she bore with her first husband. Incensed at the insult, Mrs. Jones alleged that her half-sister, May, had taken advantage of their mother while in a compromised state during her illness and unduly influenced Anna to write her firstborn out of the will. May countered that Anna and her mother had fallen out years earlier, were not on good terms, and had not seen each other in years. That their mother was not of sound mind when her lawyer drew up the will was a ludicrous notion according to May.

The audience in the courtroom couldn't wait for the drama to unfold. It was packed with entertainment seekers "tittering" with amusement. A large retinue of May's friends occupied a block of seats in the crowd and would visibly shake their heads in unison and turn their noses in haughty disgust anytime their friend's character was besmirched.[20] They would be shaking their heads a lot.

In answer to May's charge that Anna had not visited their mother in many years, Anna implied that her lack of visitation was the result of not feeling welcome by her stepfather or May, but that she still saw her mother regularly out in the town. She further claimed to have noticed changes in her mother's mental state as early as 1896 when she feared Anna was being manipulated at home by both Frank and May. It wouldn't have been out of character. Mrs. Jones alleged that Frank had once coerced her mother into giving him bonds that rightly belonged to his stepdaughter and sold them. Anyone familiar with Frank's many legal troubles could easily have believed such a claim. Anna further claimed that May would regularly swear at their mother and be violent with her, such that their mother was afraid of May.[21]

Several other witnesses took the stand including a neighbor, a nurse, and several of the Hootons' former domestic servants. They all attested to May's harsh treatment of her mother, telling her who she could and couldn't speak to, forcing her to clean up after the dogs she kept in their smoking room, and supposedly shoving her into the bathtub on

The Socialite Niece: Mary "May" Hooton (Detail)
Courtesy of the Chester County History Center, West Chester, PA

one occasion. "May was the boss of that whole shootin' match," said Caroline Price, the Hootons' former cook who affirmed the charge that Anna was afraid of her daughter. Another former cook, John Wesley, claimed that May routinely cussed out both her parents and on one occasion threw water in Frank's face. He also testified that May complained about her half-sister almost daily and specifically related dinner-time conversations in which May ranted loudly that Mrs. Jones would not get "one damn cent" of their money.[22]

May denied all the accusations, but if any character witnesses took the stand in her defense, the paper never reported on them. Anna Jones ultimately lost the suit, not because May was found to be innocent of the allegations made of her, but because she simply could not prove her mother's state of mind. When Anna Hooton's lawyer produced previous versions of the will, they were not much different, which challenged the claim that it had been adjusted under duress during her last days.[23] Mott was never called to testify and upon hearing about it no doubt appreciated no longer being in town where he did not have to feel any public mortification by the spectacle of it all.

The truth about May's actual disposition is hard to discern, but if nothing else, she was her father's daughter. Like Frank, May grew up striving toward social betterment. She was drawn to Philadelphia and New York societies, perhaps in an effort to live up to her Penrose roots. Sometime after she died in 1933, a retrospective in Chester County's *Daily Local News* described her as "a tall, handsome blonde who had a way of doing and saying what she liked, and having her own friends. She was brilliant and refreshing, known to everybody, liked by most people, and a typical personality."[24] A stunning beauty in her day, she modeled for Wanamaker's in Philadelphia, her likeness being used to advertise the department store's "Princess May Glove," likely a dual allusion to both the model and the then Princess of Wales. For Mott, that double entendre was all too befitting of his niece's sense of entitlement.[25]

Life had not always been easy for May. Her father had all but bankrupted the family on more than one occasion during her childhood and his brief, yet very public incarceration in the early 1890s coincided with her prime days as a young, single woman making her way in society. Her love life also suffered from a series of unfortunate events. In 1898 at twenty-six years of age, May became engaged to Major Lawrence Smith, a surgeon in the United States Volunteers. Several months after announcing their engagement, Smith contracted typhoid fever and died while deployed to Puerto Rico during the Spanish-American War.[26] Four years later, she became engaged again and wed David Trumbull Lanman Robinson of New York. It was a lavish affair at the Church of the Holy Trinity in West Chester. May wore an elegant Parisian gown, and many of the scions of New York, Philadelphia, and Baltimore societies were in attendance, "several of whom count their fortunes in the six figures," the *Daily Local News* felt it necessary to report.[27] The wedding nearly didn't happen. Her fiancée battled an attack of asthma upon arrival in West Chester the day before and they feared he wouldn't be well enough to go through with the ceremony. It was a tragic omen of what was to come. After a trip to the south, the couple returned to New York City intending to make their home, but that September, just eight months after their wedding, David Robinson died in New York City having contracted Typhoid fever—the same illness that had taken her first fiancée.[28]

The third time was the charm for May. When she married Thomas Gilford in 1908, she solidified her position as a true New York socialite. The couple remained married for twenty-three years, making their homes at various times in New York, Italy, and California. Mott likely maintained at least a superficial relationship with his niece, though there is no evidence to suggest they were close. After leaving West Chester, his priorities were his sister Sallie, his niece Annie, and his nephew Hazen.

After a couple of years working as an engineer for the E. I. DuPont de Nemours Company in Wilmington, Delaware, Hazen was offered a job as a superintendent of a pulp mill in Portland, Maine.[29] Mott, Sallie, and Annie decided to break with Pennsylvania and moved with Hazen in 1908 where they took up residence in a boarding house on State Street in the center of the city.[30] A few years later, they moved to

Westbrook where Hazen joined the S. D. Warren Company in Cumberland Mills. The company transferred Hazen to Gardiner, Maine south of Augusta where he worked as office manager and assistant to the president of the company's Copsecook Mill.[31] Once again, Mott, Sallie, and Annie followed Hazen, taking up residence on Main Avenue in nearby Farmingdale.

The family continued to travel together on vacations. They returned to West Chester from time to time and even spent springs in Richmond, Virginia—no doubt an unusual feeling for Mott to vacation in a city that represented the very heart of enemy territory in his earlier years.[32] During one of these sojourns back to Pennsylvania, Hazen met and fell in love with Sarah Gray Park whose family owned Cloverly Farm just north of the West Chester borough. The couple married at the farm in 1917 and returned to Maine to start their life together.[33] Within a year, Sarah fell pregnant and in March 1918, she gave birth to a boy, Hazen Park Chase. It was a hard labor and Sarah became gravely ill. Just ten days later, she died leaving Hazen a widower with a newborn.[34] The family returned to West Chester and laid Sarah to rest in Oaklands Cemetery and Hazen's sister Annie promised to help her brother with the baby, continuing the family tradition of maiden aunts stepping up to help with their sibling's children.[35]

As the years wore on, Mott finally slowed down. Where once he had planned to travel abroad, he now stayed closer to home. He occupied himself with genealogical research allowing his correspondence to do the traveling as he sent requests for information to various repositories both in the United States and the United Kingdom. On the Carpenter side of the family, he wrote to shirttail relatives and genealogists to establish his descent of the family from William Carpenter, his immigrant ancestor from England.[36] On the Hooton side, he was less concerned with their history in America, particularly because much of that history involved fighting against the United States as both British Loyalists during the Revolution and Confederate sympathizers during the War between the States. Instead, he cared more about tracing the family back within England and locating a Hooton coat of arms. He wrote to the Department of Heraldry at the Bailey, Banks, and Biddle Company; to Meredyth Burke, son of the Ulster King of Arms who had written several books on the peerage of the untitled landed classes of Great Britain; and to John Matthews, author of Matthew's American Armory and Blue Book.[37] He also reached out to Earnest A. Hooton, a noted American physical anthropologist – and likely distant relative – who sent Mott a hand-drawn copy of a crest he had located in a book along with an old engraving of a manor building in Cheshire England known as Hooton Hall, but he could not confirm the connection to Mott.[38]

Mott enjoyed relatively good health in his later years, except for some trouble with his eyes beginning in 1907 for which he sought out a treatment he had read about that employed "magnetic forces."[39] The following year, he received a medical exam in Philadelphia where his doctor pronounced him in good health telling him, "there is no reason another fifteen years shouldn't be added to your allotted portion."[40] His clean bill of health was positive news, but it also served as a reminder that he would continue to outlive many of those he had come to know over his long, adventurous life. Mott began reaching out to those he had known trying to reconnect. He wrote to Dr. Charles Gray, his old friend from the 22nd and was pleased to get a warm response. Gray was a proud grandfather by that point and looked forward to a day when he and Mott could catch up face-to-face. "I have changed in all these years, all except my heart, which I hope is alright," Gray remarked about his own advancing years.[41] But Mott quickly learned that such responses were becoming more and more infrequent. In 1905, Mott attempted to reach out to Frank Cowen, the eccentric former patent clerk of President Johnson and jack of all trades with whom he traveled in China and parts of Southeast Asia. He received a reply from Frank's brother, James, sadly informing Mott that Frank had passed.[42] Frank had spoken to his brother about Mott and their travels many times, but that fact came as little consolation.

Of course, given Mott's upbringing in West Chester and his service in the Civil War, he could still count many friends in his home county.

The veteran Brandywines living in West Chester occasionally reunited over a drink and they followed their old captain's career with much interest. When Mott was promoted to colonel in 1901, several of the old Brandywine Guards got together to celebrate "Captain Hooton" getting his eagle.[43] But as the years went on, such reunions became smaller and smaller. By 1910 there were few Brandywines left.

Even where his family was concerned, Mott continued to outlive members of his generation as he began receiving telegrams from cousins that more often portended loss. In September 1910, for example, Mott learned that Kate Blackiston Stille, the cousin whose impassioned letter to Mott in 1862 exposed the deep ideological divide in the family over the question of secession, had passed away of stomach cancer.[44] Mott's prophesied longevity was a double-edged sword and the longer he lived, the more he lost. He had finally reached the age when people began leaving his life in far greater numbers than they were entering it.

Mott lived out the remainder of his years in Gardiner, Maine with Sallie and Annie. The doctor who had told him to expect another fifteen years was not far off the mark. In the late 1910s, Mott's health started to decline. He developed interstitial nephritis, an incurable kidney disease in which inflammation prevented the kidneys from properly filtering urine.[45] Being still twenty-some years away from the invention of dialysis, his prognosis was grim, but he held on for several more years until May of 1920 when Mott suffered a severe stroke. For a week he lingered before passing away on May 30, 1920, at the age of eighty-two.[46]

***

Sallie brought Mott's body back to West Chester. Mott had spent so much of his life on the move rarely settling anywhere for longer than a year or so at a time, yet despite the transience of his existence and the relatively little time he spent in West Chester throughout his long life, his heart was never truly connected to anywhere else. Funeral services were conducted at the Episcopal Church of the Holy Trinity on June 3rd. After the service, a small group of pallbearers bore his body through town to Oaklands Cemetery. Mott had had many friends and relations throughout his life, but they were either scattered across the country or had previously passed and so there were not enough friends or relations left to bear the casket. Mott's family had no choice but to hire pallbearers for the funeral. At the head of the funeral cortege, a firing squad from the Bernard Schlegel post of the American Legion dressed in full military uniform led the procession into the cemetery.[47]

As his casket entered the graveyard, the retinue of mourners followed the winding paths past the resting place of Sarah Chase, his nephew's first wife. They moved around the small hill on top of which his brother Frank and sister-in-law Anna lay. Down through the small valley, across the creek, and over the hills, the cortege was suddenly surrounded by so many Mott had known in his life. "Old Bollie," his militaristic French headmaster; Aunt Em and Uncle Tommy Rhoads; Henry McIntire, founder of the Brandywine Guards and the first military commander under whom he had ever served; and nearly a dozen former members of his small company of faithful ones. At the gravesite, in a back corner of the cemetery, Edmund Jones, a veteran of the US Navy played Taps while the American Legion squad fired three volleys into the air.[48] The plot included the resting places of his grandfather Carpenter and his Uncle John. Right beside his beloved Aunt Susan, the perpetual wanderer had finally come home.

Medals of a decorated veteran: (Top) Civil War, Grand Army of the Republic, Indian Wars; (Bottom) Spanish American War, Philippine Insurrection, Sons of the American Revolution

Courtesy of Clay Chase

MOTT HOOTON MADE
A BRIGADIER-GENERAL

Achievement of a lifetime: Mott Hooton made Brigadier General
San Francisco Chronicle, April 22, 1902

Epilogue

After her brother's funeral, Sallie Rhoads returned to Maine where she sold the home in Farmingdale she had shared with Mott and their niece. The last of her generation, she moved in with Hazen and his family in nearby Gardiner.[1] Except for some arteriosclerosis in her later years, Sallie remained quite healthy until October of 1922 when she came down with bronchitis that developed into pneumonia. A week later, on October 17, she died.[2] Annie and Hazen brought their aunt's body home to Pennsylvania where she was laid to rest beside her parents and sister in the Media Cemetery near Media, Pennsylvania.

Annie and Hazen's father, Mort, finally retired and settled down with the family and by 1920 had moved in with Hazen.[3] Mort savored his time with his family, taking pride in tottering about with his grandchildren and making up for so much time spent away, traveling for work. Morton Chase died a year after Sallie in 1923.

Hazen did not stay in Maine long after his uncle's passing. In 1920, he left his aunt and sister in Gardiner and took a job with the American Writing Paper Company in Holyoke Massachusetts as the assistant to the vice president overseeing manufacturing in four of the company's mills.[4] While still in Maine, he had hired a nurse, Nellie Schuman, to help look after his son. Hazen eventually fell in love with Nellie and the couple were married and had a daughter, Elizabeth.[5] In 1927, Hazen joined with several other businessmen in forming the Harris Silk Hosiery Company in Holyoke, Massachusetts as clerk and treasurer.[6] He remained with the company throughout the 1930s eventually taking the reins as president.[7]

Last of a generation: Sallie Rhoads (presumed) with Mott (left), Morton Chase (right)
Courtesy of Clay Chase

On a crisp day in early January 1938, Hazen suffered a massive heart attack while working in his garage. His wife and children became concerned when he didn't respond to the call for dinner and found him on the ground still clutching the tools he had been working with. Nellie immediately called for their neighbor who was a doctor, but it was clear to the physician when he arrived that Hazen was gone. He was only fifty-three years old.[8]

Annie remained in New England, but the rest of her life remains a bit of a mystery. She had been engaged once in the 1910s, but after hearing about the dangers of childbirth from her Aunt Sallie, she called it off resolving never to marry so she would never have to face it herself.[9] Seeing her brother's first wife die following childbirth in 1918 would only have reinforced that fear. It may also have been why Sallie herself never married. Annie, or 'Nan' as she became known in the family, stayed true to her convictions and never married. She continued to live

Mott's legacy: Hazen (left), Annie (right) later in life
Courtesy of Clay Chase

in New England until her death in 1961. She, too, was buried in the Media Cemetery by her parents and grandparents.

Mott's other niece, May, achieved in life what her father could not. Her marriage to New York socialite and financier Thomas Buchanan Gilford had brought her into a world of high society—hosting luncheons for debutants, vacationing in the Berkshires, and traveling frequently between their home on 53rd Street in the heart of Manhattan and far-off haunts in California and Italy.[10] Despite her glamorous life, May never forgot her attachment to West Chester. She and her husband purchased a grand, gothic-revival house on West Virginia Avenue at the north end of town, which she filled with antiques. Constructed with a locally sourced Serpentine stone, theirs was one of four such houses on the block known collectively as "the four sisters." May's husband died in 1931 after twenty-three years of marriage.

Despite May's success, she had inherited her father's penchant for becoming embroiled in public scandal, the scale of which far surpassed anything her father had endured. In 1932 a Hollywood actress sued May for $250,000. During her time in New York, May had become acquainted with John Eshlemen Lloyd, a wealthy New York lumber-man and president of the American Lumber Association. Lloyd was also a cousin of Walter Edge, the American ambassador to France.[11] Lloyd was born in Germantown in Philadelphia and his mother was a native of Downingtown in Chester County, just one town over from West Chester.[12] Lloyd had been a bachelor until the age of forty-two when he attended a performance of "Ladies' Night" on Broadway and became smitten with the Spanish-born lead actress, Judith Vosselli. In 1918, Lloyd and Vosselli married.[13] They would never have children of their own, but Vosselli had two children from a previous marriage, whom Lloyd adopted. At the encouragement of her husband, Vosselli expanded her career into movies and the couple split their time between New York and California so she could continue to perform on Broadway. She made her Hollywood debut in the 1926 film "The Prince of Tempters" and went on to have roles in over thirty-five feature films between 1926 and 1935, including "Rogue Song," a Lionel Barrymore film starring Lawrence Tibbett, Stan Laurel, and Oliver Hardy.[14]

In early 1932, after nearly fourteen years of marriage, Lloyd left New York and flew to Reno, Nevada where he filed for divorce in the state's district court. While in Nevada, Lloyd fell critically ill and traveled to San Francisco to seek treatment. After several attempts to deliver the divorce summons to Vosselli at her Hollywood home, and her husband being too sick to travel, Lloyd sought a divorce decree by default.[15] On April 27, the divorce was granted.

Lloyd cited cruelty in his divorce complaint against his wife, though Vosselli contended she had no idea there was anything wrong in their marriage.[16] No sooner was the divorce finalized than May, widowed for less than a year, hopped on the first plane to San Francisco. St. Francis Hospital. With a municipal judge as officiant and a congregation of nurses, Lloyd and May were married at the groom's bedside in St. Francis Hospital. Lloyd's doctor served as Best Man.[17] The groom had been divorced for just nine days. "We are gloriously happy today," May told reporters from Lloyd's hospital room. "With his courage and hope of happiness to carry him through this illness, I believe my husband will win his way back to health."[18] May arranged a private car to bring them back across the country to West Chester as soon as his doctor approved Lloyd's discharge.

May's sudden marriage to Lloyd, particularly so soon after her previous husband's death, raises many questions about both her relationship with Thomas Gilford and her relationship with John Lloyd. The urgency with which she traveled to San Francisco after the divorce suggests she had planned for this before Lloyd left New York. There are no public reports of infidelity or a souring marriage while Thomas was still alive, but the circumstances are suggestive. Certainly, it was an assumption Lloyd's ex-wife made. Filled with rage, Vosselli filed an alienation lawsuit against May the next month for a staggering quarter of a million dollars claiming May had "unlawfully appropriated John Eshlemen Lloyd to herself" and bankrolled both Lloyd's travel and the divorce.[19]

May had returned to West Chester with her new husband to begin his convalescence, however, he continued to deteriorate and died on October 20, just five months later. An autopsy revealed Lloyd's body to be riddled with cancer. What started as a rare form of bowel cancer of the cecum (the junction between the small and large intestines), had metastasized to his liver and throughout his abdomen.[20] May had Lloyd buried in Oaklands Cemetery beside her previous husband whose plot she would share. May would not live much longer herself. As 1933 wore on, she became increasingly ill until she died at home on September 9th. An autopsy revealed she was suffering from ovarian cancer.

May never paid Vosselli as the suit was thrown out in January 1933. While the circumstances of the divorce and sudden remarriage may have been scandalous and disreputable, Vosselli could not prove any actionable wrongdoing. But not even death would stop Vosselli from the restitution she believed she deserved. On February 14, 1934,

The scorned Hollywood actress: Judith Vosselli
Library of Congress

New York's *Daily News* ran a sensational article entitled "Ex-Wife Asks $250,000 Balm of Dead Rival." Vosselli had filed a new lawsuit in Brooklyn to get her money from May's estate. "Reaching behind the portals of death—where the law has forbidden such claimants to enter," wrote *Daily News* contributor Warren Hall, "a Broadway actress prepared yesterday to collect $250,000 from the estate of her dead love rival for the theft of her dead ex-husband." Hall clearly relished in the scandal reporting dramatically that the sum of the damages equated to "$1,250 for every day that Mrs. Mary Penrose Gilford Lloyd enjoyed the affections of John Eshlemen Lloyd."[21]

Vosselli failed in her second lawsuit, particularly as there was no precedent for such an alienation suit against a deceased defendant. Still, the entire affair illustrated just how much of Frank Hooton's daughter May really was. Her ability to avoid financial liability was in her blood, particularly since Vosselli's was not the only suit to come out of the situation. Lloyd's doctor in California, after serving as his patient's best man, sued the couple for skipping town without paying the $7,500 hospital fees.[22] If Mott had been alive, he might have taken solace in the fact that between the higher profile of her Penrose middle name and the multitude of married surnames she had collected over the years, the Hooton name was almost always left out of accounts in the national press.

✳✳✳

In 1912, Mott wrote to his cousin, Mary Jane Blackiston, that it was a "pity we were ever born."[23] Perhaps it was a touch of melancholy in the seventy-four-year-old general whose diminishing social circle reminded him of his own mortality. Whatever the reason for the dour self-reflection, his cousin refused to entertain the idea responding emphatically, "I think we can all be useful to someone if we try. I know it would have been very different for your sister and the children if you had never been born."[24] Mott would have done well to take his cousin's wisdom to heart. After all, his life touched many around him and continues to inspire people to this day.

It is a hackneyed phrase to say, "history is written by the winners." Though generally accurate, one might also add that it is written about the famous. Mott left his mark within certain circles—the army, his family, his friends—but he was not famous. Were it not for the chance encounter with his headstone during a casual walk through Oaklands Cemetery, his story would largely have been lost to time. And yet in life, he witnessed and took part in so many impactful moments in the late-nineteenth century that writing this book at times felt like writing a textbook for a college survey course in American history—the bitter fight over slavery; the continued struggles of race relations during southern Reconstruction; westward settlement and the displacement of America's indigenous people; expansion of the railroads to connect "sea to shining sea;" the tumultuous crucible from which the American labor movement arose; and the beginnings of American imperialism. He traveled the world and encountered some of the most influential and colorful people of his time and he found himself in precarious situations with his life on the line on many occasions. His was a full life.

The study of history often involves an examination of broad social and political forces. The cause and effect of these forces over time teach us about who we are as a people. History can warn us of repeating a past danger or guide us into making better choices for the future. But the individual is often lost in this work. Most people are not the drivers of the times in which they live and so to some, the study of an obscure historical figure is little more than a curiosity, unworthy of serious investigation. However, history can also inspire. It is difficult for people to relate to "broad historical forces" and many of the famous or exceptional individuals who do rise to prominence because they were the great movers and shakers of significant events are inaccessible to the average person. Part of the value in history for the average individual is in the example of how everyday people navigated the historic moments of their time. To learn about even the most mundane lives of those in one's own local community during times long past is to see a piece of ourselves in the larger continuum of humanity. It makes us not just observers of history as if our lives were an ahistorical existence divorced from the past, but active participants in it. Like Mott, most of us will live in reaction to events that occur beyond our control, but the experiences of people in our past who are like us can show us by example how to react and rise to the times into which we were born.

Admittedly, Mott is still an exceptional person. Most people will not have lived a life as full of adventure as he and the source material, however incomplete, is still far more than will exist for many people in their local historical societies. But the value in local history—which is often poorly funded and little appreciated—or local biography is not in the ability to fill a book on an individual, but in the greater understanding and relation to everyday life and our role in it. Local history makes national or even international history more relatable because it allows us to see the major events and trends of history through the eyes of a community we know. It reminds us that we too play a role in the historical continuum of our communities, which are affected by the larger events happening all around us. It makes us less divorced from the history we only experience in classrooms, textbooks, or large museums. The Smithsonians of the world can teach us much about history, but it is our local historical institutions that can teach us about ourselves.

The Victorians who conceived of cemeteries like Oaklands where Mott rests believed in the self-reflective power of cemeteries. On the one hand, they were a reminder of one's own mortality and to use oneself well in the time they had. On the other hand, they encouraged the visitor to appreciate and reflect on the lives behind the stones to inspire the lives of those whose stories have not yet concluded. Mott's story is one of adventure, one of family, and one of many more just waiting to be uncovered.

THE END.

Bibliography

Primary Sources

Chase, Annie E. to Hazen Park Chase, n.d. Private Collection.

Cleveland, Henry. *Alexander H. Stephens in Public and Private: With Letters and Speeches, Before, During, and , Since the War.* Philadelphia: National Publishing Company. 1866.

Consolidated Military Officer's File of 1st Lieutenant Mott Hooten [sic], 22nd U.S. Infantry. RG 94. Letters Received, 1871-1894, National Archives Identifier 7423592. National Archives and Records Administration, Washington, D.C.

Cort, Mary Lovina. *Siam: The Heart of Farther India.* New York: Anson D. Randolph & Company. 1886.

Darlington, Joseph B. Correspondence. Chester County Historical Society.

Darlington, William Henry. Correspondence. Chester County Historical Society.

"Gilford-Robinson Nuptuals." *New York Tribune.* October 6. 1908.

"The Grant Off for Manila." *Waterbury Democrat.* November 16, 1901.

Halderman, John A. "Royal Cremation in Siam." In *Reports from the Consuls of the United States on the Commerce, Manufactures, etc. of their Consular Districts.* Washington: Government Printing Office. 1881.

Hoopes, Abner. Correspondence. Chester County Historical Society.

Hooton, Francis C. Correspondence. Chester County Historical Society.

Hooton, Mott. "Certain Historical Data Regarding Extended Order." *Journal of the Military Service Institution* 16. 1895.

—"From Gettysburg to the Battle of the Wilderness." Unpublished Diary. Private Collection. 1863-1864.

—*Military Memoirs of Mott Hooton.* 1900.

—*Military Memoirs of Mott Hooton.* Unpublished Draft. Private Collection. 1899.

"In re Neely's Estate, Appeal of Hooton." *The Atlantic Reporter.* 1892-1893.

Kennan, George F. *Tent Life in Siberia: An Incredible Account of Siberian Adventure, Travel, and Survival.* 1870. Reprint. New York: Skyhorse Publishing. 2007.

Lamborn, Charles. Correspondence. Chester County Historical Society.

Livingston Seaman, Louis. "Why the Canteen Should Be Restored." *The North American Review*, January. 1903.

McClernand, E. J. "Edward W. Casey," *Report of the Twenty-Second Annual Reunion of the Association of the Graduates of the United States Military Academy.* June 12, 1891.

Mott Hooten [sic] Correspondence, 1866-1867. Ms 1988-100. Special Collections. Virginia Polytechnic Institute and State University.

Mott Hooton Papers, MS. Coll. 171. Chester County Historical Society.

Powell, William Henry. *Officers of the Volunteer Army and Navy who Served in the Civil War.* Philadelphia: L. R. Hamersly & Co. 1893.

Price, Philip. Correspondence. Chester County Historical Society.

Report of the Secretary of War; Being Part of the Message and Documents Communicated to the Two Houses of Congress at the Beginning of the Second Session of the Forty-Fifth Congress. Washington, D.C.: Government Printing Office. 1877.

Report of the Twenty-Second Annual Reunion of the Association of the Graduates of the United States Military Academy, June 12, 1891.

Rhoads. Family File. Chester County Historical Society.

Rupert, Alfred. Correspondence. Chester County Historical Society.

Sheaff, Charles. Correspondence. Chester County Historical Society.

Speakman, Charles. Correspondence. Chester County Historical Society.

Stanley, David S. *Report on the Yellowstone Expedition of 1873.* Washington, D.C.: Government Printing Office. 1874.

Taylor, Bayard. *Life and Letters of Bayard Taylor.* Vol. 1. Boston: Houghton, Mifflin, and Co. 1895.

Trobriand, Philippe Regis de,. *Military Life in Dakota: The Journal of Philippe Regis de Trobriand.* 1951. Reprint. Edited by Lucile M. Kane. Translated by Lucile M. Kane. Lincoln, Nebraska: University of Nebraska Press. 1982.

United States Federal Census, 1850-1930.

United States War Department. *The War of the Rebellion: A Compilation of the Official Records of the Union and Confederate Armies.* Vol. 27. Washington, D.C.: Government Printing Office. 1880.

Uriah Hunt Papers. Ms. Coll. 174. Chester County Historical Society.

Way, Joseph. Correspondence. Chester County Historical Society.

Wiley, Samuel T. *Biographical and Portrait Cyclopedia of Chester County, Pennsylvania.* Philadelphia: Gresham Publishing Co. 1893.

Wood, Leonard. "Civil Report of the Military Governor, 1899-1902." 1902.

Secondary Sources

Brands, Benjamin D. "Unsatisfactory and Futile: The Officer's Lyceum Program and U.S. Army Reform." *The Journal of Military History* 83 (4). 2019.

Brown, Dee. *Bury My Heart at Wounded Knee: An Indian History of the American West.* New York: Open Road Integrated Media. 2012.

Brown, Kevin M., and Amy L. King. *A Small Company of Faithful Ones: The*

Brandywine Guards of Chester County, Company A, 1st Pennsylvania Reserves. Create-Space. 2011.

Busey, John W. *These Honored Dead: The Union Casualties at Gettysburg.* Hightstown, New Jersey: Longstreet House. 1988.

Chase, Dorothy. Personal Correspondence with the author. 2007-2011.

Chudacoff, Howard P. *The Age of the Bachelor: Creating an American Subculture.* Princeton: Princeton University Press. 1999.

Dixon, Mark E. "West Chester's Own Napoleon." *Main Line Today.* Newtown Square, Pennsylvania, June 8, 2016. https://mainlinetoday.com/life-style/west-chesters-own-napoleon/.

Dobbin, Robert F. *The Cynic Philosophers: From Diogenes to Julian.* Edited by Robert F. Dobbin. Translated by Robert F. Dobbin. New York: Penguin Books Limited. 2012.

Fitzpatrick, Kevin C. *Governor's Island Explorer's Guide: Adventure and History in New York Harbor.* Guilford, Connecticut: Globe Pequot. 2016.

Greene, Jerome A. *Battles and Skirmishes of the Great Sioux War, 1876-1877: The Military View.* Edited by Jerome A. Greene. Norman, Oklahoma: University of Oklahoma Press. 1993.

—*Yellowstone Command: Colonel Nelson A. Miles and the Great Sioux War, 1876-1877.* Norman, Oklahoma: University of Oklahoma Press. 2006.

Harper, Douglas. *If Thee Must Fight.* West Chester, Pennsylvania: Chester County Historical Society. 1990.

Hazbund, Waleed. "The East as an Exhibition: Thomas Cook & Son and the Origins of the International Tourism Industry in Egypt." In *The Business of Tourism: Place, Faith, and History,* edited by Philip Scranton and Janet F. Davidson. Philadelphia: University of Pennsylvania Press. 2007.

Hennessy, John J. *Return to Bull Run: The Campaign and Battle of Second Manassas.* Norman, Oklahoma: University of Oklahoma Press. 1993.

Innis, Ben. *Bloody Knife: Custer's Favorite Scout.* Bismarck, North Dakota: Smoky Water Press. 1994.

Johansen, Bruce Elliott. *The Native Peoples of North America: A history.* Vol. 1. New Brunswick, New Jersey: Rutgers university press. 2006.

Linn, Brian McAllister. *The Philippine War, 1899-1902.* Lawrence, Kansas: University Press of Kansas. 2000.

Lubetkin, M. John. *Jay Cooke's Gamble: The Northern Pacific Railroad, The Sioux, and the Panic of 1873.* Norman, Oklahoma: University of Oklahoma Press. 2006.

Nankivell, John H. *Buffalo Soldier Regiment: History of the Twenty-Fifth United States Infantry, 1896-1926.* 1927. Facsmile Reprint. Edited by Quintard Taylor. Lincoln, Nebraska: University of Nebraska Press. 2001.

Nystrom, Justin A. *New Orleans After the Civil War: Race, Politics, and a New Birth of Freedom.* Baltimore: Johns Hopkins University Press. 2010.

O'Toole, George J. A. *The Spanish War: An American Epic, 1898.* New York: W. W. Norton and Company. 1984.

Powell, Pamela C. "French Schoolmaster Turns Borough into Athens." *Chester County Living,* January 22, 2006.

Rhea, Gordon C. *Cold Harbor: Grant and Lee, May 26-June 3, 1864.* Baton Rouge: Louisiana State University Press. 2002.

—*The Battle of the Wilderness, May 5-6 1864.* Baton Rouge: Louisiana State University Press. 1994.

Richardson, James D., ed. *Messages and Papers of Jefferson Davis and the Confederacy, Including Diplomatic Correspondence, 1861-1865.* Broomall, Pennsylvania: Chelsea House Publishers, LLC. 1985.

Ritchie, Donald A. *Press Gallery: Congress and the Washington Correspondents.* Cambridge, Massachusetts: Harvard University Press. 1992.

Sandage, Scott A. *Born Losers: A History of Failure in America.* Cambridge, Massachusetts: Harvard University Press. 2005.

Seaman, Louis Livingston. "Why the Canteen Should Be Restored," In *The North American Review, Vol. 176, N. 554. University of Northern Iowa. January, 1903.*

Sears, Stephen W. *Gettysburg.* New York: Mariner Books. 2003.

—*To the Gates of Richmond: The Peninsula Campaign.* New York: Haughton, Mifflin Co. 1992.

Shelton, Jim. "Part of the Family- Handsome Dan and Friends Have a Special Place in Elm City Lore." *New Haven Register*, October 22, 2010.

Smith, Duane A. *A Time for Peace: Fort Lewis, Colorado, 1878-1891.* Boulder, Colorado: University Press of Colorado. 2006.

Stackpole, Edward J., Wilbur Sturtevant Nye, and Bradley M. Gottfried. *The Battle of Gettysburg: A Guided Tour.* Mechanicsburg, Pennsylvania: Stackpole Books. 1998.

Stowell, David O., ed. *The Great Strikes of 1877.* Chicago: University of Illinois Press. 2008.

Tucker, Spencer C. ed. *The Encyclopedia of North American Indian Wars, 1607-1890: A Political, Social, and Military History.* Vol. 1: A-L. Denver, Colorado: ABC-CLIO. 2011.

White, W. Thomas. "Montana and the Pullman Strike of 1894: A Response to Industrial Warfare." Thesis, University of Montana. 1975.

Wilkerson, Dan. *Colt's Double Action Revolver, Model 1878.* Marceline, Missouri: Walsworth Publishing Company. 1998.

Wittenberg, Eric J. *The Union Cavalry Comes of Age: Hartwood Church to Brandy Station, 1863.* Charleston, South Carolina: The History Press. 2017.

Yenne, Bill. *Indian Wars: The Campaign for the American West.* Yardley, Pennsylvania: Westholme Publishing. 2006.

Zuelow, Eric G. E. *A History of Modern Tourism.* New York: Palgrave. 2015.

Primary Source Newspapers/Periodicals

The United States Army and Navy Journal, and Gazette of the Regular and Volunteer Forces, New York, New York

Anaconda Standard, Anaconda, Montana

The Atlantic Reporter

Augusta Chronicle, Augusta, Georgia

Chicago Daily Tribune, Chicago, Illinois

Daily Local News, West Chester, Pennsylvania

Daily News, New York, New York

Delaware Gazette and State Journal, Wilmington, Delaware

Denver Post, Denver, Colorado

Evening Bulletin, Providence, Rhode Island

Evening Herald, Shenandoah, Pennsylvania

Evening Public Ledger, Philadelphia, Pennsylvania

Evening Star, Washington, D.C.

The Evening Times, Washington, D.C.

The Jeffersonian, West Chester, Pennsylvania

Midland Journal, Rising Sun, Maryland

The Morning Republican, Chester County, Pennsylvania

National Gazette and Literary Register, Philadelphia, Pennsylvania

The National Tribune, Washington, D.C.

New Haven Register, New Haven, Connecticut

The New York Herald, New York, New York

New York Tribune, New York, New York

The North American Review

The Norwalk Hour, Norwalk, Connecticut

The Norwich Bulletin, Norwich, Connecticut

The Outlook: A Weekly Newspaper, New York, New York

Philadelphia Inquirer, Philadelphia, Pennsylvania

Pittsburgh Daily Post, Pittsburgh, Pennsylvania

Pittsburgh Dispatch, Pittsburgh, Pennsylvania

Richmond Times Dispatch, Richmond, Virginia

San Francisco Chronicle, San Francisco, California

The Silver Blade, Rathdrum, Idaho

Springfield Republican, Springfield, Massachusetts

The Sun, New York, New York

The Times, Philadelphia, Pennsylvania

The Times-Democrat, New Orleans, Louisiana

The Topeka State Journal, Topeka, Kansas

The Village Record, West Chester, Pennsylvania

Washington Herald, Washington, D.C.

Washington Star, Washington, D.C.

The Washington Times, Washington, D.C.

Waterbury Democrat, Waterbury, Connecticut

Wauwatosa News, Wauwatosa, Wisconsin

Archival Repositories

Army Military History Institute, Carlisle, PA

Chester County Historical Society, West Chester, PA

Chester County Archives, West Chester, PA

Civil War Museum of Philadelphia

Delaware County Archives, Media, PA

Delaware County Historical Society, Chester, PA

Hagley Manuscripts and Archives, Greenville, DE

Library of Congress

Maine Division of Public Health, Vital Statistics Office

Massachusetts Commandery, Military Order of the Loyal Legion of the United States

National Archives and Records Administration, Washington D.C.

Pennsylvania Reserve Volunteer Corps Historical Society (PRVCHS)

Private Collection of Clay Chase

Private Collection of Richard Chase

Private Collection of Decker Landry

Private Collection of Ed & Faye Max

Private Collection of Richard Palamar

Union League Legacy Foundation

Virginia Polytechnic Institute and State University Special Collections, Blacksburg, VA

Online Resources

Ancestry.com

Chronicling America, Library of Congress

FamilySearch.org

Fold3.com

GenealogyBank.com

Newspapers.com

Pennsylvania State Archives- Civil War Veterans Card File

Notes

Preface

1. In the intervening years, this has changed somewhat as additional repositories and collections have appeared online, however, without deep research what remains is still very surface level information about the basic elements of his career.

2. William Henry Darlington to Family, February 1, 1862, William H. Darlington Papers, Chester County Historical Society.

Introduction

1. "Major Matt[sic] Hooton," *Anaconda Standard*, September 24, 1895, pg. 8.

2. Francis C. Hooton to Uriah Painter, April 28, 1898, Mott Hooton Papers, Ms. Coll. 171, Chester County Historical Society. Mott's brother, Frank, referenced Meade's letter of recommendation at this time in an effort to assist Mott in obtaining a promotion to Brigadier General.

3. For Siam reference, see U.S. Department of State, *Reports from the Consuls of the United States on the Commerce, Manufactures, Etc. of their Consular Districts, No. 9, 1881,* John A. Halderman [Washington, D.C.: Government Printing Office, 1881], 45. For Siberia reference, see George, Kennan, "Regeneration of Cuba: Santiago de Cuba Revisited," in *The Outlook: A Weekly Newspaper, January-April, 1899, Four Months,* ed. Lyman Abbot et al. [New York: The Outlook Company, 1899], 499.

4. *Daily Local News* (PA), n.d. This article was clipped from the *Daily Local News,* Chester County, Pennsylvania's local newspaper, and filed under Mott's name in the clippings file at the Chester County Historical Society. The date was not retained when the article was clipped, however, context clues suggest it dates to the 1880s.

5. Justine Ingersoll to Mott Hooton, August 2, 1871, Mott Hooton Papers, Ms. Coll. 171, Chester County Historical Society.

6. Robert Dobbin, trans., *The Cynic Philosophers: From Diogenes to Julian,* [New York: Penguin Books Limited, 2012], introduction, 3

7. Ibid., introduction, 2

8. Ibid.

9. Ibid.

1. A Childhood of Opportunity

1. *National Gazette and Literary Register,* October 20, 1838, pg. 2.

2. *American Sentinel,* November 25, 1835, pg. 3.

3. St. Andrew's Episcopal Church is now St. George's Orthodox Church. The cemetery at Fifth and Spruce no longer exists. The remains were supposedly relocated to the St. Andrew's Collegiate Church at 42nd and Spruce Street in 1938. However, it is not known if they were moved yet again when the church was deconsecrated in the 1970s.

4. *National Gazette and Literary Register,* October 20, 1838, pg. 2. Today, Union Street is known as Delancey Street. The home is just down the block from the Physick House.

5. Not much is known of Mott Sr.'s siblings. Rebecca married Collins West in Philadelphia and remained in the city when most of the rest of her family moved south. Nothing else is known of Elizabeth, Catherine, or Isaac. Mott Jr. would never be as close with his father's family as he would be with his mother's family. He was perhaps closes to his Aunt Rachel's family with whom he corresponded frequently.

6. Samuel T. Wiley, *Biographical and Portrait Cyclopedia of Chester County, Pennsylvania,* (Philadelphia: Gresham Publishing Co., 1893), 288.

7. Gilbert Cope, "Elizabeth Hooton," in *Daily Local News,* June 29, 1915.

8. Wiley, 288.

9. Ibid.

10. Ibid., 287.

11. Orange Street was renamed Manning Street in the latter half of the nineteenth-century. The meeting house stood on grounds now occupied by the Farm Journal Building, which is a part of Pennsylvania Hospital.

12. Rhoads Family File, Chester County Historical Society. Peter McCall was the first cousin of George A. McCall who would become Mott's next door neighbor growing up and commanding officer during the Civil War. Peter was a so-called Copperhead, a pro-slavery northern Democrat, during the war, an irony considering his cousin would command the state's entire volunteer corps. for the Union.

13. Pam Powell, "French Schoolmaster Turns Borough into Athens," *Chester County Living,* January 22, 2006, p. 12. Ann continued the precedent of prioritizing education many years later when, after a brief relocation to West Chester, she elected to leave her daughters behind to complete their education in the borough rather than return to Delaware County with her.

14. *Public Ledger,* June 12, 1852, pg 3.

15. "Francis C. Hooton," Biographical Sketch promoting his candidacy for Prothonotary, 1899. Notes that the farm belonged to John Carpenter Sr., but a property sale notice in 1852 shows it was owned by the son. See *Public Ledger,* June 12, 1852, pg 3. The farm was located at the corner of Goshen and Fern Hill Roads, currently the site of the Fern Hill Medical Campus.

16. Wiley, 563-564. While this specifically describes Frank's education, it is likely Mott being just eighteen-months younger, attended the same institutions.

17. Powel, 12.

18. Today this is West Chester University, part of the Pennsylvania system of higher education.

19. Powel, 12.

20. Mark E. Dixon, "West Chester's Own Napoleon," *Main Line Today,* June 8, 2016.

21. Powel, 12.

22. Ibid.

23. Ibid.; Eric J. Wittenberg, *The Union Cavalry Comes of Age: Hartwood Church to Brandy Station, 1863,* (Charleston, SC: The History Press, 2017).

24. Powel, 12. Today, an apartment complex, The Metropolitan, sits on the former school site across the street from the Chester County Hospital.

25. Ibid.,

26. See United States Federal Census, 1850, West Goshen Township, Chester County; United States Federal Census, 1850, Springfield Township, Delaware County; United States Federal Census, 1850, Radnor Township, Delaware County.

27. United States Federal Census, 1850, West Goshen Township, Chester County, PA.

28. United States Federal Census, 1870, West Chester, Chester County, PA. Although Mott was not living in West Chester in 1870, he was still recorded with his brother's household.

29. For Chester County farms see Mott Hooton to Ann Eliza Rhoads, February 7, 1877, Mott Hooton Papers, Ms. Coll. 171, Chester County Historical Society. For St. Paul property, see Mott Hooton to Sallie Rhoads, May 16, 1901, Mott Hooton Papers, Ms. Coll. 171, Chester County Historical Society.

30. Mott Hooton to Ann Eliza Rhoads, June 10, 1878, Mott Hooton Papers, Ms. Coll. 171, Chester County Historical Society and *Daily Local News,* August 8, 1893.

31. Susan Carpenter, Last Will and Testament, 1872. For letters about the store, see for example, Charles Muirhead to Ann Eliza Rhoads, November 14, 1878, Chester County Historical Society; Mott to Ann Eliza Rhoads, November 25, 1878, January 10, 1879, July 2, 1879, February 7, 1877, Mott Hooton Papers, Ms. Coll. 171, Chester County Historical Society.

32. Mott Hooton to Ann Eliza Rhoads, October 27, 1878, Mott Hooton Papers, Ms. Coll. 171, Chester County Historical Society.

33. Mott Hooton unpublished farm diary, 1854, Mott Hooton Papers, Ms Coll. 171, Chester County Historical Society.

34. *Daily Local News,* April 19, 1889.

35. George A. McCall to War Department, November 24, 1865, Consolidated Military Officer's File of 1st Lieutenant Mott Hooten [sic], 22nd U.S. Infantry. RG 94. Letters Received, 1871-1894, National Archives Identifier 7423592. National Archives and Records Administration, Washington, D.C.

36. *Public Ledger,* June 12, 1852, pg 3.

37. *Village Record,* May 10, 1859.

38. Matt [sic] Hooton, Pennsylvania Civil War Veterans Card File.

39. While this is ultimately conjecture, his family's resistance to his joining the army after the Civil War suggests a possibility that even at this early date he might have anticipated some disapproval of the army as a vocation.

2. *The Brandywine Guards*

1. Kate Blackiston to Mott Hooton, February 1, 1862, Mott Hooton Papers, Ms. Coll. 171, Chester County Historical Society.

2. Ibid.

3. Rachel Blackiston to Mott Hooton, April 8, 1862, Mott Hooton Papers, Ms. Coll. 171, Chester County Historical Society.

4. Jefferson Davis to Provisional Congress of the Confederate States of America in J.D. Richardson, *Messages and Papers of Jefferson Davis and the Confederacy, Inclduing Diplomatic Correspondence, 1861-1865.*

5. Henry Cleveland, *Alexander H. Stephens in Public and Private: With Letters and Speeches, Before, During, and Since the War* (Philadelphia: National Publishing Company, 1866), 721.

6. Ibid.

7. William Henry Darlington, letter, July 23, 1861, Chester County Historical Society.

8. Rachel Blackiston to Mott Hooton, April 8, 1862, Mott Hooton Papers, Ms. Coll. 171, Chester County Historical Society.

9. Ibid.

10. Kate Blackiston to Mott Hooton, February 1, 1862, Mott Hooton Papers, Ms. Coll. 171, Chester County Historical Society.

11. Andrew Hooton to Mott Hooton, January 24, 1862, Mott Hooton Papers, Ms. Coll. 171, Chester County Historical Society.

12. Andrew Hooton to Mott Hooton, April 29, 1868, Mott Hooton Papers, Ms. Coll. 171, Chester County Historical Society and Andrew Hooton to Mott Hooton, September 28, 1864, Mott Hooton Papers, Ms. Coll. 171, Chester County Historical Society.

13. Andrew Hooton to Mott Hooton, January 19, 1864, Mott Hooton Papers, Ms. Coll. 171, Chester County Historical Society.

14. Bayard Taylor to R. H. Stoddard, April 21, 1861, in Taylor, Bayard, *Life and Letters of Bayard Taylor,* Vol. 1, (Boston: Houghton, Mifflin and Company, 1895), 375-376.

15. Douglas R. Harper, *If Thee Must Fight,* (West Chester, PA: Chester County Historical Society, 1990), 47.

16. Kevin Brown and Amy King, *A Small Company of Faithful Ones: The Brandywine Guards of Chester County, Company A, 1st Pennsylvania Reserves,* (CreateSpace, 2011), 15-16.

17. William Bowen to Mott Hooton, May 9, 1861, Ed and Faye Max Collection.

18. Brown and King, 15-16. The war was a great leveler, however. The men would all intermingle and there is no evidence of any feelings of class strife among the Brandywines.

19. Philip Price to Mott Hooton, August 1, 1863, Mott Hooton Papers, Ms. Coll. 171, Chester County Historical Society.

20. Philip Price to Elizabeth Pratt, November 10, 1861, Chester County Historical Society.

21. Joseph Way to brother, February 13, 1862, Chester County Historical Society.

22. *Village Record,* May 4, 1861.

23. Harper, 86.

24. Alfred Rupert to George Rupert, July 20, 1861.

25. Harper, 86.

26. Ibid.

27. Mott Hooton to Francis C. Hooton, October 5, 1863, Mott Hooton Papers, Ms. Coll. 171, Chester County Historical Society.

28. Alfred Rupert to George Rupert, August 16, 1862, Chester County Historical Society.

29. Alfred Rupert to George Rupert, September 21, 1861, Chester County Historical Society.

30. Charles Speakman to Abbie Speakman, September 8, 1861, Chester County Historical Society.

31. *American Republican,* July 16, 1861.

32. Alfred Rupert to George Rupert, July 20, 1861, Chester County Historical Society.

33. Susan Carpenter to Mott Hooton, September 22, 1863, Ed and Faye Max Collection.

3. A Feather Bed Company

1. William Henry Darlington, July 25, 1861, Chester County Historical Society. Darlington, a member of the Brandywine Guards serving with Mott described "Camp Carroll" as it was known, in great detail and related the unusual feeling he and the other Brandywines felt in this comfortable camp while others were locked in combat.

2. Charles Speakman to Abbie Speakman, July 25, 1861, Chester County Historical Society.

3. Charles Sheaff to Charlotte Sheaff, July 27, 1861, Chester County Historical Society.

4. Charles Speakman to Abbie Speakman, September 1, 1861, Chester County Historical Society.

5. Charles Speakman to Abbie Speakman, September 8, 1861, Chester County Historical Society.

6. William Henry Darlington, September 21, 1861, Chester County Historical Society.

7. William Henry Darlington, September 21, 1861, Chester County Historical Society. There is no direct evidence to corroborate the rumor Darlington heard regarding Nields' alcoholism.

8. Joseph Way to Albert Way, October 3, 1861, Chester County Historical Society.

9. Alfred Rupert to George Rupert, September 29, 1861, Chester County Historical Society.

10. Alfred Rupert to George Rupert, September 29, 1861, Chester County Historical Society.

11. Charles Lamborn, letter, October 16, 1861, Chester County Historical Society.

12. Joseph Way to brother, February 19, 1862, Chester County Historical Society.

13. Joseph Way to Albert Way, January 7, 1862, Chester County Historical Society.

14. Joseph Way to Mother, February 13, 1862, Chester County Historical Society.

15. Harper, Douglas, *If Thee Must Fight: A Civil War History of Chester County, Pennsylvania*, (West Chester, PA: Chester County Historical Society, 1990), 97.

16. Charles Speakman to Abbie Speakman, February 16, 1862, CCHS.

17. Stephen W. Sears, *To the Gates of Richmond: The Peninsula Campaign*, (New York: Haughton, Mifflin Company, 1992), 6-7.

18. Charles Speakman to Abbie Speakman, June 19, 1862, CCHS.

19. Charles Speakman to Abbie Speakman, July 11, 1862, CCHS.

20. Ibid.

21. Charles Speakman to Abbie Speakman, July 11, 1862, CCHS. Speakman related the scene as they all experienced that night.

22. Ibid., 282.

23. Ibid., 306.

24. Joseph Way to Albert Way, August 20, 1862, CCHS.

25. Mott Hooton to Francis C. Hooton, August 20, 1862, Mott Hooton Papers, Ms. Coll. 171, Chester County Historical Society.

26. Mott Hooton to Francis C. Hooton, August 20, 1862, Mott Hooton Papers, Ms. Coll. 171, Chester County Historical Society.

27. John J. Hennessy, *Return to Bull Run: The Campaign and Battle of Second Manassas,* (Norman, OK: University of Oklahoma Press, 1993), 330-331.

4. On the Front Lines

1. W. D. Hartman, letter, October 17, 1862. National Archives and Records Administration.

2. W. D. Hartman, letter, November 25, 1862. National Archives and Records Administration.

3. W. D. Hartman, letter, December 24, 1862. National Archives and Records Administration.

4. Francis C. Hooton to Sallie Rogers, February 25, 1863, Mott Hooton PMs. Coll. 171, Chester County Historical Society.

5. *Washington Star,* February 27, 1863, reprinted in *Village Record,* March 3, 1863.

6. Ibid.

7. *Village Record,* March 10, 1863.

8. John Harvey to Alfred Rupert, March 11, 1863, CCHS.

9. Mott Hooton to Susan Carpenter, March 27, 1863, Mott Hooton PMs. Coll. 171, Chester County Historical Society.

10. Ibid.

11. Ibid.

12. Ibid.

13. Ibid.

14. Ibid.

15. The Guards gained one member, Private Andrew Madden, in September of '62 which accounts for the extra man that makes up 78 members as opposed to only 77. Madden was not only the last person to enlist in the company, but he was the only person to be enlisted after 1861.

16. Sears, 6-14.

17. Ibid., 15-16.

18. Edward J. Stackpole, Wilbur Sturtevant Nye, Bradley M. Gottfried, *The Battle of Gettysburg: A Guided Tour* (Mechanicsburg, PA: Stackpole Books, 1998), 38. Some sources have suggested that Philadelphia could have proved an

appealing target for Lee as well. Either way, Chester County would still have stood in the army's path.

19. Mott Hooton, Diary, June 26, 1863 – June 30, 1863.

20. Mott Hooton, Diary, July 1, 1863.

21. Mott Hooton, Diary, July 2, 1863.

22. Sears, 321-322.

23. Mott Hooton, Diary, July 4, 1863.

24. *Official Records*, Series I. Vol. 27, Part I, Reports. Serial No. 43.

25. Mott Hooton, Diary, 1863-1864, July 5, 1863- July 15, 1863.

26. Mott Hooton, Diary, 1863-1864, July 27, 1863.

27. Mott Hooton, Diary, 1863-1864, August 3, 1863.

28. Mott Hooton, Diary, 1863-1864, August 15, 1863.

29. Joseph B. Darlington to Harvey Darlington, October 1, 1863, CCHS.

30. Mott Hooton, Diary, 1863-1863, September 28, 1863.

31. Mott Hooton to Francis C. Hooton, October 5, 1863, Mott Hooton Collection, CCHS.

32. Mott Hooton, Diary, 1863-1864, September 14, 1863 – September 15, 1863.

33. Mott Hooton, Diary, 1863-1864, August 24, 1863.

34. Joseph B. Darlington to Sister, October 22, 1864.

35. Mott Hooton, Diary, 1863-1864, October 19, 1863.

36. Ibid.

37. Ibid.

38. Ann E. Rhoads to Mott Hooton, October 6, 1863, Ed and Faye Max Collection.

39. Susan Carpenter to Mott Hooton, September 22, 1863, Ed and Faye Max Collection.

40. Mott Hooton, Diary, 1863-1864, November 26, 1863.

41. Ibid.

42. Mott Hooton, Diary, November 27, 1863.

43. Mott Hooton, Diary, November 29, 1863.

44. Mott Hooton, Diary, November 30, 1863.

45. Ibid.

46. Mott Hooton, Diary, December 1, 1863.

47. Mott Hooton, Diary, December 2, 1863.

48. Mott Hooton, Diary, 1863-1864, December 27, 1863.

49. Mott Hooton, Diary, December 28, 1863.

50. Mott Hooton, Diary, December 29, 1863.

51. Mott Hooton, Diary, April 7, 1864.

52. Mott Hooton, Diary, 1863-1864, January 31, 1864.

53. Among his list of literature was *The Pickwick Papers* by Charles Dickens; *Shoulder Straps: A Novel of New York* and *The Army and The Days of Stroddy* both by Henry Morford; *Gil Blas* by Alaine-René Lesage; Thackeray's *Irish Sketchbook*; Geraldine

Jewsbury's *Zoe: The History of Two Lives; Conseulo* and *The Countess of Rudolstadt* by George Sand. See Mott Hooton, Diary, 1863-1864, February 3 – April 15.

54. Mott Hooton, Diary, March 18, 1864.

55. Mott Hooton, Diary, April 14, 1864.

56. Mott Hooton, Diary, 1863-1863, February 4, 1864.

57. Mott Hooton, Diary, February 5, 1864.

58. Mott Hooton, Diary, April 11, 1864.

59. Mott Hooton, Diary, February 12, 1864.

60. Mott Hooton, Diary, March 16, 1864.

61. Ibid.

62. Mott Hooton, Diary, March 17, 1864.

63. Mott Hooton, Diary, 1863-1864, May 4, 1864.

64. Gordon C. Rhea, *The Battle of the Wilderness, May 5-6, 1864,* (Baton Rouge: Louisiana State University

Press, 1994), 51.

65. Mott Hooton, Diary, 1863-1864, May 5, 1864.

66. Ibid.

67. Mott Hooton, Diary, May 6, 1864.

68. Ibid.

69. Mott Hooton, Diary, May 7, 1864.

70. Mott Hooton, Diary, May 8, 1864.

71. Mott Hooton, Diary, May 9, 1864.

72. Mott Hooton, Diary, May 10, 1864.

73. Ibid.

74. Mott Hooton, Diary, May 12, 1864.

75. Ibid.

76. Mott Hooton, Diary, May 13, 1864.

77. Mott Hooton, Diary, May 18, 1864.

78. Mott Hooton, Diary, 1863-1864, May 29, 1864.

79. Gordon C. Rhea, *Cold Harbor: Grant and Lee, May 26-June3, 1864* (Baton Rouge, Louisiana State

University Press, 2002), 139-140.

80. Ibid., 140.

81. Ibid.

82. Mott Hooton, Diary, 1863-1864, May 30, 1864.

83. Rhea, *Cold Harbor*, 141.

84. Ibid.

85. Rhea, *Cold Harbor*, 143.

86. Ibid., 145.

87. Ibid., 147.

88. Mott Hooton, Diary, 1863-1864, May 31, 1864.

89. Ibid.

90. Ibid.

91. This was probably Mott's shorthand for "When Johnny Comes Marching Home."

92. Mott Hooton, Diary, 1863-1864, June 5, 1864

5. *Prospects*

1. Mott Hooton telegram, June 7, 1864.

2. Mott Hooton to Francis C. Hooton, telegram, June 7, 1864, Uriah Hunt Painter Papers, Ms. Coll. 174, Chester County Historical Society.

3. *Village Record,* June 11, 1864.

4. Ibid.

5. Ibid.

6. Ibid.

7. Ibid. A tiger refers to a long howl or holler given after the more formal 'hurrahs' have been shouted.

8. Thomas Maloney to Mott Hooton, July 7, 1864, Mott Hooton Papers, Ms. Coll. 171, Chester County Historical Society.

9. Catherine Jenkins to Mott Hooton, November 1, 1864, Mott Hooton Papers, Ms. Coll. 171, Chester County Historical Society.

10. James Mooney to Mott Hooton, July 7, 1864, Mott Hooton Papers, Ms. Coll. 171, Chester County Historical Society. Mooney did not actually mention Eli Catren by name as he was at the time unaware of Catren's capture.

11. Ibid.

12. *Village Record,* July 12, 1864.

13. *Village Record,* July 19, 1964.

14. Ibid.

15. Hampton Hildeburn to Mott Hooton, August 17, 1866, Mott Hooten Correspondence, 1866-1867, Ms 1988-100, Special Collections, Virginia Tech.

16. Mott's property holdings are a little sketchy and hard to trace, however, later correspondence suggests he owned at least two separate farms, which he presumably leased out to tenant farmers. It is not clear when he acquired the properties nor if he possessed them at this time.

17. J. Kershaw to Mott Hooton, February 15, 1865, Mott Hooton Papers, Ms. Coll. 171, Chester County Historical Society.

18. Mott's relationship with Bowen is unclear. By this time, Bowen's family was living in Nebraska, but based on correspondence, the Bowens had a connection to Chester County and were at least acquaintances of Mott's family. How close Mott and Bowen is not clear. The tone of Bowen's letters suggests a close familiarity, yet

the frequent references to letters being unreciprocated by Mott makes one question if Mott's feelings toward Bowen were mutual. Mott may also have simply been a poor correspondent.

19. William R. Bowen to Mott Hooton, July 9, 1864, Mott Hooton Papers, Ms. Coll. 171, Chester County Historical Society.

20. Ibid.

21. Emmor B. Cope to Mott Hooton, July 28, 1864, Mott Hooton Papers, Ms. Coll. 171, Chester County Historical Society.

22. Ann Eliza Rhoads to Mott Hooton, September 24, 1864, Mott Hooton Papers, Ms. Coll. 171, Chester County Historical Society.

23. Emmor B. Cope to Mott Hooton, July 28, 1864. For all of Cope's jaded attitude about the army, went on to have an illustrious career in the army corps of engineers, eventually attaining the rank of Lieutenant Colonel. Among his more notable accomplishments, he became an early superintendent of the Gettysburg Battlefield national park, helping in the lay out of the park and designing the few large, metal observation towers still used by visitors to the battlefield to this day. The particular construction method of the towers is known as a "Cope truss."

24. William R. Bowen to Mott Hooton, December 11, 1864, Mott Hooton Papers, Ms. Coll. 171, Chester County Historical Society.

25. Luther Mendenhall to Mott Hooton, October 24, 1864, Mott Hooton Papers, Ms. Coll. 171, Chester County Historical Society.

26. William Henry Darlington to Mother, August 6, 1861, William Henry Darlington Letters, Chester County Historical Society.

27. Ann Eliza Rhoads to Mott Hooton, August 7, 1863, Mott Hooton Papers, Ms. Coll. 171, Chester County Historical Society.

28. Ibid.

29. Susan Carpenter to Mott Hooton, September 22, 1863, Ed and Faye Max Collection.

30. Emmor B. Cope to Mott Hooton, January 24, 1865, Mott Hooton Papers, Ms. Coll. 171, Chester County Historical Society.

31. Consolidated Military Officer's File of 1st Lieutenant Mott Hooten [sic], 22nd U.S. Infantry. RG 94. Letters Received, 1871-1894, National Archives Identifier 7423592. National Archives and Records Administration, Washington, D.C.

32. William McCandless to War Department, November 28, 1865, Consolidated Military Officer's File of 1st Lieutenant Mott Hooten [sic], 22nd U.S. Infantry. RG 94. Letters Received, 1871-1894, National Archives Identifier 7423592. National Archives and Records Administration, Washington, D.C.

33. William Cooper Talley to War Department, December 19, 1864, Consolidated Military Officer's File of 1st Lieutenant Mott Hooten [sic], 22nd U.S. Infantry. RG 94. Letters Received, 1871-1894, National Archives Identifier 7423592. National Archives and Records Administration, Washington, D.C.

34. George A. McCall to War Department, November 24, 1865, Consolidated

Military Officer's File of 1st Lieutenant Mott Hooten [sic], 22nd U.S. Infantry. RG 94. Letters Received, 1871-1894, National Archives Identifier 7423592. National Archives and Records Administration, Washington, D.C.

35. Truman Seymour to War Department, December 13, 1864, Consolidated Military Officer's File of 1st Lieutenant Mott Hooten [sic], 22nd U.S. Infantry. RG 94. Letters Received, 1871-1894, National Archives Identifier 7423592. National Archives and Records Administration, Washington, D.C.

36. Ibid.

37. Francis C. Hooton to Uriah Painter, April 28, 1898, Mott Hooton Papers, Ms. Coll. 171, Chester County Historical Society.

38. Ibid.

39. See George Meade to Moot Hooton, January 23, 1871, Mott Hooton Papers, Ms. Coll. 171, Chester County Historical Society. Meade served in the 22nd Infantry and likely served for a time with Mott. Later this year, while on recruiting duty in New York, Mott assisted Meade with obtaining a new saddle. See George Meade to Mott Hooton, June 28, 1871, Mott Hooton Papers, Ms. Coll. 171, Chester County Historical Society and George Meade to Mott Hooton, July 25, 1871, Mott Hooton Papers, Ms. Coll. 171, Chester County Historical Society.

40. *Village Record,* July 11, 1865.

41. Ibid.

6. Into the West

1. Hampton Hildeburn to Mott Hooton, September 17, 1866, Mott Hooten [sic] Correspondence, 1866-1867, Ms 1988-100, Special Collections, Virginia Polytechnic Institute and State University.

2. Mott Hooton, *Military Memoirs of Col. Mott Hooton* (1900), 4.

3. Bill Yenne, *Indian Wars: The Campaign for the American West* (Yardley, PA: Westholme Publishing, 2006), 109.

4. Ibid.

5. Ibid., 110. The army would be further reduced by another 25,000 by 1874.

6. Mott Hooton, *Military Memoirs of Col. Mott Hooton* (1900), 4.

7. For general information on post-war strategic doctrine and the reservation system, see Yenne, 111-114.

8. Although Fort James was the official name of the post, Mott only ever referred to it as Firesteel. For consistency, this book will reference it as Mott knew it.

9. Mott Hooton, *Military Memoirs of Col. Mott Hooton* (1900), 4.

10. Fort Stevenson was named in honor of Brigadier General Thomas G. Stevenson who fell at the Battle of Spottsylvania in 1864.

11. Mott Hooton, *Military Memoirs of Col. Mott Hooton* (1900), 4.

12. Mott Hooton, *Military Memoirs of Col. Mott Hooton* (1900), 5. Though unclear in

significance, Mott also mentions that the man's heart was sent to the Army Medical Museum, then in Washington D. C.

13. Trobriand, Philippe Regis de, *Military Life in Dakota: The Journal of Philippe Regis de Trobriand,* trans. And ed. Lucile M. Kane (Lincoln, NE: University of Nebraska Press, 1951), 41.

14. Ibid., 41-44. Virtually all of the descriptions of Fort Stevenson are taken from de Trobriand's journal.

15. Ibid., 69.

16. Ibid., 41.

17. Ibid.

18. Ibid., 49.

19. Ibid., 80.

20. Within seven years, this area would become a designated reservation for the Three Affiliated Tribes and it remains so today. Also, de Trobriand and his contemporaries often referred to the Hidatsa as the Gros Ventre, or Gros Ventre of the Plains/Missouri. The Arikara are sometimes referred to as the Ree in many sources.

21. Bad Lands here refers generally to the particular type of geological formations of the landscape, not the National Park of the same name in present day South Dakota.

22. De Trobriand, 80.

23. Ibid., 83.

24. Ibid.

25. De Trobriand continually refers to Crow's Breast as "Crow Belly."

26. De Trobriand, 86.

27. Ibid.

28. Ibid., 83.

29. Ibid., 88.

30. Ibid., 89.

31. As with Crow's Breast, de Trobriand refers to White Shield as "White Parefleche."

32. De Trobriand, 95.

33. According to de Trobriand, neither the Mandan nor the Hidatsa ever put on such performances. See pg. 98.

34. Hooton, Mott, Unpublished writing regarding his thoughts on the American Indian, n.d., Mott Hooton Papers, Ms. Coll. 171, Chester County Historical Society.

35. De Trobriand, 98.

36. Ibid., 98-99.

37. Ibid., 100-101.

38. For a more in depth description of the powwow, see De Trobriand, 100-107.

39. Hooton Military Memoirs, 5.

40. Ibid.

41. De Trobriand, 219.

42. Hooton Military Memoirs, 5.

43. De Trobriand, 263.

44. Ibid., 284.

45. Ibid., 287-289.

46. Ibid., 289.

47. Ibid., 341.

48. Ben Innis, *Bloody Knife: Custer's Favorite Scout,* (Bismarck, ND: Smoky Water Press, 1994), 64.

49. Hooton Military Memoirs, 6.

50. Ibid.

51. William Bowen to Mott Hooton, March 17, 1869, Mott Hooton Papers, Ms. Coll. 171, Chester County Historical Society.

52. Ann Eliza Rhoads to Mott Hooton, October 1870, Mott Hooton Papers, Ms. Coll. 171, Chester County Historical Society.

53. Sallie Rhoads to Mott Hooton, December 14, 1866, Mott Hooton Papers, Ms. Coll. 171, Chester County Historical Society.

54. Ibid.

55. Susan Carpenter to Mott Hooton, May 28, 1866, Mott Hooton Papers, Ms. Coll. 171, Chester County Historical Society.

56. Ibid.

57. Susan Carpenter to Mott Hooton, November 6, 1870, Mott Hooton Papers, Ms. Coll. 171, Chester County Historical Society.

58. Susan Carpenter to Mott Hooton, November 27, 1870, Mott Hooton Papers, Ms. Coll. 171, Chester County Historical Society.

59. Susan Carpenter to Mott Hooton, October 16, 1870, Mott Hooton Papers, Ms. Coll. 171, Chester County Historical Society.

60. Ibid.

61. Susan Carpenter to Mott Hooton, January 6, 1867, Mott Hooton Papers, Ms. Coll. 171, Chester County Historical Society.

62. Susan Carpenter to Mott Hooton, January 17, 1868, Mott Hooton Papers, Ms. Coll. 171, Chester County Historical Society.

63. Susan Carpenter to Mott Hooton, April 15, 1867, Mott Hooton Papers, Ms. Coll. 171, Chester County Historical Society.

64. Susan Carpenter to Mott Hooton, January 17, 1867, Mott Hooton Papers, Ms. Coll. 171, Chester County Historical Society.

65. Susan Carpenter to Mott Hooton, November 27, 1870, Mott Hooton Papers, Ms. Coll. 171, Chester County Historical Society.

66. Simon Cameron to Mott Hooton, October 31, 1870, Mott Hooton Papers, Ms. Coll. 171, Chester County Historical Society.

67. Kevin C. Fitzpatrick, *Governor's Island Explorer's Guide: Adventure and History in New York Harbor* (Guilford, CT: Globe Pequot, 2016), 14.

7. A Confirmed Bachelor

1. "Maj. Matt [sic] Hooton," *Anaconda Standard*, Anaconda, MT, September 24, 1895, pg. 8.

2. "'Tiny,' Yale's Toast, Famed Beauty, Dead," *Evening Bulletin*, Providence, RI, August 30, 1909.

3. "Trouble of a Pinafore Company," *New York Herald*, New York, NY, May 14, 1891, pg. 6.

4. Justine Ingersoll to Mott Hooton, August 2, 1871, Mott Hooton Papers, Ms Coll. 171, Chester County Historical Society.

5. Ibid.

6. Justine Ingersoll to Mott Hooton, n.d., Mott Hooton Papers, Ms Coll. 171, Chester County Historical Society.

7. Justine Ingersoll to Mott Hooton, September 2, 1871, Mott Hooton Papers, Ms Coll. 171, Chester County Historical Society.

8. Justine Ingersoll to Mott Hooton, n.d., Mott Hooton Papers, Ms Coll. 171, Chester County Historical Society.

9. Charles Gray to Mott Hooton, May 19, 1871, Mott Hooton Papers, Ms Coll. 171, Chester County Historical Society.

10. Justine Ingersoll to Mott Hooton, August 2, 1871, Mott Hooton Papers, Ms Coll. 171, Chester County Historical Society.

11. Ibid.

12. Duane A. Smith, *Time for Peace: Fort Lewis, Colorado, 1878-1891*, (Boulder, CO: University Press of Colorado, 2006), 80.

13. Smith, 81.

14. Stevens Norvell to Mott Hooton, February 10, 1869, Mott Hooton Papers, Ms. Coll. 171, Chester County Historical Society.

15. Mott Hooton to Susan Carpenter, November 30, 1861, Mott Hooton Papers, Ms Coll. 171, Chester County Historical Society.

16. Francis C. Hooton to Sallie Rogers, February 25, 1863, Chester County Historical Society.

17. Sallie Rogers to Mott Hooton, April 21, 1864, Mott Hooton Papers, Ms Coll. 171, Chester County Historical Society.

18. Hampton Hildeburn to Mott Hooton, August 17, 1866, Mott Hooten[sic] Correspondence, 1866-1867 Ms 1988-100, Special Collections, Virginia Polytechnic Institute and State University.

19. James M. Good to Mott Hooton, August 13, 1866, Mott Hooton Papers, Ms Coll. 171, Chester County Historical Society.

20. Hampton Hildeburn to Mott Hooton, August 17, 1866, Mott Hooten[sic] Correspondence, 1866-1867 Ms 1988-100, Special Collections, Virginia Polytechnic Institute and State University.

21. Ibid.

22. Sallie Rogers to Mott Hooton, June 18, 1863, Mott Hooton Papers, Ms Coll. 171, Chester County Historical Society.

23. Ibid.

24. Ann Eliza Rhoads to Mott Hooton, June 24, 1869, Mott Hooton Papers, Ms. Coll. 171, Chester County Historical Society.

25. Susan Carpenter to Mott Hooton, October 16, 1870, Mott Hooton Papers, Ms. Coll. 171, Chester County Historical Society.

26. Fannie Bemis to Mott Hooton, November 24, 1871, Mott Hooton Papers, Ms. Coll. 171, Chester County Historical Society.

27. Carrie's surname or relation to the family is not clear. In one of her letters she references her brother, Mort. However, Mott's family was acquainted with two Morts- Morton Jefferis and Morton Chase. Carrie was often referenced in connection with the Chases, however she likewise refers to the Chases in third person as if they are not her immediate family. In which case, she could be Carrie Jefferis. If she is the former, she would eventually become the sister-in-law of Mott's own sister, Annie, who married Mort Chase.

28. Carrie to Mott Hooton, October 22, 1870, Mott Hooton Papers, Ms. Coll. 171, Chester County Historical Society.

29. Susan Carpenter to Mott Hooton, November 6, 1870, Mott Hooton Papers, Ms. Coll. 171, Chester County Historical Society.

30. Carrie to Mott Hooton, April 24, 1871, Mott Hooton Papers, Ms. Coll. 171, Chester County Historical Society.

31. Carrie to Mott Hooton, May 1, 1871, Mott Hooton Papers, Ms. Coll. 171, Chester County Historical Society.

32. Ibid.

33. Carrie to Mott Hooton, October 22, 1870, Mott Hooton Papers, Ms. Coll. 171, Chester County Historical Society.

34. Carrie to Mott Hooton, May 1, 1871, Mott Hooton Papers, Ms. Coll. 171, Chester County Historical Society.

35. Carrie to Mott Hooton, October 22, 1870, Mott Hooton Papers, Ms. Coll. 171, Chester County Historical Society.

36. Carrie to Mott Hooton, May 1, 1871, Mott Hooton Papers, Ms. Coll. 171, Chester County Historical Society.

37. Marselis to Mott Hooton, January 1, 1870, Mott Hooton Papers, Ms. Coll. 171, Chester County Historical Society.

38. Oskaloosa Smith to Mott Hooton, February 5, 1872, Mott Hooton Papers, Ms. Coll. 171, Chester County Historical Society.

39. Mott Hooton to Ann Eliza Rhoads, July 21, 1876, Mott Hooton Papers, Ms. Coll. 171, Chester County Historical Society.

40. Mott Hooton to Ann Eliza Rhoads, September 28, 1877, Mott Hooton Papers, Ms. Coll. 171, Chester County Historical Society.

41. "'Tiny,' Yale's Toast, Famed Beauty, Dead," *Evening Bulletin,* Providence, RI, August 30, 1909.

42. Ibid.

43. Ibid.

44. "Fifteen Hundred Present at Brilliant Opening Performance of the Sokoloff Symphonies at 'Music Hill,' Weston," *The Norwalk Hour,* July 7, 1933, pg. 18.

45. "Musicians' Relief Group Appointed," *Evening Star,* Washington D.C., October 26, 1935, pg. 5.

46. "An Opera Company of Her Own: How Miss Justine Ingersoll of New Haven Came to Have Such a Thing," *The Sun,* New York, NY, June 5, 1892, 4.

47. "'Tiny,' Yale's Toast, Famed Beauty, Dead," *Evening Bulletin,* Providence, RI, August 30, 1909.

48. "New Books: Brief Review of Important and Interesting New Publications," *The Sun,* New York, NY, July 6, 1895, 7.

49. "'Tiny,' Yale's Toast, Famed Beauty, Dead," *Evening Bulletin,* Providence, RI, August 30, 1909.

50. *The Norwich Bulletin,* Norwich, CT, November 30, 1909, 10.

51. Shelton, Jim, "Part of the Family—Handsome Dan and Friends have a Special Place in Elm City Lore," *New Haven Register,* October 22, 2010, https://www.nhregister.com/news/article/Part-of-the-family-Handsome-Dan-and-friends-11611806.php#photo-13462744.

52. "'Tiny,' Yale's Toast, Famed Beauty, Dead," *Evening Bulletin,* Providence, RI, August 30, 1909.

53. "Yale's 'College Widow' Who Is Dead," *Chicago Daily Tribune,* Chicago, IL, August 30, 1909.

54. "'Tiny,' Yale's Toast, Famed Beauty, Dead," *Evening Bulletin,* Providence, RI, August 30, 1909.

8. Expedition and Insurrection

1. Ann Eliza Rhoads to Mott Hooton, September 8, 1872, Mott Hooton Papers, Ms. Coll. 171, Chester County Historical Society.

2. Susan Carpenter to Mott Hooton, April 5, 1869, Mott Hooton Papers, Ms. Coll. 171, Chester County Historical Society.

3. Susan Carpenter to Mott Hooton, October 16, 1870, Mott Hooton Papers, Ms. Coll. 171, Chester County Historical Society.

4. M. John Lubetkin, *Jay Cooke's Gamble: The Northern Pacific Railroad, The Sioux, and the Panic of 1873,* (Norman, OK: University of Oklahoma Press, 2006), 5.

5. Ibid., 6.

6. Ibid., 11.

7. Ibid., 4.

8. Ibid., 75-76.

9. Ibid., 42.

10. Ibid., 175.

11. Ibid., 175.

12. Ibid., 176.

13. Ibid., 177-179.

14. David D. Stanley, *Report on the Yellowstone Expedition of 1873*, (Washington: Government Printing Office, 1874), 3.

15. Ibid.

16. Lubetkin, 188-189.

17. Stanley, *Report on the Yellowstone Expedition of 1873*, 4.

18. Hooton, Mott, *Military Memoirs of Col. Mott Hooton*, 7.

19. Stanley, *Report on the Yellowstone Expedition of 1873*, 6.

20. Hooton, Mott, *Military Memoirs of Col. Mott Hooton*, 7.

21. Lubetkin, 259-264.

22. Stanley, *Report on the Yellowstone Expedition of 1873*, 7.

23. Ibid., 8.

24. Hooton, Mott, *Military Memoirs of Col. Mott Hooton*, 7.

25. Stanley, *Report on the Yellowstone Expedition of 1873*, 17.

26. Lubetkin, 276-277.

27. Hooton, Mott, *Military Memoirs of Col. Mott Hooton*, 7.

28. Mott Hooton to Ann Eliza Rhoads, December 14, 1876, Mott Hooton Papers, Ms Coll. 171, Chester County Historical Society.

9. *Wanderlust*

1. Mott Hooton to Ann Eliza Rhoads, December 25, 1875, Mott Hooton Papers, Ms. Coll. 171, Chester County Historical Society.

2. Eric G. E. Zuelow, *A History of Modern Tourism*, (New York: Palgrave, 2015), see Chapter 2.

3. Ibid., 39.

4. Based on context from other letters, this could be Tom Stellwagen.

5. Thomas Stellwagen to Mott Hooton, June 7, 1863, Mott Hooton Papers, Ms. Coll. 171, Chester County Historical Society.

6. Tom's father, Captain Henry Schreiner Stellwagen, also saw much of the world during his life. As a young man, he served aboard a merchant vessel that travelled to Calcutta, India and upon entering the US Navy served aboard ships that saw service along the coast of Africa to enforce the ban on slave trading. He also fought in the fleet with Commodore Matthew Perry during the Mexican War. Although Mott was

friends with Captain Stellwagen's son, likely through the latter's marriage to Mott's cousin Annie (daughter of his Uncle Francis Carpenter) we do not know if he was at all acquainted with the Captain himself. Though it is quite possible Mott had heard of the man's career through Tom.

7. Zuelow, 21.

8. Ibid., 25.

9. "On To Europe: Pleasure Seekers for the Old Country on the Increase," *The New York Herald,* July 4, 1875, page 8.

10. Norway Heritage: Hands Across the Sea, website, http://www.norwayheritage.com/p_ship.asp?sh=scyth. This website is dedicated to providing historical passenger manifests, documents, and photographs related to ships used by Norwegian emigrants.

11. Zuelow,

12. Mott Hooton to Ann Eliza Rhoads, October 28, 1875, Mott Hooton Papers, Ms. Coll. 171, Chester County Historical Society.

13. Ibid.

14. Mott Hooton to Ann Eliza Rhoads, November 19, 1875, Mott Hooton Papers, Ms. Coll. 171, Chester County Historical Society.

15. Mott Hooton to Ann Eliza Rhoads, October 28, 1875, Mott Hooton Papers, Ms. Coll. 171, Chester County Historical Society and Mott Hooton to Ann Eliza Rhoads, November 19, 1875, Mott Hooton Papers, Ms. Coll. 171, Chester County Historical Society.

16. Mott Hooton to Ann Eliza Rhoads, October 28, 1875, Mott Hooton Papers, Ms. Coll. 171, Chester County Historical Society.

17. Mott Hooton to Ann Eliza Rhoads, December 25, 1875, Mott Hooton Papers, Ms. Coll. 171, Chester County Historical Society.

18. Ibid.

19. Ibid.

20. Ibid.

21. Mott Hooton to Ann Eliza Rhoads, n.d., Mott Hooton Papers, Ms. Coll. 171, Chester County Historical Society.

22. Mott Hooton to Ann Eliza Rhoads, December 25, 1875, Mott Hooton Papers, Ms. Coll. 171, Chester County Historical Society.

23. Mott Hooton to Ann Eliza Rhoads, January 31, 1876, Mott Hooton Papers, Ms. Coll. 171, Chester County Historical Society.

24. Ibid.

25. Mott Hooton to Ann Eliza Rhoads, January 31, 1876, Mott Hooton Papers, Ms. Coll. 171, Chester County Historical Society.

26. Ibid.

27. Ibid.

28. Ibid.

29. Ibid.

30. *Wilmington Daily Commercial,* August 6, 1875, pg. 1.

31. Zuelow, 63.

32. Waleed Hazbun, "The East as an Exhibition: Thomas Cook & Son and the Origins of the International Tourism Industry in Egypt" in *The Business of Tourism: Place, Faith, and History,* ed. Philip Scranton and Janet F. Davidson, (Philadelphia: University of Pennsylvania Press, 2007), 5.

33. Ibid., 6.

34. Ibid., 23.

35. Ibid., 25.

36. Ibid., 13.

37. Mott Hooton to Ann Eliza Rhoads, March 1, 1876, Mott Hooton Papers, Ms. Coll. 171, Chester County Historical Society.

38. Ibid.

39. Ibid.

40. Ibid.

41. Ibid.

42. Ibid.

43. Ibid.

44. Ibid.

45. Mott Hooton to Ann Eliza Rhoads, November 19, 1876, Mott Hooton Papers, Ms. Coll. 171, Chester County Historical Society.

46. Mott Hooton to Ann Eliza Rhoads, March 12, 1876, Mott Hooton Papers, Ms. Coll. 171, Chester County Historical Society.

47. Ibid.

48. Ibid.

49. Ibid.

50. Mott Hooton to Ann Eliza Rhoads, March 1, 1876, Mott Hooton Papers, Ms. Coll. 171, Chester County Historical Society.

51. Mott Hooton to Ann Eliza Rhoads, April 15, 1876, Mott Hooton Papers, Ms. Coll. 171, Chester County Historical Society.

52. Ibid.

53. Ibid.

54. Ibid.

55. Ibid.

56. Ibid.

57. Ibid.

58. Ibid. Though Mott does not specifically mention it, often the Dervishes in this particular kind of ceremony would also inflict self-harm, cutting themselves or piercing their flesh, a kind of self-flagellation, when in the midst of their frenzied movements.

59. Mott Hooton to Ann Eliza Rhoads, April 15, 1876, Mott Hooton Papers, Ms. Coll. 171, Chester County Historical Society.

10. Peril at Clear Creek

1. Yenne, 176.

2. Ibid.

3. Ibid., 177-178.

4. *Battles and Skirmishes of the Great Sioux War, 1876-1877: The Military View,* ed. Jerome A. Greene, (Norman, OK; University of Oklahoma Press, 1993), xvi.

5. *Battles and Skirmishes of the Great Sioux War,* xvii.

6. *Battles and Skirmishes of the Great Sioux War,* xviii – xix.

7. Mott Hooton to Ann Eliza Rhoads, July 21, 1876, Mott Hooton Papers, Ms Coll. 171, Chester County Historical Society.

8. Ibid.

9. *Battles and Skirmishes of the Great Sioux War,* xxii.

10. Mott Hooton to Ann Eliza Rhoads, September 5, 1876, Mott Hooton Papers, Ms Coll. 171, Chester County Historical Society.

11. Oskaloosa M. Smith in *Battles and Skirmishes of the Great Sioux War, 1876-1877: The Military View,* ed. Jerome A. Greene, (Norman, OK; University of Oklahoma Press, 1993), 117.

12. Mott Hooton to Ann Eliza Rhoads, October 6, 1876, Mott Hooton Papers, Ms Coll. 171, Chester County Historical Society.

13. Ibid.

14. Ibid.

15. Jerome Greee, *Yellowstone Command: Colonel Nelson A. Miles and the Great Sioux War, 1876-1877,* (Norman, OK: University of Oklahoma Press, 2006), 81-82.

16. Hooton, Mott, *Military Memoirs of Col. Mott Hooton,* 8.

17. Alfred C. Sharpe in *Battles and Skirmishes of the Great Sioux War, 1876-1877: The Military View,* ed. Jerome A. Greene, (Norman, OK; University of Oklahoma Press, 1993), 124.

18. Ibid., 125-126.

19. Greene, *Yellowstone Command,* 85.

20. Ibid.

21. Ibid., 86.

22. Ibid.

23. Alfred C. Sharpe in *Battles and Skirmishes of the Great Sioux War, 1876-1877: The Military View,* ed. Jerome A. Greene, (Norman, OK; University of Oklahoma Press, 1993), 129.

24. Mott Hooton to Ann Eliza Rhoads, October 26, 1876, Mott Hooton Papers, Ms Coll. 171, Chester County Historical Society.

25. Alfred C. Sharpe in *Battles and Skirmishes of the Great Sioux War, 1876-1877: The

Military View, ed. Jerome A. Greene, (Norman, OK; University of Oklahoma Press, 1993), 129.

26. Mott Hooton to Ann Eliza Rhoads, October 26, 1876, Mott Hooton Papers, Ms Coll. 171, Chester County Historical Society.

27. Alfred C. Sharpe in *Battles and Skirmishes of the Great Sioux War, 1876-1877: The Military View,* ed. Jerome A. Greene, (Norman, OK; University of Oklahoma Press, 1993), 130.

28. Mott Hooton to Ann Eliza Rhoads, October 26, 1876, Mott Hooton Papers, Ms Coll. 171, Chester County Historical Society.

29. *Report of the Secretary of War; Being Part of the Message and Documents Communicated to the Two Houses of Congress at the Beginning of the Second Session of the Forty-Fifth Congress,* Vol. I, (Washington: Government Printing Office, 1877), 491. And Mott Hooton to Ann Eliza Rhoads, October 27, 1876, Mott Hooton Papers, Ms Coll. 171, Chester County Historical Society.

30. *Report of the Secretary of War,* 491.

31. Mott Hooton to Ann Eliza Rhoads, October 26, 1876, Mott Hooton Papers, Ms Coll. 171, Chester County Historical Society.

32. Hooton, *Military Memoirs of Col. Mott Hooton,* 10.

33. Mott Hooton to Ann Eliza Rhoads, February 2, 1877, Mott Hooton Papers, Ms Coll. 171, Chester County Historical Society.

11. *Fires of Unrest*

1. Mott Hooton to Ann Eliza Rhoads, September 28, 1877, Mott Hooton Papers, Ms Coll. 171, Chester County Historical Society.

2. Ibid. Mott's letter was written on Wyoming Valley Hotel letterhead.

3. Mott Hooton to Ann Eliza Rhoads, August 12, 1877, Mott Hooton Papers, Ms Coll. 171, Chester County Historical Society.

4.] Mott Hooton to Ann Eliza Rhoads, October 2, 1877, Mott Hooton Papers, Ms Coll. 171, Chester County Historical Society.

5. Ibid.

6. Mott Hooton to Ann Eliza Rhoads, October 2, 1877, Mott Hooton Papers, Ms Coll. 171, Chester County Historical Society.

12. *Cain and Abel*

1. Ann Eliza Rhoads to Mott Hooton, January 4, 1864, Mott Hooton Papers, Ms Coll. 171, Chester County Historical Society.

2. Ibid.

3. Mott Hooton to Ann Eliza Rhoads, December 11, 1863, Ed and Faye Max Private Collection.

4. Bill Bowen to Mott Hooton, April 8, 1864, Mott Hooton Papers, Ms Coll. 171, Chester County Historical Society.

5. "Colonel Hooton's Canvass for the Office of Prothonotary," *The Times*, Philadelphia, June 23, 1895, pg. 15.

6. For Clerk of the House, see: "For Clerk of the House," *Daily Local News*, December 1, 1881. For Prothonotary see: "Col. Francis C. Hooton," *Morning Republican*, February 1, 1899. For State Senate see: Unknown Newspaper, November 4, [no year given], newspaper clippings file, Chester County Historical Society.

7. There is no evidence that Mott ever begrudged Frank his rank. On the contrary, when Frank applied for the Lieutenant Colonelcy of the 175th in 1862, he did so on Mott's advice. "I would advise you to try and [get] a commission in the line for it is no fun being a Private in this army. It is, like all armies, a despotism." Mott Hooton to Francis C. Hooton, August 20, 1862, Mott Hooton Papers, Ms Coll. 171, Chester County Historical Society.

8. Sallie Rogers to Mott Hooton, August 24, 1862, Mott Hooton Papers, Ms Coll. 171, Chester County Historical Society.

9. Sallie Rogers to Mott Hooton, April 1864, Mott Hooton Papers, Ms Coll. 171, Chester County Historical Society. Sallie would offer dubious reassurance saying "all is fair in love and war."

10. Sarah Carpenter to Mott Hooton, March 1, 1864, Mott Hooton Papers, Ms Coll. 171, Chester County Historical Society.

11. Susan Carpenter to Mott Hooton, November 27, 1870, Mott Hooton Papers, Ms Coll. 171, Chester County Historical Society. Susan references a letter she had received from Mott writing "you remarked in your last if you were me or I [emphasis hers] you would not have much to do with the Penrose[s]. Have you heard anything? If so, tell me."

12. "Episcopalian worldly lot" see Mott Hooton to Ann Eliza Rhoads, January 10, 1879, Mott Hooton Papers, Ms Coll. 171, Chester County Historical Society. For "might as well be dead as to be poor," see Mott Hooton to Ann Eliza Rhoads, February 25, 1878, Mott Hooton Papers, Ms Coll. 171, Chester County Historical Society.

13. Mott Hooton to Sallie Rhoads, January 13, 1901, Mott Hooton Papers, Ms Coll. 171, Chester County Historical Society.

14. United States Patent, US 117884A

15. "Fruit Preservative," *The Jeffersonian*, August 26, 1871.

16. United States Patent, US164371A

17. "A Non-Explosive Lamp," *Daily Local News*, January 14, 1875 and "The Petroleum Safety Lamp," *Daily Local News*, March 3, 1875.

18. "Col. Hooton's Anti-Death Petition," *Daily Local News*, January 21, 1891.

19. *Morning Republican,* March 28, 1894.

20. Ibid.

21. Ibid.

22. Mott Hooton to Francis C. Hooton, August 20, 1862, Mott Hooton Papers, Ms Coll. 171, Chester County Historical Society.

23. Mott Hooton to Ann Eliza Rhoads, February 7, 1877, Mott Hooton Papers, Ms Coll. 171, Chester County Historical Society.

24. Mott Hooton to Ann Eliza Rhoads, March 8, 1878, Mott Hooton Papers, Ms Coll. 171, Chester County Historical Society.

25. Mott Hooton to Ann Eliza Rhoads, June 10, 1878, Mott Hooton Papers, Ms Coll. 171, Chester County Historical Society. It is not clear what Mott was alluding to regarding his grandfather, Andrew Hooton, though it suggests perhaps the elder Hooton similarly faced financial troubles of his own doings at some point.

26. Mott Hooton to Ann Eliza Rhoads, July 13, 1878, Mott Hooton Papers, Ms Coll. 171, Chester County Historical Society.

27. Francis C. Hooton to Mott Hooton, July 9, 1878, Mott Hooton Papers, Ms Coll. 171, Chester County Historical Society.

28. Ibid.

29. Ibid.

30. Ibid.

31. Francis C. Hooton to Mott Hooton, July 24, 1878, Mott Hooton Papers, Ms Coll. 171, Chester County Historical Society.

32. Ibid.

33. Ibid.

34. Ibid.

35. Ibid.

36. Mott Hooton to Ann Eliza Rhoads, September 28, 1878, Mott Hooton Papers, Ms Coll. 171, Chester County Historical Society.

37. Ibid.

38. Mott Hooton to Ann Eliza Rhoads, July 2, 1879, Mott Hooton Papers, Ms Coll. 171, Chester County Historical Society.

39. Mott Hooton to Ann Eliza Rhoads, June 23, 1879, Mott Hooton Papers, Ms Coll. 171, Chester County Historical Society.

40. Mott Hooton to Ann Eliza Rhoads, November 15, 1879, Mott Hooton Papers, Ms Coll. 171, Chester County Historical Society.

41. Francis C. Hooton to Ann Eliza Rhoads, February 18, 1884, Mott Hooton Papers, Ms Coll. 171, Chester County Historical Society.

42. Ibid.

43. Ibid.

44. Scott A. Sandage, *Born Losers: A History of Failure in America,* (Cambridge, MA: Harvard University Press, 2005), 233.

45. Ibid., see chapter 8.

46. "A Politician's Good Fortune," *The Times*, Philadelphia, July 10, 1889, pg. 1.

47. Ibid.

48. See both "A Politician's Good Fortune," *The Times*, Philadelphia, July 10, 1889, pg. 1 and "James Neely's Strange Bequest," *Pittsburgh Dispatch*, July 11, 1889, pg. 4.

49. "In re Neely's Estate, Appeal of Hooton," *The Atlantic Reporter*, Vol. 25, November 2, 1892 – March 15, 1893, (St. Paul, MN: West Publishing Co., 1893), 1055.

50. No relation to Frank Hooton's step daughter, Anna Ralston Jones.

51. "In re Neely's Estate, Appeal of Hooton," *The Atlantic Reporter*, Vol. 25, November 2, 1892 – March 15, 1893, (St. Paul, MN: West Publishing Co., 1893), 1055.

52. *The Times*, Philadelphia, April 30, 1891, pg. 2.

53. "In re Neely's Estate, Appeal of Hooton," *The Atlantic Reporter*, Vol. 25, November 2, 1892 – March 15, 1893, (St. Paul, MN: West Publishing Co., 1893), 1055.

54. Ibid.

55. Ibid.

56. "Colonel Hooton in Court Again," *The Times*, Philadelphia, March 12, 1893, pg. 10.

57. "Colonel Hooten Weakens," *Evening Herald*, Shenandoah, Pennsylvania, August 25, 1893, pg. 3.

58. *Daily Local News*, August 8, 1893.

59. "A Lawyer in Jail," *Delaware Gazette and State Journal*, Wilmington, Delaware, August 3, 1893, pg. 4.

60. *Daily Local News*, August 3, 1893.

61. Ibid.

62. Ibid.

63. "Col. Hooton in Prison," *The Times*, Philadelphia, August 2, 1893, pg. 1.

64. "Colonel Hooton's Troubles," *Daily Local News*, August 2, 1893.

65. "Colonel Hooten Weakens," *Evening Herald*, Shenandoah, Pennsylvania, August 25, 1893, pg. 3.

66. *Daily Local News*, August 25, 1893.

67. Mott Hooton to Ann Eliza Rhoads, February 8, 1879, Mott Hooton Papers, Ms Coll. 171, Chester County Historical Society.

68. Hooton, Mott, *Military Memoirs of Col. Mott Hooton*, 10.

13. Paranoia in the Animas Valley

1. Mott Hooton to Ann Eliza Rhoads, November 2, 1879, Mott Hooton Papers, Ms Coll. 171, Chester County Historical Society.

2. Mott Hooton to Ann Eliza Rhoads, June 7, 1879, Mott Hooton Papers, Ms Coll. 171, Chester County Historical Society.

3. Mott Hooton to Ann Eliza Rhoads, September 9, 1879, Mott Hooton Papers, Ms Coll. 171, Chester County Historical Society.

4. Mott Hooton to Ann Eliza Rhoads, July 2, 1879, Mott Hooton Papers, Ms Coll. 171, Chester County Historical Society; and Mott Hooton to Ann Eliza Rhoads, July 25, 1879, Mott Hooton Papers, Ms Coll. 171, Chester County Historical Society.

5. Mott Hooton to Ann Eliza Rhoads, August 24, 1879, Mott Hooton Papers, Ms Coll. 171, Chester County Historical Society.

6. Smith, 5-7.

7. Ibid., 24.

8. Ibid., 6.

9. Ibid., 11.

10. Ibid., 7.

11. Ibid., 8-12.

12. Ibid., 24.

13. Ibid., 25.

14. Ibid., 26.

15. Ibid.

16. Ibid., 27.

17. Ibid., 29.

18. Ibid., 30.

19. Mott Hooton to Ann Eliza Rhoads, October 26, 1879, Mott Hooton Papers, Ms Coll. 171, Chester County Historical Society.

20. Ibid.

21. Mott Hooton to Ann Eliza Rhoads, November 2, 1879, Mott Hooton Papers, Ms Coll. 171, Chester County Historical Society.

22. Ibid.

23. Mott Hooton to Ann Eliza Rhoads, December 7, 1879, Mott Hooton Papers, Ms Coll. 171, Chester County Historical Society.

24. Ibid.

25. Hooton, Mott, *Military Memoirs of Col. Mott Hooton*, 11.

26. Ibid.

14. The Captain and the King

1. Mott Hooton to Ann Eliza Rhoads, February 14, 1880, Mott Hooton Papers, Ms Coll 171, Chester County Historical Society.

2. Mott Hooton to Ann Eliza Rhoads, February 7, 1877, Mott Hooton Papers, Ms Coll 171, Chester County Historical Society.

3. "Duties of Army Officers," *Sacramento Daily-Record-Union,* August 28, 1880, 8.

The Special Order was published in numerous papers throughout the country. This is just one example.

4. Mott Hooton to the Adjutant General, June 12, 1881, Consolidated Military Officer's File of 1st Lieutenant Mott Hooten [sic], 22nd U.S. Infantry. RG 94. Letters Received, 1871-1894, National Archives Identifier 7423592. National Archives and Records Administration, Washington, D.C.

5. *Military Memoirs of Mott Hooton,* Unpublished Draft, 1899, Private Collection.

6. Mott Hooton to Ann Eliza Rhoads, October 26, 1879, Mott Hooton Papers, Ms Coll 171, Chester County Historical Society.

7. Mott's report was submitted to the Adjutant General's Office in 1882. While it was transferred to the National Archive and Records Administration, its current location has been lost over several rounds of re-filing. The latest known file was 6947-ACP-1885 within Record Group 165, noted in a 1983 dissertation from Ohio State University: Skirbunt, Peter Daniel, "Prologue to Reform: The 'Germanization" of the United States Army, 1865-1898," Ph.D. dissertation, Ohio State University, 1983, 125.

8. *Military Memoirs of Mott Hooton,* Unpublished Draft, 1899, Private Collection.

9. Mary Lovina Cort, *Siam: The Heart of Farther India,* (New York: Anson D. Randolph & Company, 1886), 73.

10. William Henry Powell, ed., *Officers of the Volunteer Army and Navy who served in the Civil War,* (Philadelphia: L. R. Hamersly & Co., 1893), 84.

11. John A. Halderman, "Royal Cremation in Siam, *Reports from the Consuls of the United States on the Commerce, Manufactures, etc., of their Consular Districts,* No. 9, July 1881, (Washington: Government Printing Office, 1881), 37-38.

12. Ibid., 38.

13. "Cremation Ceremonies," *Siam Weekly Advertiser,* March 18, 1881, in Halderman, John A., "Royal Cremation in Siam, *Reports from the Consuls of the United States on the Commerce, Manufactures, etc., of their Consular Districts,* No. 9, July 1881, (Washington: Government Printing Office, 1881), 45.

14. Cort, 83.

15. Cort, 86.

16. "Cremation Ceremonies," 42.

17. *The United States Army and Navy Journal, and Gazette of the Regular and Volunteer Forces,* Vol. 18, (New York), 1880-1881, 871.

18. *Daily Local News,* n.d.

19. *The United States Army and Navy Journal,* Vol. 18, 871.

20. *Daily Local News,* n.d.

21. Dan Wilkerson, *Colt's Double Action Revolver, Model 1878,* (Marceline, MO: Walsworth Publishing Company, 1998), 44.

22. *Military Memoirs of Mott Hooton,* Unpublished Draft, 1899, Private Collection.

23. James B. Cowan to Mott Hooton, February 3, 1905, Mott Hooton Papers, Ms. Coll. 171, Chester County Historical Society.

24. An eccentric to the end, Cowan devised one last hoax before his death in 1904. He announced he would be buried under a high hill on his estate, Tollgate Hill beneath a modern replica of a Viking longboat, which would be burned according to the old Viking funeral rites. He went so far as to have the boat built, but it was just a story for the media. When he passed, he received a conventional, Christian burial in St. Clair Cemetery.

25. Mott Hooton to the Adjutant General, June 12, 1881, Consolidated Military Officer's File of 1st Lieutenant Mott Hooten [sic], 22nd U.S. Infantry. RG 94. Letters Received, 1871-1894, National Archives Identifier 7423592. National Archives and Records Administration, Washington, D.C.

26. *Daily Local News*, n.d.

27. *Military Memoirs of Mott Hooton*, unpublished draft, 1899. Private Collection. It is not known if the ship from St. Petersburg sailed direct to Philadelphia or if he stopped in England or elsewhere in Europe first.

15. *Peacekeeper*

1. Smith, 98.

2. Ibid., 38-39.

3. Ibid., 94-95.

4. Ibid., 50.

5. Ibid., 121.

6. Ibid., 108.

7. Ibid., 109.

8. Ibid., 109-110.

9. Ibid., 110.

10. Ibid., 111.

11. Ibid., 119.

12. Ibid.

13. Ibid., 120.

14. Maris' exact cause of death was listed as "heart clot following diphtheria." Morris [sic] Chase, Death Registry Entry, Pennsylvania, Philadelphia City Death Certificates, 1803-1915, page 101, familysearch.org; and Morris [sic] Chase, Death Certificate, Pennsylvania, Philadelphia City Death Certificates, 1803-1915, page 234, familysearch.org. Susan's cause of death was listed as "Pseudo memb[ranous] laryngitis, a form of croup caused by diphtheria. Susie Chase, Death Registry Entry, Pennsylvania, Philadelphia City Death Certificates, 1803-1915, page 90, familysearch.org and Susie Chase, Death Certificate, Pennsylvania, Philadelphia City Death Certificates, 1803-1915, page 923, familysearch.org.

15. Dorothy Chase, Personal Correspondence with the Author, June 21, 2011.

16. Morton Chase, United States Federal Census, 1910.

17. Annie E. Chase to Hazen Park Chase, n.d., Private Collection.

16. End of the Frontier

1. Bruce Elliott Johansen, *The Native Peoples of North America: A History*, Vol. 1 (New Brunswick, NJ: Rutgers University Press, 2006), 303.

2. Spencer C. Tucker, ed., *The Encyclopedia of North American Indian Wars, 1607-1890: A political, Social, and Military History*, Vol. 1: A-L (Denver, CO: ABC-CLIO, 2011), 1223.

3. Hooton, Mott, Unpublished writing regarding his thoughts on the American Indian, n.d., Mott Hooton Papers, Ms Coll. 171, Chester County Historical Society.

4. Ibid.

5. Ibid.

6. E. J. McClernand, "Edward W. Casey," *Report of the Twenty-Second Annual Reunion of the Association of the Graduates of the United States Military Academy*, June 12, 1891, 47-49.

7. Hooton, Mott, Unpublished writing regarding the death of Plenty Horses, June 1909, Mott Hooton Papers, Ms Coll. 171, Chester County Historical Society.

8. Hooton, Mott, Unpublished writing regarding his thoughts on the American Indian, n.d., Mott Hooton Papers, Ms Coll. 171, Chester County Historical Society.

9. Ibid.

10. Ibid.

11. Ibid.

12. Ibid.

13. Ibid.

14. Mott Hooton to Ann Eliza Rhoads, March 12, 1876, Mott Hooton Papers, Ms Coll. 171, Chester County Historical Society.

15. Hooton, Mott, Unpublished writing regarding his thoughts on the American Indian, n.d., Mott Hooton Papers, Ms Coll. 171, Chester County Historical Society.

16. Mary Jane Blackiston to Mott Hooton, 1912, Mott Hooton Papers, Ms Coll. 171, Chester County Historical Society.

17. See work by Benjamin D. Brands, "Unsatisfactory and Futile': The Officer's Lyceum Program and U. S. Army Reform," *The Journal of Military History*, Vol. 83 No. 4 (October 2019).

18. Unpublished recitation summarizing lectures by Colonel Lazeux, n.d., Private Collection and Scheibert, J., "The Civil War in America Considered from a Military Point of View for the Officers of the German Army," unpublished manuscript, n.d., Private Collection; R. C. Drum to Mott Hooton, February 21, 1888, Private Collection. This last letter references translations Mott had requested from a book

on military tactics from 1875 by Baron Wechmar, General Major and Brigade Commander of the German army.

19. Robert Lincoln to War Department, February 19, 1883, Private Collection; John Davis to Robert Lincoln, July 24, 1883, Private Collection.

20. 1888—File No. 695—Hooton, Allott [sic]—California, Record Group 94: Records of the Adjutant General's Office, 1762 – 1984, Series: Letters received, 1805-1889, Identifier 146615638, National Archives and Records Administration, Washington D.C.

21. J. O. Gilmore to Mott Hooton, March 11, 1895, Private Collection.

22. "Certain Historical Data Regarding Extended Order," *Journal of the Military Service Institution,* Vol. 16 (1895), 549. Extended Order refers to a form of troop formation during skirmishing whereby the soldiers of a unit are spaced widely apart at varying intervals depending on their surrounding geography. This is in contrast to "Close Order" formation such as shoulder-to-shoulder marching.

23. David S. Stanley to Adjutant General of the US Army, August 16, 1894, Private Collection.

24. Circular, F. B. Jones on behalf of Peter Swaine, Circular, Post of Fort Keogh, June 9, 1894, Private Collection.

25. White, W. Thomas, "Montana and the Pullman Strike of 1894: A Western Response to Industrial Warfare," unpublished thesis, (The University of Montana, 1975), 21-22.

26. Ibid., 24-25.

27. Ibid., 49.

28. Ibid., 50.

29. M. V. Sheridan on behalf of Wesley Merritt, July 7, 1894. Private Collection.

30. Ibid.

31. F. B. Jones to Mott Hooton, July 13, 1894. Private Collection.

32. White, 56.

33. Ibid., 65.

34. "The Post at Helena," *The Silver Blade,* (Rathdrum, Idaho), September, 28, 1895.

17. *New Priorities*

1. Nelson A. Miles to the President and Members of the Examining Board, August 16, 1894. Private Collection.

2. Elwell S. Otis to Examining Board, August 13, 1894. Private Collection.

3. David S. Stanley to Adjutant General, US Army, August 16, 1894, Private Collection.

4. Ibid.

5. Elwell S. Otis to Examining Board, August 13, 1894. Private Collection.

6. Taylor, Quintard, introduction in Nankivell, John H., *Buffalo Soldier Regiment: History of the Twenty-Fifth United States Infantry, 1896-1926*, (Lincoln, NE: University of Nebraska Press, 2001), x.

7. Ibid., xi.

8. Ibid.

9. Ibid., xi -xii.

10. "Colored Troops Go Through," *Chicago Tribune*, October 2, 1898, pg. 14.

11. Mott Hooton to Ann Eliza Rhoads, December 14, 1876, Mott Hooton Papers, Ms Coll. 171, Chester County Historical Society.

12. Mott threatened to expatriate on more than one occasion in reference to national politics. Once during the contentious 1876 Presidential election, and again a year and a half later in which he identified England as his desired destination. It is anyone's guess how serious his threat was, but clearly he had no love for politics. See Mott Hooton to Ann Eliza Rhoads, December 14, 1876, Mott Hooton Papers, Ms Coll. 171, Chester County Historical Society and Mott Hooton to Ann Eliza Rhoads, February 25, 1878, Mott Hooton Papers, Ms Coll. 171, Chester County Historical Society.

13. For more information on Uriah Hunt Painter, see Ritchie, Donald A., *Press Gallery: Congress and the Washington Correspondents*, (Cambridge, MA: Harvard University Press, 1992).

14. Francis C. Hooton to Uriah Hunt Painter, April 9th, 1898, Mott Hooton Papers, Ms Coll. 171, Chester County Historical Society.

15. Mott Hooton to Francis C. Hooton, May 31, 1898, Mott Hooton Papers, Ms Coll. 171, Chester County Historical Society.

16. George J. A. O'Toole, *The Spanish War: An American Epic, 1898*, (New York: W. W. Norton and Company, 1984), 20.

17. Ibid.

18. Ibid., 21.

19. Ibid., 22.

20. Ibid., 21.

21. Ibid., 27.

22. Ibid., 127.

23. Ibid., 139.

24. Ibid., 161. Incidentally, the Spanish conducted their own independent investigation and declared the incident an accident originating inside the ship as they found no evidence of a mine, however, no one paid much attention to the Spanish report.

25. Ibid., 163.

26. Ibid., 168.

27. Ibid., 170.

28. Ibid., 173.

29. John H. Nankivell, *Buffalo Soldier Regiment: History of the Twenty-Fifth United States Infantry, 1869-1926,* (Lincoln, NE: University of Nebraska Press, 2001), 66.

30. Ibid.

31. Mott Hooton to Francis C. Hooton, May 31, 1898, Mott Hooton Papers, Ms. Coll. 171, Chester County Historical Society.

32. *Military Memoirs of Mott Hooton,* Unpublished Draft, 1899. Private Collection. One newspaper article from June 23, 1898 reported gout as Mott's affliction and that he was treated and recovered aboard the *Olivette.* However, given the subsequent transfer and sick leave, this was likely either a separate matter or a mistake on the part of the paper. *The Sun,* New York, NY, June 23, 1898, page 1.

33. Nankivell, 80.

34. Ibid., 85.

35. O'Toole, 374-375.

36. Leonard Wood, *Civil Report of the Military Governor, 1901,* (Cuba, Military Governor, 1899-1902), 41-43.

37. George F. Kennan, "Regeneration of Cuba" in *The Outlook,* Vol. 61, January—April, 1899, (New York: The Outlook Company, 1899), 498-499.

38. *Military Memoirs of Mott Hooton,* Unpublished Draft, 1899. Private Collection.

39. Mott Hooton to Sallie Rhoads, February 23, 1901, Mott Hooton Papers, Ms. Coll. 171, Chester County Historical Society.

40. "Mourn Loss of Canteen," *The Topeka State Journal,* January 12, 1901, page 5. Mott's reference to military discipline being compromised during Secretary Proctor's tenure is not clear. Mott clearly had strong opinions about Proctor and his policies, but what they were is not known.

41. Louis Livingston Seaman, "Why the Army Canteen Should Be Restored," in *The North American Review,* Vol. 176, No. 554 (University of Northern Iowa, January, 1903), 80.

18. Uncle Mott

1. Mott Hooton to Morton Hazen Chase, September 25, 1901, Mott Hooton Papers, Ms. Coll. 171, Chester County Historical Society.

2. Ibid.

3. Ibid.

4. Ibid. Interestingly, Mott specifically told Hazen to avoid football saying "there he would draw a line." What his aversion to football was, he never said.

5. Ibid.

6. Mott Hooton to Annie Chase, April 8, 1900, Mott Hooton Papers, Ms. Coll. 171, Chester County Historical Society.

7. Mott Hooton to Annie E. Chase, May 17, 1900, Mott Hooton Papers, Ms. Coll. 171, Chester County Historical Society.

8. Ann Eliza Rhoads to Mott Hooton, January 1, 1864, Mott Hooton Papers, Ms. Coll. 171, Chester County Historical Society.

9. Mott Hooton to Sallie Rhoads, April 24, 1899, Mott Hooton Papers, Ms. Coll. 171, Chester County Historical Society.

10. Ann Eliza Rhoads to Mott Hooton, August 7, 1863, Mott Hooton Papers, Ms. Coll. 171, Chester County Historical Society.

11. Susan Carpenter to Mott Hooton, June 30, 1869, Mott Hooton Papers, Ms. Coll. 171, Chester County Historical Society.

12. Ibid.

13. Ann Eliza Rhoads to Mott Hooton, June 24, 1869, Mott Hooton Papers, Ms. Coll. 171, Chester County Historical Society.

14. Susan Carpenter to Mott Hooton, June 30, 1869, Mott Hooton Papers, Ms. Coll. 171, Chester County Historical Society.

15. Ibid.

16. Mott Hooton to Sallie Rhoads, January 13, 1901, Mott Hooton Papers, Ms. Coll. 171, Chester County Historical Society.

17. Mott Hooton to Sallie Rhoads, April 26, 1901, Mott Hooton Papers, Ms. Coll. 171, Chester County Historical Society. That the name of the gloves was the same as their model, it was likely just an ironic coincidence. The gloves were undoubtedly named for Princess Mary of Teck, wife of the future King George V of England who was known in the royal family as May.

18. Mott Hooton to Sallie Rhoads, May 10, 1901, Mott Hooton Papers, Ms. Coll. 171, Chester County Historical Society.

19. Mott Hooton to Ann Eliza Rhoads, October 6, 1876, Mott Hooton Papers, Ms. Coll. 171, Chester County Historical Society and Mott Hooton to Ann Eliza Rhoads, November 8, 1877, Mott Hooton Papers, Ms. Coll. 171, Chester County Historical Society.

20. Annie E. Chase to Hazen Park Chase, n.d. Private collection.

21. Mott Hooton to Annie E. Chase, April 8, 1900, Mott Hooton Papers, Ms. Coll. 171, Chester County Historical Society.

22. Mott Hooton to Sallie Rhoads, March 2, 1901, Mott Hooton Papers, Ms. Coll. 171, Chester County Historical Society.

23. Ibid.

24. Mott Hooton to Sallie Rhoads, March 5, 1899, Mott Hooton Papers, Ms. Coll. 171, Chester County Historical Society.

25. Ibid.

26. Mott Hooton to Sallie Rhoads, April 24, 1901, Mott Hooton Papers, Ms. Coll. 171, Chester County Historical Society.

27. Ibid.

28. Mott Hooton to Henry A. DuPont, March 22, 1872, Manuscripts and Archives, Hagley Museum and Library.

29. Ibid.

30. Ibid.

31. Ibid.

32. A bronze statue to Malsee's ancestor is still standing in the town of Lurgan in County Armagh, Northern Ireland. Pedigree documents are located in the Mott Hooton Papers, Ms. Coll. 171, Chester County Historical Society.

33. Mott Hooton to Sallie Rhoads, May 19, 1901, Mott Hooton Papers, Ms. Coll. 171, Chester County Historical Society.

34. Mott Hooton to Sallie Rhoads, June 5, 1900, Mott Hooton Papers, Ms. Coll. 171, Chester County Historical Society.

35. Mott Hooton to Sallie Rhoads, March 25, 1900, Mott Hooton Papers, Ms. Coll. 171, Chester County Historical Society.

36. Mott Hooton to Sallie Rhoads, January 24, 1901, Mott Hooton Papers, Ms. Coll. 171, Chester County Historical Society.

37. Mott Hooton to Sallie Rhoads, December 6, 1900, Mott Hooton Papers, Ms. Coll. 171, Chester County Historical Society.

38. Mott Hooton to Sallie Rhoads, April 16, 1901, Mott Hooton Papers, Ms. Coll. 171, Chester County Historical Society.

39. Mott Hooton to Sallie Rhoads, November 5, 1901, Mott Hooton Papers, Ms. Coll. 171, Chester County Historical Society.

40. See *Midland Journal,* Rising Sun, Maryland, November 5, 1909, p. 6; *Washington Herald,* Washington, D.C., July 19, 1909, p. 5; *Wauwatosa News,* Wauwatosa, Wisconsin, July 9, 1909, p. 3.

41. Mott Hooton to Sallie Rhoads, September 30, 1900, Mott Hooton Papers, Ms. Coll. 171, Chester County Historical Society.

42. Mott Hooton to The Honorable Members of the Military Committees of the Senate and House of Representatives, March 1899, Private Collection.

43. "Railroading Veterans upon the Retired List," *The Times-Democrat,* April 24, 1902.

44. "Army Promotions," *Augusta Chronicle,* April 20, 1902, pg. 12.

45. Mott Hooton to Sallie Rhoads, January 13, 1901, Mott Hooton Papers, Ms. Coll. 171, Chester County Historical Society.

46. Ibid.

47. Mott Hooton to Sallie Rhoads, February 4, 1901, Mott Hooton Papers, Ms. Coll. 171, Chester County Historical Society.

19. One Last Mission

1. Brian McAllister Linn, *The Philippine War, 1899-1902,* (Lawrence, KS: University Press of Kansas, 2000), 16.

2. Ibid., 17.

3. Ibid.

4. Ibid., 19.

5. Ibid., 20.

6. O'Toole, George J. A., *The Spanish War: An American Epic, 1898*, (New York: W. W. Norton & Company, 1984), 386.

7. Linn, Brian McAllister, *The Philippine War, 1899-1902*, (Lawrence, KS: University Press of Kansas, 2000), 24.

8. O'Toole, 370-371.

9. Linn, 386.

10. Ibid., 185.

11. Ibid., 185-186.

12. Mott Hooton to Sallie Rhoads, March 6, 1901, Mott Hooton Papers, Ms. Coll. 171, Chester County Historical Society.

13. Henry Clark Corbin to Thomas Butler, February 28, 1901, Consolidated Military Officer's File of 1st Lieutenant Mott Hooten [sic], 22nd U.S. Infantry. RG 94. Letters Received, 1871-1894, National Archives Identifier 7423592. National Archives and Records Administration, Washington, D.C.

14. Mott Hooton to Adjutant General, June 12, 1901, Consolidated Military Officer's File of 1st Lieutenant Mott Hooten [sic], 22nd U.S. Infantry. RG 94. Letters Received, 1871-1894, National Archives Identifier 7423592. National Archives and Records Administration, Washington, D.C.; and John H. Mitchell to Elihu Root, June 21, 1901, Consolidated Military Officer's File of 1st Lieutenant Mott Hooten [sic], 22nd U.S. Infantry. RG 94. Letters Received, 1871-1894, National Archives Identifier 7423592. National Archives and Records Administration, Washington, D.C.

15. "The Grant Off for Manila," *Waterbury Democrat*, November 16, 1901, page 3.

16. Mott Hooton to Sallie Rhoads, December 16, 1901, Mott Hooton Papers, Ms. Coll. 171, Chester County Historical Society.

17. Ibid.

18. Ibid.

19. Linn, 295.

20. Ibid., 286.

21. Ibid.

22. Ibid., 302-303.

23. See Consolidated Military Officer's File of 1st Lieutenant Mott Hooten [sic], 22nd U.S. Infantry. RG 94. Letters Received, 1871-1894, National Archives Identifier 7423592. National Archives and Records Administration, Washington, D.C.

24. Addison G. Foster to Theodore Roosevelt, March 7, 1902, Consolidated Military Officer's File of 1st Lieutenant Mott Hooten [sic], 22nd U.S. Infantry. RG 94. Letters Received, 1871-1894, National Archives Identifier 7423592. National Archives and Records Administration, Washington, D.C.; and John H. Mitchell to William McKinley, October 5, 1901, Consolidated Military Officer's File of 1st Lieutenant Mott Hooten [sic], 22nd U.S. Infantry. RG 94. Letters Received, 1871-1894, National

Archives Identifier 7423592. National Archives and Records Administration, Washington, D.C.

25. *Daily Local News*, April 10, 1902.

26. *Daily Local News*, April 7, 1902.

27. Theodore Roosevelt to Elihu Root, n.d. Consolidated Military Officer's File of 1st Lieutenant Mott Hooten [sic], 22nd U.S. Infantry. RG 94. Letters Received, 1871-1894, National Archives Identifier 7423592. National Archives and Records Administration, Washington, D.C.

28. Elihu Root to H. C. Corbin, April 14, 1902, Consolidated Military Officer's File of 1st Lieutenant Mott Hooten [sic], 22nd U.S. Infantry. RG 94. Letters Received, 1871-1894, National Archives Identifier 7423592. National Archives and Records Administration, Washington, D.C. The note is not signed. That it came as Root's order is inferred by the additional documents in the file.

29. Henry Clark Corbin, Memo from War Department, April 14, 1902, Consolidated Military Officer's File of 1st Lieutenant Mott Hooten [sic], 22nd U.S. Infantry. RG 94. Letters Received, 1871-1894, National Archives Identifier 7423592. National Archives and Records Administration, Washington, D.C.

30. "Now a Brigadier General: Col. Mott Hooton, Retired Today, Promoted by the Senate," *The Washington Times*, April 16, 1902. See also *The National Tribune*, Washington DC, April 10, 1902, page 4 and *The Evening Times*, April 15, 1902, page 1.

31. Mott would not be the only Colonel promoted to General just prior to retirement. The Senate made numerous "last minute" promotions around this time for active military officers who had served in the Civil War. The *Evening Star* reported that additional Colonels with Civil War service would similarly by promoted in the days following, one of whom to fill the vacancy left by Mott. "Col. Hooton Promoted," *Evening Star*, April 15, 1902.

20. General Hooton

1. "The Army and Navy, President and Mrs. Roosevelt's Guests Last Night. A Brilliant Event," *The Evening Star*, February 12, 1904, pages 17 and 20.

2. Ibid. The paper printed the entire, lengthy guest list, which listed Brig. Gen. Moot [sic] Hooton and Miss Annie E. Chase.

3. "The Social World: Another White House Function Becomes History," *Evening Star*, January 23, 1904, page 5.

4. Francis C. Hooton to Sallie Rhoads, March 13, 1901, Mott Hooton Papers, Ms. Coll. 171, Chester County Historical Society.

5. Ibid.

6. C. C. Bowman to Mott Hooton, September 12, 1904, Mott Hooton Papers, Ms. Coll. 171, Chester County Historical Society. See also A. L. Lee to Mott Hooton,

September 12, 1904, Mott Hooton Papers, Ms. Coll. 171, Chester County Historical Society and J. A. Wilkinson to Mott Hooton, September 13, 1904, Mott Hooton Papers, Ms. Coll. 171, Chester County Historical Society.

7. A photograph of Mott with Captain Webster exists in the photo archives of the Chester County Historical Society as part of Ms. Coll. 171.

8. "Col. Hooton's Funeral," *Daily Local News*, January 12, 1904.

9. *Daily Local News*, January 23, 1904.

10. "Attachment Against Colonel Hooton," *The Times*, Philadelphia, February 19, 1897, pg. 3.

11. *The Times*, Philadelphia, May 17, 1896, pg. 18.

12. "Col. Francis Hooton Dead at West Chester," *Philadelphia Inquirer*, January 12, 1904, pg. 3.

13. "Politics in Chester County: Colonel Hooton's Canvass for the Office of Prothonotary," *The Times*, Philadelphia, June 23, 1895, pg. 15. "Coventries" and "Nottinghams" refer to townships within Chester County.

14. Ibid.

15. "Colonel Hooton Gets Gay," *Philadelphia Inquirer*, August 23, 1903, pg. 7.

16. "Pennypacker Boom, that Fell Flat," *Philadelphia Inquirer*, May 23, 1902, pg. 2.

17. See Miscellaneous Receipts, Mott Hooton Papers, Ms. Coll. 171, Chester County Historical Society. Also, United States Federal Census, 1910, West Chester, Pennsylvania.

18. "Gilford-Robinson Nuptuals," *New York Tribune*, October 6, 1908.

19. *Daily Local News*, June 13, 1916.

20. Ibid.

21. Ibid.

22. Ibid.

23. *Daily Local News*, June 14, 1916.

24. *Daily Local News*, n.d.

25. Mott Hooton to Sallie Rhoads, April 26, 1901, Mott Hooton Papers, Ms. Coll. 171, Chester County Historical Society. Also Mott Hooton to Sallie Rhoads, May 10, 1901, Mott Hooton Papers, Ms. Coll. 171, Chester County Historical Society.

26. *Morning Republican*, August 20, 1898.

27. *Daily Local News*, n.d.

28. *Daily Local News*, n.d.

29. It is not clear which paper company initially employed Hazen. Later career summaries, such as when he joined the American Writing Paper Company in Massachusetts, reference employment at one time or another with the Ontario Paper Company and the Brompton Paper and Pulp Company both out of Canada. However, his primary employer would have been the S. D. Warren Company. See "M. Hazen Chase Appointed," *Springfield Republican*, December 4, 1920, pg 8.

30. 1910 United States Federal Census. Interestingly, Mott was enumerated twice in the 1910 census, once in West Chester in his sister-in-law's family and once in

Maine. However, correspondence from Mott as early as 1908 bear the Portland address. See Mott Hooton to Franklin Conrad Woolman, October 30, 1908, Mott Hooton Papers, Ms. Coll. 171, Chester County Historical Society.

31. "M. Hazen Chase Appointed," *Springfield Republican,* December 4, 1920, pg 8. Mott's 1920 death certificate also lists his length of residence in Farmingdale as five years, further supporting the 1915 move.

32. *Richmond Times Dispatch,* June 19, 1913, pg. 5.

33. *Evening Public Ledger,* April 3, 1917, pg. 14.

34. *Philadelphia Inquirer,* March 23, 1918, pg. 17.

35. Dorothy Chase, Personal Correspondence with Author, September 26, 2007. The exact sequence of events is unclear. As Dorothy Chase had heard, Hazen had married and moved to Maine first, while Mott, Sallie, and Annie followed once Sarah died to help him with the baby. However, Mott's death certificate notes that Mott had been living in Maine since 1915, two years before Hazen and Sarah had even married. What is presented here, then, is what we believe to be the most likely scenario given the primary source evidence.

36. See S. S. Evans to Mott Hooton, November 10, 1909, Mott Hooton Papers, Ms. Coll. 171, Chester County Historical Society; S. S. Evans to Mott Hooton, December 28, 1909, Mott Hooton Papers, Ms. Coll. 171, Chester County Historical Society; S. S. Evans to Mott Hooton, June 23, 1912, Mott Hooton Papers, Ms. Coll. 171, Chester County Historical Society;

37. Bailey, Banks, and Biddle to Mott Hooton, March 30, 1904, Mott Hooton Papers, Ms. Coll. 171, Chester County Historical Society; Arthur Meredyth Burke to Mott Hooton, February 20, 1904, Mott Hooton Papers, Ms. Coll. 171, Chester County Historical Society; John Matthews to Mott Hooton, July 22, 1911, Mott Hooton Papers, Ms. Coll. 171, Chester County Historical Society; John Matthews to Mott Hooton, August 2, 1917, Mott Hooton Papers, Ms. Coll. 171, Chester County Historical Society.

38. Earnest A. Hooton to Mott Hooton, August 27, 1910, Mott Hooton Papers, Ms. Coll. 171, Chester County Historical Society.

39. Pat Pequet to Mott Hooton, September 15, 1907, Mott Hooton Papers, Ms. Coll. 171, Chester County Historical Society.

40. J. H. Musser to Mott Hooton, October 14, 1908, Mott Hooton Papers, Ms. Coll. 171, Chester County Historical Society.

41. Charles C. Gray to Mott Hooton, May 7, 1901, Mott Hooton Papers, Ms. Coll. 171, Chester County Historical Society.

42. James B. Cowan to Mott Hooton, February 3, 1905, Mott Hooton Papers, Ms. Coll. 171, Chester County Historical Society.

43. *Daily Local News,* February 7, 1901. Eagle refers to the rank insignia symbol of an army colonel.

44. Mary Jane Blackiston to Mott Hooton, September 23, 1910, Mott Hooton Papers, Ms. Coll. 171, Chester County Historical Society.

45. Mott Hooton, Death Certificate, May 30, 1920.

46. Ibid.

47. *Daily Local News*, June 5, 1920.

48. Ibid.

Epilogue

1. Sallie S. Rhoads, Death Certificate, October 17, 1922. The address on the certificate is Hazen's Gardiner home. Not the Farmingdale residence she share with Mott.

2. Sallie S. Rhoads, Death Certificate, October 17, 1922.

3. 1920 United States Federal Census, Gardiner, Maine.

4. "M. Hazen Chase Appointed," *Springfield Republican*, pg. 8.

5. Dorothy Chase, Personal Correspondence with Author, September 26, 2007. Nellie is also listed as a nurse in Hazen's household in the 1920 United States Federal Census, Gardiner, Maine.

6. *Springfield Republican*, April 24, 1927, pg. 12.

7. "M. Hazen Chase Dies," *Springfield Republican*, January 9, 1938.

8. Ibid.

9. Dorothy Chase, Personal Correspondence with Author, September 26, 2007.

10. *Philadelphia Inquirer*, October 25, 1914, pg. 11. See also *Daily Local News*, n.d.

11. "Ex-Wife Asks $250,000 Balm of Dead Rival," *Daily News*, February 14, 1934.

12. John Eshleman Lloyd, Death Certificate, October 20, 1932.

13. "Ex-Wife Asks $250,000 Balm of Dead Rival," *Daily News*, February 14, 1934.

14. "Called Cruel: Philadelphia Society Man Seeks Reno Divorce from Actress," *San Francisco Chronicle*, February 19, 1932.

15. "Wife Dodges Divorce Suit," *San Francisco Chronicle*, April 20, 1932, pg. 22.

16. "Called Cruel: Philadelphia Society Man Seeks Reno Divorce from Actress," *San Francisco Chronicle*, February 19, 1932; and "Ex-Wife Asks $250,000 Balm of Dead Rival," *Daily News*, February 14, 1934.

17. "Former Wife Sues Hospital Wedding Bride," *San Francisco Chronicle*, May 19, 1932.

18. "Society Woman Flies Across U.S. to Wed Man in Hospital," *San Francisco Chronicle*, May 6, 1932, pg. 17.

19. "Judith Vosselli Seeks $250,000 For Love Theft," *Daily News*, June 3, 1932.

20. John Eshleman Lloyd, Death Certificate, October 20, 1932.

21. "Ex-Wife Asks $250,000 Balm of Dead Rival," *Daily News*, February 14, 1934.

22. "Best Man Sues Newlyweds To Collect $7500 Doctor's Bill"

23. Mary Jane Blackiston to Mott Hooton, 1912, Mott Hooton Papers, Ms. Coll. 171, Chester County Historical Society.

24. Ibid.

Index

ABOUT THE AUTHORS

Kevin Brown holds a BA in History from West Chester University and an MA in American History from the University of Delaware. Having grown up in West Chester, he became fascinated by his home county's rich history while a student at WCU. He lives in London with his wife and two daughters.

Amy King holds a BA in History from West Chester University. A native of northern Delaware, she has always had an insatiable appetite to learn about the lives and experiences of everyday people, a passion she brings with her in her job as an archaeologist. She lives in Wilmington with her son.

Also by Kevin Brown & Amy King

A Small Company of Faithful Ones: The Brandywine Guards of Chester County, Company A, 1st Pennsylvania Reserves

They were not soldiers. They were farmers, laborers, teachers, lawyers, and tradesmen. Even a dentist could be counted among the ranks. In the spring of 1861, one hundred thirteen men from Chester County, Pennsylvania, calling themselves the Brandywine Guards, organized in West Chester to fight for the Union during the Civil War. As Company A, 1st Pennsylvania Reserves, these young men proved their mettle in some of the most horrific battles of the war- Second Bull Run, Antietam, Fredericksburg, Gettysburg, and the Wilderness, to name a few. Though forever linked to one another through the shared experience of war, when the dust settled, the lives they each created for themselves were many and varied. Follow this small company of faithful ones through the hardships of war and learn about the men they each became, the families they raised, and the many legacies they left behind. This is not the retelling of the Civil War, nor is it a military history- although there are elements of both. It is a very personal history. It is a story that reveals what the ordinary person is capable of when the human body and spirit are pushed to the limit and beyond. After one hundred fifty years, the Brandywine Guards are reunited once more.